AT THE MARGINS

M E D I E V A L
C U L T U R E S

SERIES EDITORS
RITA COPELAND
BARBARA A. HANAWALT
DAVID WALLACE

Sponsored by the Center for Medieval Studies at the University of Minnesota

Volumes in the series study the diversity of medieval cultural histories and practices, including such interrelated issues as gender, class, and social hierarchies; race and ethnicity; geographical relations; definitions of political space; discourses of authority and dissent; educational institutions; canonical and noncanonical literatures; and technologies of textual and visual literacies.

For more books in the series, see pages 285–88.

AT THE MARGINS

MINORITY GROUPS IN PREMODERN ITALY

STEPHEN J. MILNER, EDITOR

Medieval Cultures, Volume 39
University of Minnesota Press
Minneapolis
London

Published by the University of Minnesota Press
111 Third Avenue South, Suite 290
Minneapolis, MN 55401-2520
http://www.upress.umn.edu

Library of Congress Cataloging-in-Publication Data

At the margins : minority groups in premodern Italy / Stephen J. Milner, editor.
    p.   cm. — (Medieval cultures ; v. 39)
    Includes bibliographical references and index.
    ISBN 0-8166-3820-9 (hc : alk. paper) — ISBN 0-8166-3821-7 (pb : alk. paper)
    1. Marginality, Social—Italy—History.   2. Minorities—Italy—Social conditions.
3. Italy—Social conditions—1268–1559.   4. Italy—Social conditions—16th century.
5. Italy—Social conditions—17th century.   6. Italy—Social life and customs—To 1500.
7. Italy—Social life and customs—16th century.   8. Italy—Social life and customs—
17th century.   I. Milner, Stephen J., 1963–   II. Series.
    HN490.M26A82   2005
    305.5'6'0945—dc22   2004021957

Printed in the United States of America on acid-free paper

The University of Minnesota is an equal-opportunity educator and employer.

12 11 10 09 08 07 06 05   10 9 8 7 6 5 4 3 2 1

For Nikki and Nola

Contents

Part III. Marginal Voices

Part IV. Minority Groups

Editor's Preface

The initial catalyst for commissioning this series of essays on the subject of margins and minority groups in premodern Italy was a half-day conference I organized back in 1998 as part of the continuing program of events within the Centre for Medieval Studies at the University of Bristol. Given the success of the initial event and the interesting dialogue that ensued, it was decided to approach a number of scholars working in the field whose research addressed issues of social or political marginalization and identity formation in the context of late medieval and Renaissance Italy. Thanks are due to all those who subsequently accepted the invitation to join the small group involved in the original event—namely myself, Michael Rocke, and Samuel K. Cohen Jr.—in putting together such a collaborative enterprise.

The volume itself is divided into four sections that address different aspects of the relation of margins to centers. The scope of the first section is to provide a framework for the more focused studies that follow by examining the centrality of margins to contemporary cultural theory and thinking concerning identity formation. Given that the Italian Renaissance has often been characterized as the source of the hegemonic discourse of Western Civilization as "center," focusing renewed attention on its margins might not only question the universality of such a grand narrative, but also serve to open up new vistas and perspectives upon a past constantly subject to reinvention.

In the sections that follow, attention is focused in turn upon the negotiation of such margins in spatial terms, in textual and rhetorical terms, and in terms of accommodating outsiders and those considered marginal to the political center. In this context, the use of the term "premodern" within the title of the volume is a conscious decision. For as the project evolved it became increasingly clear that contemporaries within late medieval and Renaissance Italy were as conscious of the porous nature of identity and the lack of clearly identifiable lines of demarcation differentiating them from alien "others" as they were of the ambiguity of their own subjectivity, and as knowing in their management of space as they were in their patterns of resistance. In this sense, the insights of a contemporary cultural theory that is largely hostile toward what it terms the "rationalizing impulse of modernity" finds suggestive application in rereading a period and place often described as the birthplace of the modern state and modern man. It is precisely in the otherness of the premodern that cultural theory and postmodernism provide illuminating vistas into ways of writing about the distant past and the possibility of re-presenting the Italian Renaissance in a manner that questions its stereotyping as cultural "center."

The collective work brought together in this volume was made possible by the continued support of Rita Copeland and David Wallace, both of whom gave generously of their time and talents while Rita was a Benjamin Meaker Visiting Professor within the Centre for Medieval Studies at the University of Bristol. Thanks are also due to the University's Arts Faculty Research Fund for financial support, to my colleagues within the Department of Italian, and to Richard Morrison and the rest of the editorial team at the University of Minnesota Press. This book is dedicated to Nikki and Nola with love.

PART I

THE CENTRALITY OF MARGINS

1

IDENTITY AND THE MARGINS OF
ITALIAN RENAISSANCE CULTURE

STEPHEN J. MILNER

Margins, borders, frontiers, thresholds, edges, limits, perimeters, frames, boundaries, peripheries, limina. These terms are all well established within both the lexis of anthropology and more recently the critical vocabulary of postmodernism and cultural studies. From the writings of Arnold Van Gennep, Clifford Geertz, and Victor Turner to the postmodern critiques of Jürgen Habermas, Jean-François Lyotard, and Fredric Jameson, the process of reading culture and producing meaningful narratives of human activity has focused considerable attention on the manner in which societies, groups, and individuals define themselves in terms of what they share in common and in terms of their differentiation from others. The examination of these processes of communal, collective, and self-identification, and the attendant concern with issues of difference, has seen particular attention paid to the limits that serve to describe or circumscribe these identities. The essays in this volume seek to examine some of these processes of description in late medieval and early modern Italy by investigating how, and by whom, the material and symbolic lines of differentiation were drawn. Yet the differentiation between some of these identities is not as clear-cut as some of the above terms might suggest. In many cases it is impossible to point to a clearly identifiable limit or edge. Indeed there is often a degree of overlap or a merging of dividing lines that renders a clear differentiation impossible.

This area is the margin, the porous grey area, or buffer zone, in which the integrity and permanency of identities are questioned and contested.

MARGINS, CENTERS, AND SOCIAL ORDERING

If the margin is a place of ambiguity and transgression, its correlative, the center, is a place where normative values and structures are more firmly rooted and clearly expressed and the contingency of identities less apparent. In the fields of anthropology and sociology, the focus on margins has underpinned many attempts to map the organizing principles and structures of communities through the analysis of their ritual and social practices. Arnold van Gennep, in his pioneering work on rights of passage published in 1908, identified the margin as representing the transitional stage between separation from and incorporation into successive social statuses, a form of social limbo prior to assuming the attributes and titles of a more clearly defined social position within an established form of social ordering.[1] Victor Turner's development of these observations in his classic studies of ritual processes and social performance in the 1960s and 1970s sought to examine the tension created by the play between what he termed "structure" and "anti-structure." While the former represented society as a clearly differentiated and hierarchically organized whole, the latter was more closely associated with the transitional, or liminal, stage in which society was envisaged as a rudimentary and relatively undifferentiated "communitas."[2] Social life, for Turner, was therefore characterized by the dialectical play between established forms and the anti-structures that come to the fore during liminal moments when the freedom afforded by the leveling and erasure of identifying attributes of status permitted what Turner called "ludic invention." As he stated, "the primordial and perennial agonistic mode is the social drama."[3] Transition, the crossing of boundaries, therefore, obviated the processes whereby states were defined: against the mediacy and rigidity of structure stood the immediacy and freedom of "communitas." Turner's analysis of the dynamics of social interaction, therefore, provided a model in which the social whole remained healthy so long as the creative tension between structure and anti-structure, center and margin, order and disorder, remained in balanced relation.

In his extensive critique of modernity, the French critic Michel Foucault characterized the margin as a designated site that required constant surveillance rather than a place for ludic invention. In his early
writings in particular, Foucault sought to reveal the means whereby the
rationalizing impulses of the early modern state and its policing of the
individual sought to maintain the integrity of the established form of
social ordering by consigning to the margin those considered a threat to
the normative structures of political ordering. He illustrated the manner
in which this repressive discourse of power operated in his classic studies
of the hospital and the prison.[4] For Foucault, the stability and norms of
the center were only ever secured in dialogue with the margin understood as the place where those considered a threat were contained or kept
within limits. Although coming from a very different disciplinary background, the English anthropologist Mary Douglas was similarly interested in the tension between center and margin. In her influential work
on pollution and taboo she examines the processes whereby cultures
differentiate between the pure and the polluted in their descriptions of
social integrity and cleanliness. For Douglas, the ritual activity of separation sorts the clean from the dirty, the acceptable from the unacceptable, in a process that symbolically describes the normative boundaries
of a healthy community while simultaneously admitting to the perennial
anxiety of contagion. In this case, the margin becomes the site of the displaced to which matter out of place can be banished, a place where objects identified as threatening decompose and rot, losing their identity
as they lose their form, joining the undifferentiated mass of dirt.[5]

In the work of the historian Benedict Anderson, on the other hand,
limits are an essential component in the cultural identification of nation-
states. For Anderson, all nations are inherently limited "because even
the largest of them . . . has finite, if elastic boundaries, beyond which lie
other nations." Given their size and relative impersonality, Anderson
argues, a sense of communality can only be generated through a process
he describes as "the imagination of communities," the marshaling of a
range of symbolizing practices to create a specific identity so that "in the
minds of each lives the image of their communion."[6] The attention paid
to spatial and symbolic margins in these influential studies of social description has helped carry margins to the center of recent sociological
and cultural analysis. And the emphasis here lies very much on the term
"description" understood not only as the process of writing down, but also

as a form of delineation, the tracing of a line or establishment of limits and their function in describing centers.

MARGINS, OTHERS, AND DISPLACEMENT: THE RENAISSANCE AND MODERNITY

In offering a variety of methods for the reading of representational practices, cultural studies has made one particularly significant contribution in focusing attention on the "Other," understood as that which lies beyond the limits and the experiences of those who pass through the legitimating structures of a given society.[7] Amongst the consequences of the attention paid to that which lies beyond is a heightened awareness of the importance of identifying the subject position of the cultural reader. In place of Clifford Geertz's famous definition of culture as "the ensemble of stories we tell ourselves about ourselves," cultural studies encourages us to focus upon the ensemble of stories we tell ourselves about others in the process of our own self-identification.[8] The focus upon processes of cultural stereotyping and the means whereby differences are naturalized within our explanatory narratives has made us aware of the dangers of carrying our own cultural assumptions into our reading of the cultures of others.[9] It is almost impossible when "reading in" to another culture not to place the values of one's own culture as the norm, the cultural "Other" being assessed in terms of its deviation from the "normal" center. As a consequence, many interpretations, or cultural readings, end up constructing what is alien in oppositional terms: as barbarous or uncivilized.[10]

This spatial awareness of culture's place has resulted in a different conceptualization of the margin. Rather than facilitating in the explanation of a transitional stage within a particular cultural configuration, it is now seen as the porous and permeable interface between cultures, the area, both physically and symbolically, where the lines of differentiation and limits are not as crisp and clear as they seem from the center. The postcolonial critic Homi K. Bhabha, for example, has not only questioned as overly prescriptive the limits of the modern Western nation as described by Anderson, but also suggested that the sheer diversity of cultural forms resists universalist narratives, such as Marxist historicism or liberal democracy, that seek to contain culture within specific symbolic or territorial boundaries.[11] For Bhabha, culture exists in a "third space" that he terms "hybridity," thereby becoming a displaced phenomenon that resists domination and provides a site where new identities, representations, and meanings can be expressed through cultural "translation."[12] This displacement of culture from the boundaries of nation-states is nowhere more evident than in the study of so-called "diaspora," minority communities in exile. At once settled and yet away from home, the tensions that arise between native and adopted cultures "produce 'diaspora space' where boundaries of inclusion and exclusion, of belonging and otherness, of 'us' and 'them,' are contested."[13] This problematizing of the notion of a clearly identifiable culture per se finds parallels in the postmodern questioning of the idea of an "essential" self. In place of the alienated individual of modernism, postmodern critics have focused attention on the decentered and fragmentary nature of human subjectivity itself, or on what has been referred to as "the displacement of the ego."[14]

This questioning of the fundamental integrity of the subject and the universality of humanity as described within the Enlightenment project strikes at the heart of the enduring characterizations of the Renaissance as the period that witnessed the birth of modern man and the rise of the culture of Western civilization. For behind much of the writing of postmodernism and cultural studies lies a critique of the centrality of modernity and by implication its Renaissance roots. Yet seeking to clarify the relationship between modernity and the Renaissance is by no means an easy task. For modernity, as configured by most postmodern critics, has seemingly little to do with the Renaissance period but rather with what Habermas characterized as the Enlightenment's impulse toward "the rational organisation of everyday social life."[15] In much the same vein, Foucault's critique of modernity is premised upon the belief that the development of the human sciences, the time when "human beings came to be interpreted as knowing subjects, and, at the same time, objects of their own knowledge," took place in the late eighteenth century.[16] However, for many critics the Renaissance shares some of the attributes associated with more broad-ranging descriptions of modernity. According to David Harvey, "the Renaissance revolution in concepts of space and time laid the conceptual foundations in many respects for the

Enlightenment project."[17] The discovery of perspective, the development of cartography, and the means of measuring space enabled man to rationalize and order nature, all key stepping-stones in the modernizing process. Political historians of Renaissance Italy have also charted the increasing bureaucratization and rationalizing tendencies of the northern Italian city-states, remarked upon by Max Weber, as evidence of the increasing sway of impersonal government over people's lives. While among literary historians Stephen Greenblatt is not alone in recognizing a perceived change "in the intellectual, social, psychological, and aesthetic structures that govern the generation of identities" in sixteenth-century England.[18] Taken together, and united with the nineteenth-century creation of the notion of universal "Renaissance Man," these observations trace the origins of modernity itself back to the fifteenth century in Italy. In the words of Tony Davies: "It is the myth of the *modern;* the *Renaissance* is its infancy; and its guiding ethos, its watchword, is *humanism.*"[19]

The classic statement of the Renaissance's status as threshold or transitional moment in the passage to modernity remains Jacob Burckhardt's *The Civilization of the Renaissance in Italy.*[20] For it is there that Burckhardt celebrated the Renaissance as a time of cultural reawakening that witnessed the emergence of both the individual as a self-conscious subject and the state as an objective entity. The combination of his historical methods and acceptance of the humanists' own rhetoric of renewal and rebirth resulted in the construction of a subject who was not only educated and male, but also responsible for the production of those masterworks that best demonstrated the spirit of the age, namely the ability to realize forms conceptualized by an unfettered imagination. What was unique about the Renaissance in Burckhardt's terms was how it was culture that determined the shape of things, not politics, economics, or religion.[21] The individual, the state, festivals, social activities, all became works of art, processes in which sublime forms were expressed and realized by unbounded egos. Unafraid of neighbors, of difference, of what others thought and saw, such individuals worked within a "free intellectual mart."[22] Burckhardt's Renaissance, therefore, inhabited a space between two periods of repression; it was postmedieval and premodern. On the one side the veil of superstition and corporate belonging, on the other "the domestication of the individual" by the determining forces of the nation-state and religious dogma.[23] Yet even within the Renaissance itself

Burckhardt noted a difference between the despotic governments that sought "the control of the individual" and were organized to ensure the glorification of the ruler in question, and the republican forms of Venice and Florence that sought their own glorification: "The most elevated political thought and the most varied forms of human development are found united in the history of Florence, which in this sense deserves the name of the first modern State in the world."[24]

The figure who best embodied the attributes of "Renaissance Man" for Burckhardt was the polymath and master of all arts Leon Battista Alberti, an individual Burckhardt characterized as believing in the power of his own agency to fashion his destiny. Yet as has been pointed out by subsequent critics, such a triumphalist celebration of his creative genius and disciplinary mastery overlooked the consequences of such mastery on the lives of others. Indeed, in his famous tract on family management, *I Libri della famiglia,* Alberti has been read as furnishing the perfect example of the subjugating discourse of patriarchal bourgeois humanism.[25] The ideology of the active life of civic participation as articulated within this text at least was addressed to a powerful patriarchal minority whose power was not solely governmental but also conditioned the practices of cultural production and education. From this perspective, the Renaissance Man "unafraid of difference" becomes a member of the ruling elite "indifferent to others."

From this standpoint, the rediscovery of classical texts and forms that threw new light on the classical traditions of Rome and Greece only served to further enhance the emergent narrative of Western civilization.[26] The humanities became the discipline areas that dealt with the secular and practical orientation of these classical works as transmitted by the teaching of the humanists. The Renaissance, therefore, has been characterized as the time when the canon of great works by great men *[sic]* was established. Under these conditions a recognizable humanist consensus was formed that became embedded with an educational program that privileged a certain canon as the proper object of study for the human sciences.

In addition, the most vibrant cultural centers of the period were often mercantile and republican. Renaissance political forms and cultural concerns, therefore, occupied an important position in the genealogy of republican liberal capitalism as found within the Atlantic republican tradition and in successive accounts of the origins of what has been termed "western bourgeois individualism."[27]

MARGINALIZING THE RENAISSANCE

Described in these terms, the Renaissance occupies an important place in postmodern critiques of the hegemonic discourse of "western, euro-centric humanism" and its subjugating discursive practices that effec-tively silenced its marginalized "Others."[28] This is reflected, for example, in the characterization of literary modernism as a movement that has "predominantly been represented in white, male, heterosexist, Euroamer-ican middle-class terms."[29] The potential contribution of postmodernism to the re-visioning of Italian Renaissance studies lies, therefore, in its questioning of this supposed cultural hegemony, by focusing upon the processes whereby such an account of the Renaissance was constructed as a historical narrative. In seeking to marginalize or destabilize the Renaissance configured as center, the insights of postmodernism serve to reveal the extent to which such representations of the Renaissance are in fact functions of a particular reading of the Renaissance as historically perpetuated within the Academy. One of the consequences of such an approach is to reveal how European humanism and the Renaissance understood as cultural center are in fact vital to the self-identification of those seeking to differentiate themselves from its apparent dominating discourse. Could it be that the durability of such a culturally "centered" characterization of the Renaissance is in part due to its necessity for those writing the histories of groups they perceive as marginalized or silenced?

So what impact might these debates within contemporary cultural theory have on our own reading of Italian culture during the period from the late Trecento to the early seventeenth century? One answer might be that they encourage us as historians to reexamine the boundaries and norms of our own discipline area, to look beyond traditional parameters in order to question the extent to which disciplines in the very act of description shut out as much as they embrace. This possibility is partic-ularly worth considering in relation to the identification of Renaissance cultural history. For part of the scope of this volume is to continue the process of marginalizing the Renaissance itself with a view to redescrib-ing its center by taking the question of limits and margins back to that center—and more particularly to centers within that center, specifically Florence and Venice.[30] As many of the studies in this volume prove, the Renaissance always had its own margins. In marginalizing the Renaissance by focusing upon its edges we can bring it back to the center of cultural debate. In its elitist embodiment it has been critically exiled and taken to represent the old way of doing things, ironically facilitating the identification of new approaches to cultural history.

For understood as center, the Renaissance has in fact furnished the means whereby other discipline areas have been able to construct their own identities through difference. Medieval studies, in particular, has taken advantage of the insights of postmodernism to address its seeming marginality relative to a discourse that characterized it as a dark age caught between the enlightenment of the classical and Renaissance periods.[31] Significantly, it is in the process of decentering the Renaissance and examining its own edges that it can rejoin a debate concerning the politics of culture where the emphasis lies more on the contingent play between constantly shifting centers and margins, at an individual, group, and societal level, than a static model in which the Renaissance itself as threshold of modernity becomes the stigmatized "Other." For as Lee Patterson has pointed out, postmodernism has furnished tools for the consideration of the history of premodern culture in a manner that seeks to avoid the traditional binary opposition of medieval/Renaissance through a focus on the shared concerns with the interrelation of spatial and discursive positions in the constitution of subjectivities. Whereas previously accounts of medieval selfhood were rendered almost impossible by the manner in which the subject as subject was identified as a Renaissance creation, the postmodern concern with issues of identity has reconfigured the point of departure through a focus on issues of difference in a manner that has thrown into clear relief the extent to which Renaissance narratives of individualism were themselves necessarily predicated on their establishment of difference from what went before.[32] It is precisely in the otherness of the premodern that postmodernism provides illuminating vistas into ways of writing about the distant past, as many of the texts in this current series demonstrate.

In terms of reading culture, therefore, postmodernism has carried the margin back to the center by focusing attention on groups and voices that previously had been marginalized by the hegemonic discourse of traditional "mainstream" elitist culture. It is here that its insights can be of service in our re-visioning of the Renaissance through the provision of alternative critical perspectives that destabilize the traditional representation of the "Renaissance" as hegemonic center. In this context, the choice of the term "premodern" in the title of this volume is deliberate. Postcolonialism, women's studies, ethnic studies, queer studies, and cultural studies more generally have all opened up previously unexplored areas of study through the formation of alternative canons and the writing of histories of groups and peoples previously excluded by traditional Western historiography.[33] In focusing on specific minority groups and marginal voices in premodern Italy, several of the essays in this volume pursue approaches not incompatible with what Phillip Brian Harper has defined as "the social logic of post-modern culture."[34] For minority groups were at the margins, sociopolitically decentered, long before the contemporary critical concern with the decentered subject. In much the same way as Harper has sought to add the experience of the socially marginal to the postmodern debate concerning decentered subjectivity, so the essays in this volume seek to illustrate how those at the sociopolitical margins of Italian cultural life in the premodern period were also implicated within the construction and contesting of established forms of social ordering.

In reexamining the center, therefore, the intention is not solely to tell the story of how "Others" were subjugated and subjectified by Western humanistic discursive practices but to begin the process of recovering the lost voices of the period through pursuing different pathways, re-searching the past. For although the ability to hear past (minority) voices is necessarily a function of the hegemonic nature of the remaining documents, traces and fragments still remain that when painstakingly pieced together help overcome such institutional forgetting.[35] Even the silences of the archive tell a story, as Carolyn Steedman has noted: "Its condition of being deflects outrage: in its quiet folders and bundles is the neatest demonstration of how state power has operated, through ledgers and lists and indictments, and through what is missing from them."[36] So as those previously silenced or marginalized by mainstream culture seek to construct their own identities, they are also producing new histories.

The importance for scholars of the Renaissance of taking up what Peter Burke refers to in his essay as the "challenge" of postmodernism, therefore, is apparent from the current status of Renaissance studies within the Academy. For one consequence of bringing the margin to the center has been the displacement of the center to the margin. In part, I would argue that those writing such revisionary history, consciously or otherwise, actually have a vested interest in maintaining a culturally "centered" characterization, or stereotype, of the Renaissance as part of their own subject positioning. Yet more importantly, with a few notable exceptions, Italian Renaissance studies in particular has proved resistant to engaging with the questions being raised in current cultural and literary theory. This may in part be due to the continuing weight of the classical tradition that has fostered the continued study of elite and canonical literary, political, and artistic practices. As I began my own postgraduate studies I recall being reminded that as a Renaissance scholar I was working at the coal face of civilization, a process that required training in Latin and Italian at least if I was to be able to mine the past successfully. Such skills are still relevant, but the key issue concerns their subsequent deployment. In the intervening years the field has become assimilated, some would say lost, within the resurgent fields of medieval and early modern studies as the Italian Renaissance undergoes its own identity crisis. In the face of the articulate and assertive voices that have moved to the center of the academic arena, Renaissance studies has apologetically stepped aside either cowed by the identification of their field as the source of the oppressive colonial discourse of Western humanism or consciously resistant to joining wider debates within cultural studies that they often characterize with patrician disdain as intellectual dumbing down and devoid of real scholarship. In the process they have been left in the wake of a cultural criticism that has adopted the insights of postmodernism and postcolonialism and dispensed with the universal Western rational subject constructed in the nineteenth century and first sighted by the likes of Burckhardt in Quattrocento Florence. Iain Chambers has gone so far as to give this new approach to cultural history a name: "post-humanism."[37]

Yet in the process of being marginalized, the Renaissance is actually beginning to rewrite itself through a heightened awareness of its own margins. For the Italian Renaissance, and centers such as Florence and Venice, has always had its own margins, and the insights afforded by anthropology and sociology have had a clear impact upon the study of the social, ritual, and economic history of the peninsula from the late Trecento to the early seventeenth century. The humanism of Renaissance urban centers was always the discourse, however hegemonic and articulate, of a numerical minority. In concentrating sustained attention on the marginalized majority within late medieval and Renaissance Italy this volume seeks to further displace the outdated, yet obdurate, characterization of "modern" Renaissance Man constructed in the nineteenth century.[38] This process is already underway. Attempts, in the words of Claire Farago, to "reframe the renaissance" by examining its encounter with the "Other" cultures of Latin America have been undertaken, while other studies have sought to shift attention away from specific centers to an examination of the modifying process of cultural translation that took place between them.[39] Others have sought to rewrite the Renaissance through examining voices and texts produced by women outside the circle of rhetorically trained male patrician elites or, in another form of decentering, to queer the Renaissance by questioning its normative heterosexuality.[40]

Within Renaissance studies itself, however, certain cultural centers have continued to predominate in terms of the volume of scholarship undertaken and the extent of the critical focus afforded them. Florence, Venice, and Rome still enjoy a disproportionate quantity of critical attention, and the prevalence of the so-called "Florentine model" both in humanistic and art historical terms is often lamented by scholars working on other cities or subject communes.[41] In taking the margins back to these centers of a Renaissance understood as center, the essays in this volume seek to show that they themselves not only were shaped by their encounters with both their material and symbolic margins, but also partook in marginalizing practices that sought to ensure the integrity and stability of their patrician-dominated forms of social ordering. Subjection and marginalization, therefore, took place at the very source of "centered" Western Eurocentric humanism. In this context it is worth focusing attention on how perceived threats to the stability of such centers were managed by those in authority, the manner in which dissident "Others" were silenced or contained by them, and the traces and fragments that exist that indicate the presence, however muted, of other voices.

Such work has been pioneered in the Florentine context by Richard Trexler and his many writings on the dispossessed and urban poor. In his seminal study of Florentine formal behavior, *Public Life in Renaissance Florence,* for example, Trexler argues that Florentine civic identity in the fifteenth century was transformed by the involvement of "new ritual groups" in the festivals and ritual processions and events that constituted the city's ritual framework.[42] Drawn from liminal groups of children, youths, and the working poor "living on the edge of the communal society," the "forced absorption" of these groups effected a transformation in Florentine civic identity, "for the *communitas florentia* found it could not do without the processional presence of these outsiders. Once the procession included them, Florence was no longer the same."[43] Similarly, the imagination of the city as community was enhanced by the participation, specifically during the feast of the city's patron saint, of the subject cities that constituted the Florentine territorial state. Coming from outside, they helped objectify and define Florence as dominant center.[44] Trexler's concern with charismatic centers and marginal groups is not surprising given his use of social anthropology as the critical prism through which he read Florentine civic life, yet to date, the use of such critical tools furnished by anthropology, and more recently postmodernism, has remained limited.

In this context it is worth considering some of the paths of enquiry that the critical perspectives assumed by postmodernism and contemporary cultural theory might open up, how they might recondition the terms of research, the questions asked of the archive: in sum, what a decentered Renaissance might look like. Significantly, it would involve the extensive traversal of traditional disciplinary boundaries. In this context Burckhardt himself, the author often held responsible for the cult of "Renaissance Man" and the association of the period with elite Western culture, was himself aware of the possibility of alternative readings of the past and the particularity of his own subject position.

While his own work has been characterized by many as defining the center, Burckhardt was alive to, and embraced, the possibility of its displacement: "In the wide ocean upon which we venture, the possible ways and directions are many; and the same studies which have served for this work might easily in other hands, not only receive a wholly different treatment and application, but lead also to essentially different conclusions."[45] Indeed, the universality of "Renaissance Man" was always partial. There is ample irony in the fact that Alberti, the quintessential secular "Renaissance Man" of Burckhardt's text, was himself shaped by his encounters with cultural marginalization, from his illegitimacy to the political exile of his family. Burckhardt's secular and bourgeois family man was in fact a celibate, beneficed cleric.[46] Far from seeing him standing alone as creative genius, the more recent characterizations of Alberti have stressed the intersubjective and relational dimension of his life and his writings. His codification of the arts of painting, building, grammar, and family management were constituted through, if not always in the literary form of, dialogue, permitting the articulation of multiple voices, and it is striking that Burckhardt's egocentric "Genius" should have penned an anonymous autobiography in a confusing attempt to call himself into being.[47] The disciplinary structures of the Renaissance arts and the humanism of the humanities, therefore, were never as prescriptive as they have been represented. The agency of the subject was, and is, exercised within conditioning, rather than determining, contexts.[48]

In this spirit, the current volume takes up the invitation issued by Burckhardt in his introduction to *The Civilization of the Renaissance in Italy:* "Such indeed is the importance of the subject that it still calls for fresh investigation, and may be studied with advantage from the most varied points of view."[49] This applies to the consideration of the problems posed by both senses of the term, namely the "subject" as discipline area and the subject as "self." Through re-searching the Renaissance archive, both the priorities that governed its constitution and the eloquence of its silences are acknowledged.[50] The aim of the following essays is to bring the margins to the fore in examining Renaissance culture and in the process furnish alternative narratives that question the modernity of Renaissance Man and the rationality of the Renaissance state.

NOTES

1. Arnold van Gennep, *The Rites of Passage,* trans. Monika B. Vizedom and Gabrielle L. Caffe, intro. Solon T. Kimball (London: Routledge, 1977).

2. Victor Turner, *The Ritual Process: Structure and Anti-Structure* (London: Routledge, 1969), 94–130.

3. Victor Turner, *From Ritual to Theatre: The Human Seriousness of Play* (New York: PAJ Publications, 1982), 11. See also pp. 20–60, "Liminal to Liminoid in Play, Flow, and Ritual: An Essay in Comparative Symbology."

4. See Michel Foucault, "Of Other Spaces," *Diacritics* 16 (1986): 22–27; *The Birth of the Clinic: An Archaeology of Medical Perception,* trans. A. M. Sheridan Smith (London: Tavistock Publications, 1973); and *Discipline and Punish: The Birth of the Prison,* trans. Alan Sheridan (Harmondsworth: Penguin, 1977).

5. Mary Douglas, *Purity and Danger: An Analysis of the Concepts of Pollution and Taboo* (London: Routledge, 1995 [1966]).

6. Benedict Anderson, *Imagined Communities: Reflections on the Origin and Spread of Nationalism* (London: Verso, 1983), 6–7.

7. Of the many introductions to Cultural Studies, see Ziauddin Sardar and Borin Van Loon, eds., *Cultural Studies for Beginners* (Cambridge: Icon Books, 1997); and Simon During, ed., *The Cultural Studies Reader* (London: Routledge, 1993).

8. See Clifford Geertz, *The Interpretation of Cultures* (London: Fontana Press, 1993).

9. See the essays in Kathryn Woodward, ed., *Identity and Difference* (London: Sage, 1997); and Michael Pickering, *Stereotyping: The Politics of Representation* (Basingstoke: Palgrave, 2001).

10. See Stuart Hall, "The Spectacle of the 'Other,'" in *Representation: Cultural Representations and Signifying Practices*, ed. Stuart Hall, 223–79 (London: Sage, 1997).

11. See Homi K. Bhabha, "DissemiNation: Time, Narrative and the Margins of the Modern Nation," in *Nation and Narration*, ed. Homi K. Bhabha, 291–322 (London: Routledge, 1990).

12. Homi K. Bhabha, *The Location of Culture* (London: Routledge, 1994).

13. Sardar and Van Loon, *Cultural Studies for Beginners*, 134. See also Raymond Chow, *Writing Diaspora* (Bloomington: Indiana University Press, 1993); and Jonathan Rutherford, ed., *Community, Culture, Difference* (London: Lawrence and Wishart, 1990).

14. See Kenneth J. Gergen, *The Saturated Self: Dilemmas of Identity in Contemporary Life* (New York: Basic Books, 1991).

15. Jürgen Habermas, "Modernity–An Incomplete Project," in *The Anti-Aesthetic: Essays on Postmodern Culture*, ed. Hal Foster (Port Townsend, WA: Bay Press, 1983), 9. For example, Charles Taylor in *Sources of the Self: The Making of the Modern Identity* (Cambridge: Cambridge University Press, 1989) makes no mention of Renaissance humanism.

16. See Hubert L. Dreyfus and Paul Rabinow, *Michel Foucault: Beyond Structuralism and Hermeneutics* (Brighton: Harvester Press, 1986), xv. For Foucault's description of the "Renaissance *episteme* of similitude" as the primary means of organizing knowledge in the sixteenth century, see Michel Foucault, *The Order of Things: An Archaeology of the Human Sciences* (London: Tavistock Publications, 1980), 17–30. A useful critique is provided by Ian Maclean, "The Process of Intellectual Change: A Post-Foucauldian Hypothesis," *Arcadia* 33 (1998): 168–81.

17. David Harvey, *The Condition of Postmodernity* (Oxford: Blackwell, 1989), 242–49 (quote at p. 249).

18. See Max Weber, *The City*, ed. and trans. Don Martindale and Gertrud Nuwith (New York: Free Press, 1958). See also the collection of papers in Julius Kirshner, ed., *The Origins of the State in Italy, 1300–1600* (Chicago: University of Chicago Press, 1996). On the increasing bureaucratization of the Florentine state and its imposition of "ego restraints" on individuals, see the thesis of Marvin B. Becker, *Florence in Transition*, 2 vols. (Baltimore: Johns Hopkins University Press, 1967–68), and his "Individualism in the Early Italian Renaissance: Burden or Blessing," *Studies in the Renaissance* 19 (1972): 273–97. Stephen Greenblatt, *Renaissance Self-fashioning: From More to Shakespeare* (Chicago: University of Chicago Press, 1980), 1.

19. Tony Davies, *Humanism* (London: Routledge, 1997), 15–25 (quote at p. 22) and 72–104.

20. Jacob Burckhardt, *The Civilization of the Renaissance in Italy*, trans. S. G. C. Middlemore (Oxford: Phaidon Press, 1945).

21. Jacob Burckhardt, *Reflections on History*, trans. M. D. H (London: George Allen & Unwin, 1944).

22. Burckhardt, *Civilization of the Renaissance*, 82: "not one of them was afraid of singularity, of being and seeming unlike his neighbours."

23. See Lionel Gossman, *Basel in the Age of Burckhardt: A Study in Unseasonable Ideas* (Chicago: University of Chicago Press, 2000); and Jörn Rüsen, "Jacob Burckhardt: Political Standpoint and Historical Insight on the Borders of Post-Modernism," *History and Theory* 24 (1985): 235–46.

24. Burckhardt, *Civilization of the Renaissance*, 48.

25. Leon Battista Alberti, *I Libri della famiglia*, ed. Ruggiero Romano and Alberto Tenenti (Turin: Einaudi, 1980). See the comments of Constance Jordan, *Renaissance Feminism: Literary Texts and Political Models* (Ithaca: Cornell University Press, 1990), 51–53; and Carla Freccero, "Economy, Woman, and Renaissance Discourse," in *Refiguring Women: Perspectives on Gender and the Italian Renaissance*, ed. Marilyn Migiel and Juliana Schiesari, 192–208 (Ithaca: Cornell University Press, 1991).

26. See the classic study of Roberto Weiss, *The Renaissance Discovery of Classical Antiquity* (Oxford: Basil Blackwell, 1969); and more recently Leonard Barkan, *Unearthing the Past: Archaeology and Aesthetics in the Making of Renaissance Culture* (New Haven: Yale University Press, 1999).

27. For a classic example of this tradition, see J. G. A. Pocock, *The Machiavellian Moment: Florentine Political Thought and the Atlantic Republican Tradition* (Princeton: Princeton University Press, 1975). For a more Eurocentric discussion of the republican tradition, see Martin van Gelderen and Quentin Skinner, eds., *Republicanism: A Shared European Heritage* (Cambridge: Cambridge University Press, 2002). For an alternative presentation of the Atlantic as a medium of cultural transmission and as an analytical category, see Paul Gilroy, *The Black Atlantic* (London, Verso, 1993); and for a critique of "bourgeois individualism," see Richard Levin, "Bashing the Bourgeois Subject," *Textual Practice* 3 (1989): 81–94.

28. See the introduction to Abdul R. JanMohamed and David Lloyd, eds., *The Nature and Context of Minority Discourse* (New York: Oxford University Press, 1990); and Robert Young, *White Mythologies: Writing History and the West* (London: Routledge, 1990).

29. Peter Childs, *Modernism* (London: Routledge, 2000), 12.

30. For a recent "decentered" view of the Renaissance, see Peter Burke, *The European Renaissance: Centres and Peripheries* (Oxford: Blackwell, 1998).

31. See, for example, Jeffrey Jerome Cohen, ed., *The Postcolonial Middle Ages* (New York: St. Martin's Press, 2000).

32. Lee Patterson, "On the Margin: Postmodernism, Ironic History, and Medieval Studies," *Speculum* 65 (1990): 87–108; and such volumes as Michael Goodrich, ed., *Other Middle Ages: Witnesses at the Margins of Medieval Society* (Philadelphia: University of Penn-

sylvania Press, 1998); and Jeffrey Richards, *Sex, Dissidence and Damnation in Minority Groups in the Middle Ages* (London: Routledge, 1990).

33. See, for example, the texts published in the University of Chicago Press series *The Other Voice in Early Modern Europe*, edited by Margeret L. King and Albert Rabil Jr.

34. Phillip Brian Harper, *Framing the Margins: The Social Logic of Postmodern Culture* (New York: Oxford University Press, 1994).

35. See Iain Chambers, *Border Dialogues: Journeys in Postmodernity* (London: Routledge, 1990), 103–17.

36. Carolyn Steedman, *Dust* (Manchester: Manchester University Press, 2001), 68.

37. Iain Chambers, *Culture after Humanism: History, Culture, Subjectivity* (London: Routledge, 2001), 2–5.

38. On the marginality of the majority, see the comments of Michel de Certeau, *The Practice of Everyday Life*, trans. Steven Rendall (Berkeley: University of California Press, 1984), xvi–xvii.

39. See Claire Farago, ed., *Reframing the Renaissance: Visual Culture in Europe and Latin America 1450–1650* (New Haven: Yale University Press, 1995); Germaine Warkentin and Carolyn Podruchny, eds., *Decentring the Renaissance: Canada and Europe in Multidisciplinary Perspective 1500–1700* (Toronto: Toronto University Press, 2001); and Stephen J. Campbell and Stephen J. Milner, eds., *Artistic Exchange and Cultural Translation in the Italian Renaissance City* (Cambridge: Cambridge University Press, 2004). In the context of the more highly theorized arena of English Renaissance studies, see David Norbrook, "Life and Death of Renaissance Man," *Raritan* 8 (1989): 89–110; and Viviana Comensoli and Paul Stevens, eds., *Discontinuities: New Essays on Renaissance Literature and Criticism* (Toronto: University of Toronto Press, 1998).

40. Margaret Ferguson, Maureen Quilligan, and Nancy Vickers, eds., *Rewriting the Renaissance: The Discourses of Sexual Difference in Early Modern Europe* (Chicago: University of Chicago Press, 1986); and Jonathan Goldberg, ed., *Queering the Renaissance* (Durham: Duke University Press, 1994).

41. See, for example, the essays collected in Paula Findlen, Michelle M. Fontaine, and Duane J. Osheim, eds., *Beyond Florence: The Contours of Medieval and Early Modern Italy* (Stanford: Stanford University Press, 2002).

42. Richard C. Trexler, *Public Life in Renaissance Florence* (New York: Academic Press, 1980).

43. Ibid., 368. See also the three volumes published by Trexler under the title *Power and Dependence in Renaissance Florence* (Binghamton, NY: Medieval and Renaissance Texts and Studies, 1993), which deal in turn with the city's children, women, and workers.

44. Trexler, *Public Life*, 256–62.

45. Burckhardt, *Civilization of the Renaissance*, 1.

46. See Thomas Kuehn, "Reading between the Patrilines: Leon Battista Alberti's *Della Famiglia* in Light of His Illegitimacy," in *Law, Family, and Women: Toward a Legal Anthropology of Renaissance Italy* (Chicago: University of Chicago Press, 1991), 157–75.

47. See Michael Baxandall, "Alberti's Cast of Mind," in *Words for Pictures: Seven Papers on Renaissance Art and Criticism* (New Haven: Yale University Press, 2003), 27–38; Anthony

Grafton, *Leon Battista Alberti: Master Builder of the Italian Renaissance* (London: Penguin, 2002); and John M. Najemy, "Giannozzo and His Elders: Alberti's Critique of Renaissance Patriarchy," in *Society and Individual in Renaissance Florence,* ed. William J. Connell, 51–78 (Berkeley: University of California Press, 2002).

48. Calvin O. Schrag, *The Self After Postmodernity* (New Haven: Yale University Press, 1997).

49. Burckhardt, *Civilization of the Renaissance,* 1.

50. See Stephen J. Milner, "Partial Readings: Addressing a Renaissance Archive," *History of the Human Sciences* 12 (1999): 89–105.

2

Margins and Minorities

Contemporary Concerns?

Derek Duncan

There is a short passage in Umberto Eco's medieval thriller *The Name of the Rose* that illustrates a number of the issues relating to current debates on marginality that seem so pervasive in cultural criticism.[1] The passage alludes particularly to the function that the margin might have for the center and to the relationship between the two. Shortly after their arrival at the unnamed Abbey somewhere in the north of the Italian peninsula, William and Adso, the novel's detective heroes, interrupt their tour of the Abbey's grounds to peer over a parapet. Far below lies what appears to be a pile of straw partially covered by snow. Adso's reflections on what they see are worth considering, for they transform this apparently insignificant and chance sighting into a metaphor for the way in which life in the Abbey is organized, understood, and experienced: "I [Adso] say straw, because it was a great heap of decaying matter, the smell of which reached the parapet I was looking over; clearly the peasants came from lower down to take from it to use on their fields. But other solid waste was mixed in with the human and animal excrement, the whole flood of dead matter that the Abbey expelled from its own body in order to keep itself clean and pure in its dealings with the mountain summit and with heaven."[2] The Abbey's ejection of all its waste products has more than just a practical function. On a symbolic level, the removal of potentially contaminating material ensures the spiritual as well as physical well-being of the Abbey. Yet this procedure has ambiguous results: the Abbey is never truly free of its waste; out of sight its smell acts as a reminder of its insidious presence. Moreover the status of the waste as "dead matter" is relativized by the use the local peasants make of it to fertilize their fields. It returns as an important element in the local economy.

In his novel, Eco constructs a society that is rigidly ordered on both an ideal and day-to-day level. The symbolism of the Abbey's architectural structure with the lofty library situated antagonistically in relation to the lowly and visceral kitchen, the way in which entry to various parts of the edifice is controlled by those in power, and the hierarchies that structure not only life in the Abbey, but also its relations with the surrounding territory are examples of how extensive the process of social ordering is. Adso's pile of straw is a compelling metaphor for an imperfect and complicated social order that strives in vain to achieve a clear sense of differentiation between a pure center (the Abbey) and an impure margin or exterior. The process of social ordering and the implications that such ordering has for individuals outside the center is a major concern of the novel. As a means of approaching the condition of "otherness," the pile of straw is suggestive in a number of ways. First, it reveals much about what the other is perceived to be (waste); second, it points to where it should be found (outside/below); and third, it alludes to the feeling it evokes (disgust). Yet as Adso's remarks indicate, the other cannot be removed so easily from the social body. The waste's smell is indicative of how it might return, physically insinuating itself back into the center.

The passage shares important elements with this volume of essays, whose project in some respects is to try to recover the waste matter of the past. First, it raises the question of how a given society projects itself onto the landscape and organizes its spaces. Space is not a passive medium simply awaiting occupation but something that is expressive of the social fabric. This leads to a broader question of how space is occupied and, eventually, to a consideration of possible structural connections between identification and habitation. Does space in some sense confer an identity? If so, how do different spaces/identities interact with each other? How self-contained can they in fact be? Finally, the passage alludes to the fact that from the perspective of the center what lies at the margin is concealed. The hidden nature of the margin's presence means that it is only recoverable through the faintest of traces. From a researcher's point of view the assessment of its historical specificity is therefore a complex and potentially fraught process. Although the margin's concealment is not absolute, a certain critical energy is required, not just to look over the parapet, but to attempt, as Adso does, actively, yet attentively, to interpret the social document he sees. Location, identity, and text move to the center in the essays that follow as they bring to the fore other histories through a rereading of the textual and contextual margin.

In developing some of these concerns, I want to keep Eco's novel as a point of reference for a number of reasons. It is a text that is very knowing about its status as a bridge between the present and a distant, obscure past. Eco is well aware that there are many ways in which the Middle Ages can be written and that even the most philologically precise is never wholly innocent.[3] Moreover, it is a novel that can be said to be about order, but more especially about the process of ordering. This is demonstrated in countless ways; the arrangement of the books within the library, the arrangement of manuscripts within a book, the codification of the meaning of precious stones, the debates over laughter and heresy are just some examples. *The Name of the Rose* reveals that the various inclusions and exclusions that this ordering entails are often arbitrary, yet never insignificant, for the attribution of meaning to perceived difference has political and social consequences. Nor does the process give any guarantee of permanence even as it aspires to it. At the highest level, the novel demonstrates that the center itself is contested terrain. Who is at the center? The pope or the emperor? How marginal are the warring factions within the church compared to the impoverished hoards that live outside? How do marginalities differ? Events in the novel take place at a time when ecclesiastical learning was being challenged by the growth of secular universities. Economically, too, the power of the abbeys was being supplanted by that of the urban centers. As the center is reconfigured, what happens at the margins? Or indeed to the margins? Whose margins? Whose center?

My aim here is to sketch out some of the potential difficulties encountered in thinking and writing about those people who appear to be very distant from the center of power in a given society and whose lives have gone largely unrecorded. Mostly they appear not as clearly defined individuals, but as members of some group linked by an apparently defining characteristic that rendered them and their lives intelligible to their contemporaries, or retrospectively made them significant to modern-day scholars. Information about their lives tends to come from hegemonic sources—legal documents, conduct manuals, tax records, sermons—

that necessarily shape them according to their own requirements. In many respects, these texts are prescriptive rather than descriptive. What is largely missing are sources that allow these lives to be expressed in their own terms in order to give the reader some idea of what it was like to have inhabited the periphery. This desire for some subjective record is doubtless anachronistic in that it belongs to our present rather than the past. It is certainly, in part at least, a symptom of cultural criticism's current interest in questions of identity, how they are formed, and their role in social practice. Yet these theoretical and political concerns are not presentist; the editors of one important collection of essays on identity argue that they are fundamental to an understanding of the project of European expansionism from the Early Modern period onward.[4] The projection of European ideas onto "discovered" territories and peoples, and their subsequent "invention" through this process of misrecognition, can be understood as characteristic of how place and identity are given meaning within a regime of power.[5] The claim, for example, that the United States of America is a "nation of migrants" depends on the persistence of the belief that no one was there to begin with. The often occluded processes of negotiation through which identities are established, and as a result of which may prematurely crystallize, is a recurrent theme of the essays in the current volume as they attempt to investigate the complexity of the variegated means through which identities are conferred and assumed.

The democratic imperative to shift attention away from the center and onto the center's others is an expression of contemporary concerns about the periphery and, I would suggest, is profoundly at odds with any totalizing desire somehow to complete the past through fitting together yet more pieces of its complex jigsaw. Paradoxically, it serves to underline the very incompleteness of the past that, like identity, is always partial and never whole. Stuart Hall argues that identities come into being at the point where discourse and subjectivity meet, the terrain on which the psychic and the social come together.[6] This division (although it is a fictive or conventional division) allows for contrasting sets of questions. First, with an emphasis on the social constitution of identities, it raises issues of definition and categorization. How were groups defined? How stable and inclusive were such definitions? In whom did the power of designation reside? Were such designations reinforced by legal statute? Were they simply the banal expressions of a commonsense notion of social differentiation? To what extent were the categories contested? These are questions that belong not solely to the historical moment under investigation but also to that of the researcher. To what extent are the categories of identity we deploy now to describe our own society applicable to other contexts?

The second, related area of investigation will focus on the question of subjectivity, or identification. To what extent, and in what ways, were those deemed part of socially marked groups conscious of their status? If there was such a consciousness did this result in a sense of common purpose or action? What links are there between identification and contestation? Again these are questions pertaining not solely to the time of the subject under scrutiny, but also to that of the researcher. What motivates a scholarly interest in one grouping rather than another? What identifications are being made over time, and what effect do they have on how the object of study is invoked and animated?[7]

What links these two aspects are the questions of power and of agency. How is power distributed in a given context? Does power emanate from above and assert itself through its own force, or are there more subterranean networks in play? What form of power attaches itself to the apparently powerless? Can they become powerful through association, or enhance their status at some other group's expense? And what is at stake for researchers in turning our attention to those groups that may still in some way be stigmatized today? What do we gain or lose through this kind of association? Is there more to it than the desire to leave no stone unturned in the selfish quest for academic novelty?

The terms "margins" and "center" are by now so familiar that it is easy to lose sight of the metaphorical nature of the terms and the connotations they possess. The reliance on metaphor to trace relations of power between dominant and subordinate groups is itself suggestive of the allusive nature of such networks. To describe, for example, a grouping as "marginal" or "at the center" ascribes to it a geographical location that is at the same time a hierarchical one. Nevertheless, it implies that the grouping does inhabit a space that is proper to it and that its space is identifiable. This draws attention to the question of space and to its role in consolidating regimes of power. Additionally, these metaphorical, social spaces are attributed with symbolic resonances. Very often the margin carries associations of resistance and transgression while the center is seen in terms of stasis and constraint. From this perspective, the very existence of the margin challenges the hegemonic order. This idea depends on a belief that the marginal constitutes an order containing different values and norms from the dominant one and does not simply exist in a hierarchical relationship to it. While this may indeed be the case it seems important not to assume in advance that the margin is inevitably a place of anarchic delight or revolutionary practice, and the center one of uniform conservatism and conformity. Neither can it be assumed that the two (if the binary is to be retained) are wholly separate and noncoextensive. Whatever the margin might mean for the center, and vice versa, that relational axis will not fully determine their constitution, for at the very least they will have mechanisms of internal ordering and organization that may in effect create their own margins and effects of exclusion.[8] Such caution needs also to be exercised in the too literal understanding of the terms "majority" and "minority," for majorities can be disenfranchised and minorities can wield power. Ania Loomba gives a very pertinent and resonant reminder of the potential imprecision of such terminology when she refers to the black communities in South Africa under apartheid as a "marginalised majority."[9]

The excerpt from *The Name of the Rose* quoted above could almost be read as an introduction to the central thesis of Mary Douglas's book *Purity and Danger*, a work of social anthropology whose insights have played a key, if sometimes unacknowledged, role in subsequent debates on the functions and constructions of identity.[10] The book's primary aim is to examine social rituals around what is perceived to be dirt in so-called primitive cultures. Dirt, Douglas insists, is relative, and its designation as such and subsequent management occupies an important place in how societies organize themselves and imagine themselves to operate. For Douglas, attempts to eradicate dirt are most profitably seen as attempts to effect control over the environment. They are critical in establishing boundaries demarcating a clear divide between the clean or pure inside and the polluted exterior. For this reason, what constitutes the boundary may often be afforded totem or sacred status. Douglas argues from the outset that the type of material most commonly perceived as polluted and polluting is that which has been evacuated from the human body (excrement, urine, blood, and semen). The human body, she contends, is a powerful symbol of any "bounded system" that on the one hand appears contained and autonomous yet is susceptible to leakage and also infiltration. The symbolic body is a vulnerable body whose margins need to be policed in order to ensure their integrity.

In order to appreciate the implications of Douglas's argument, it is necessary to move outward away from the human body to consider what it represents, and to consider how procedures adopted to maintain the purity of the individual body are also deployed in social terms to keep the boundaries and borders of society intact. The structural principle that prizes the discarding of bodily waste is replicated through the discarding, or disavowal, of those bodies deemed socially impure. In an obvious sense, this can entail closing geographical frontiers, limiting or strictly controlling entry. Internally, however, this principle operates to stigmatize and exclude individuals or groups that are somehow believed to pose a threat to social integrity. What counts is not the verifiable nature of that threat, but rather the result of its purging. The ritualized removal of the infected parts strengthens that which remains. It is an act of social and psychological fortification.

Although Douglas does not attempt to pursue the political or social implications of her work, it has been taken up by a number of theorists who see in it a mechanism to elucidate the psychological dynamics of power relations in the social field.[11] However, there is a danger that the too rigid application of this model insinuates a static and totally inflexible model of the dynamic of domination. What Douglas describes is best seen as a process rather than as the creation of a definitive product. The "purity and danger" of her book's title do not represent an antithetical and exclusive pairing. The relationship between the terms is one of complicity rather than opposition, for they are different aspects of what is at stake in the construction and maintenance of identity.

Again Eco's novel gestures toward Douglas's thesis but on this occasion also moves beyond it. One of the principal concerns in *The Name of the Rose* is heresy: how it operates within the body of the church, and how powerfully the attribution of a heretical identity to an individual or group works to ensure an often violent exclusion. William is in the Abbey to take part in talks between representatives of the pope and the Franciscan minority who argue that Christ's vow of poverty must be taken literally. Yet, it soon emerges that what is at stake in this theological dispute is the temporal role of the church and its entitlements. The novel's political dimensions relate primarily to struggles internal to the church, but these struggles are themselves part of the broader conflict between church and empire that, in turn, open out onto the tension between religious and secular authority in the burgeoning city-states of Europe. At the level of high politics, the debates over Christ's poverty seem mere pretexts for the articulation and resolution of issues of temporal power.

Eco is less interested in the debate itself than in the mechanism used to force a resolution. As an expression of theological dissent, heresy can be seen as a practice of dissident reading, the production of textual interpretation that is not simply incorrect, but rather is believed to challenge, or at least have the power to challenge, existing configurations of the permissible. Heresy is the politicization of reading and transforms a potentially solitary activity into one that is primarily social in both its intent and its effects. The charge of heresy is not invoked to classify a set of beliefs or ideas according to some set of objective criteria, but to determine and outlaw opposition. The designation of heresy constructs what it claims to describe. The heretic cannot by definition be simply ignored.

Yet for Eco, heresy is not solely about the subtleties of learned disputation and the practice of reading nor about power and the deployment of force within the church itself. The accusation of heresy is employed as a means of social control. In the novel this is represented most graphically by the torturing of alleged heretics and the burning at the stake of the unnamed peasant girl suspected of witchcraft.[12] Their heresy is not primarily theological, but a response to their social condition. The accusation of heresy is most commonly directed against those whose religious unorthodoxy is expressed through a resistance to the temporal authority of the church.

This broader definition of the heretic can be used to understand the marginalization of other groups in different contexts whose social exclusion is justified through a rhetoric of demonization. In his introduction to a collection of essays on the construction of "race," Henry Louis Gates at one point writes starkly: "Blacks and other people of color could not write."[13] His deceptively straightforward announcement of a historical situation relating to the position of the early black population in the United States stands, in his essay on "race" and its cultural inscriptions, as a paragraph in its own right. The enormity of this statement's implication can barely be estimated, for it points not to a historical situation in which a group of people had been denied the chance to acquire literacy skills, but to one in which a notion of "race" had been deployed that had determined blacks unable to learn. This inherent inability could then be used to justify the tyranny of slavery and naturalize a social hierarchy. It is all the more startling given that the participants in the debates referred to by Gates were themselves so central to the foundation of supposedly progressive Enlightenment thought. Consequently, arbitrary and ferociously divisive notions of racial difference nestle within modernity itself and give lie to the liberal ambitions of its project.

Yet, as Gates demonstrates, it was also known that blacks could read and write, for the law threatened to punish those who learned as well as those who presumed to teach them. Black-authored texts from this period are few, and, as Gates infers, when they did exist were often imitative of those written by white men. What Gates describes is a violent intensification of the situation in which many marginalized groups may find themselves. Much is written about them yet little by them; this discursive imbalance creates the subsequent problem that very often the dominant center has constructed the terms through which a group can express itself. To speak consciously from the margins implies an acknowledgment of a socially intelligible and significant position of alterity. On a similar level, just as disempowered groups tend to be the objects rather than subjects of hegemonic discourse, they tend to be written about in terms that presuppose a singularity of identity and experience.[14] Where such groups do possess a cultural tradition through which to articulate some form of self-definition, this is usually perceived to lack credibility; it is necessarily partial from the perspective of the center.

Nonetheless, it is now a commonplace of cultural criticism that whatever inhabits the margins of a given social formation is far from marginal (in the sense of unimportant) to how that formation operates. Margins are dangerous precisely because of their capacity potentially to reform the center, and thus are seen as lawless territories in need of stern regulation. One issue that is often overlooked, however, is the experience of living in a marginal space, or the lived consequences of bearing a marginal identity. What does it mean to be the object of fascinated disgust and inhabit the perilous borderlands?[15] For one must ask exactly who is fascinated or imperiled by such lives. While Douglas's work successfully draws together psychic and social aspects of identity construction, it does not seek to go beyond the social symbolism of tainted identities to explore what it was like to be tainted. As such, the centrality of the center remains paramount, for the margin is significant precisely to the degree that it remains encapsulated by its marginal position. Only by looking for other axes of location and signification can the marginal literally move away from the center. While it would be naive to assume that any group could ever be wholly autonomous, by shifting the angle of vision from which it is seen other perspectives might emerge that rewrite accounts from the center.[16]

For those who have been able to speak from the margins, Foucault's idea of "reverse discourse" suggests a partial solution to the problem.[17] He argues that those who find themselves confined by external modes of categorization can nevertheless exert some limited form of agency by speaking back through these same categories. For example, in modern Western societies, stigmatized groups can utilize the juridical and pathologizing terms used to define them negatively in order to argue for legal entitlements on the basis of post-Enlightenment notions of human rights. Never entirely self-defining, the subject, in Foucault's terms, can deploy some element of influence through acting out a contestational subjectivity within given formulations of identity. Yet, it is this almost retrospective assumption of identity that has led some critics to comment on the belatedness of identity formations.[18] These formations invariably preexist those that inhabit them.

While the Foucauldian notion of a "reverse discourse" allows the subject at least the possibility of negotiating identity, it does not mean that identity can ever become full or even representative. Hall writes of the excess that extends beyond identity's limits, an excess that has led some recent cultural theorists to question the value of retaining "identity" as a useful tool. The case against identity has received greatest impetus from the work of Judith Butler.[19] While endorsing a feminist politics, Butler questions the apparently timeless stability that attends the term "woman" on whose behalf feminism has claimed to speak. She argues that the category cannot precede its discursive formation but instead that "woman" is produced and fashioned by discourse. Butler's antifoundationalism offers another take on the misgivings voiced within feminism that the singularity of the term "woman" has too often had white, middle-class, educated, first-world women as its principal referent. Factors such as race, class, location, and generation complicate the universal signifier and the claims made on its behalf. Just as there is conflict between prescriptive notions of identity imposed from above and their contestation from below, so too can what might be termed lateral identities overlap and clash. Distinctions of, say, race and gender do not necessarily reside comfortably in a single body. Different contexts alter the saliency of specific differences that, in any case, are never singular. It needs to be remembered that even from within, such identities will be partial and exclusive. A self-elected identity will still have its own margin or minority, its own uncomfortable and complicating excess.

If it is the case that identity demands purification, it is not solely the identity of the dominant that does so; less obviously powerful groups can effect exclusions of their own, exclusions that may not translate into a social system, but that, nevertheless, create other patterns of influence, knowledge, and coercion in the social framework. In the normal run of things no one person or group will be equally and consistently empowered and no one will suffer uniform disempowerment although the chances are clearly not the same for everyone. In attempting to study the links between identity and power, it is important to bear in mind the shifting parameters in which power operates and the provisional contingency of identity in a given situation.

The problem of definition is not, however, one that belongs solely to the past in the sense that, nowadays, the theoretically aware are so attuned to the stakes of cultural difference that "we" can stand above the confusions and delusions of our naively partial ancestors. Iain Chambers makes this precise point: "Our interpretations of society, culture, history and our individual lives, hopes, dreams, passions and sensations, involve attempts to *confer* sense rather than to *discover* it. For it is we, with our histories, languages, memories and constraints, who make sense. We never arrive at the bottom of things: the analysis always remains open."[20] The determination to "make sense" has been apparent in much of the cultural analysis that has been generated in recent years by critics themselves "marked" by identity. Those inspired to produce work contesting normative understandings of history and text through drawing attention to the role played by categorizations of issues such as gender, race, and sexuality are often, though not inevitably, marked by these categories themselves. Yet the simple fact of belonging to one of these categories guarantees little in itself, least of all a research project. Nor does it guarantee that such categorizations will be contested rather than reevaluated. The point again is not to reverse the center/margin hierarchy.

Writing from inside the discursive context of queer studies, Margaret Hunt warns very appositely that, for example, an overemphasis on the growth of homosexual subcultures in Renaissance cities can lead to an all too easy narrative that moves toward "the progressive attainment of a unitary homosexual identity."[21] This move both underwrites a certain notion of the Renaissance as the birthplace of the modern world, and also delimits the very variegated and complex history of homosexuality both male and female. She also cautions against the wish to see in the ill-defined nature of male friendships of the period a kind of erotic golden age that has since fallen into sad decline. Apart from anything else, the freedoms we might imagine to have obtained necessarily formed part of a more complex social network of relations and cannot be held in approving isolation from it. While alternative narratives of subaltern experience have undoubted appeal, the task is to retain a critical sense of the whole without falling for the claims of a new totality.

If Eco's postmodern meditation on the past has any message for the reader it is perhaps to reiterate such a warning. The novel abounds in examples of how to read astutely, and also of how to be enslaved to the false authority of the text. The Abbot is the main exponent of the practice of enslaved reading. His lecture to the novice Adso on the language of precious stones exemplifies the work of reading as an act of homage to received belief: "The language of gemstones takes many forms, each one expresses several truths, according to the sense of the interpretation one chooses, according to the context in which it appears. And who decides on the correct level of interpretation, and on the correct context? You know, my boy, you've been taught this: it is authority, the surest commentator of all, and the one most invested with prestige, and therefore with sanctity."[22] His aim is to still the questioning energies of the young reader through the reassertion of the prerogatives of the center. Adso is not silenced, for William, his master, intervenes. In many respects, William is the novel's ideal reader. His constant interrogation of the world as text makes him an exemplary critic and historian. William refuses ever to believe absolutely in a single interpretation, preferring to operate through conjecture, always retaining the sense of alternative possibilities. It is when he abandons this principle that he fails as a detective, for he invests too much in a single interpretation of the series of murders that had occurred in the Abbey. Too late, he discovers that they were linked, not by a single narrative thread, but by a network of contingencies that created the semblance of an order when, in fact, what was going on was a complex and contradictory process of negotiation between participants not always aware that a dialogue was taking place.

Consequently, it is Adso, the novel's naive narrator, who reveals himself to be Eco's most astute and circumspect reader by virtue of his very tentativeness. Toward the end of the novel, Adso, by now an old man, sifts through the sparse fragments of text that have been salvaged after fire engulfed the Abbey and its great library. His memory clouded by age, his understanding bolstered by the illusion of hindsight, Adso questions the meanings he has attributed to the past, wondering if they are the effects of chance rather than divine design. His narrative becomes a lamentation as he realizes that what he cannot in any way name is his one earthly love, the girl he had sex with in the Abbey's kitchen and who was subsequently burned at the stake as a witch. Adso and William were powerless to intervene and save her from the zeal of the Inquisition. Yet, their powerlessness is of an entirely different order from that of the girl herself, who experiences power as absolute domination over her body. Adso's narrative cannot resurrect the unnamed girl, who is in effect unnameable, and whose very abjection cemented relationships in the center of power. For the detectives, powerlessness is negotiated and potentially reversible. Adso's identification over time with the girl is also that of the historian looking at the pieces of the past unsure of how to name and commemorate what was there.

Eco's narrative seems to me to pose the types of question we might consider when approaching areas of scholarly inquiry that demand some degree of tact and respect for what in many ways are lost objects, if they were ever objects at all. What is perhaps needed is an informed openness to a network of problems that are necessarily insoluble. As a corollary to this I would propose what might be termed an ethics of reading combining scrupulous attention to source, and crucially to context; a practice of reading that recognizes the lacunary nature of its object yet does not remain daunted by it. Its supplement would be a cautious empathy that admits the limitations of its own locatedness yet is open to the possibility of connection. To approach lives lived on the periphery requires an ability to read and interpret what is at the textual margin. It also demands that an attempt is made to understand these lives in their variegated complexity, and not primarily with the pretext of creating an even fuller picture of the center by examining how the center is reflected from its margins.

NOTES

1. Umberto Eco, *Il nome della rosa* (Rome: Bompiani, 1980).

2. Ibid., 93. The translation is mine: "Dico strame, perché si trattava di una gran frana di materia puteolente, il cui odore arrivava al parapetto da cui mi affacciavo; evidentemente i contadini venivano ad attingervi dal basso onde usarne per i campi. Ma alle deiezioni degli animali e degli uomini, si mescolavano altri rifiuti solidi, tutto il rifluire di materie morte che l'abbazia espelleva dal proprio corpo, per mantenersi limpida e pura nel suo rapporto con la sommità del monte e col cielo."

3. See Umberto Eco, "The Return of the Middle Ages," in *Faith in Fakes: Travels in Hyperreality* (London: Minerva, 1986), 59–85.

4. Kwame Anthony Appiah and Henry Louis Gates, "Introduction: Multiplying Identities," in *Identities*, ed. Appiah and Gates, 1–6 (Chicago: University of Chicago Press, 1995).

5. The idea that places are constructed through discourse, the ways in which they are talked, thought, and written about, is associated particularly with Edward Said's groundbreaking *Orientalism* (London: Routledge, 1978).

6. Stuart Hall, "Who needs 'Identity'?" in *Questions of Cultural Identity*, ed. Stuart Hall and Paul du Gay, 1–17 (London: Sage, 1996).

7. For a discussion of the experience of archival research and of how that experience broadens social and psychological uses of the past, see Carolyn Steedman, "The Space of Memory: In an Archive," *History of the Human Sciences* 11 (1998): 65–83. For an exploration of the potential uses the past might have for the contemporary queer historian and political activist, see Scott Bravmann, *Queer Fictions of the Past: History, Culture and Difference* (Cambridge: Cambridge University Press, 1997).

8. The inevitability of this is suggested by Gayatri Spivak, the postcolonial feminist critic, who in reference to her own practice notes: "by pointing to a feminist marginality, I have been attempting, not to win the centre for ourselves, but to point out the irreducibility of the margin in all explanations." Quoted in Lidia Curti, *Female Stories, Female Bodies: Narrative, Identity, Representation* (Basingstoke: Macmillan, 1998), 3.

9. Ania Loomba, *Colonialism/Postcolonialism* (London: Routledge, 1998), 14.

10. Mary Douglas, *Purity and Danger: An Analysis of Concepts of Pollution and Taboo* (London: Routledge, 1995 [1966]).

11. See most notably Julia Kristeva, *Pouvoirs de l'horreur* (Paris: Seuil, 1980). For an application of this model in a more specialized sense, see Jackie Stacey, *Teratologies: A Cultural Study of Cancer* (London: Routledge, 1997). Her influence is also felt in a study drawing largely on Bakhtin's notion of the carnivalesque: Peter Stallybrass and Allon White, *The Politics and Poetics of Transgression* (London: Methuen, 1986). Examining the social valences of symbolic distinctions between high and low, this work can be read as a useful gloss on Eco's *The Name of the Rose*.

12. For a discussion of the links between power, torture, and the visual, see Elaine Scarry, *The Body in Pain: The Making and Unmaking of the World* (New York: Oxford University Press, 1985). Also Michel Foucault, *Discipline and Punish: The Birth of the Prison*, trans. Alan Sheridan (Harmondsworth: Penguin, 1977), 3–69.

13. Henry Louis Gates Jr., "Writing 'Race' and the Difference It Makes," in *Writing "Race" and Difference* (Chicago: University of Chicago Press, 1986), 9.

14. Much recent work on autobiographical writing, for example, attempts to overcome the leaden sameness that is often attributed to those belonging to specific groupings. For a discussion of this issue in reference to working-class expressions of identity, see Regenia Gagnier, *Subjectivities: A History of Self-Representation in Britain, 1832–1920* (Oxford: Oxford University Press, 1991).

15. For a complex and moving account of what it might mean, for example, to inhabit the marginal space of a lesbian/Chicana identity, see Gloria Anzaldùa, *Borderlands/ La Frontera: The New Mestiza* (San Francisco: aunt lute books, 1987).

16. This enterprise necessarily calls into question the subject position of the writer/ historian. For an extended meditation on the hidden yet omnipresent white self expressed obliquely through representations of blackness, see Toni Morisson, *Playing in the Dark: Whiteness and the Literary Imagination* (London: Picador, 1993).

17. Michel Foucault, *History of Sexuality*, vol. 1, *An Introduction*, trans. Robert Hurley (Harmondsworth: Penguin, 1990), 101.

18. This sense of "belatedness" is commented on by Rosi Braidotti, *Nomadic Subjects: Embodiment and Difference in Contemporary Feminist Theory* (New York: Columbia University Press, 1994), esp. 35. It is also a key element in the construction of colonialist identity mapped out by Homi K. Bhabha, *The Location of Culture* (London: Routledge, 1994).

19. Judith Butler, *Gender Trouble: Feminism and the Subversion of Identity* (New York: Routledge, 1990), and *Bodies that Matter* (New York: Routledge, 1994).

20. Iain Chambers, *Border Dialogues: Journeys in Postmodernity* (London: Routledge, 1990), 11. See also the essays in Lynn Hunt, ed., *The New Cultural History* (Berkeley: University of California Press, 1989).

21. Margaret Hunt, "Afterword," in *Queering the Renaissance*, ed. Jonathan Goldberg (Durham: Duke University Press, 1994), 360.

22. Eco, *Il nome della rosa*, 451: "Il linguaggio delle gemme è multiforme, ciascuna esprime più verità, a seconda del senso di lettura che si sceglie, a seconda del contesto in cui appaiono. E chi decide quale sia il livello di interpretazione e quale il giusto contesto? Tu lo sai ragazzo, te l'hanno insegnato: è l'autorità, il commentatore tra tutti più sicuro e più investito di prestigio, e dunque di santità."

3

Decentering the
Italian Renaissance

The Challenge of Postmodernism

Peter Burke

This case study of the implications of postmodernism is presented from the point of view of a practicing historian rather than that of a philosopher or critic, despite occasional trespassing into other disciplines from time to time. To begin with the assumption on which the following discussion depends: every generation has to rewrite history, not because the past has changed, even if there is always a little more of it than before, but essentially because the present is changing, and with it the assumptions and the needs of readers of history. In other words, like the anthropologist, the historian is a kind of interpreter, a "cultural translator" we might say, who attempts to make the language of the past intelligible to the present.[1] And our present happens to be the age of postmodernity.

We may not all be very happy with that period label. Curiously enough, historians, comparatively speaking, have not contributed their share to the interdisciplinary and international debate on postmodernity, despite the fact that periodization is their professional concern and it is, after all, always good to know what age one is living in. There have of course been discussions of the postmodern challenge to historical knowledge.[2] However, historians surely ought to be discussing other issues as well. From a cultural historian's point of view, at least, the term "postmodern" looks somewhat odd, for several reasons. It is a label for a period that distrusts labels, or better, in which some people like to parade their distrust of labels. Like the modernity against which the postmoderns — or at least the postmodernists — define themselves, the concept should be viewed as a rhetorical device for a given generation to present itself as special. The label should not be taken too seriously, although it may still be adhering to us a hundred years from now, in the same way that the term "Renaissance," once employed by a handful of Italian artists and writers such as Giorgio Vasari to describe their own age, has been transformed into the common currency of later historians.

However, this chapter is concerned not so much with postmodernity as with postmodernism, in other words the cultural movement, or cluster of movements, in architecture, philosophy, literature, and so on, that launched the idea of postmodernity in the first place.[3] Two characteristics of these movements are particularly relevant to anyone interested in European cultural history, including the Italian Renaissance. The remainder of this chapter will focus on these two characteristics: the critique of Grand Narrative and the linguistic turn.

THE CRITIQUE OF GRAND NARRATIVE

The first phrase refers in particular to the critique of what is sometimes called the "Master Narrative" of the rise of modernity and of Western civilization via ancient Greece and Rome, Christianity, the Renaissance, the Reformation, the Scientific Revolution, the Enlightenment, and the French and Industrial Revolutions. The recent vogue of "microhistory" might be regarded as an implicit critique of this kind of narrative, since the shift of interest from "great men" such as Martin Luther to ordinary people like Martin Guerre clearly has egalitarian implications. Another implicit critique is the movement for the "decanonization" of the classics in literature departments in universities in the United States and elsewhere.

The explicit critique of Grand Narrative, which like other narratives is also an interpretation, is associated with the late Jean-François Lyotard in particular. However, related problems to Lyotard's were raised at virtually the same time, the late 1970s, in a lecture by an American historian of the Renaissance, William Bouwsma. Both authors concentrated on the problem of defining modernity.[4]

Modernity is indeed an ambiguous concept. It is one that has been in almost continuous use ever since the twelfth century, if not before. The problem is that in almost every successive century it has acquired a somewhat different meaning. One cannot expect any term or concept to carry such a burden of meaning without cracking under the strain. For this reason it might be a good idea for historians to abandon the word "modern" altogether, or at the very least to discriminate more systematically between its different meanings.

The traditional view of the Italian Renaissance as the origin of modernity, the view made famous by Jacob Burckhardt, is particularly vulnerable to criticism. Of which modernity was the Renaissance the origin? Since Burckhardt's day we have come to associate modernity less with the individualism of which he approved and more with the industrialization, railways, and democracy that he hated.[5]

The fundamental problem is the tradition of identifying ourselves, readers of history, with the humanists and artists of the Renaissance. If we are to understand the Renaissance (or the Middle Ages or the ancient world), we would surely be well advised to view it as an alien culture. At the very least (since there surely are degrees of otherness), we should view the culture of the Renaissance as a half-alien culture, one that is distant from us and indeed receding from us, becoming more alien every year.[6]

For example, the very idea of a movement to revive the culture of the distant past, the desire to return to the past, not to mention the faith in the possibility of going back, has become an alien one. It contradicts the expectation of progress that has long been important in our own culture and has not yet disappeared, however deeply its foundations may have been undermined in the last generation or so.

As an example of this otherness, one might take the famous world chronicle compiled by the Nuremberg physician Hartmann Schedel at the end of the fifteenth century and illustrated by Dürer's master Michael Wolgemut and others. The chronicle includes a number of views of Italian cities. The view of Venice is instantly recognizable, but it is somewhat disconcerting for modern readers to discover that the same image is used to represent more than one city, such as Naples, Siena, Verona, and Mantua.[7] It is if anything even more disconcerting to find an equivalent for this practice in the case of portraits. For instance, Schedel's chronicle used the same woodcut to portray Homer, the prophet Isaiah,

Hippocrates, Terence, the medieval lawyer Accursius, and the Renaissance philosopher Filelfo. In other words, these representations contradict our assumptions of the uniqueness of the individual.[8]

The ambiguities of the term "modernity" are only a part of the problem raised by the critique of master narratives in general and in particular by the critique of the narrative of the Rise of Western Civilization as a triumphalist story that passes over the achievements and contributions of other cultures. How can and how should historians of the Renaissance react to this challenge?

There would seem to be three options. The first is to ignore the challenge and go on as before. After all, most readers of history books, at least in Britain, are probably indifferent to the debate over postmodernism and may even be unaware of its existence. All the same, many of them are not the readers of (say) thirty years ago. Come to that, the place of reading in our culture is not the same as it was thirty years ago. The problem of representing the Renaissance to a new generation, re-presenting the Renaissance, will not go away.

The second extreme option is to stop speaking about the Renaissance altogether; in other words to treat it as an obsolete concept, whether because it does not apply to popular culture, because women did not have a Renaissance (though some did, in my view at least), because the major breaks in European cultural history came earlier or later, in the thirteenth and seventeenth centuries rather than around 1400 and 1600, or finally because the younger generations have lost interest in the topic. It is doubtless for this last reason that a number of gifted scholars teaching in American or Canadian universities have abandoned the Renaissance and turned to subjects with more obvious relevance to the lives of their students.[9]

All the same, in many parts of the world Italian high culture of the fifteenth and sixteenth centuries has not lost its appeal. On the contrary, the *Birth of Venus* and the *Mona Lisa* have never been so well known as they are today, and no one has so far produced a better name than Vasari's for the movement of which they are a part. That leaves only the third or moderate option, which is to try to revise or reframe or rewrite the Renaissance.

There is more than one way of doing this. One way might be to forget about modernity and present the Renaissance as a "postmedieval" movement. One advantage of this move is that a number of leading humanists defined their own culture by contrast to that of the "Middle Ages," a period that they in a sense invented as a foil to their own, to define themselves by contrast to the recent past. The culture created by the artists and humanists was in important respects different from what went before, even if it was not necessarily similar to what came after.

Another possibility, to be explored further in this chapter, is to present the Renaissance in a "decentered" fashion, that is, as a movement that coexisted and interacted with other movements and indeed with other cultures in a process of permanent cultural exchange across geographical, social, and chronological boundaries, including the boundaries that are both described and transgressed by other contributors to this volume.

This approach emphasizes Renaissance exchanges with Gothic, for instance, with scholasticism, with popular culture, with Byzantine culture, and so on. At a time when debates on multiculturalism are in progress, it may be easier than before to notice the Renaissance exchanges between the Christian, Jewish, and Muslim worlds. Interestingly enough, the German art historian Edgar Wind was already using the now fashionable term "hybridization" in the 1950s, to refer to the interaction of classical and Christian culture.[10]

In an age of increasing globalization it may also be helpful to look at the Renaissance in an explicitly comparative perspective. Take the case of European ambivalence to Italy, for example, a combination of admiration and envy for Italian cultural achievements with a deep suspicion of Italian morals and perhaps also a fear of loss of identity, expressed in phrases like "Tedesco" (or "Inglese") "Italianato diavolo incarnato." It might be interesting to compare this reaction, or mixture of reactions, with (say) traditional Japanese ambivalence to Chinese cultural models.[11] One might even extend the comparison to the contemporary Third World's ambivalence to the West, which has led to a debate on "aping" and "ideas out of place" (the classic Brazilian phrase) without the participants expressing any awareness of the fact that they are echoing—not to say aping—European debates of the sixteenth century.[12]

A decentered or polycentric view of the Renaissance has become associated with the concept of "reception." The term is not a recent coinage, but goes back to the late nineteenth century, when German-speaking scholars in particular discussed the reception of Roman law and that of the Italian Renaissance in Northern Europe.[13] What is new is

the centrality of the idea, linked to the current concern—if not obsession—with interaction, encounter, dialogue, and so on. Also new is the
view of "receiving" (in the wake of the voluntarist cultural theory of
Michel de Certeau) as a process of creative adaptation or reinterpreta-
tion.[14] Studies of the spread of the Renaissance beyond Italy are taking
this line more and more.[15] Italy itself might also be analyzed in this way,
placing more emphasis than before on interaction between regions (the
Neapolitanization of the Florentine Renaissance, say), interaction between
social groups, and so on.

An interest in interaction is associated with an interest in stylistic
pluralism at the level of the individual as well as the culture. Aby Warburg's famous essay on the last will of Francesco Sassetti, a microhistori-
cal study of an individual who took what he wanted from medieval and
Renaissance culture, now looks astonishingly fresh, so well does it fit
current preoccupations.[16] Some recent studies of fifteenth- and sixteenth-
century art show the same artists shifting styles from "Gothic" to "Renaissance" according to the demands of different patrons or the conventions of different genres and settings.[17]

It is tempting to borrow from seventeenth-century Catholic theology
and to describe this recent shift in the practice of cultural historians as
the rise of "Occasionalism." Earlier cultural historians, especially the
Marxists, had assumed that a noble or a bourgeois would behave in a predictably consistent way. Frederick Antal, for example, argued that the
feudal worldview of the early fifteenth-century Florentine nobility was
associated with a taste for Gentile da Fabriano, while the bourgeois worldview was expressed by the realism of Masaccio.[18] In contrast, some recent
studies suggest that the same artist or patron behaved differently on different occasions, in different social settings or cultural contexts. For example, Gentile's pupil Pisanello produced paintings in the international
Gothic style at the same time as making his famous Renaissance medals.
Even the handwriting of some artists and humanists varied between
Gothic and Renaissance scripts according to the occasion.[19]

A vivid illustration of occasionalism comes from Japan in the late
nineteenth century, when at least part of the upper classes lived what
has been called a "double life," having adopted Western culture without
giving up their own traditions. They compartmentalized the two cultures
rather than mixing them, eating and dressing in the Western manner
on certain occasions and furnishing a single room in Western style in

their houses (just as their more Westernized descendants sometimes furnish a single room in the traditional manner in their apartments).[20] These Japanese were "bicultural," just as many people were and are bilingual, and like bilinguals they were able to switch from one code to another. The linguistic analogy brings us inevitably to the linguistic turn, the second characteristic of postmodernity to be discussed in this chapter.

THE LINGUISTIC TURN

The so-called "linguistic turn" in the humanities is a useful piece of shorthand, although—as usual with such slogans—it refers to a number of different phenomena or trends that really need to be distinguished, three in particular. In the first place, a greater concern with the language (including the rhetoric) of historical documents, from Machiavelli's *Prince* (say) to wills or petitions or graffiti. In the second place, the idea of culture as a text. In the third place, an emphasis on the power of language in everyday life, indeed on "discursive construction," rejecting and even inverting social determinism.

This third emphasis goes with a greater concern with "invention," as seen in a number of book titles of the 1980s and 1990s—the invention of Tradition, of Athens, of George Washington, of Argentina, of Scotland, and so on. However, the invention of invention is not as recent as many people seem to think; a Mexican historian, the late Edmundo O'Gorman, was already thinking in terms of the invention (as opposed to the discovery) of America at the end of the 1950s.[21] This reaction against social determinism and its accompanying stress on the power of human inventiveness may well have gone too far, but it has surely been illuminating, not to say liberating, in its time.

To return to the Renaissance. A few at least of the concerns of a postmodern age do seem to help in interpreting a postmedieval one. For example, current concerns with the cultural construction of masculinity and femininity might lead us to a rereading of Castiglione's *Book of the Courtier* as a set of implicit or explicit directions for this purpose, or more exactly for the reconstruction of noble masculinity and femininity in the new age of gunpowder and print. At a time of intense preoccupation with the body, it is easier than before to notice the importance of new bodily practices in the Renaissance, from dancing or fencing to the gestures considered appropriate for public speaking. At a time when books and printing are declining in importance, it is perhaps easier than it used to be to understand the age of the rise of print, since we are necessarily more aware than fifty years ago of the interaction between oral and visual media—an interaction important for understanding the Renaissance dialogue, for example.[22] At a time when we hear so much about the power of language, the reasons for the Renaissance interest in rhetoric become easier to appreciate than before.[23] At a moment when it has become increasingly difficult to draw a line separating high culture and popular culture, there is one barrier less between ourselves and certain writers of the Renaissance, such as Pietro Aretino, François Rabelais, and Thomas Nashe, all of whom combined and transformed elements from both worlds.[24]

However, of all the ways in which the recent linguistic turn has illuminated Renaissance culture, the most important has surely been its undermining of the notion of fixed social identities. Today, identities now seem much more fluid or fragile than they did as little as a generation ago. Studies of the rhetoric of autobiographies, for instance, represent a reaction against earlier interpretations that—with few exceptions, such as Tindall's classic study of Bunyan—now seem literal-minded and positivist.[25] More emphasis is now placed on the idea of role models in helping us to find ourselves or construct ourselves. The idea of plural or unstable selves, once virtually confined to Buddhists, has become more general. The reaction against traditional interpretations may sometimes have gone too far. We have shifted from an interest in self-expression to an awareness of self-presentation to a concern with self-fashioning and finally to the idea of "inventing" the self, prompting the awkward question, Who is doing the inventing?

Whether or not it has been exaggerated, this changing view of identity is surely of great relevance to any view of the Renaissance, an age of famous autobiographies as of biographies, portraits, self-portraits, letters, and other "ego-documents." In the case of Italy, one thinks not only of the humanist Pope Pius II, of Benvenuto Cellini, of the Milanese physician Girolamo Cardano, but also of a host of minor figures who kept some kind of diary or journal or memoranda (known at the time as *ricordanze*).[26] Jacob Burckhardt saw this habit as evidence of what he called "the development of the individual." For some time Burckhardt's contrast between a medieval collective consciousness and an individual Renaissance consciousness has been coming to seem implausible. On one side, scholars have pointed to individualism in the Middle Ages, the autobiographies of Abelard and Guibert of Nogent, the presentation of individuals in the Icelandic sagas, and so on. Meanwhile another group of scholars has been emphasizing the importance of identifications with family or faction or fraternity or city in the Italian Renaissance.[27] They have reminded us that *ricordanze* are as much local chronicles or family histories as they are autobiographies.

To return to language. Today we are more likely than thirty years ago to see the autobiography of (say) Benvenuto Cellini in terms of the rhetoric of self-presentation rather than assuming that that compulsive boaster did everything he claimed.[28] In similar fashion we are quick to note Petrarch's self-definition by means of Saint Augustine, or Pope Pius II's self-definition by means of the model of Caesar, or Emperor Maximilian's by means of King Arthur. The literary use of these role models has its visual parallel in the so-called "allegorical portrait" or "identification portrait" in which Laura Battiferri appears as Petrarch's Laura, fra Giovanni Andrea (painted by Lotto) as Saint Peter Martyr, and so on.[29]

Again, Petrarch's autobiography in dialogue form, the *Secretum*, does not or should not seem so odd as it once did before we came to think of the self as unstable or fragmented. Petrarch was simply talking to his self or to one of them and creating personae such as "Franciscus" or "Augustinus." In similar fashion, he was concerned to rewrite his letters in order to present a better image of himself to contemporaries and posterity. Erasmus also rewrote his letters for the sake of posterity. He was able to do this more effectively because he lived in the age of print, but his aims may not have been as new as was recently argued.[30]

For a sense of the changes taking place it may be instructive to turn back to Karl Weintraub's study in the history of autobiography published in 1978, in particular the chapters on Petrarch, Cellini, and Cardano. Weintraub is sensitive to what we might call fault lines or cracks in all three of these Renaissance selves, but all the same, his emphasis falls on synthesis. The *Secretum*, for instance, is viewed as an exercise in "self-discovery." The "diverse strains" in the personality of Cellini are duly noted, but in order to discuss the way in which he communicates "a unified view of his self." Cardano is described as having "a profound sense of the complexities of life," so much so that it was difficult for him to see himself as "coherent," but this view on the part of Cardano is treated by Weintraub as a weakness, a failure to delineate his personality.[31]

Recent work on the art of biography in the Renaissance points in a similar direction.[32] The "category of the person" has been problematized.[33] More exactly, it has been reproblematized, since there is evidence that it was already seen as problematic by at least some people in the fifteenth century. As evidence for this assertion one might cite an anonymous fifteenth-century Florentine novella in which a group of friends, described as a "gang" *(brigata)* and led by no less a figure than the architect engineer Filippo Brunelleschi, try to persuade a certain carpenter, nicknamed "the fat man" *(il Grasso),* that he is not himself but a certain Matteo, a man on the edge of the group who owes money to the victim.[34] Brunelleschi breaks into the carpenter's house, locks himself in, and when the fat man arrives, imitates his voice and speaks to him as Matteo. Then Brunelleschi's friend Donatello arrives and addresses the carpenter as "Matteo." Some municipal officials, invited to join in the deception, also treat the fat man as Matteo and so arrest him for not paying the money he owes to himself. A priest contributes to the hoax, telling "Matteo" in a nicely ambiguous phrase that "pare che tu sia uscito di te" ("it seems that you are beside yourself," or more literally, "outside yourself"). The carpenter is first incredulous, then confused and stupefied, then more or less persuaded, then convinced, and finally, when he learns that he has been the victim of a hoax, he is at once relieved and furious.

This novella recounts a classic practical joke or *beffa* in the style of the period, a common social practice in Tuscany as well as a favorite theme for short stories at this time.[35] It suggests that some fifteenth-century Florentines did not have to wait for twentieth-century psychologists to tell them about the importance of the peer group in establishing what an individual believes. However, its significance goes beyond this. Just as Brunelleschi was playing with the carpenter, so the novella itself plays with the idea of the fragility of identity, with what the text calls "a fantasy of ambiguity" *(una fantasia d'ambiguità)* at the very time and in the very place where Burckhardt located what he called "the development of the individual." This example raises the possibility that the function of role models such as Caesar or Virgil or Augustine, not to mention the

increasing interest in biography evident in humanist circles, was to sta-
bilize fragile identities.[36]

To sum up. In some recent historical writing, the Renaissance has
been decentered in at least three respects: geographical, thematic, and
social. It has been decentered geographically in the sense that historians
now take a less "Florentinocentric" and even a less Italocentric view of
the movement than before. They are coming to emphasize contributions made outside Tuscany, outside Italy, and even, on occasion, outside Europe.[37] The Renaissance has also been decentered thematically in
the sense of being extended from "art" to material culture, and from
"literature" to a wide range of performances.[38] The movement has also
been decentered socially, and this in two different ways. In the first place,
popular culture is beginning to find a niche in histories of the Renaissance.[39] In the second place, there is less stress than there used to be on
the achievements of heroic individuals, even Leonardo and Michelangelo, and there is more emphasis on the collaboration of small groups.[40]
This shift in emphasis is much less dramatic than the notorious postmodern slogan of "the death of the author," but it is a shift in the same
direction.

This chapter began with the idea of cultural translation, and it ends
with another idea about the relation between past and present. There is
of course a serious danger of our projecting our postmodern concerns
onto the Renaissance. After all, it is now clear that Burckhardt projected
onto the Renaissance some of his typically mid-nineteenth-century concerns about modernity, the private individual, and so on. However, Burckhardt's position in his own culture, as a Basel patrician turned professor,
gave him insights into Italian culture in the fifteenth and sixteenth centuries, and these insights have outlasted him. Let us hope that, as in
Burckhardt's case, the change in our standpoint on the escalator of time
has given us a fresh angle of vision on the past.

NOTES

1. Thomas O. Beidelman, ed., *The Translation of Cultures* (London: Routledge, 1971);
and Sanford Budick and Wolfgang Iser, eds., *The Translatability of Cultures* (Stanford: Stanford University Press, 1996).

2. Joyce Appleby, Lynn Hunt, and Margaret Jacob, *Telling the Truth about History*
(New York: Norton, 1994); Richard Evans, *In Defence of History* (London: Granta, 1996);
and Gérard Noiriel, *Sur la "Crise" de l'histoire* (Paris: Belin, 1996).

3. Hans Bertens, *The Idea of the Post-modern* (London: Routledge, 1995).

4. Jean-François Lyotard, *La Condition post-moderne* (Paris: Minuit, 1979); William J. Bouwsma, "The Renaissance and the Drama of Western History," in *A Usable Past: Essays in European Cultural History* (Berkeley: University of California Press, 1990), 348–65; Bouwsma, "The Eclipse of the Renaissance," *American Historical Review* 103 (1998): 115–17; and Lee Patterson, "On the Margin: Postmodernism, Ironic History and Medieval Studies," *Speculum* 65 (1990): 87–108.

5. Jörn Rüsen, "Jacob Burckhardt: Political Standpoint and Historical Insight on the Borders of Post-Modernism," *History and Theory* 24 (1985): 235–46.

6. Stephen Medcalf, "On Reading Books from a Half-Alien Culture," in *The Later Middle Ages* (London: Methuen, 1981), 1–55. See also Peter Burke, "Anthropology of the Italian Renaissance," *Journal of the Institute of Romance Studies* 1 (1992): 207–15.

7. Hartmann Schedel, *Liber Chronicarum* (Nuremberg: Koberger, 1493), fols. 43r, 68r, 80r, 84r.

8. Peter Burke, "The Renaissance, Individualism and the Portrait," *History of European Ideas* 21 (1995): 393–400.

9. Examples include Jerry Bentley and Robert Finlay, who have turned to world history, and Mark Phillips, who has turned to eighteenth- and nineteenth-century historiography.

10. Edgar Wind, *Pagan Mysteries in the Renaissance* (Oxford: Clarendon Press, 1958), 29.

11. David Pollack, *The Fracture of Meaning: Japan's Synthesis of China from the Eighth through the Eighteenth Centuries* (Princeton: Princeton University Press, 1986).

12. Roberto Schwarz, ed., *Misplaced Ideas: Essays in Brazilian Culture* (London: Verso, 1992).

13. Gustav Bauch, *Die Rezeption des Humanismus in Wien* (Breslau: Marcus, 1903).

14. Michel de Certeau, *The Practice of Everyday Life,* trans. Steven Rendall (Berkeley: University of California Press, 1984).

15. A recent example is Peter Burke, *The European Renaissance: Centres and Peripheries* (Oxford: Blackwell, 1998).

16. Aby Warburg, "Francesco Sassettis letztwillige Verfügung" (1907), repr. in his *Gesammelte Schriften,* 2 vols. (Leipzig: Teubner, 1932), 1:213–46.

17. Thomas da Costa Kaufmann, *Court, Cloister and City: The Art and Culture of Central Europe, 1450–1800* (London: Weidenfeld and Nicolson, 1995).

18. Frederick Antal, *Florentine Painting and Its Social Background* (London: Routledge and Kegan Paul, 1947).

19. Hélène Michaud, *La Grande Chancellerie et les écritures royales au 16e siècle* (Paris: Presses Universitaires de France, 1967), 210 and 308.

20. Johannes Witte, *Japan zwischen zwei Kulturen* (Leipzig: Hinrichs, 1928); and Edward Seidensticker, *Low City, High City: Tokyo from Edo to the Earthquake, 1867–1923* (London: Allen Lane, 1983).

21. Edmundo O'Gorman, *The Invention of America* (Bloomington: Indiana University Press, 1961); Eric J. Hobsbawm and Terence O. Ranger, eds., *The Invention of Tradition* (Cambridge: Cambridge University Press, 1983).

22. Peter Burke, "The Renaissance Dialogue," *Renaissance Studies* 3 (1989): 1–12; Virginia Cox, *The Renaissance Dialogue: Literary Dialogue in its Social and Political Contexts,*

Castiglione to Galileo (Cambridge: Cambridge University Press, 1992); Judith Bryce, "The Oral World of the Early Accademia Fiorentina," *Renaissance Studies* 9 (1995): 77–103; and Peter Burke, "Oral Culture and Print Culture in Renaissance Italy," *Arv: Nordic Yearbook of Folklore,* 1998, 7–18.

23. Brian Vickers, *In Defence of Rhetoric* (Oxford: Clarendon Press, 1988).

24. Paul Larivaille, *Pietro Aretino fra Rinascimento e Manierismo* (Rome: Bulzoni, 1980); and Mikhail Bakhtin, *Rabelais and His World,* trans. Helene Iswolsky (Cambridge, MA: MIT Press, 1968).

25. Erving Goffman, *The Presentation of Self in Everyday Life* (New York: Doubleday, 1958); Stephen Greenblatt, *Sir Walter Raleigh: The Renaissance Man and His Roles* (New Haven: Yale University Press, 1973); and Greenblatt, *Renaissance Self-Fashioning: From More to Shakespeare* (Chicago: University of Chicago Press, 1980); William Y. Tindall, *John Bunyan Mechanic Preacher* (New York: Columbia University Press, 1934).

26. Marziano Guglielminetti, *Memoria e scrittura: L'autobiografia tra Dante e Cellini* (Turin: Einaudi, 1977); Gian-Mario Anselmi, Fulvio Pezzarossa, and Luisa Avellini, eds., *La memoria dei mercatores: Tendenze ideologiche, ricordanze, artigianato in versi nella Firenze del Quattrocento* (Bologna: Pàtron, 1980); Angelo Cicchetti and Raul Mordenti, "La scrittura dei libri di famiglia," in *Letteratura Italiana,* ed. Alberto Asor Rosa, 9 vols., 3.2:1117–59 (Turin: Einaudi, 1984); and Peter Burke, "The Self from Petrarch to Descartes," in *Rewriting the Self: Histories from the Renaissance to the Present,* ed. Roy Porter, 17–28 (London: Routledge, 1997).

27. F. William Kent and Dale Kent, *Neighbours and Neighbourhood in Renaissance Florence* (Locust Valley: Augustin, 1982); Ronald F. E. Weissman, "Reconstructing Renaissance Sociology," in *Persons in Groups: Social Behaviour as Identity Formation in Medieval and Renaissance Europe,* ed. Richard C. Trexler, 39–46 (Binghamton, NY: Medieval and Renaissance Texts and Studies, 1985); and Burke, "Anthropology."

28. Jonathan Goldberg, "Cellini's *Vita* and the Conventions of Autobiography," *Modern Language Notes* 89 (1974): 71–83; and Dino S. Cervigni, *The Vita of Benvenuto Cellini: Literary Tradition and Genre* (Ravenna: Longo, 1979).

29. Edgar Wind, "Studies in Allegorical Portraiture," *Journal of the Warburg and Courtauld Institutes* 1 (1937–38): 138–53; and Peter Burke, "The Presentation of Self in the Renaissance Portrait," in *The Historical Anthropology of Early Modern Italy: Essays on Perception and Communication* (Cambridge: Cambridge University Press, 1987), 150–67.

30. Nicholas Mann, *Petrarch* (Oxford: Oxford University Press, 1985); and Lisa Jardine, *Erasmus: Man of Letters* (Princeton: Princeton University Press, 1993).

31. Karl J. Weintraub, *The Value of the Individual: Self and Circumstance in Autobiography* (Chicago: University of Chicago Press, 1978), 98, 133, 147, 156.

32. Patricia L. Rubin, *Giorgio Vasari: Art and History* (New Haven: Yale University Press, 1995).

33. Marcel Mauss, "The Category of the Person" (1938), in *The Category of the Person: Anthropology, Philosophy, History,* ed. Michael Carrithers, Steven Collins, and Steven Lukes, 1–25 (Cambridge: Cambridge University Press, 1985).

34. "Il Grasso Legnaiuolo," in *Prosatori volgari del '400,* ed. Claudio Varese, 767–802 (Milan: Ricciardi, 1955).

35. Peter Burke, "Frontiers of the Comic in Early Modern Italy," in *A Cultural History of Humour*, ed. Jan Bremmer and Herman Roodenburg, 61–75 (Cambridge: Polity Press, 1997).

36. Peter Burke, "Individuality and Biography in the Renaissance," *European Legacy* 2 (1997): 1372–82, and Burke, "Reflections on the Frontispiece Portrait in the Renaissance," in *Bildnis und Image*, ed. A. Köstler and E. Seidl, 151–62 (Cologne: Böhlau, 1998).

37. See Burke, *European Renaissance*.

38. Richard Goldthwaite, "The Empire of Things: Consumer Demand in Renaissance Italy," in *Patronage, Art and Society in Renaissance Italy*, ed. F. William Kent and Patricia Simons, 153–75 (Oxford: Clarendon Press, 1987); Peter Thornton, *The Italian Renaissance Interior 1400–1600* (London: Zwemmer, 1991); and Dora Thornton, *The Scholar in His Study: Ownership and Experience in Renaissance Italy* (New Haven: Yale University Press, 1997). See also Paula Findlen, "Possessing the Past: The Material World of the Italian Renaissance," *American Historical Review* 103 (1998): 83–114.

39. Peter Burke, "Learned Culture and Popular Culture in Renaissance Italy," in *Varieties of Cultural History* (Cambridge: Polity Press, 1997), 124–35.

40. Burke, *European Renaissance*, 10–12.

PART II

NEGOTIATING MARGINS

4

The Ambivalence of Policing Sexual Margins

Sodomy and Sodomites in Florence

Michael Rocke

In late medieval and early modern Italy, no sexual practice was more deeply feared and reviled—at least in the official pronouncements of church and state—or more rigorously persecuted than was sodomy. One of several carnal sins that the church declared to be *contra naturam*, supposedly outside the realm of natural law because they prevented procreation, sodomy most commonly referred to sexual relations between persons of the same sex, though its meaning was typically extended to include "unnatural" relations between men and women as well. Moralists and lawmakers alike regularly branded sodomy as an abomination, the object of extreme hatred, to both God and mankind. Even its very mention was said to be defiling. As it was often portrayed, sodomy so offended God that it threatened to provoke his terrifying vengeance not only against those who perpetrated the sin but also against whole communities, the model, of course, being the misinterpreted biblical account of the destruction of Sodom and Gomorrah. Because of this vice, a Florentine law of 1418 stated, "the anger of the omnipotent God is incited in terrible judgment not only against the sons of men, but also against the fatherland and against inanimate objects." Indeed, sodomy was proclaimed to induce a host of misfortunes that afflicted society. According to a court sentence from the same city against a sodomite in 1436, this practice was to blame for wars, plague, conspiracies, and disorders of all kinds. In his *Summa theologica,* Antoninus Pierozzi, the archbishop of Florence from 1436 to 1459, cataloged the many calamities that sodomy reputedly produced: it hastened the Last Judgment when the world would be consumed by fire; it caused the great flood at the time of Noah; it perverted the reproductive purpose of the genitals; it made men more base than beasts; it provoked the indignation of the saints and the fatal retribution of God; finally, it brought on pestilence and plague, more devastating in Italy than elsewhere because the practice, he said, was so prevalent there.[1]

Those individuals who committed the sin of sodomy, and who consequently were said to bear such heavy responsibility for endangering the peace, safety, and welfare of their societies, came in for relentless condemnation. Their vices were so evil, the 1436 sentence cited above stated, that God declared sodomites to be "sinners against nature, renegades from his divine and everlasting mercy, and condemned to the everlasting flames." According to Archbishop Antoninus, these wretched creatures "died in the greatest abomination to the people of God."[2]

In Renaissance Italy this was not merely idle rhetoric. The governments of numerous Italian states gave concrete form to these expressions of fear and loathing by mounting the most widespread and systematic repression of sodomy ever known up to then in Christian Europe. Three of the peninsula's leading republics—Venice in 1418, Florence in 1432, and Lucca in 1448—took the unusual measure of creating special judiciary commissions to pursue and to castigate sodomites, and in these three cities, well into the sixteenth century, no single sexual crime was more frequently prosecuted or more heavily penalized. Throngs of people, mainly males, were hauled before the courts to be accused or tried for their illicit sexual acts, and several thousand were convicted. Commonly they had to pay ruinous fines or to endure long prison sentences or exile, while the less fortunate among them were forced to undergo raucous ritual shamings or to suffer appalling forms of mutilation, dismemberment, or the ultimate and most highly symbolic torment of death by burning.[3]

As they were represented in legal and religious discourse, and punished by the courts in Italian cities, then, sodomy and sodomites were made to appear dangerously far beyond the margins of what was morally and sexually proper, or even tolerable. The confine between "natural" and "unnatural" sexual behaviors was staked out clearly, and the consequences of violating it could be, and often were, extreme. Nonetheless, as local communities attempted to patrol and to enforce these margins, and to police the activities of the sexual outlaws in their midst, they were forced, perhaps inevitably, to adopt less clear-cut and intransigent stances. For despite the opprobrium and censure that this sexual practice officially evoked, despite the severe punishments and rigorous surveillance, sodomy—and above all male homosexual activity—was a social and sexual reality in many Italian societies that was evidently quite extensive and difficult to eradicate. Here I would like to focus on the case of Florence, a city where male same-sex relations were indeed extraordinarily common, so much so as to have earned the city an infamous reputation across Europe. Partly as a result, the ambiguities and contradictions of policing sodomy there were particularly evident.

The Florentine state in the fifteenth century deployed an innovative and remarkably prolific strategy to control sodomy that was centered on the evocatively titled Officers of the Night (*Ufficiali di notte*), the special magistracy created for this purpose in 1432 and suppressed in 1502. In these seventy years, as many as seventeen thousand different individuals were incriminated for homosexual relations alone, and some three thousand were convicted. In the century's last forty years, when prosecutions were most frequent, every year an average of approximately four hundred men and adolescents came to the attention of the courts, and fifty-five to sixty of them were condemned. These astonishing figures, especially for an urban population of around only forty thousand, far exceed those so far known for any other contemporary European city. Moreover, they demonstrably represent only the publicly visible tip of a much broader phenomenon of same-sex sodomy in this city that is largely hidden from historical view. The evidence suggests, in fact, that most fifteenth-century Florentine males would have had some form of same-sex sexual encounter at some point in their lives.[4] In the sexual culture and the social world of late medieval and early modern Florence, then, homosexual relations were anything but marginal. Rather, they were an integral feature of male experience, which is one of the reasons why their control, from a political perspective, proved so troublesome in that city.

The ubiquity of sodomitical activity in Florence in itself cautions against regarding sodomites, in anything but an abstract sense, as a separate category at the margins of social life. But there are other considerations, too, that render the identification of the people who engaged in sodomy as a distinctive and marginal group fairly hazardous. In premodern European sexual culture, sodomites did not, in the first place, constitute a discrete *sexual* class of beings; they clearly cannot be equated with the very modern categories of "homosexuals" or "gays."[5] Sodomites were defined not by the biological sex of their erotic partners, in other words, but strictly by the sexual acts they performed. People who had sexual relations that fell within the parameters of what was considered sodomy were termed sodomites, no matter whether they coupled with members of their own sex or with the opposite sex. And in fact, although the vast majority of the sodomy cases prosecuted in Florence and elsewhere dealt with sex between males, many also involved unauthorized relations between men and women, and their perpetrators were all indistinctly labeled "sodomites."

If this gender-blind usage obliterates the sexual classifications of the "homosexual" and "heterosexual" that are familiar to us, however, another popular semantic practice reveals a contemporary conception of the sodomite that narrows the definition of the category and shifts it in a different direction. In Florentine vernacular sources, the term "sodomite" referred exclusively to the so-called active or dominant partner in an erotic encounter, who normally played the role of phallic inserter. This term was almost never used to refer to the subordinate partner who took the so-called passive role, that is, the woman or, as was predominantly the case, the adolescent boy who was the object of a man's illicit erotic attentions. It was not the act alone, in other words, but above all the *role* one took in it that mattered. Paradoxical as it may seem, not everyone who engaged in sodomy, therefore, was considered a sodomite.

Moreover, while a single sexual act or relation might have gained the perpetrator the epithet of "sodomite" in a judiciary proceeding, it is questionable whether this was a designation that could have stuck for long, a possibility that further undermines the "sodomite" as a discrete and marginal category. The Florentine evidence strongly suggests that for the vast majority of people incriminated, sodomy was a rare, sporadic, or temporary transgression, by no means a lifetime or personally defining practice. Same-sex relations among males were commonly abandoned altogether after a period of youthful license, and at any age they might have been (and probably were) interspersed more or less regularly with sexual relations with women, both outside and within marriage.[6] It cannot

be assumed that a single denunciation or even conviction for sodomy—
to limit the field only to those caught in the judiciary net—meant that a
person was consequently regarded as a committed and incorrigible sodomite. The only clear ways that Florentines distinguished men who apparently had an acknowledged reputation for sodomy were as "public
and notorious" or "inveterate" sodomites, appellations that appear quite
seldom in the sources.[7] If the category of the sodomite, then, were to be
imagined in too rigid or determined a fashion, it would fail to capture the
variety of most males' sexual experience over the course of their lives and
would exaggerate the relatively little space within it that sodomy occupied.

Finally, sodomites did not constitute a distinguishable, let alone marginal, social group in the same sense that women, children, the poor,
prostitutes, persons with certain illnesses, and so forth might be considered to do. As mentioned earlier, the single defining feature of sodomites
was the consummation of a sexual act that, more often than not, was
clandestine and invisible, rendering them difficult even to notice and to
classify without some form of public prosecution. And unsurprisingly,
those males who engaged in sodomy also had no common social profile.
The evidence shows that they represented the entire spectrum of ages,
marital conditions, occupations, and statuses typical of the complex urban
world of fifteenth- and sixteenth-century Italy.[8] Although preachers and
lawmakers commonly portrayed sodomites as a well-defined and dangerous group that personified evil, as a genuine category of social and
sexual actors they were ephemeral and elusive.

However difficult they were to categorize, over the course of the later
Middle Ages sodomites became an increasingly common feature of the
public scene and the collective mentality of Florence as a result of vast
changes in the ways that the sexual margin defining them was policed.
The system of controlling sodomy that the Florentines developed in the
fifteenth century considerably shifted the boundaries that delineated
their community's sexual landscape. Within the space of just a few years
in that century's early decades, sodomy was transformed from a crime
that was brutally punished but seldom prosecuted, to one that was mildly
penalized but tried routinely on practically a daily basis. Until 1415, the
law prescribed that convicted sodomites be either fully castrated or
burned alive. These extreme penalties, typical for this crime throughout
Europe, not only stressed the monstrous character of this "unnatural"

act but also disarmed the sodomite's potential threat, either by emasculating him, and thus removing him to the shamed margins of male society, or by expelling him permanently through execution. Though certainly spectacular, however, in Florence such punishments seem to have had a severely limiting effect on the number and kind of sodomitical relations prosecuted. Trials for sodomy in this early period were rare and sporadic, and they generally involved only the most abhorrent cases of ferocious assaults and anal rape or the abuse of very young children, or cases involving several different serious crimes in addition to sodomy. Much evidence suggests, in contrast, that the authorities willfully ignored less offensive and less conspicuous forms of simple consensual sexual relations between males, which must have been much more widespread than the infrequent trials would indicate.[9]

In the early fifteenth century, mounting pressures to police this sexual practice more effectively finally led the government, after much vacillation, to come up with novel and less draconian alternatives. In 1415 new statutes expressly prohibited the exile, mutilation, or execution of sodomites for a first conviction, substituting these penalties with a huge fine of one thousand lire and mandating the death penalty for a second offense. The stated purpose of this humane revision was to encourage judges to enforce the law, so that they would not allow sodomy to go unpunished, as it was candidly admitted in an early version of the text, "out of fear of the truth."[10] Faced with persistent sporadic enforcement, however, the government was soon forced to adopt even more radical measures. In 1432 it instituted the special civic magistracy over sodomy, the Officers of the Night, whose lay officials were authorized to carry out summary proceedings on the basis largely of anonymous denunciations. Yet at the same time that it moved to intensify the surveillance and repression of sodomy, the government also drastically reduced the penalties for it. The new law prescribed a series of relatively low, graduated fines that increased with successive convictions; the penalty of death was now to be imposed only for a sodomite's fifth offense. To induce sodomites to confess their crimes, the law also offered incentives of reduced fines to persons indicted who admitted their guilt, plus the unique guarantee of full immunity from prosecution to those persons who appeared spontaneously before the officials and incriminated themselves, divulging their sexual relations.[11]

With these sweeping reforms the Florentine ruling class had finally hit upon the right balance, it seems, between the perceived need to control sodomy in a more comprehensive way and widespread reluctance within the community to crack down too severely. The results were swift in coming and highly persuasive. From a previous average of less than one per year, convictions by the Night Officers for same-sex sodomy suddenly proliferated, reaching an unprecedented high of thirty-seven in 1436 and settling to an annual average of thirteen through the 1450s. At the end of that decade a further substantial cut in fines, resulting in probably the most lenient penalties for sodomy in all of Italy, produced yet another surge of convictions, to an average of nearly fifty every year over the next three and a half decades, with an astonishing all-time record in the single year of 1473 of 161 men condemned.[12] It appears, somewhat paradoxically, that in order to police this ostensibly most nefarious and feared vice in a more widespread fashion, the Florentine state was compelled to make sodomy seem little more than a mundane peccadillo.

The system of relatively low and graduated penalties for multiple offenses of sodomy that originated in 1432 underwent numerous adjustments over the next seventy years, up to the abolition of the Night Office in 1502, and it continued to fluctuate thereafter through the middle of the sixteenth century. Fine levels rose and fell, and the number of convictions permitted before the severe sentences of exile or death came into effect varied. But the basic principle remained intact, and the few attempts to challenge it and to revive more oppressive alternatives met with little or no success. The most notable exception comes from the 1490s, when the charismatic Dominican reformer, Girolamo Savonarola, condemned the practice of issuing fines for sodomy and called instead for "pretty little bonfires" of sodomites. Although he himself had to admit that such grotesque pleas fell on deaf Florentine ears, the friar's influence was decisive in making penalties for sodomy much harsher.[13]

In general, the governing class of Florence preferred to discipline sodomy in a relatively benign and pragmatic way, which allowed men to indulge over time in limited sexual transgressions—for a price, certainly, but without risking life and limb. This strategy was perhaps a tacit but shrewd acknowledgment of the transitory nature in their society of most homosexual behavior, which was associated mainly with the periods of adolescence and youthful bachelorhood before marriage.[14]

Though they were intent on patrolling this sensitive sexual margin, real-
istic city fathers—many of whom might well have had same-sex experiences themselves when young—ensured through the fairly lenient penalties that most men who overstepped this confine had the possibility
eventually of "outgrowing" and abandoning the vice, as most in fact
would. Rather than punishing sodomites in a permanently marginalizing fashion, either by maiming them physically or by expelling them
from the community through exile or execution, the provision of a series
of graduated fines permitted them, in effect, to be discreetly reintegrated.
Lax enforcement helped reinforce this process even further. Not only were
the vast majority of males incriminated for sodomy never convicted, but
even those who were condemned, at least through much of the fifteenth
century, were accorded a good deal of clemency. One notorious sodomite
in the 1470s and 1480s, the young baker Jacopo di Andrea called "il Fornaino," chalked up a remarkable twelve recorded convictions.[15]

Not all acts of sodomy were dealt with so indulgently, however. The
government carefully maintained the full range of repressive options
available so that certain crimes could be punished with greater severity.
By law, the application of the new, more lenient penalties created in 1432
was restricted to the Office of the Night; the unwritten assumption, borne
out by its records, was that these officials would deal predominantly with
the vast extent of more or less consensual sodomy that the community,
within limits, could tolerate. Offenses that were more threatening and
detestable—such as keeping same-sex brothels, assaults that resulted in
anal injuries, sodomy between Jews and Christians, or sodomy committed in churches—were reserved to other courts and usually received exemplary corporal or capital punishments.[16] On a few occasions, notorious
sodomites were also treated to ritualized public shaming, such as the
one inflicted in 1486 on an infamous man nicknamed "Pacchierotto":
wearing a large defamatory miter, or fool's cap, he was whipped around
the government square up to the statue of the lion, the civic symbol,
where he received twelve lashes; then he was processed to the commercial center of the New Market, where he got twelve more; and lastly he
was led to the Street of the Furriers, site of many of his own trysts and a
well-known nightly haunt of sodomites, where he was given another
twelve lashes, before being jailed for several years.[17] The abuse of young
children was often punished with similar defaming publicity: in 1488
four men who had sodomized a ten-year-old boy were stripped bare and

tied together to the column in the central market, whipped severely, and then paraded nude to the city gates and exiled.[18] In 1520 a man who had incestuously sodomized his own son was pulled around the city on a cart while his flesh was being ripped off with red-hot pincers, and finally what was left of him was burned.[19] Overall, however, such scenes of ritual derision against sodomites or the hideous spectacles of sodomites being tortured and burned were uncommon in Florence. Of roughly three thousand men convicted for sodomy between 1432 and 1502, only around one in twenty was sentenced to some form of public humiliation, which in any case they often avoided by paying an alternative fine. And the sodomites who were put to death in the fifteenth and sixteenth centuries could be counted practically on the fingers of one hand.[20]

In any case, what seems important to stress in this context is that, by creating a special judiciary niche—in the form of the unique Office of the Night—for the fairly lax disciplining of most sodomitical relations, Florentines publicly acknowledged that the moral category of sodomy was not, in fact, uniformly sinful or objectionable. The margin between sodomy and fully licit sexual practices remained firm, but judiciary practice in Florence made it appear considerably more nuanced. Indeed, a policy of discretionary court practice was a prominent characteristic of local efforts in general to police sodomy, reinforcing the impression of Florentines' reluctance to deliver a blanket condemnation of sodomy. A noteworthy theoretical statement of this approach comes from a law of 1520, which observed that the delinquents who commit

the detestable vice of sodomy...are persons of various conditions, and the crimes are committed in different ways and with diverse characteristics, such that...some should be punished with heavier penalties and some with lighter penalties...and it is deemed a good thing that such crimes are punished according to the quality of the persons and the gravity of the offense, and that to a certain extent the penalties prescribed by law can, with the authority and severity of the magistrates, be regulated and adjusted.[21]

Rather than collapsing sodomy and sodomites into indefinite moral categories, in other words, Florentines consistently paid close attention to various kinds of concrete social and sexual distinctions, which were then reflected in their public disciplinary actions. In policing one of the most sharply drawn and vigorously defended boundaries in Western sexual morality, they persistently blurred the margins, insisting on mapping onto and across them their own socially and culturally significant confines. In the remainder of this essay I would like to chart some of these differently situated borders. Three in particular merit special attention: boundaries related to age, to gender, and to political or civic status.

Age, and especially distinctions among generational cohorts, had a fundamental influence in shaping both the character of same-sex sexual behavior and the policing of sodomy in Florence. The prevalent, indeed virtually normative, form of homosexual relations was what might be termed "pederasty," that is, a hierarchical relationship determined by a strict separation of sexual roles to which corresponded an equally clear difference in the ages of the two partners. In the vast majority of cases, an adult man over the age of eighteen took the dominant sexual role with a "passive," sexually receptive adolescent between the ages of thirteen and eighteen or at most twenty, in other words, roughly between the onset of puberty and the full growth of a beard. There were few exceptions to this conventional pattern. Reciprocal or age-reversed relations were rare, limited mainly to cases in which both partners were adolescents, while relations in which adult men took the receptive role, though not unknown, were rarer still.[22]

These conventions of age and sexual role difference inherent in same-sex sodomy were closely bound up with the social identity of males. In the first place, they helped define the cultural and social boundaries between the life stages of adolescence and youth. As the records show, the number of passive partners dropped off sharply after the age of eighteen, and even further at age twenty, with very few youths over this age appearing in the receptive role. Around this age young males passed an unwritten but widely recognized border marking two sociosexual periods of life: on one side was what Florentines called the *fanciullo,* or boy, whose sexual passivity was considered somehow "natural," appropriate to his age and status; and on the other was the *giovane,* or youth, who was expected to display the domineering virility of an adult and who could no longer allow men to sodomize him without jeopardizing his manly identity and reputation. The documented sexual behavior of numerous individuals in fact corresponded to these expectations; that is, as adolescents they were passive to many men, but as youths they made the transition, without a single exception, to an exclusively active role in sodomizing boys. The age of eighteen to twenty for males thus marked a critical sexual and social passage, indicated by other social markers as well, from boyhood to adulthood.[23]

The Florentine community carefully observed young males' sexual comportment around this margin and acted to defend the social and cultural divide that it staked out. When authors of denunciations reported abnormal cases in which a youth past his adolescent prime, or on rare occasions an older man, was accused of taking the receptive sexual role, they commonly spoke of them with scorn and derision or stressed the ignominy of such shameful behavior. One informer, to cite a typical example, wrote contemptuously of a youth who was a sodomite's kept companion, "by now he's grown up, which is a disgrace."[24] The judiciary authorities were also especially attentive to violations of this sort and sought to reinforce proper behavior by punishing overaged passives, often with unusually harsh sentences. Normally the courts did not penalize boys who took the passive role, since they were typically legal minors aged eighteen or under, and minors, at least in judiciary practice regarding sodomy, were almost wholly exempt from punishment. Once again this was an ambiguous characteristic peculiar, it seems, to Florence, or at any rate sharply distinct from the situation in Venice, where teenagers were regularly punished as adults; is it possible that Florentines believed that sodomy committed by the young angered God less than that practiced by their elders?[25] Once they became adults, however, their penalties for taking the receptive part could be severe, even in comparison with their dominant partners. In 1497 one passive youth of twenty-two was given twenty-five lashes in the Old Market and then exiled for two years, while another the same age was fined the large sum of fifty florins and also exiled for two years. In 1506 two lovers, both unusually around thirty years of age, were convicted, and while the one who took the active part was simply fined, his companion was publicly shamed by being paraded and whipped through the city wearing a defamatory miter. The rationale that supported such exemplary punishments was made clear in a sentence in 1493 against a twenty-six-year-old youth who confessed that many men had sodomized him: he was convicted, the sentence reads, "because he could be called a man, not a boy."[26] This young man, and the others like him, had violated one of the sexual norms that, in Florentine eyes, helped separate mature men from mere boys, and the officials, in punishing them as they did, assisted in upholding and buttressing that critical margin.

Intimately related to such concerns about demarcating biological and social stages in life was an equally strong preoccupation about clarifying and reinforcing gender boundaries. The sexual passivity of grown men evoked such derisive or alarmed reactions among informers and encouraged such forceful disciplining by the authorities not only because it was inappropriate behavior for adult men, in contrast to boys, but because it was considered unacceptable *masculine* behavior that challenged and threatened to defame the virility not only of the offender himself but of the entire male community. The metaphors and images that Florentines employed when speaking and writing about sodomy, mainly in denunciations but in other sources as well, reveal plainly that they understood the opposing sexual roles in sodomy as gendered, as womanly or manly. To their way of thinking, to be penetrated sexually reduced a male to the submissive and subjugated role of woman. Informers stressed this disgrace by denigrating supposedly passive boys with a variety of pejorative feminine terms, ranging from *bardassa,* a feminine noun that was derived from an Arabic word for slave and denoted a male prostitute, to *puttana,* a "female whore," and from *cagna* or *cagna in gestra,* "bitch" or "bitch in heat," to simply *donna,* "woman," or even *moglie,* "wife." Such terms, it should be stressed, were never applied to the boys' active companions. The dominant role of the penetrator was never so explicitly gendered, probably because it conformed fully to expectations of suitable virile behavior, regardless of the sex of his partner. A man who committed sodomy with a boy, in other words, did not imperil his own virile identity, and indeed he may have enhanced it. The boy's passivity, in contrast, was deplorable and womanly, but in the end tolerable and unpunished, since it was recognized as simply a temporary deviation along his path to full manhood.[27]

When adult men allowed others to sodomize them, however, they dangerously challenged their culture's protocols of masculinity, posing a threat that added urgency to the community's efforts to police and to defend the conventional boundaries of pederasty. The best illustration known to me of the high gender stakes involved in such transgressions comes from a law passed in 1516 in Venice, but the sentiments it expressed would have been equally at home in Florence. The Venetian legislators, with language verging on hysteria, observed that "an absurd and unheard-of thing has recently become known, which can in no way be tolerated, that several most wicked men of 30, 40, 50, 60 years and more have given themselves like prostitutes and public whores to be passives in such a dreadful excess." This revelation deeply humiliated local commentators, especially because foreigners, as a result, were now maliciously deriding the masculinity of the entire male populace.[28] A case just like that feared by the Venetians had been uncovered in Florence only two decades earlier, in 1496, and there, too, reactions were predictably both harsh and embarrassed. In this instance, sixty-three-year-old Salvi Panuzzi, an affluent, office-holding citizen and a notorious sodomite with a thirty-year record of importuning and sodomizing boys, confessed now that, despite his ripe age, he had unusually allowed several young men to penetrate him. For this flagrant defiance of the most elementary norms of manly comportment, the scandalized Night Officers singled him out for exemplary punishment and made him one of only three men, out of the several thousand overall that they convicted, whom they sentenced to death, by burning after beheading. Yet as much as they abhorred his actions, the officials were also acutely worried that his execution, by rendering public his womanish "evil ways" threatened to "bring shame on the entire city," suggesting that they feared his case would make a mockery of Florentine manhood. They therefore commuted his sentence, after payment of a very large fine, to life imprisonment on bread and water, securely hidden away in the city's prison ward for the insane.[29] By defusing the publicity of Panuzzi's execution, and secluding this violator of manly ideals among the criminally mad, the magistrates acted to defend the conventions and boundaries that helped fashion masculine identity.

The manner in which the Florentine community dealt with sodomites who were office-holding citizens, like Panuzzi, provides a final illustration both of the ambiguous marginality of sodomites in this society and of how the policing of sodomy helped to erect or reinforce other kinds of nonsexual margins. Beginning in the early fifteenth century, when sodomy first came to be seen as a high-priority problem of public morality, the governing class took measures not to relegate citizen-sodomites to the margins of civic life, but, on the contrary, to ensure that they continued to enjoy full political rights and privileges. The statutes of 1415, which first introduced the penalty of a fine for a first conviction, also guaranteed that men condemned for sodomy could not for this reason be denied civic office or other municipal honors, not even if their sexual activity were so outrageous that it provoked "talk, scandal, uproar, or disturbances."[30] The 1432 law that instituted the Office of the Night and the new series of graduated fines also substantially upheld the civic privileges of citizens who committed sodomy. Only sodomites who were condemned a third time were prohibited from holding office, and then for a mere two years; only a fourth conviction brought a lifetime ban.[31] This noteworthy defense of the office-holding rights of convicted sodomites remained intact during the following six decades, until 1494, when the protoprincely Medici family fell from power and the sodomy laws were drastically reformed.

One result of this indulgent, inclusive policy—which lax enforcement of the laws especially against members of the city's many families who made up the dominant political class only reinforced—was that throughout most of the fifteenth century, countless sodomites must have served regularly in municipal offices and even sat in the highest councils of state. To take perhaps only the most striking example, even the infamous Salvi Panuzzi—first indicted for sodomy in 1466 and several times since then, including a self-denunciation in 1478—was selected three times between 1485 and 1491 to the city's most prestigious and powerful magistracies, and he also occupied positions as the city's chief judiciary representative numerous times in towns throughout the Florentine territory.[32] At least a couple of prominent citizens who were convicted of sodomy, in addition to collecting several other indictments, served either before or after their condemnations even as Officers of the Night, adjudicating charges of sodomy against others.[33] The influence wielded by sodomites in public office occasionally attracted the angry reproach of people who made denunciations to the Night Officers, and back in the 1420s had also fuelled the ire of Bernardino da Siena, who roundly condemned it in his series of Florentine Lenten sermons.[34]

After the Medici were driven into exile in 1494, in the new climate of moral rigor championed by Savonarola and his followers, this decades-old policy of detaching sodomites' sexual crimes from their public activities came temporarily to an end. New laws made penalties for sodomy much harsher than before and stripped all convicted sodomites of their civic rights, which could thereafter be restored only with the favor of a two-thirds majority of the Great Council.[35] Very soon after this so-called popular regime fell and the Medici were restored in 1512, however, sodomites were partially reintegrated into civic life, but with some significant novelties. For the first time in local legal history, in laws passed in 1514, 1520, and 1527, graduated penalties for sodomy were differentiated in part according to whether the person condemned was eligible or not to hold public office, and in part according to their age. At the outset, prescribed punishments flagrantly benefited citizens, especially youths, not only by guaranteeing their right to hold office but also by allowing them a greater number of convictions, compared with men ineligible for office, before the severest sanctions applied. Later laws corrected this discrimination somewhat, but continued to protect sodomites' civic privileges and to maintain penal distinctions between those sodomites within and those outside of the governing class, above all by reserving corporal punishments and exile to the latter.[36] These different modes of disciplining men of disparate classes and ages for the practice of sodomy probably reflect the growing social and political divisions of early sixteenth-century Florentine society and the more openly aristocratic outlook of its patriciate. But in any case, one of their effects was to inscribe new social and political boundaries around and across the margin between licit and illicit sexual behavior. In policing this sexual confine, Florentines continued to modify and mold it by superimposing on it their own significant categories of social and civic identity.

Certainly the prevalence in Florence of sodomy, which according to some contemporaries was defended by many local men as a deeply entrenched tradition, goes a long way toward explaining why its practical control was characterized by such blatant ambiguities.[37] Confronted with this widespread sexual custom, the governing class in the fifteenth and early sixteenth centuries pragmatically adopted a strategy aimed at containing it within acceptable bounds rather than repressing it outright. In doing so, they substantially softened the contours of the absolute moral condemnation of sodomy and sodomites that the church, and even their own legal rhetoric, continued to propagate. In practical terms, what was reputedly the greatest abomination known to God and man appeared quite mundane and fairly innocuous. Again in contrast to the categorical, one-dimensional depiction of sodomy and sodomites in official pronouncements, Florentines were also very alert to the distinctions that, in tangible experience, defined this sexual practice and those who engaged in it, distinctions determined by ages, sexual roles,

genders, and civic status, and they fashioned their disciplinary efforts accordingly. Not only did they shift, or at any rate destabilize and articulate, the seemingly fixed moral and sexual margin between the licit and
the illicit, but they also established and policed diverse, intersecting, and
sometimes conflicting boundaries that were no less significant in mapping out their community's social, political, and cultural parameters.

NOTES

1. Law of 1418: Archivio di Stato di Firenze (hereafter ASF), *Provvisioni, Registri*,
108, fol. 2v (15 Apr. 1418). Sentence of 1436: ASF, *Giudice degli appelli e nullità*, 79 (pt. 2),
fol. 57r (15 Feb. 1435 in Florentine calendar, 1436 in modern calendar; henceforth such
dates will be rendered, for example, 1435/6). Antoninus Pierozzi, *Sancti Antonini summa
theologica*, 4 vols. (Graz: Akademische Druck- u. Verlagsanstalt, 1959), tit. quintus, cap. IV,
para. 2 (2:667–68).

2. Sources cited in note 1.

3. Comprehensive studies of the prosecution of sodomy in late medieval and early
modern Italian cities include Guido Ruggiero, *The Boundaries of Eros: Sex Crime and Sexuality in Renaissance Venice* (New York: Oxford University Press, 1985), 109–45; and Michael
Rocke, *Forbidden Friendships: Homosexuality and Male Culture in Renaissance Florence* (New
York: Oxford University Press, 1996). See also Elisabeth Crouzet-Pavan, "Police des moeurs,
société et politique à Venise à la fin du Moyen Age," *Revue historique* 264 (1980): 241–88;
Patricia Labalme, "Sodomy and Venetian Justice in the Renaissance," *Legal History Review*
52 (1984): 217–54; Barisa Krekic, "Abominandum Crimen: Punishment of Homosexuals
in Renaissance Dubrovnik," *Viator: Medieval and Renaissance Studies* 18 (1987): 337–45;
Gabriele Martini, *Il "vitio nefando" nella Venezia del Seicento: Aspetti sociali e repressione di
giustizia* (Rome: Jouvence, 1988); Luciano Marcello, "Società maschile e sodomia: Dal
declino della 'polis' al Principato," *Archivio storico italiano* 150 (1992): 115–38.

4. On the institution and operation of the Office of the Night, see Rocke, *Forbidden
Friendships*, 45–84, and also p. 115 for an indication of the probable extent of sodomy. My
estimate there that "by the time they reached the age of thirty, at least one of every two
youths in the city of Florence had been formally implicated in sodomy to this court [the
Ufficiali di notte] alone; by the age of forty, at least two of every three men had been incriminated," has been unconvincingly challenged by Samuel K. Cohn Jr. in a review of *Forbidden Friendships* that appeared in *Speculum* 74 (1999): 481–83. For my detailed rebuttal, see
Michael Rocke, "*L'amor maschio è fanciullo*: Hierarchical Same-sex Paradigms in Renaissance Italy," forthcoming in *The Trouble with Boys*, ed. Gilbert Herdt (Chicago: University
of Chicago Press).

5. See Rocke, *Forbidden Friendships*, 10–12. The historical literature on the development of the modern sexual categories of "homosexual" and "heterosexual" is extensive;
among the finest recent examples are George Chauncey, *Gay New York: Gender, Urban
Culture, and the Making of the Gay Male World, 1890–1940* (New York: Basic Books, 1994);

and Randolph Trumbach, *Sex and the Gender Revolution: Heterosexuality and the Third Gender in Enlightenment London* (Chicago: University of Chicago Press, 1998).

6. See esp. Rocke, *Forbidden Friendships*, 113–32.

7. For examples, see ibid, 23–24, 124 n. 51.

8. Ibid., 134–47.

9. Ibid., 20–26.

10. ASF, *Statuti*, 23, fol. 86v. The revised version of this statute, without the incriminating phrase, was promulgated in 1415: *Statuta populi et communis florentiae publica auctoritate collecta castigata et praeposita anno salutis MCCCCXV*, 3 vols. (Fribourg: apud Michaelem Kluch, 1778–83), 1:320–23.

11. The law instituting the *Ufficiali di notte* and outlining its regulations is in ASF, *Provvisioni, Registri*, 123, fols. 31v–36v (17 Apr. 1432); for a detailed discussion, see Rocke, *Forbidden Friendships*, 45–54.

12. Figures on convictions are in ibid., 57–60, 198; see also Figure 6.1 (p. 199).

13. On the changes in the 1490s and the impact of Savonarola and his reform movement, see ibid., 195–226; see also Umberto Mazzone, *"El buon governo": Un progetto di riforma generale nella Firenze savonaroliana* (Florence: Olschki, 1978).

14. Rocke, *Forbidden Friendships*, 113–32.

15. On lax enforcement by the Night Officers, see ibid., 66–80; on "il Fornaino," pp. 72–73 and elsewhere.

16. Ibid., 53–54, 66.

17. ASF, *Otto di guardia e balìa, Repubblica*, 74, fol. 20r (17 July 1486); a remarkable description of Pacchierotto's punishment is in Simone Filipepi, *Cronaca*, in *Scelta di prediche e scritte di fra Girolamo Savonarola*, ed. Pasquale Villari and Eugenio Casanova (Florence: Sansoni, 1898), 501–2. See also Rocke, *Forbidden Friendships*, 78 and n. 188.

18. ASF, *Otto di guardia e balìa, Repubblica*, 79, fol. 12v (12 Mar. 1487/8).

19. Giovanni Cambi, *Istorie di Giovanni Cambi cittadino fiorentino*, in *Delizie degli eruditi toscani*, ed. Ildefonso Da San Luigi, 24 vols. (Florence, 1770–86), 23:178.

20. Rocke, *Forbidden Friendships*, 76–80.

21. ASF, *Provvisioni, Registri*, 205, fol. 12r (23 May 1520).

22. The basic norms and social configurations of same-sex sexual relations are discussed in Rocke, *Forbidden Friendships*, 87–101.

23. Ibid., 99–101.

24. Ibid., 102, and generally on similar remarks in denunciations, pp. 102–4.

25. Ibid., 51–52, 63. On Venetian practice and a comparison with Florence, see Labalme, "Sodomy," 236; Ruggiero, *Boundaries*, 123; Michael Rocke, "Il fanciullo e il sodomita: Pederastia, cultura maschile e vita civile nella Firenze del Quattrocento," in *Infanzie: Funzioni di un gruppo liminale dal mondo classico dall'Età moderna*, ed. Ottavia Niccoli (Florence: Ponte alle Grazie, 1993), 214–15. The 1432 law instituting the Officers of the Night justified the creation of a lower scale of penalties for minors with the argument that "youth is less capable of deceit": ASF, *Provvisioni, Registri*, 123, fol. 33r–v (17 Apr. 1432).

26. ASF, *Otto di guardia e balìa, Repubblica*, 106, fols. 39v and 40r (1 Feb. 1496/7); 136, fol. 236v (12 Dec. 1506); ASF, *Ufficiali di notte e conservatori dei monasteri* (hereafter *Ufficiali di notte*), 28, fol. 67r (29 July 1493).

27. Rocke, *Forbidden Friendships*, 105–10.

28. Labalme, "Sodomy," 251 n. 160, and 234 n. 73.

29. ASF, *Ufficiali di notte*, 30, fols. 87r–89v (22 Sept.–7 Oct. 1496) and fols. 130v–132r (8 Oct. 1496). On Panuzzi, see Rocke, *Forbidden Friendships*, 79, 129, 202–3.

30. *Statuta populi et comunis florentiae*, 1:321.

31. ASF, *Provvisioni, Registri*, 123, fols. 32v–33r (17 Apr. 1432).

32. Rocke, *Forbidden Friendships*, 79.

33. See the examples of Nofri d'Antonio Lenzoni and Bernardo di Taddeo Lorini in ibid., 74.

34. See, for example, ibid., 41–43, 74.

35. Ibid., 205–9.

36. Ibid., 226–35.

37. In Florence in 1425, the Franciscan preacher Bernardino da Siena claimed that sodomy was considered a "custom" in Tuscany and was justified with this excuse: *Le prediche volgari*, ed. by Ciro Cannarozzi, 5 vols. (Florence: Libreria editrice fiorentina, 1940–58), 4:116. On Bernardino's critique of sodomy, see Michael Rocke, "Sodomites in Fifteenth-Century Tuscany: The Views of Bernardino of Siena," in *The Pursuit of Sodomy: Male Homosexuality in Renaissance and Enlightenment Europe*, ed. Kent Gerard and Gert Hekma, 7–31 (New York: Haworth Press, 1989). An excellent recent study of Bernardino, with a substantial chapter on sodomy, is Franco Mormando, *The Preacher's Demons: Bernardino of Siena and the Social Underworld of Early Renaissance Italy* (Chicago: University of Chicago Press, 1999).

5

STIGMA, ACCEPTANCE,

AND THE END TO LIMINALITY

JEWS AND CHRISTIANS IN EARLY MODERN ITALY

KENNETH R. STOW

Qui stan li gand[dissi]mi becco
ferdinando .racamator
e putanissima sua moglie
rifiuto de' giudei
che sol il boia resta
chi ne vol de infami
venga con pochi quatrin
dami la querela beccone
che te ho in culo
ove solete tenere il cazzo
che ve se tagliara li mosticci

These verses, appearing on a *cartello infamante,* a placard tacked on the door of one Ferdinando Fredini, Milanese weaver resident in Rome, in 1620, calling him the "refuse of the Jews," neatly point out the place of the Jews in the social pecking order of Early Modern Italy.[1] What the placard expresses is neither hate nor fear nor disdain. It is a mordant satire, and its clarity reveals how deceptive is the portrait painted by Cecil Roth of brilliant light turned dark: achievement, social acceptance, then repression. No less deceptive is the alternative view of a gray world—informed by Franciscan venom—turned black by ghetto isolation.[2]

Yet what assurance is there that a single placard, one of about ninety such placards whose existence was known to the *Tribunale di Governatore* in Rome from the middle of the sixteenth century through the middle of the seventeenth, represents the norm? Even taken verbatim, these imprecations are hyperbole. Just as their writer surely did not consider Ferdinando's wife truly to be the queen of whores, "putanissima," so he did not turn up his nose when he passed a Jew on the street. However, there were those who did. One fifteenth-century preacher insisted that "[Jews] be treated as public prostitutes, who because of their filth are tolerated [only] while they live in a bordello ... so Jews should live their stinking lives in some stinking place, separate from Christians."[3] Yet lampooning Jews was the more frequent posture, sarcastically or raucously mocking Jewish practice for contravening right social values. Jewish rites of passage were considered especially notorious. Weddings and funerals evoked derisive glee, and the latter sometimes provoked stoning by jeering throngs. Jews were also mocked in the races of the pre-Lenten Carnival. These scenes were formalized in written satire and dramas known as *giudiate.*

But such mockery might also reflect deep concern, functioning as a vehicle to project internal misgivings. Jewish practice more than once was judged emblematic of that which Renaissance (Christian) contemporaries questioned or disliked in their own actions. Medievals called this transfer of self-criticism onto others the *iudicio alienum.* The practice continued into the Renaissance. In the drama and *giudiata Gnora Luna,* the Christian author (the surviving version is from somewhat later) has the young, beautiful Jewish Gnora Luna married off to a decrepit octogenarian, whose demise she demonstrably hastens. In fact, the author appears merely to have changed the names and the religion of the personae in Pietro Aretino's sixteenth-century satire on marriage, the *Sei giornate,* where Nanna the whore is matched by her mother with "an old man, who only lived because he was still eating." The predictable result was adultery and the fulfillment of her husband's wish "to have me for his wife or die." Nanna "buried a little knife that I had in his chest and his pulse beat no more."[4]

The step from such transposed self-criticism and judgment to a desire to be relieved of the Jewish presence was not large. In 1556, the town elders of Udine seized on what they called an *occasione scacciare gli ebrei* and received permission from the Venetian overlord to do this. The Venetians themselves had never made peace with their own consciences about Jews. The 1519 debate in the Venetian Senate on renewing the charter of 1516 allowing Jews to reside in Venice, as reported in the diary of Marino Sanuto, was replete with cries that a Jewish presence provoked divine anger and endangered the Republic's well-being. Jews had never lived in Venice itself previous to 1516 and entry even then was contingent on the Jews living apart on the island of the Ghetto, whence the source of the name.[5]

This debate was still going on as late as 1638, when Simone Luzzatto wrote his *Discorso* on Venetian Jewry. Praising the Jews' unique mercantile (and mercantilistic) value to the Venetian Republic, Luzzatto compared them to the foot of the body politic (as he invoked the metaphor) on which everything and everyone stands, and he depicted their commerce as the blood that keeps the heart pumping,[6] inverting fifteenth-century Franciscan propaganda that likened Jewish lending to gangrene in the body politic's arteries.[7] Luzzatto was touting the new kind of mercantilist Jew who was found in Venice, Livorno, and Ancona.[8] But this vision might also be upended to attack Jews, especially those who continued to lend and were accused of being unproductive. They were robbing rather than contributing to the common weal and also impeding ultimate salvation, for their accrued riches were a deterrent to conversion. This accusation presages Karl Marx's no less utopian denigration of Jewish "finance capital," whose disappearance was to herald a new world order.[9]

Apprehensiveness was paralleled by anxiety. Anxiety might be produced by manipulation, which was the case in 1475, when Bishop Hinderbach of Trent willfully exploited the accusation that the town's Jews had murdered the child Simon. But in the so-called darker side of the Renaissance,[10] the line separating real from dissimulated anxiety was thin. People were rereading Tacitus, linking his words to what had been libeled about Jews, magic, and blood in the Middle Ages, and creating a vision of Jewish terror wrought against Christian social integrity, of perverse Jewish practice corrupting Christian purity.[11] This was the current version of the anxiety about Judaizing first expressed by Paul in Galatians and Corinthians. But Paul had meant Judaizing on the part of, and stimulated by, various groups of Jewish Christians. By the time of John

Chrysostom (ca. 387), the culprits had become the Jews themselves.[12] Eventually, Judaizing was the charge laid at the doorstep of baptized Jews in Visigothic Spain (seventh century) and, again, immediately following the First Crusade, of converts returned easily to Judaism with no mechanisms to control them. Eventually, the charge was applied to the far more threatening—from Christian society's viewpoint—New Christians, the conversos and Marranos, as they are all too readily called, of fifteenth-, sixteenth-, and seventeenth-century Spain and Portugal. The concept of Judaizing, with the same meaning of the pollution of social values and virtues through the penetration of Jewish practices—and now Jewish blood, through intermarriage—was again invoked in late nineteenth- and twentieth-century anti-Semitic discourse.[13] Content and context had evolved, but the essential pattern remained a constant.

JEWS, ECCLESIASTICS, AND THE LAW

It was precisely this anxiety about contamination through Judaizing that fueled humanist concerns. It was they, including Hinderbach, who orchestrated the libel at Trent. Franciscan Observantines like Bernardino da Feltre, who are often credited with this libel, only seconded it as their obsession was Jewish lending. Humanists were also responsible for a new accusation. "Marranos," they said (by which they meant Jews) had imported syphilis, then a new disease, into Europe. Judaizing, by implication, was being equated with physical infection (a forerunner of nineteenth-century racial theory). By contrast, the Jews' defenders at Trent, after the fact—the fact being the brutal execution of the town's Jewish males and the equally brutal conversion of their surviving wives— were respectively the Dominican Bishop de' Giudici and the Franciscan Pope Sixtus IV. They acted out of love of the church, not the Jews, as well as canonical consistency dating back to Innocent IV's condemnation of the blood libel in 1253. The former, nonetheless, had to be defended against charges of Judaizing, which was done by proclaiming him a good Christian, for was it not known that he had never desecrated the purity of the Christian altar by dining with Jews.[14]

It was again the question of purity that exercised the Franciscan preacher Bernardino da Feltre about Jewish moneylending despite his understanding of capital and finance. Certain laypeople were disturbed no less, as Marino Sanuto's diary explains. Opponents of lending believed that it destroyed the wholeness of the Christian polity that was embodied by the civic fabric. Sanuto responded, regardless of his personal suspicions, by citing Alessandro da Imola, Baldus, and other leading jurists. All professors at Perugia, they saw Jewish lending as a virtue: it benefited the poor, to whom no Christian banker cared to lend. In fact, Jewish and Christian banking were often complementary, not adversarial. But none of this deterred the Franciscans, whose initially interest-free *Monti di pietà* competed with Jewish banking, a competition they finally won in 1682, when the Jewish banks of Rome were closed, their fate sealed also by millenarianly oriented mercantilist argument. Complementary to the Franciscans, legal cudgels against lending were taken up in the fifteenth century by the same humanist circles—in particular by the law faculty at Padua and the legist Alexander de Nievo—that spawned the charges at Trent in 1475.[15]

Something about the Jews seems to have been unacceptable to everybody, including those who shunned radicalism. But this was not a one-way downhill street. The Renaissance was a period during which for Jews and others what metaphorically ought to have been light, in particular, humanist learning and scientific discovery, was often the source of darkness. Thus the Jesuit confessor Von Spee said that it was immoral and un-Christian to torture suspected witches, for the tortured normally confessed, whether justly or not, but those who did not confess were considered aided by the devil through a *maleficium silentii*. The result, invariably, was false testimony and confession, a mortal sin, damning eternally the souls of all who were tortured.[16] Where, then, did justice reside? Where did light begin and darkness end? The same pattern, differently construed, was played out by the Jews' mendicant protagonists and humanist antagonists at Trent in 1475.

In the same vein, the displeasure Sixtus IV expressed regarding the humanists—who were not only attacking Jews, but also, as de' Giudici pointed out, papal prerogatives—did not prevent the pope from speaking angrily, charging the Jews with offending Christianity and corrupting Christians: "they open their filthy mouths and, because of their wholly erroneous dogma, invent depraved, obscene diabolic visions." He was more preoccupied about "the Jewish contagion ... which enables them to seduce Christians away from the faith [the reference is to reconversion, not direct proselytism] and make them accomplices of their lewdness."[17]

Equally instructive about contradiction is the case of *ius commune,* Roman law as applied in Italy. This law categorized Jews as *cives* living under civil law and enumerated Jewish privileges and limitations, uniquely granting Jews a precisely defined legal status. The absence of legal precision elsewhere exposed Jews to being labeled (correctly) as instruments of arbitrarily exercised governmental authority. By contrast, precise definition in Italy removed ambiguity about Italian Jewish legal status, whether in old or new settlements. Yet new settlements in the Italian North had to contend with legal arguments emanating from Paduan (trained) lawyers like Alexander de Nievo intended to choke Jews economically. The Franciscan Bernardino da Busti asserted that Jews had violated the terms law established and, therefore, should be expelled.[18] Paradoxically, however, when Paul IV issued his bull of 1555, *Cum nimis absurdum,* establishing the Roman ghetto and imposing a series of canonical restrictions, he was guided not by legal radicalism but by his belief that punctiliously observed regulations would encourage conversions. His specific demands were not new; the ghetto, as in Venice, was intended to conserve a difficult Jewish presence, not to anticipate expulsion.[19] Similarly, the Roman Papal Vicar, albeit for his own political ends, often supported halachic arbitration (on the basis of Jewish law). The initiative of the Medici Pope Leo X, archpersonification of the so-called Renaissance papacy, is nevertheless mystifying. De facto he violated papal and canonical precedent (only Gregory XI had spoken directly of "compulsion" in 1375) and sanctioned measures (indirectly) to force Jews to attend conversionary sermons.[20]

One might expect budding scientific investigation to have promoted rapprochement. Jews studied medicine alongside Christians in Padua and were active scientific inquirers. Nonetheless, Jews were affected by the growing apprehension of the unknown. Together with the anxieties and irrationalities that are said to have marked the sixteenth century so visibly, this apprehension generated fears of magic, divination, and poisoning.[21] Such fears may underlie the charges of Pius V, whose 1569 bull expelling Jews from all areas of the Papal States, save Rome, Ancona, and Avignon, accused them of "sorcery, enchantment, magic and idolatrous worship and wickedness."[22] The pope may have been specially moved by the involvement of Jewish "diviners" in popularly sought out calculations, on whose basis bets, *scomesse,* were regularly placed on the date of the coming papal conclave, that is, on the date of the current pope's death.

One of these diviners allegedly possessed a crystal ball in which an evil spirit, *spirito maligno*, was said to be entrapped. The popes, Pius V in particular, may have entertained visions of conjuring against their lives.[23]

Yet, how great is the distance between fears like these of Pius V and fears of revenge from the supernatural for what was deemed an affront to both civic purity and the unity of the body politic? Was it not fears like these that had moved the modern(istic) government of Venice long to ponder admitting Jews—despite the possible advantage that Jewish bankers and Jewish merchants might bring to the *corpus economicum*? Mercantilist economic politics may have prompted (in part) Jewish resettlement in England, or even Holland, but Italy was mired in the static introspection prompted by residual medieval attitudes, which, in turn, was reinforced by new Counter-Reformation preoccupations, whose effects and directions deepened as time passed.

The apogee of Counter-Reformation Jewry policy was not reached until 1751, when Benedict XIV issued bulls that rigorously renewed prior restrictions on Rome's Jews and expressed concerns that loans being made by Polish bishops to Jewish borrowers "were contaminating the Polish church."[24] Papal economic perceptions where Jews were involved had already demonstrated their unique logic in 1682, when the same mercantilist perception that sustained Jewish economic activity elsewhere was applied to justify closing down the Papal States' Jewish banks. The popes, who had uninterruptedly supported a restricted form of Jewish lending since the twelfth century, even during the reigns of Paul IV and Pius V, had reversed course completely.[25]

This shift was not sudden. By 1682, Roman Jewish banks had been vanquished by the Roman *Monte di pietà,* which, until the beginning of the seventeenth century, had not been viable. Yet they were vanquished not by free competition, but by a broader ecclesiastical policy to which economic logic was harnessed. The expansion of the Roman *Monte di pietà* thus was only partly fueled by the original Franciscan goal of providing the poor with interest-free loans. The real motivation was the Counter-Reformation goal of "disciplining"—which meant placing everything from liturgy to confraternities to the conjugal bed under church control.[26] Once again, the rest of Europe was moving on to something else, whether in economics, statecraft, or social policy. But Italy, driven by an ecclesiastical ethos of "disciplining," was seeking to resolve its Jewish problem through a scheme of overall control: through isolation, through establishing ever sharper lines of demarcation, and by usurping Jewish activities that had once been supervised by—but were not directly the province of—governmental establishments. In Venice, too, Jewish banking became an instrument of governmental (welfare) policy. The banks, wholly unprofitable by about 1600, were nevertheless forced to remain open, their capital derived from a banking tax to which all of Venetian Jewry contributed.[27]

The Jews, as Simone Luzzatto's *Discorso* implies, were growing ever more aware of their predicament. They certainly had some sense of danger's newer levels, albeit they often failed to grasp danger's true proportions. At Rome, the ghetto was first noted in the simple statement, "the pope [Paul IV] has ordered the Jews to sell our homes...[and] to live together."[28] This statement perhaps should not be taken literally, but made by a widow pleading a private case it was unlikely to be a smokescreen. Jews were twice as careful about public activities, especially commercial ones. One Hebrew chronicler berated the greedy Jew who purportedly imported infected feather-beds into Udine, the antecedent to the 1556 expulsion.[29] More often, Jews feared publicizing the dates of events like circumcisions and weddings.[30] They also made rules forbidding women to participate in funeral corteges, such as the one promulgated in 1620.[31] The principal aim was to avoid the mockery and stone pelting that often were the fortune of these ritualized events.

NEGOTIATION, ANXIETY, AND TENSION

All of these provisions were the product of a tacit negotiation between Jews and Christians, the aim of which was to moderate anxiety. Even the lampooning of the *giudiata* may be so viewed, minimizing anxieties—even low level ones—by transference and projection into stories like that of *Gnora Luna* or *The Wedding of Barucabbà*.[32] These acts were salutary, letting out steam, and therefore to be protected. Their quintessence was in the annual Easter time "ritual stonings," a practice widespread in medieval Spain as well as Italy.[33] Here, moreover, the scenario was left neither to chance nor to inherent traditional ritual process. At Urbino, in 1519, negotiation was explicit, framed by a ducal decree, in which the duke agreed that no youths older than fifteen might participate in the drama, lest violence become unrestrained and the resulting damage real.[34] True anger emerged when once, in violation of prior arrangement—not to mention the annual ritual—a Jew threw the stones back, rewriting the script.

Negotiated or even scripted processes thus mediated between stigma, in the sense of an assigned negative symbolic identity, and acceptance, the moderation of stigma's threatening or anxiety-producing implications. Mediation was even attempted to resolve crises, if only temporarily, or theoretically. At Trent, in 1475, so emblematic of Renaissance-Jewish vectors, Pope Sixtus IV, effectively acting as mediator, called for due legal process to be observed. Punctilious legal observance was the keystone that had anchored the equilibrium, the balance between privilege and restriction that had traditionally enabled a Jewish presence in Christian society. This balance had great tenacity. The bull *Antiqua improbitas* of 1581 gave the papal inquisition jurisdiction over nearly all Jewish canonical offenses. But punishments, as seen in the activities of the early seventeenth-century Modenese inquisitional tribunal, were not arbitrary. Often they were only fines. Similarly, many cases were dropped for want of evidence.[35]

Yet, by its constant probing, this same Modenese tribunal was militating against the status quo and toward the establishment of a Modenese ghetto, which the Este rulers refrained from decreeing until 1638. The exigencies of behavioral uniformity and clear lines of demarcation that were driving the Counter-Reformation church could no longer remain at peace with the old and perennially renegotiated balance. Thus, the idealized equilibrium of the Middle Ages as described by Thomas Aquinas in his *Summa Theologica*—in which Judaism and the (defeated and canonically restricted) Jews are iconographic of the absence of faith and its just recompense, while Christianity and Christian civilization represent true faith and its rewards—ceded to the sharp lines concretized by the ghetto wall.[36] The heightened yearning for differentiation and the need for control bespoken by Counter-Reformation discourse was, it seems, rendering all Jewish expression potentially intolerable, as illustrated by the Bolognese (papal) inquisitor who asked Rabbi Yishmael Haninah, being tortured by the cord, whether the Jewish use of *'An* rather than *San* was an intentional slight of Christian saints, *'an* purportedly standing for *agnello*, or sheep. Rabbi Yishmael rebutted the charge by asking how a collective noun could modify an individual name. Possibly he did not know that the usage *'an* may have been a dialectical idiosyncrasy as the term appears indiscriminately in Roman Jewish (Hebrew) notarial texts and these, one suspects, were regularly shown to representatives of the Apostolic Camera in the presence of Hebrew (mostly apostate) readers. But the essence here is that this hairsplitting inquiry far exceeded the pursuit of purportedly undisguised blasphemies that characterized the thirteenth-century assault on Rabbinic talmudic texts. It so far exceeded past inquiries, was in fact so startingly new, that the charge simply could not hold, and Rabbi Yishmael was freed.[37]

This did not always happen. In acts drawn by sixteenth-century rabbinic notaries, Jews invariably called Christians by the name of *Goi*, including Christian arbiters appointed at the request of one of the disputing parties in disputes between two Jews. The antagonism implicit in this name made it a subject of the inquisitional inquiry of Rabbi Yishmael Haninah, and its constant invocation suggests that Jews pictured themselves as living simultaneously both within and outside of (Christian) Roman society, regardless of how thin the line of demarcation was. Roman Jews and Christians may have eaten the same foods and thought in the same Italian language, as the acts of rabbinic notaries whose grammar is impeccably Italian reveal. Hence they wrote, for example, *casa sua*, although *bayyit* (house, *casa*) is masculine in Hebrew, and the personal pronoun's gender in Hebrew is that of the actor, not of the modified noun. In addition, Jews and Christians may have jostled, bought, and sold from each other in the marketplace.[38] Yet as one scholar has put it incisively, no matter how intense the contact, Rome's Jews remained perpetually "intimate outsiders."[39]

Nor could the gap be bridged by cultural negotiation. Demonstrably, Rome's Jews (and Jews elsewhere in Italy, too) modeled their process of matrimony on the Christian one, separating—unlike Jews elsewhere—the betrothal from the wedding by months.[40] They were also developing contracts of (true) adoption following models and concepts visible in Christian texts, in which adoptive parents were said "to love the child as their own" and to act as though the child had been "born of their own bodies." Jewish contracts in Rome said the same things. Yet, in both cases, Jews added something unique. With respect to matrimony, sons and daughters were afforded the unimpeachable privilege of rejecting a proposed match when in the Christian world children's marital rights were being restricted. With respect to adoption, the Jewish child itself, rather than an accompanying sum guaranteeing the Christian adoptee's well-being, became a *donatio inter vivos*, an "irrevocable gift," which, instructively, is the legal and verbal equivalent of the Talmudic *mattanah gemurah*. In addition, following popular Roman Jewish practice, the Jewish child's name was changed from that of a biological grandparent to that of an adoptive one.[41] Similarly, a Jewish element was actively at work, not simple—and maddening—imitation, when David Arbi tried to save his daughter's floundering engagement (the result of David's bankruptcy) by claiming: What God hath joined, let no man put asunder. The Gospel citation may have been Arbi's way of framing the rabbinic idea that "matches are made in heaven" and under no circumstances should man—namely Arbi's prospective in-laws—interfere.[42]

JEWISH CULTURE AND ITS CHALLENGE

Jewish culture thus differed, and this cultural difference aroused protest. The mockery of the *giudiata* was directed not so much against specific offending behavior as against Jewish behavior as a whole. This behavior may once have been tolerable and somehow familiar, but during the Counter-Reformation, some of its aspects were beginning to disturb, at all social levels, lay and ecclesiastic: to wit, the contrast between the stately Renaissance funereal ideal and the still raucous Jewish funeral, replete (admittedly to rabbinic chagrin, but only from the seventeenth century) with women's uncontrolled wailing.[43] It is likely not coincidental that the *giudiata* flowered at roughly the same time that such behavioral contrasts appeared.

Jewish behavior had the potential to offend. Jews saw fit to compensate monetarily young women whose virginity was impugned. Christian rules, at least in Venice, compensated the father.[44] Jewish society viewed the release of (at least some) maledictions, such as the ligature, or the knotting of the groom, causing impotence, as secular matters. Christians often viewed this release as part of the sacral process.[45] Priests, in particular, viewed marital sacrality as under their direct jurisdiction, while Jews viewed it as achievable through interspousal, including sexual, relations.[46] Christian secular society was, in principle, intent on limiting women's (legal) privileges, while Jewish women might be their own legal agents, entitled to undertake legal and economic initiatives.[47]

How conscious people were of these contrasts or the precise extent to which they were deemed offensive is unknown. It is hard to imagine these contrasts were the primary cause of radical programmatic change, certainly with respect to medieval postures. But social and behavioral differences no doubt functioned like accelerants heightening the flames that anxieties associated with such matters as lending, civic integrity, and, most of all, ritual murder ignited. Together, these greater and lesser causes put the old medieval balance into sustained shock, as evidenced by disdain and rejection: the *occasione,* or "desire for separation," in Udine, or the worry over syphilitic infection in humanist writings.

These Christian attitudes had Jewish counterparts. In 1589, following Sixtus V's enlargement of the ghetto, which indicated its permanence, the Roman Jewish notary Pompeo (Rabbi Moise) del Borgo, writing in Italian, having previously consistently referred to the Roman ghetto as the *seraglio ebreorum,* abruptly declared that Rome's Jews were living in *nostro ghet.*[48] He was punning on the name ghetto, deliberately conflating it (eventually to the point of writing it in Hebrew letters) with the Hebrew *get,* or "bill of divorce." Indicatively, the *get* is always "delivered" by the husband (*ha-megaresh* [active]) to the wife (*ha-gerushah* [passive]), and perhaps Rabbi del Borgo was intent on conveying the ambivalence and sense of rejection divorce often entails. But he was also implying that the *ghet* was strictly a Jewish preserve, which was correct. In 1621, out of convenience but perhaps also callous disregard, a Christian miller galloped his horse and wagon through the ghetto. He was attacked by a boisterous angry crowd and kicked to death.

However, before an investigating magistrate this expression of "justified Jewish rage" was quickly transformed into pleas of "ignorance." The Jews had learned apprehensiveness. Caution—if not cowardice— led them to blame the incident on a marginal (Jewish) youth, whose fate is unknown.[49] A similar apprehensiveness was demonstrated by a number of Jewish youths in Modena at Easter time in 1604. Summoned before the local inquisition and charged with creating a noisy disturbance, they vigorously demurred. Yes, they were playing a rowdy game, swinging on a rope and singing lustily in an attic located within earshot of a church, but they had not intended to mock the Passion.[50] From within closed quarters Jews might be uninhibited; only there might they mock Christians and their faith, at least vicariously.

This rule had both its limits and its exceptions. Annually, Venetian Jews pelted a baker's errand boy with the bread he had just carried into the ghetto at Passover's end,[51] and at least once in the early seventeenth century, Jews and Christians in Rome freely tossed stones at each other.[52] Nevertheless, the time had passed when Jews might feel free to masquerade as Roman *sbirri*, the papal police, as some of them had done in 1551 on the festival of Purim, noted for behavioral abandonment and inversion.[53] And one year a Venetian baker's boy complained about the pelting, and the inquisition promptly launched an investigation.

Still, nothing, including the ghetto, was hermetically sealed. The gates opened in the morning to let Jewish and Christian traffic pass out and in. Yet, the ghetto did end an era when stigma and acceptance coexisted, a time of physical (no longer attitudinal) segregation and disciplining had been inaugurated. What may be called the liminality of the medieval Jewish equilibrium was replaced by the sense of *nostro ghet,* "our bill of divorce." Also indicative was the strong sense, expressed best by the policies of Paul IV and his followers, that with the firm line of the ghetto wall in place, large-scale conversion of Jews to Christianity might at last occur. The interaction and constant cultural intermingling that typified the medieval equilibrium had also raised doubts about the ability of converts to complete a religious rite of passage.[54] The Spanish tradition of *convivencia,* of "living together," however it had deteriorated by 1492, had certainly fostered the religious and cultural ambivalence that characterized so many New Christians; the need to quash this ambivalence is the principal message, and goal, of the edict of expulsion in that year.[55]

At Rome, converts may have maintained frequent contacts with Jews and they often lived just on the other side of the ghetto wall, but they were also locked out at night.[56] Symbolically, the limina had been crossed. Various, if imperfectly observed, laws were also enacted to ensure that physical separation be thorough. However, suspicions never disappeared. Cardinal Charles Borromeo in the sixteenth century, as well as the ecclesiastical protector of the Turin House of Converts in the eighteenth century, saw venality as conversion's moving force.[57] The sixteenth-century popes were more optimistic—and it was the popes who were the real founders of the ghetto era. Their view was represented in 1558, perhaps officially, by the Udinese jurist Marquardus de Susannis. In his highly influential manual of Roman and canon Jewry law, de Susannis insisted that true conversion was possible, that converts did become "new men," and that conversionary rites of passage might be complete. Accordingly, Jews should be invited repeatedly to "enter the church," both physically and spiritually to espouse the faith.[58]

Most Jews refused this "invitation." Nonetheless, the ghetto wall did affect Jewish behavior. It has been suggested that the same ghetto wall that ruled out liminality may also have facilitated accepting Italian ways, for example by writing even communal documents in Italian instead of in Hebrew, as previously.[59] The ghetto wall had made Italian into a neutral tool, no longer a symbol of cultural challenge. Yet this absence of challenge may also have stunted the progress of acculturation, which the level of Italian philological tracts produced in the eighteenth-century ghetto reveals.[60]

The ghetto was decisive, however, and functioned as a true border in provoking a sense of Jewish social space, a physically separate, even "holy space." The walls of the ghetto substituted for those of the Holy City, Jerusalem,[61] and made the ghetto into an arena for purely Jewish activity. It was also a locus for Jewish fantasy, a (virtually theatrical) illusion—not a delusion—that Jews consciously fostered. To perfect this illusion, they sought assiduously to ensure that litigation be carried out exclusively through Jewishly supervised arbitration. Through such arbitration, they likely convinced themselves that irrespective of other realities, they somehow controlled their own fate.[62] Modern sociologists refer to similar phenomena as the creation of a "sociological wall."[63] Some Jews actually celebrated the founding of ghettos, calling it the Purim of the ghetto, metaphorically converting isolation into liberation and deliverance. More subtly, the time of mystic prayer was changed from morning to night, as though the time of closure were the time of real freedom.[64] These, to be sure, were means of figurative escape. They were also a means for coping with the ghetto as a permanent institution.

DENOUEMENT

Prior to the ghetto, there had been no uniform pattern of Jewish Italian settlement. Many cities had never accepted Jews at all. Conversely, by 1492 and 1510–41, Jews had been banished from Sicily and the Kingdom of Naples, as they also were from the Duchy of Milan in 1597. The founding of the ghetto further reduced Jewish settlement. Jews in Tuscany were restricted to Florence and Siena until the ducal founding of the unique Livornese community in 1591. The Jews of papal Bologna were expelled, first, in 1569, then, definitively, in 1593, and one-third of the Jews of

Ferrara fled about 1597. The large ghettos, Rome and Venice, numbered over three thousand, never surpassing four thousand, while other centers numbered in the hundreds. Florence, however, grew to about 1,500, an enormous increase from pre-ghetto times (1571). Modena may have expanded to over one thousand and Mantua to two thousand. Yet ghettoization progressed slowly. It reached Modena only in 1638, and Alessandra, Asti, and Turin in Piedmont only in the early eighteenth century.[65]

There were significant exceptions, most importantly Livorno where, in 1591, the Tuscan dukes invited Sefardi and Portuguese merchants, all former New Christians, to settle in order to develop Livorno's southern Mediterranean trade—which they duly did. These Jews were not ghettoized. This successful Livornese experiment was preceded by a similar one in Piedmont in 1572.[66] It failed. Opposition arose from the adjacent and Spanish-ruled Duchy of Milan, and the proposed conditions of settlement in Piedmont were also as unworkably medieval as they were modern. The first to attempt a commercial settlement of Portuguese ex–New Christians was Pope Paul III. In 1534, he issued a license for them to settle in Ancona directly to compete with Venice. But in 1556, Paul IV undid this initiative by burning twenty-four of these Portuguese at the stake, all of whom he charged with marranism. The port city recovered but never flourished as Paul III had originally hoped.[67]

Otherwise, the ghetto was ubiquitous and endured. So too did the mentality of stigmatization, which did not wane despite the approach of modernity. In some circles, notably nineteenth-century ecclesiastical ones and, subsequently, the initiators of Mussolini's racial laws, stigmatization persevered into the twentieth century. The end of the physical ghetto, which was simultaneous with the demise of the Papal States on 20 September 1870, witnessed, if it did not catalyze, a torrent of ecclesiastical vituperation. The papal church again began to move in the direction once taken by Hinderbach and Pavini at Trent. Pope Leo XIII even turned his back on seven hundred years of tradition, reaffirmed as recently as 1758 by the Franciscan Pope Clement XIV Ganganelli, by refusing to denounce the blood libel made at Polna in Bohemia in 1899. Notably, Leo XII was supported by a commission of the Holy Office, at whose head stood Cardinal Merry del Val. The cardinal's ancestor, it was said, a young boy, "had been crucified by the Jews."[68]

The ritual murder accusation has, in fact, never died. Linked to an unmitigated anti-Zionism, the libel still flourishes, most conspicuously, but not exclusively, on the Italian-driven Web site Holywar.org. Tellingly, this site also denigrates Pope John Paul II, accusing him of promoting the heresy of the freedom of religious conscience, a freedom first Gregory XVI and then Pius IX, in the nineteenth century, had labeled a "delirium."[69] Yet there is also the other side, embracing broad educated circles, including many clergy, for whom being Jewish is meritorious, Jewish practice often a sought-out experience. For these latter, the direction of the passage through the limina has been wholly reversed.

NOTES

1. Reprinted in "Insult and Blasphemy in Early Modern Italy," in Peter Burke, *The Historical Anthropology of Early Modern Italy: Essays on Perception and Communication* (Cambridge: Cambridge University Press, 1987), 95 and 246n.

2. Cecil Roth, *The Jews in the Renaissance* (Philadelphia: Jewish Publication Society, 1959); David Ruderman, "Cecil Roth, Historian of Italian Jewry: A Reassessment," in *The Jewish Past Revisited: Reflections on Modern Jewish Historians*, ed. David Myers and David Ruderman, 128–43 (New Haven: Yale University Press, 1998); Moses A. Shulvass, *The Jews in the World of the Renaissance*, trans. Elvin Kose (Leiden: Brill, 1973); and Robert Bonfil, *Jewish Life in Renaissance Italy* (Berkeley: University of California Press, 1992).

3. Cited and trans. by Diane Owen Hughes, "Distinguishing Signs: Ear-rings, Jews and Franciscan Rhetoric in the Italian Renaissance City," *Past and Present*, no. 112 (1986): 29. Adinah Miller alerted me to this citation.

4. On *giudiate*, see Lynn Gunzberg, *Strangers at Home: Jews in the Italian Literary Imagination* (Berkeley: University of California Press, 1992); also Paolo Toschi, *Le origine del teatro italiano* (Turin: Borighieri, 1976); and Giovanni Giannini, *La poesia popolare a stampa nel secolo XIX*, 2 vols. (Udine: Istituto delle edizioni accademiche, 1938), 1:61–65. On Baruccabà and Gnora Luna, see the late version *Diana infedele di Baruccabà*, in Rome, Biblioteca apostolica vaticano (henceforth BAV), *Raccolta Generale Miscellanea*, IV, 94, insert n. 2. See, too, Attilio Milano, *Il Ghetto di Roma* (Rome: Staderini editore, 1964), 327, and on funerals, pp. 261–68; and Abraham Berliner, *Storia degli ebrei di Roma*, trans. Aldo Audisio (Milan: Rusconi, 1992), 221–24. On Aretino, see Guido Ruggiero, *Binding Passions: Tales of Magic, Marriage, and Power at the End of the Renaissance* (Oxford: Oxford University Press, 1993), 24–26.

5. On Udine, see Kenneth Stow, "The Jew as Alien and the Diffusion of Restriction: An Expulsion Text from Udine in 1556," in *Jews in Italy*, ed. Haim Beinart, 55–72 (Jerusalem: Magnes Press, 1988); and the extracts from Sanuto's diary cited in Bonfil, *Jewish Life*, 39–42. On the Venetian Ghetto, see Benjamin Ravid, "Republica nifredet mikol shilton 'aher" [in Hebrew], in *Thought and Action*, ed. Alfred A. Greenbaum and Alfred Ivry, 27–53 (Tel Aviv: University of Tel Aviv, 1983); Ravid, "The Religious, Economic, and Social Background and Context of the Establishment of the Ghetti of Venice," in *Gli Ebrei e Venezia: Secoli XIV–XVIII, atti del convegno internazionale organizzato dall'Istituto di storia della soci-*

età e dello Stato Veneziano della Fondazione Giorgio Cini, Venezia, Isola di San Giorgio Maggiore, 5–10 giugno 1983, ed. Gaetano Cozzi, 211–59 (Milan: Edizioni Comunità, 1987). For bodily metaphors of the state, see Guido Ruggiero, "Constructing Civic Morality, Deconstructing the Body: Civic Rituals of Punishment in Renaissance Venice," in *Riti e rituali nelle Società Medievali,* ed. Jacques Chiffoleau, Lauro Martines, and Agostino Paravicini Bagliani, 175–90 (Spoleto: Centro Italiano di Studi sull'alto Medioevo, 1994).

6. Simone Luzzatto, *Discorso, Ma'amar 'al Yehudaei Veneziah,* ed. Alfredo Ascoli and trans. Riccardo Bachi and Moshe Shulvass (Jerusalem: Mossad Bialik, 1951), 8th "Investigation." Analyzed by Benjamin Ravid, *Economics and Toleration in Seventeenth-Century Venice: The Background and Context of the "Discorso" of Simone Luzzatto* (Jerusalem: American Academy for Jewish Research, 1979).

7. On Franciscan activity, particularly of Bernardino da Feltre, see Renata Segre, "Bernardino da Feltre, i Monti di pietà e i banchi ebraici," *Rivista storica italiana* 90 (1978): 818–33; and Bonfil, *Jewish Life,* chapter 1.

8. On mercantilism, see Jonathan Israel, *European Jewry in the Age of Mercantilism* (Oxford: Oxford University Press, 1985).

9. See Kenneth Stow, "The Good of the Church, The Good of the State: The Popes and Jewish Money," in "Christianity and Judaism," ed. Diana Wood, special issue, *Studies in Church History* 29 (1992): 237–52.

10. See the essays in Robert Kinsman, ed., *The Darker Vision of the Renaissance: Beyond the Fields of Reason* (Berkeley: University of California Press, 1974).

11. See Anna Foa, "The New and the Old: The Spread of Syphilis (1494–1530)," in *Sex and Gender in Historical Perspective,* ed. Edward Muir and Guido Ruggiero (Baltimore: Johns Hopkins University Press, 1990), 36–37.

12. On the concepts Judaizing and Judaization, see John Gager, *The Origins of Anti-Semitism* (New York: Oxford University Press, 1983).

13. Ritchie Robertson, "Historicizing Weininger: The Nineteenth-Century German Image of the Feminized Jew," in *Modernity, Culture, and "the Jew,"* ed. Bryan Cheyettte and Laura Marcus (Cambridge: Polity Press, 1998), 23; Steven Ascheim, " 'The Jew Within': The Myth of 'Judaization' in German," in *The Jewish Response to German Culture from the Enlightenment to the Second World War,* ed. Jehuda Reinharz and Walter Schatzberg, 212–41 (Hanover, NH: University Press of New England, 1985). On Marrano Judaizing, see Kenneth Stow, "Church, Conversion, and Tradition: The Problem of Jewish Conversion in Sixteenth-Century Italy," *Dimensioni e problemi della ricerca storica* 2 (1996): 26–35.

14. Battista de' Giudici, *"Apologia Iudaeorum,"* ed. and trans. Diego Quaglioni (Vatican City, 1987), 55. On Trent, see Ronnie Po-Chia Hsia, *Trent 1475* (New Haven: Yale University Press, 1992); Anna Esposito and Diego Quaglioni, *Processi contro gli ebrei di Trento (1475–1478)* (Padua: CEDAM, 1990–), 1:37–41; Diego Quaglioni, "Propaganda Antiebraica e Polemiche di Curia," in *Un Pontificato ed una città: Sixto IV (1471–1484),* ed. Massimo Miglio, Francesca Niutta, Diego Quaglioni, and Concetta Ranieri (Vatican City, 1984), 264; on Sixtus IV, see Kenneth Stow, "Papal Mendicants or Mendicant Popes: Continuity and Change in Papal Policies toward the Jews at the End of the Fifteenth Century," in *The Friars and the Jews in the Middle Ages and the Renaissance,* ed. Steven McMichael (Leiden: Brill, forthcoming).

15. Diego Quaglioni, "Fra tolleranza e persecuzione: Gli ebrei nella letteratura giuridica del tardo Medioevo," in *Gli ebrei in Italia*, ed. Corrado Vivanti, 647–77, *Storia d'Italia: Annali*, vol. 11 (Turin: Einaudi, 1996). On De Nievo, see Stow, "Papal Mendicants," discussing Marquardus de Susannis, *De Iudaeis et aliis infidelibus* (Venice, 1558), 1:11: "in eius [De Nievo's] consilio quod fecit contra iudaeos fenerantes quod habeo et impressum reperitur post Pisanellum," implying its marginality. On Jewish banks and the *Monti di pietà*, see Maria Muzzarelli, "Ebrei, Bologna e sovrano-pontifice: La fine di una relazione tra verifiche, restrizioni e ripensamenti," in *Verso l'epilogo di una convivenza: Gli ebrei a Bologna nel xvi secolo*, ed. Maria Muzzarelli, 19–54 (Florence: Giuntina, 1996). On Franciscan financial acumen, see David Ruderman, *The World of a Renaissance Jew* (Cincinnati: Hebrew Union College Press, 1981), 85–97.

16. Friedrich von Spee, *Cautio Criminalis*, ed. Anna Foa (Rome: Salerno, 1986).

17. "ora sua spurcissima aperire, ac prava et obscena quedam diabolica figmenta, suis falsissimis dogmatibus confingere"; "contagione iudaica ... ut christicolas a veritate seducere et se voluptatum suarum compotes facere valeant." Sixtus IV's letter is printed in Shlomo Simonsohn, *The Apostolic See and the Jews*, 8 vols. (Toronto: Pontifical Institute of Mediaeval Studies, 1988–91), vol. 3, no. 999 and nos. 972 and 1002. For Jewish medical licenses, see nos. 945 and 951, and Ariel Toaff, *The Jews in Umbria*, 3 vols. (Leiden: Brill, 1992), vol. 3, no. 1824.

18. Kenneth Stow, "Expulsion Italian Style: The Case of Lucio Ferraris," *Jewish History* 3 (1988): 51–64.

19. Kenneth Stow, *Catholic Thought and Papal Jewry Policy* (New York: Jewish Theological Seminary, 1977); and Stow, "The Papacy and the Jews: Catholic Reformation and Beyond," in "The Frank Talmage Memorial Volume," ed. Barry Walfish, special issue, *Jewish History* 6 (1991): 268.

20. Kenneth Stow, *The Jews in Rome*, 2 vols. (Leiden: Brill, 1995–97), vol. 1, nos. 105, 106, and esp. no. 844. For Leo X de' Medici and Julius II, see Simonsohn, *Apostolic See*, vol. 3, nos. 1273 and 1210.

21. On irrationality, see Marc Bensimon, "Modes of Perception of Reality in the Renaissance," in Kinsman, *The Darker Vision*, 221–72; and on elixirs, see Ruggiero, *Binding Passions*. On Jewish science, see David Ruderman, *Jewish Thought and Scientific Discovery in Early Modern Europe* (New Haven: Yale University Press, 1995).

22. "sortilegiis, incantationibus, magicisque superstitionibus et maleficis." See Pius V's bull *Hebreorum gens* in Sebastiano Franco, H. Fory, and Henrico Dalmazzo, eds., *Bullarum diplomatum et privilegiorum sanctorum romanorum pontificum*, 25 vols. (Turin: Augustae Taurinorum, 1857–85), 7:740–42 (cited in Stow, *Catholic Thought*, 34), and for Clement VIII's bull *Caeca et obdurata* of 1593, see ibid., 10:22.

23. Recorded in the *Avvisi*, in Rome, BAV, *Codex Urbanus Latinus*, 1038, fol. 140r; 1039, fols. 104r–v, 108v, 112v, and 120r–v, amongst others.

24. *A quo primum*, the bull of Benedict XIV, is cited in Mario Rosa, "Tra tolleranza e repressione: Roma e gli ebrei nel '700," in *Italia Judaica: Gli ebrei in Italia della segregazione alla prima emancipazione, Atti del III convegno internazionale, Tel Aviv 15–20 giugno 1986* (Rome: Ministry of Culture, 1989), 3:90. See also Marina Caffiero, "'Le insidie de' perfidi

Giudei': Antiebraismo e riconquista Cattolica alla fine del settecento," *Rivista storica italiana* 105 (1993): 555–81.

25. Kenneth Stow, "Papal and Royal Attitudes toward Jewish Lending," *AJS Review* 6 (1981): 161–84; and Stow, "The Consciousness of Closure: Roman Jewry and Its *'Ghet,'*" in *Essential Papers on Jewish Culture in Renaissance and Baroque Italy,* ed. David Ruderman, 386–400 (New York: New York University Press, 1992).

26. On "disciplining," see Adriano Prosperi, "L'inquisitore come confessore," in *Disciplina dell'anima, disciplina del corpo e disciplina della società tra medioevo ed età moderna,* ed. Paolo Prodi and Adriano Prosperi, 187–224 (Bologna: Il Mulino, 1994); and Adriano Prosperi, *Tribunali di Coscienza* (Turin: Einaudi, 1976). See also William Hudon, "Religion and Society in Early Modern Italy," *American Historical Review* 101 (1996): 783–804.

27. Brian Pullan, *Rich and Poor in Renaissance Venice: The Social Institutions of a Catholic State to 1620* (Cambridge: Harvard University Press, 1971), 576–78.

28. Stow, *Jews in Rome,* no 1723. See also Simonsohn, *Apostolic See,* vol. 6, no. 2566 (Nov. 1555) and no. 2625 (Aug. 1546), for orders that prohibit Jews from living outside the area of Piazza Giudea and Via Giudea, presaging the ghetto.

29. Isaiah Sonne, *Mi-Pavolo ha-Revi'i ʿad Pius ha-Hamishi* (Jerusalem: Mossad Bialik, 1954), 195–98; and the parallel Christian account in Stow, "The Jew as Alien."

30. See Daniel Carpi, ed., *Minute Books of the Jewish Community of Padua* [in Hebrew], 2 vols. (Jerusalem: Israel Academy of Sciences, 1974–80), 2:464.

31. See Milano, *Il Ghetto di Roma,* 261–68.

32. Rome, BAV, *Raccolta Generale Miscellanea,* IV, 94, insert n. 2.

33. David Nirenberg, *Communities of Violence: Persecution of Minorities in the Middle Ages* (Princeton: Princeton University Press, 1996), 200–218.

34. Toaff, *The Jews in Umbria,* vol. 3, no. 2321.

35. Franco, Fory, and Dalmazzo, *Bullarum,* 8:378–81 (cited in Stow, *Catholic Thought,* 33). Albano Biondi, "Gli ebrei e l'inquisizione negli Stati Estensi," in *L'inquisizione e Gli Ebrei,* ed. Michele Luzzati, 265–86 (Bari: Laterza, 1994).

36. Thomas Aquinas, *Summa Theologica,* 2 vols. (New York: Benziger, 1947), II, II, 10–12.

37. Aharon Jellinek, ed., *Haqirot ʿal ʿinyanei ha-nozrim me'et R. Yishma'el Haninah* (Ha-Shahar, 1871), 17–23. See David B. Ruderman, "An Apologetic Treatise from Sixteenth Century Bologna," *Hebrew Union College Annual* 50 (1979): 253–75. On the thirteenth century, see Chen-Melekh M. Merchavia, *The Church vs. Talmudic and Midrashic Literature* [in Hebrew] (Jerusalem: Mossad Bialik, 1973); and Kenneth Stow, "The Burning of the Talmud in 1553 in the Light of Sixteenth-Century Catholic Attitudes toward the Talmud," *Bibliothèque d'Humanisme et Renaissance* 34 (1972): 435–59.

38. See Stow, *Jews in Rome,* no. 384. On foods, see Maria Luisa Lombardo, *La Dogana Minuta a Roma nel primo quattrocento* (Viterbo: Centro di studi di civiltà comunale, 1983), 133–38.

39. Term coined by Thomas V. Cohen, "The Case of the Mysterious Coil of Rope: Street Life and Jewish Persona in Rome in the Middle of the Sixteenth Century," *Sixteenth Century Journal* 19 (1988): 209 and 214.

40. On Jewish marital behavior, see Aron Freimann, *Seder kiddushin ve-nissuin 'aharei hatimat ha-Talmud* (Jerusalem: Mossad HaRav Kook, 1964), 82, 86–87; and Kenneth Stow, "Marriages are Made in Heaven: Marriage and the Individual in the Roman Jewish Ghetto," *Renaissance Quarterly* 48 (1995): 445–91.

41. Rome, Archivio Capitolino Storico (henceforth ACS), *Notai ebrei*, fascicle 2, book 3, fol. 9r–v (2 Jan. 1569). See also Stow, *Jews in Rome*, no. 271; and Kristen Gager, *Blood Ties and Fictive Ties* (Princeton: Princeton University Press, 1996), 44, 71, 75, 79, 83, 87, and 136. See also David Herlihy and Christiane Klapisch-Zuber, *Tuscans and Their Families: A Study of the Florentine Catasto of 1427* (New Haven: Yale University Press, 1985), 145–47.

42. Rome, ACS, *Notai ebrei*, fascicle 1, book 1, fol. 114v. Arbi, once actually Parnas of the Catalan-Aragonese synagogue, had fallen on hard times. See Stow, *Jews in Rome*, no. 1966.

43. On Christian funerals, see Samuel K. Cohn Jr., "Burial in the Early Renaissance: Six Cities in Central Italy," and Diane Owen Hughes, "Mourning Rites, Memory, and Civilization in Premodern Italy," in Chiffoleau, Martines, and Bagliani, *Riti e rituali*, 39–57 and 23–38. On Jewish funerals, see Sylvie-Anne Goldberg, *Crossing the Jabok: Illness and Death in Ashkenazi Judaism in Sixteenth Through Nineteenth-Century Prague*, trans. Carol Cosman (Berkeley: University of California Press, 1996); Bonfil, *Jewish Life*, 265–70; and Elliott Horowitz, "Confraternities in Seventeenth Century Verona" (Ph.D. dissertation, Yale University, 1987), 105–10. See also Ariel Toaff, *Il Vino e la carne* (Bologna: Il Mulino, 1989), 67–68 and 224–25.

44. Guido Ruggiero, *The Boundaries of Eros: Sex Crime and Sexuality in Renaissance Venice* (Oxford: Oxford University Press, 1985), 17–18; Kenneth Stow, "The Knotty Problem of Shem Tov Soporto: Male Honor, Marital Initiation, and Disciplinary Structures in Mid-Sixteenth Century Jewish Rome," in "Memorial Book for Joseph B. Sermoneta," special issue, *Italia* 13 (2001): 137–50. See also Yacov Boksenboim, ed., *Responsa of Azriel Diena*, 2 vols. (Tel Aviv: University of Tel Aviv, 1977), 1:434, no. 125.

45. David Gentilcore, *From Bishop to Witch: The System of the Sacred in Early Modern Terra d'Otranto* (Manchester: Manchester University Press, 1992), 215; and Peter Burke, "Rituals of Healing in Early Modern Italy," in *Historical Anthropology*, 211–14.

46. See the twelfth-century Abraham ben David of Posquierres, *Sefer Ba'alei ha-Nefesh*, ed. J. Kafah (Jerusalem: Mossad HaRav Kook, 1964). See also Isaiah Hurwitz, *Shenai luhot ha-berit* (Furth, 1764), 102b, and contrast with Bernardino da Siena, *Le prediche volgari*, 2 vols., ed. Ciro Cannarozzi (Florence: Rinaldi, 1958), vol. 1, sermon nos. 19–21.

47. Stow, *Jews in Rome*, no. 1743. On the *mundualdus*, see Thomas Kuehn, *Law, Family, and Women: Toward a Legal Anthropology of Renaissance Italy* (Chicago: University of Chicago Press, 1991), 216–22.

48. Stow, "Consciousness of Closure."

49. Simona Feci, "The Death of a Miller: A Trial *contra hebreos* in Baroque Rome," *Jewish History* 7 (1993): 15–20.

50. Archivio di Stato di Modena, *Fondo dell'Inquisizione*, busta 26:6 (26 Apr. 1604): *Contra Davide de Nurscia*. Reference courtesy of Katherine Aron Beller.

51. Benjamin Ravid, "Kosher Bread in Venice," *Italia* 6 (1986): 20–29; and the text in Pier Cesari Ioly-Zorattini, *Processi del S. Uffizio di Venezia contro ebrei e giudaizzanti*, 14 vols. (Florence: Olschki, 1980–97), 4:43–46.

52. Archivio di Stato di Roma, *Relazioni dei Sbirri*, no. 104; *Costituti*, busta 676, 21.1.1611. Robert Davis has graciously shown me this unpublished text. See, too, Rome, ACS, *Notai ebrei*, fascicle 18, book 1, fol. 3v (25 Sept. 1573).

53. Cohen, "Case of the Mysterious Coil of Rope," 217.

54. Stow, "Church, Conversion, and Tradition," 387.

55. Maurice Kriegel, "La Prise d'une decision: L'expulsion des juifs d'Espagne en 1492," *Revue historique* 29 (1978): 49–90; and Henry Kamen, "The Mediterranean and the Expulsion of Spanish Jews in 1492," *Past and Present*, no. 119 (1989): 30–55.

56. Kenneth Stow, "A Tale of Uncertainties: Converts in the Roman Ghetto," in *Shlomo Simonsohn Jubilee Volume*, ed. Daniel Carpi, Moshe Gil, and Yosef Gorni, 257–81 (Jerusalem: Graph-Chen Press, 1993).

57. Luciano Allegra, "A Model of Jewish Devolution," *Jewish History* 7 (1993): 29–58; and Allegra, *Identità in bilico: Il Ghetto ebraico di Torino nel Settecento* (Turin: Zamorani, 1996), 111–15.

58. Marquardus de Susannis, *De Iudaeis*, part I, chapter 11 on lending, chapters 7, 9.2, and part III, chapter 1 on Jewish machinations, and part III, chapters 2, esp. 7 and 8, on conversion, exemplifying both "light" and "dark."

59. Robert Bonfil, "Changes in the Cultural Patterns of a Jewish Society in Crisis: Italian Jewry at the Close of the Sixteenth Century," *Jewish History* 3 (1988): 11–30.

60. Joseph Sermoneta, "Jewish Culture at Rome in the XVIIIth Century as Seen Through New Documentation" [in Hebrew], in *Italia Judaica*, 3:69–96.

61. Kenneth Stow, "Sanctity and the Construction of Space: The Roman Ghetto," in *Luoghi sacri e spazi della santità*, ed. Sofia Boesch and Lucetta Scaraffia, 593–608 (Turin: Einaudi, 1990); revised in *Jewish Assimilation, Acculturation and Accommodation*, ed. Menachem Mor, 54–77 (Lanham: University Presses of America, 1992).

62. Kenneth Stow, *Theater of Acculturation: The Roman Ghetto in the Sixteenth Century* (Seattle: University of Washington Press, 2000), chapter 3.

63. See Milton M. Gordon, *Assimilation in American Life* (New York: Oxford University Press, 1964); and also Peter I. Rose, *They and We: Racial and Ethnic Relations in the United States*, 5th ed. (New York: Random House, 1997).

64. Elliott Horowitz, "Coffee, Coffee Houses, and the Nocturnal Rituals of Early Modern Jewry," *AJS Review* 14 (1989): 17–46. On the related ghetto Purim, see Milano, *Il Ghetto di Roma*, 529 and 540, and also Cecil Roth, "La festa per l'istituzione del Ghetto a Verona," *Rassegna Mensile di Israel* 3 (1928): 33–39.

65. Roberto Bachi, "The Demographic Development of Italian Jewry from the Seventeenth Century," *Jewish Journal of Sociology* 4 (1962): 172–91. On ghetto foundings, see Attilio Milano, *Storia degli ebrei in Italia* (Turin: Einaudi, 1963), 243–337.

66. Renzo Toaff, *La Nazione Ebrea a Livorno e a Pisa (1591–1700)* (Florence: Olschki, 1990). The privilege of Emanuel Filiberto of Piedmont published by Mario Lattes, "Notes et Documents," *Revue des Etudes Juives* 5 (1882): 231–37; and see Milano, *Storia*, 274.

67. Bernard Cooperman, "Venetian Policy toward Levantine Jews in Its Broader Italian Context," in Cozzi, *Gli Ebrei e Venezia*, 65–84; also Salo Baron, *A Social and Religious History of the Jews*, 16 vols. (Philadelphia: Jewish Publication Society, 1952–), 14: 39–40.

68. Giovanni Miccoli, "Santa Sede, questione ebraica e antisemitismo," in Vivanti, *Gli ebrei in Italia*, 1371–1574. For the text of Cardinal Ganganelli, see *Die Paepstlichen Bullen ueber die Blutbeschuldigung* (Munich: August Schupp, 1900), translated in Cecil Roth, ed. and trans., *The Ritual Murder Libel and the Jew: The Report by Cardinal Lorenzo Ganganelli (Pope Clement XIV)* (London: Woburn Press, 1935).

69. Pius IX, in *Quanta cura Syllabus* of 8 December 1864—citing Gregory XVI— said it was a "delirio, [especially to say that] la libertà di coscienza e dei culti essere un diritto proprio di ciascun uomo. . . ." For the full text, see http://digilander.libero.it/ magistero/p9quanta.htm/. This bull introduces the well-known "Syllabus of Errors."

6

CAST OUT AND SHUT IN

THE EXPERIENCE OF NUNS
IN COUNTER-REFORMATION VENICE

MARY LAVEN

It may seem strange to categorize female religious as a minority group in any sense other than the numerical one, or to consider nuns in the context of those whose religious, political, or moral identity situated them on the edge of society. After all, nunneries were sacred institutions, bastions of chastity whose members contributed to the spiritual assets of the wider community in which they resided. Furthermore, nuns in premodern Europe often came from the highest ranks of society, and many convents were renowned for fostering a noble pedigree. Far from being marginal, those communities of nuns that enjoyed a reputation for both piety and nobility occupied an honorable and sometimes powerful position within civic society.[1] In Venice, the fusion of spiritual and social credit was graphically displayed by the nuns of Santa Maria delle Vergini in the rituals accompanying the investiture of their abbess. The ceremony involved a symbolic marriage of Venice's supreme temporal authority with the new abbess: by an exchange of rings, the doge bestowed upon the nun temporal power with which to govern her community and the abbess invested the ducal authority with sanctity.[2] But this marriage of secular and religious interests was in many ways a fragile alliance. The combination of spiritual and social status was difficult to maintain, especially in an age of religious reform. This chapter explores the paradoxes that surrounded the status of female religious in Counter-Reformation

Venice, which rendered them at once a marginal and a central element of society.

I begin by considering the ways in which some Venetian nuns felt marginalized or excluded, situating their responses within two important historical contexts: the social and economic pressures that caused many women to take the veil against their personal inclinations, and the Counter-Reformation drive to subject all female religious to strict enclosure. But this is only one half of the story. Notwithstanding forced vocations and compulsory enclosure, women in Venetian convents were determined to reassert their position within their families and neighborhoods. The second part of the chapter will be devoted to looking at nuns' strategies for resisting marginalization.

At one level, of course, entering a religious order was all about leaving society behind. The acceptance and profession ceremonies of female religious represented in the most blatant terms their exclusion from the world. "Forget your people, and your father's home" was the injunction that some newly accepted novices received at the initial rite of clothing.[3] At the same time, the novices cast off their lay garments, allowed their hair to be cut short, and made the physical transition from the public church to the enclosed convent. The drama of the ceremony caught the imagination of more than one writer. In Aretino's dialogue *Ragionamento della Nanna e della Antonia,* published in 1534, the ex-nun turned prostitute, Nanna, reflects upon her own traumatic entry to the convent. As she passed from the church to the convent, she recalls, the door slammed behind her, shutting out the world and preventing her from saying farewell to her relations. In the words of Nanna, "I believed myself to be entering a tomb alive."[4] An equally arresting account is given by Arcangela Tarabotti, a nun at the Venetian convent of Sant' Anna in the first half of the seventeenth century and author of *Inferno monacale,* an eloquent tirade against the practice of forcing girls to become nuns against their will. Like Aretino, Tarabotti invoked the metaphor of entering a tomb in order to describe the "funereal ceremony" of profession. This is her description of the moment at which the novice takes her irrevocable vows: "with bitter resolution, . . . her lips faint with desperation, she is induced to utter her own sentence of entombment."[5] But how did the symbolic step of death to the world, intrinsic to the nun's profession, affect her standing within the wider community?

Becoming a nun in early modern Venice entailed for many women a loss of status. This was in large part to do with the circumstances in which hundreds or even thousands of women were compelled to enter convents against their will—circumstances that inform the grim accounts of profession given by both Aretino and Tarabotti. At the end of the sixteenth century, there were fifty convents in the city of Venice and the surrounding lagoon islands, accommodating over three thousand nuns.[6] The burgeoning population of female religious in Venice, as elsewhere in Italy, has been accounted for by two related socioeconomic factors. Firstly, the inflation in marital dowries from the fifteenth century onward meant that fathers often could not afford to marry all their daughters. Secondly, noble families seeking to preserve their wealth encouraged a strategy of celibacy among their sons, so as to prevent the fragmentation of the patrimony amongst a profusion of male heirs. This inevitably resulted in a shortage of eligible husbands for young noble girls. Hard-pressed patricians chose to put their daughters into convents rather than allow them to marry out of the noble caste.[7]

Females born into noble households were, therefore, divided into those who would marry and those who would become nuns. The process of selection was bound to be invidious. Doubtless some parents were more attentive to the will and disposition of their daughters than others, but there were clearly tactical considerations to be taken into account. Given the preference for young brides, elder daughters were more likely to be sent to the nunnery—a policy that enabled their fathers to conserve the hefty sum that would eventually dower their younger girls for as long as possible. Illegitimate daughters were also obvious candidates for the religious life.[8] The singling out of girls who were handicapped or deemed unattractive for some other reason attracted particular opprobrium.[9] This practice was criticized by reforming ecclesiastics, who addressed the issue of forced vocations. Writing in 1584, Silvio Antoniano exhorted parents: "do not dedicate to God in religion . . . the unfortunate girl, because she is born deformed or crippled."[10] In a work published in 1603, Pietro Giussani condemned those responsible for sending "those who are either of ill-formed body, or else of simple intellect" to the nunnery. He likened them to "impious Cain, because they sacrifice the worst to God."[11] The arguments of these men were echoed in Venice by Arcangela Tarabotti:

They do not give to Jesus their most beautiful or virtuous daughters, but rather the most repulsive and deformed ones, and if there are any girls within the family who are lame, hunchbacked, crippled or simple, they are condemned to remain in prison for their entire life, as if the defect of nature were their fault.[12]

Being lame herself, Tarabotti bitterly opposed this principle of selection. But even if the actual number of physically disabled nuns was small (and we lack the statistics to know), the association of nuns with the unattractive or incapable created a stigma around the conventual existence.

The implicit favor paid to those women who were selected as brides was underlined by the bestowal of a marital dowry perhaps ten or twenty times bigger than the religious dowries required by their sisters in the nunnery.[13] In a culture in which wealth and display played crucial roles in the construction and maintenance of honor, a large dowry and an opulent trousseau were sources of bridal power.[14] Conversely, there is evidence that some women in convents felt their material exclusion keenly. One noble nun, suor Crestina Dolfin, who escaped from the nunnery of Spirito Santo in 1561, told her friends that she had left the convent "because she wanted her share of her father's and brother's estates, and also the dowry of her mother."[15] Arcangela Tarabotti perceived the economic exclusion of nuns like Crestina as contrary to law: "there exists no law by which married women are granted a greater claim over their families' houses than women who have become nuns."[16] The problem was not simply that women destined for the convent were denied a fair share of the family's riches, but also that they were prevented from engaging in the sort of conspicuous extravagance that granted married women status. Drawing attention to the continual flouting of sumptuary laws by Venetian noblewomen, famed for their low-cut dresses and high-heeled clogs, the historians Stanley Chojnacki and Robert Davis have stressed the possibilities for self-promotion that were afforded by extravagant dress.[17] For nuns such possibilities were limited, and Tarabotti illustrates the cruelty of this distinction by contrasting the lavish festivities of a Venetian marriage with the shabby rites of profession: whereas the bride is adorned with the finest cloth from Flanders and the most precious pearls from the Orient, the nun is clad in "the grossest, roughest stuff"; worse still, "often there is insufficient material, and so the sleeves are odd and do not match the rest of the garment." The shame conveyed by this detail is revealing of the significance attached to dress as a marker of status.[18]

I have pointed to some of the ways in which an involuntary nun—excluded from the marriage market, cheapened by her dowry, and deprived of finery—suffered a blow to her social standing. But the *spiritual* status of Venetian convents was also compromised both by the practice of forced vocations and by the enduring pretensions of patrician nuns. An uncomfortable relationship existed between nuns as noblewomen—"the first blood and first born of the city," as a contemporary observer put it—and nuns as brides of Christ.[19] This tension was clearly articulated in the responses of noble nuns and their families to a series of reforming measures enacted by the patriarch Antonio Contarini in the early sixteenth century. Contarini's policy involved the transfer of "observant" nuns to the comparatively lax "conventual" houses, placing the administration of the slack and unruly convents in the hands of the new nuns. Unsurprisingly, the cohabitation of the old conventual communities with the imported observant nuns led to some fiery disputes, and the most aristocratic nuns viewed the policy as a serious affront. On 21 August 1521, four abbesses came to address the doge and patriarch, accompanied by a host of relatives. The nobleman Niccolò Michiel spoke on behalf of the nuns of San Zaccaria, where several of his daughters and sisters were nuns: he complained that the community, which for 760 years had been of exclusively noble composition, had been forced to open its doors to "bastards, Greeks, and plebs."[20]

In a situation where both the authorities and the nuns themselves were under no illusions about the factors motivating women to take the veil, it was extremely difficult to impose strict disciplinary standards. The abbess of San Biagio e Castaldo explained to the patriarchal visitor in 1593 why she stopped short of attempting to subject the women in her charge to the full rigors of convent discipline: "while I do not fail to admonish and reprove them, it is not the practice to mete out penances in these times, for the girls are put here for safekeeping rather than as nuns."[21] The link between indiscipline and forced vocations was commented upon from a variety of quarters. The papal nuncio to Venice, Alberto Bolognetti, argued in 1581 that the practice whereby fathers forced their daughters to enter the convent, "not having sufficient money to marry them on an equal social footing, and not wanting to permit them to take a social inferior for a husband, lest the splendor of their families might be diminished," was "the root from which all the disorders are born."[22] Tarabotti also warned parents that "by forcing your daughters to enter nunneries, you are participating in all their scandalous actions."[23]

The scandals arising from Venetian convents presented one of the recurring paradoxes of female religious status. All too often, high birth seemed to go together with low conduct, a consequence of the frequent incidence of forced vocations among the noble nuns. In the words of Girolamo Priuli, diarist and social critic in the early sixteenth century: "these nun-whores were the daughters or relatives of the principal Senators who governed the Venetian Republic." The convents he repeatedly dubbed "public bordellos and bawdy-houses."[24] Priuli was not the first or the last to invoke the metaphor of the brothel to describe the nunneries of Venice. In 1497, the Franciscan Timoteo da Lucca, preaching in San Marco, lamented the fact that "whenever a foreign gentleman comes to this city, they show him the nunneries, scarcely nunneries in fact but brothels and public bordellos."[25] Gasparo Contarini later made use of the same imagery, writing in his *De officio episcopi* of 1516 that "many convents of virgins, dedicated to God, take the place of bordellos."[26] The charge continued to be directed against nunneries and their occupants, as in 1620 when a denunciation remarked of S. Servolo "that it appeared not to be a place of female religious but rather of true whores."[27] That the polarized categories of "nun" and "whore" might collapse so readily suggests the ease with which female religious drifted from the center to the margins of Venetian society.

The uncertainties and ambiguities of nuns' status were intensified by the post-Tridentine efforts to reform the convents of Venice. The centerpiece of these reforms was the drive to reduce all nunneries to strict enclosure, a controversial policy laid down in the decrees of the Council of Trent and consolidated in Pius V's bull *Circa pastoralis* of 1566.[28] The measure was taken up energetically by both the Venetian state and church, suggesting not so much deference to the directives of Rome as a determination to put an end to the scandals that jeopardized the role of the city's convents in accommodating the unmarried kinswomen of the patriciate. Enjoying the endorsement of papal authority, the Venetian government fired off new laws, limiting contact between nuns and the outside world and laying down punishments for those who had transgressed the holy boundaries of enclosure. The state magistrates with special responsibility for the city's convents *(provveditori sopra monasteri)*, first appointed in 1521, busied themselves with putting the letter of the law into practice; officials of the church, meanwhile, subjected nunneries to rigorous visitations and sought to plug every gap in the convent wall. The result was that many Venetian women who had been compelled to enter the convent on account of familial pressures, rather than as a result of divine calling, found themselves subjected to an austere and segregated regime that suited them ill. In particular, they resented the attempts of the authorities to cut them off from their friends and relatives in the outside world. Compulsory enclosure rendered forced vocations a more bitter pill to swallow.

The policy of enclosing convents aimed at nothing short of physical isolation. Windows were bricked up, doors were sealed, gardens were put out of bounds, and the light was shut out with blinds and curtains. One visitation records how the nuns of San Rocco and Santa Margherita were instructed to block up the ventilation holes that aired the latrine, for fear that a nun might be able to catch a glimpse of the street below.[29] The reformers aimed to isolate nuns culturally and emotionally as well as physically. Female religious were discouraged from communicating by means of letter "because it is not conducive to the tranquility of their state to disturb it with this bother of writing."[30] All correspondence in which nuns participated was to be strictly censored by the abbess; the nuns were not allowed to keep pen and ink in their cells. The reading of literature was also predictably restricted, and the inspection of convent libraries was a standard feature of every visitation. As for music, an area that we might expect to have offered nuns opportunities for creative expression, the picture was similarly bleak. There was a crackdown on the employment of lay music-teachers to instruct nuns, and female religious were generally discouraged from singing and music making in church, particularly in the presence of a lay congregation. Ideally, nuns were to be rendered inaudible as well as invisible.[31]

The most tightly controlled area of nuns' lives was that of their personal and affective ties. The renunciation of close personal relationships was an ancient principle of monastic life. As the confessor to the nuns of Santa Marta commented in 1620, "I have always, in general, persuaded the nuns to relinquish particular friendships both inside and outside the convent: because *amicitia huius mundi est inimica Deo.*"[32] But while

there was nothing new about the confessor's injunction, in the period of
the Counter-Reformation nuns found their relationships policed to an
unprecedented extent. Endless regulations were issued controlling nuns'
contacts with outsiders—neighbors and employees, priests and doctors,
friends and family. Many of these rules and regulations related to the
parlatorio, literally the "speaking-room," where convent business was
conducted and where nuns were permitted to meet close relations. This
ambiguous site on the very edge of enclosure was considered a weak spot
in the convent defenses and was subject to increasingly strict control.[33]

The records of the authorities who sought to enclose the convents of
Venice suggest a clash between the culture of the open convent, with
its traditions of sociability and intercourse with the outside world, and
the efforts of the authorities to turn these institutions into closed communities. But they also tell the tale of resistance to enclosure on both
sides of the convent wall. In the remainder of this chapter, I shall be
pointing to the ways in which nuns defied marginalization, in their
efforts to reestablish themselves more centrally within their families
and neighborhoods.[34]

As with every other aspect of conventual life, nuns' relations with
their families came under strict regulation in the rush of legislation precipitated by the Tridentine reforms. Visits from family members were
subject to the limitations of time and place laid down in the rules governing use of the *parlatorio;* and male relatives were only allowed to visit
if they came within the required degrees of kinship.[35] But notwithstanding the limits of the law, female religious were determined to keep the
visits flowing, asserting their usefulness to their families by offering
them some small measure of material support. The patriarchal authorities constantly urged nuns to refrain from squandering their resources
in giving away food. Usually, this practice consisted in baking cakes and
biscuits for friends and relatives, but nuns were also guilty of giving
handouts directly from the larder. We learn, for example, in 1567, of one
suor Beatrice Moro, at Sant' Andrea di Zirada, sending a bag of flour to
her sister's house, hidden among the convent's dirty washing.[36] Bearing
in mind that some nunneries were powerful economic institutions, female religious might use their influence to bring more substantial benefits to their families. The 1595 visitation to Santa Croce di Giudecca revealed that a group of nuns belonging to a branch of the noble Molino
clan were serving the interests of their relatives. It was noted that these

"Molline" (significantly, Venetian nuns nearly always persisted in using their family name) had for many years been letting out houses belonging to the nunnery to their relations at a cheap rate.[37]

The efforts of female religious to court attention and affection from their families are further indicated by their response to marriages occurring among their sisters and other female relatives. Whereas Tarabotti describes such events as the ultimate humiliation for the nun, who inevitably compared the feasting and extravagance of the marital rites with her own marginalized existence, there is evidence that nuns were, in fact, anxious to be involved in the family festivities. Regulations were passed condemning the practice whereby brides would visit convents in all their splendor on their wedding day, but the nuns continued to gather round the windows of the *parlatorii* in order to view the bride and touch her hand.[38] Some nuns were unstoppable in their desire to shower gifts upon their sisters on their wedding days.[39]

Similar tactics of gift giving, hospitality, and material support were used by nuns in sustaining relationships with nonfamilial acquaintances. Repeatedly cropping up throughout the records are those lay employees and servants who did shopping and other jobs outside the enclosure for nuns. At the convent of Sant' Andrea di Zirada in 1567–68, the involvement of female religious with lay employees was the root of various disciplinary lapses being investigated by the *provveditori*. A large group of women was employed here on a casual basis, often to provide particular services for individual nuns. For example, of one Zuana it was reported that "she keeps eight or ten chickens, belonging to madonna suor Gabriela, at her own home...; she is provided with bread and wine and every other thing in return for feeding these chickens."[40] Zuana was one of a group of women described disparagingly by witnesses as gossips *(petegole)* who lived parasitically "on the shoulders of the monastery." Besides providing the occasional services for the nuns, petegole—as the word suggests—had another important commodity to offer those who lived within the enclosure of the convent. In return for material support, Zuana and company traded snippets of news and information from the world. The transaction is clearly articulated by one witness: "these women take away food, and they bring gossip backward and forward."[41] Unsurprisingly, the authorities in Venice frowned upon these sorts of relationships. Bishop Antonio Grimani of Torcello wrote contemptuously in 1592 of "the practice of many little women *(feminette)*, employed by the nuns, who speak continually at the doors and windows [of the nunneries]."[42] These gossips who took food from the nuns constituted a very real threat to the dignity and prosperity of the convent.

By consorting with lower-class women from the neighborhood, Venetian nuns furnished new links that bound their communities into the fabric of city life. However, what served to reintegrate female religious at one level of society further jeopardized their position at another. "Whores, bawds, and witches" was how one observer characterized the women who were accustomed to frequent the convent of San Servolo, in 1621.[43] While this remark was clearly an exaggeration, it suggests an association of Venetian nuns with other marginal groups that is borne out more generally by the evidence of trial records. For in their efforts to resist the isolation of enclosure, nuns welcomed into their *parlatorii* a wide variety of social outcasts, ranging from prostitutes to Jews to defrocked priests. Such exchanges suggest that the constrained existence of the enclosed nun afforded certain opportunities for social mixing that would have been denied to the laywoman of equivalent social status. Space does not allow here for a proper discussion of these fascinating interactions—interactions that flouted every decorum of the Venetian convent existence, and yet that could be as liberating as they were degrading. However, the themes of social inversion and the exchange of identities may be pursued in one specific context: the experience of Carnival in the cloister.

The high concentration of disciplinary lapses at Carnival time suggests that the convents of Venice—notwithstanding enclosure—remained in tune with the calendar of civic merrymaking.[44] During this period of disorder and release, the convent *parlatorii* functioned as semi-public spaces, in which nuns were pleased to provide hospitality and other entertainments.[45] In 1588, Patriarch Trevisan issued a general mandate "concerning the abuses and excesses that take place in the churches and *parlatorii* of nuns, especially at times of Carnival, with refreshments, eating and drinking, playing, singing, dancing; and people entering convents wearing masks to the dishonor of God and of our Religion."[46] These abuses and excesses were repeatedly condemned by the Venetian authorities throughout the period. Wholly incompatible with the dignity of female religious and with the principle of enclosure, such practices nevertheless proved enduring. Carnival revelers were evidently keen to include nunneries in their boisterous progresses. In some respects, their institutional status made religious houses more susceptible to intrusion than private households; moreover, the added subversion of creating profane confusion among Christ's brides enticed those whose goal it was to turn the world upside down.

For those nuns who craved variety in their recreation, and an escape from the unchanging routine of religious life, Carnival provided a measure of seasonal license. Two activities associated with Carnival were particularly appealing to nuns: acting and dressing up. In theory, at least, nuns were allowed to engage in convent theater, so long as the subject was pious and the participants retained their religious garb. However, visitation reports suggest that certain communities took advantage of their cloistered existence to break the rules in private. For example, at the Miracoli it was recorded in 1595, "That sometimes the nuns sing profane songs, they play the guitar and the lute, and they dress up as men in order to put on plays. . . . It is ordered that they should not wear secular clothes when they perform plays."[47] Elissa Weaver, who has worked extensively on convent theater in Tuscany, has noted that "for the most part the audience was the convent community," pointing to the laws that sought to exclude outsiders.[48] But while her own evidence for convent drama suggests that it was a largely internal affair, she has observed that the subjects nuns chose to represent were overwhelmingly concerned with life outside the convent walls. Thus at an imaginative level, "the insistence of convent theater to stage the secular world almost to the exclusion of the world the women actually knew" provided an escape from the hemmed-in life of the nunnery.[49] While research has not yet yielded manuscripts of plays performed by Venetian nuns, it would appear from the repeated orders to keep outsiders from attending convent productions, and from the cases that came before the *provveditori*, that in Venice at least a public audience was often procured. Whether or not Venetian nuns chose to represent secular scenes in their drama, they surely shared the desire of their Tuscan sisters to secure temporary relief from their oppressive conventual existence. Convent theater was an excuse for actual rather than merely metaphorical contact with the world. Besides providing a forum for autonomous creativity, theatrical events presented Venetian nuns with yet another strategy for attracting layfolk into their midst.

Dramatic representations could, and often did, involve putting on costumes for the stage, and nuns appear to have delighted in the chance to don secular clothes belonging to either sex. But even without theater,

Carnival was a time for dressing up and for flirting with alternative identities. During the course of an investigation into a scandal at San Zaccaria
in 1614, one nun freely admitted that "during Carnival, the nuns are accustomed to dress up, both as men and as women, and to walk about
the convent at night."[50] In 1612, Malipiera Malipiero, a prostitute often
to be found in the *parlatorii* of Spirito Santo, was accused of lending the
nuns "gold, silver, and all sorts of clothes" to wear during Carnival.[51]
Suor Elena Badoer from the nunnery at Malamocco on the Lido was de-
nounced by her own abbess in 1626 for having organized a party that
transgressed the boundaries between lay and religious:

> This Carnival, on three or four days, especially on the feast of
> Sant' Apolonia, she dressed up in secular clothes as a gentle-
> woman, with a veil over her face, and she went to dance in the
> *parlatorii* in the presence of her *petegole* and of a man who was
> playing the violin.[52]

Dressing up had an obvious appeal for nuns, continually warned against
the crime of vanity. But it also served to convey anonymity, and to liber-
ate those like suor Elena Badoer—face veiled—to assume alternative
identities.

This chapter has pointed to some of the ways in which Venetian
nuns resisted enclosure and exclusion. Women in convents sought visits from their relations, despite the resentment that one might have
expected from those who had been placed in nunneries at their family's
convenience. They happily opened up their *parlatorii* and gave refreshments to those making merry during Carnival, in the hope that the liber-
ties and festivities of the lay world might in some way rub off on them.
Nuns also sought to claw back some of the material status of which they
had been deprived; hence their desire to make gifts to all and sundry, a
practice repeatedly condemned by the authorities. The displays of mag-
nanimity that occurred at the convent gratings might be seen as analogous to the bequests with which, Stanley Chojnacki has argued, Venetian
laywomen empowered themselves. At the same time, the nuns' love of
clothes, jewelry, and even high-heeled footwear suggests an attempt to
emulate the self-promotional tactics of their secular sisters, as commented on by Chojnacki and Robert Davis.[53] And yet nuns' engagement
in sociable intercourse, briefly explored in this chapter, was not simply a

pale reflection of the experience of noblewomen in the lay world. The social exchanges of nuns were often more diverse, and also more subject to female control, than those enjoyed by laywomen. While the patronage systems of Venetian laywomen have been described as "parochial, private and highly personal," nuns operated within far broader networks, nurtured in the semipublic space of their *parlatorii*.[54] These sites, located at the margins of the enclosed convent, became centers of hospitality and entertainment for both the lay and religious worlds.

NOTES

1. The Florentine nuns of San Piero Martire protested their ancient right to tax exemptions in 1478, claiming that the continual prayers they offered up on behalf of the city were "more useful coming from persons of such great religion than two thousand horses": Richard Trexler, "Le Célibat à la fin du moyen âge: Les Religieuses de Florence," *Annales ESC* 27 (1972): 1329. Kate Lowe has commented on the remarkable success of another Florentine community, Le Murate, in raising funds and attracting patronage: "Female Strategies for Success in a Male-Ordered World: The Benedictine Convent of Le Murate in Florence in the Fifteenth and Early Sixteenth Centuries," in *Women in the Church: Papers Read at the 1989 Summer Meeting and the 1990 Winter Meeting of the Ecclesiastical History Society*, ed. William J. Sheils and Diana Wood, 209–21, Studies in Church History 27 (Oxford: Blackwell, 1990). The political influence of Venetian nuns was noted by the outgoing papal nuncio, Alberto Bolognetti, in his report of 1581. He believed that the nuns were able to win disciplinary concessions from government in return for their efforts to curry favor among their fathers, brothers, and other relatives: "Dello stato et forma delle cose ecclesiastiche nel dominio dei signori venetiani, secondo che furono trovate et lasciate dal nunzio Alberto Bolognetti," published in A. Stella, *Chiesa e stato nelle relazioni dei nunzi pontifici a Venezia* (Vatican City: Biblioteca Apostolica Vaticana, 1964), 117.

2. Gabriella Zarri, "Monasteri femminili e città (secoli XV–XVIII)," in *Storia d'Italia: Annali*, vol. 9, *La chiesa e il potere politico dal Medioevo all'età contemporanea*, ed. Giorgio Chittolini and Giovanni Miccoli (Turin: Einaudi, 1986), 375. For contemporary accounts of these rites, see "Cronica del Monistero delle Vergini di Venetia," Venice, Biblioteca Museo Correr (henceforth BMC), *Correr* 317, and Francesco Sansovino, *Venetia città nobilissima et singolare* (Venice: Iacomo Sansovino, 1581), fol. A6v. In his rewriting of Sansovino's guide (Venice, 1604), Giovanni Stringa included a full description of the recent investiture of abbess Sofia Malipiero in 1598: fols. 126v–128r.

3. Giovanni Badoer, *Ordo rituum et caeremoniarum tradendi velamina monialibus, Quae jam emiserunt Professionem, vel eodem tempore emittunt* (Venice: Pinelli, 1689): "oblivisci-mini populum vestrum et domum Patris vestri."

4. Pietro Aretino, *Sei Giornate*, ed. Giovanni Aquilecchia (Bari: La Terza, 1969), 11: "credetti certo di entrare viva viva in una sepoltura."

5. Arcangela Tarabotti, *Inferno monacale*, ed. Francesca Medioli (Turin: Rosenberg and Sellier, 1990), 70: "con aspra risolutione, . . . con labbra da disperatione fioche, s'induce a properir la sentenza della propria sepoltura." On the symbolic death signified by profession, see Anthony Molho, "'Tamquam vere mortua': Le professioni femminili nella Firenze del tardo medioevo," *Società e storia* 43 (1989): 1–44. For a rather different view of such ceremonies, see Kate Lowe, "Secular Brides and Convent Brides: Wedding Ceremonies in Italy during the Renaissance and Counter-Reformation," in *Marriage in Italy 1300–1650,* ed. Trevor Dean and Kate Lowe, 41–65 (Cambridge: Cambridge University Press, 1998).

6. The figure of three thousand is necessarily an estimate, since we have no consistent data for the twenty convents that were situated on the lagoon islands, and that were subject to the bishop of Torcello rather than to the patriarch of Venice. These convents served the city of Venice and accommodated at least several hundred women. For the city of Venice itself, a census of 1581 records that there were 2,508 women living in nunneries (Venice, BMC, P. D. 230 b-II: "Descrition de tutte le anime che sono nella città di Venezia"). By 1642, the number of nuns had risen to 2,905, despite a significant drop in the city's overall population (Archivio di Stato di Venezia [henceforth ASV], *Miscellanea Codici* I, Storia Veneta, filza 128, "Ristretto delle anime che sono nella città di Venezia").

7. For discussion of the socioeconomic factors behind female vocations in Venice, see James C. Davis, *The Decline of the Venetian Nobility as a Ruling Class* (Baltimore: Johns Hopkins University Press, 1963), 62–67; Stanley Chojnacki, "Dowries and Kinsmen in Early Renaissance Venice," *Journal of Interdisciplinary History* 5 (1975): 576; Alexander Cowan, *The Urban Patriciate: Lübeck and Venice, 1580–1700* (Cologne: Bohlau, 1986), 148; Giovanni Spinelli, "I religiosi e le religiose," in *La chiesa di Venezia nel seicento,* ed. Bruno Bertoli (Venice: Edizioni studium cattolico veneziano, 1992), 194–95; Volker Hunecke, "Kindbett oder Kloster: Lebenswege venezianischer Patrizierinnen im 17. und 18. Jahrhundert," *Geschichte und Gesellschaft* 18 (1992): 460–61; Jutta Gisela Sperling, *Convents and the Body Politic in Late Renaissance Venice* (Chicago: University of Chicago Press, 1999), 18–71; Mary Laven, *Virgins of Venice: Enclosed Lives and Broken Vows in the Renaissance Convent* (London: Viking, 2002), 22–42. On Florence, see Rabb B. Litchfield, "Demographic Characteristics of Florentine Patrician Families, Sixteenth to Nineteenth Centuries," *Journal of Economic History* 29 (1969): 203; Trexler, "Le Célibat," and Molho, "'Tamquam vere mortua,'" 37. On Bologna, see Craig Monson, *Disembodied Voices: Music and Culture in an Early Modern Convent* (Berkeley: University of California Press, 1995), 8. On Genoa, see Michele Rosi, "Le monache nella vita genovese dal secolo XV al XVII," *Atti della società ligure di storia patria* 27 (1895): 67–74.

8. Julius Kirshner and Anthony Molho, "The Dowry Fund and the Marriage Market in Early Quattrocento Florence," *Journal of Modern History* 50 (1978): 425; Hunecke, "Kindbett oder Kloster," 449.

9. Trexler, "Le Célibat," 1343; Kirshner and Molho, "Dowry Fund," 424.

10. Cited in Enrico Cattaneo, "Le monacazioni forzate fra cinque e seicento," in *Vita e processo di suor Virginia Maria de Leyra, Monaca di Monza,* ed. Umberto Colombo (Milan: Garzanti, 1985), 167: "non si dedichi a Dio nella religione . . . la povera zitella, perché sia nata deforme, o storpiata."

11. In Ibid., 168: "quelli, o che sono mal formati del corpo, o che sono scemi d'intelletto"; "imitando l'empio Caino fanno sacrificio al Signore Dio del peggio."

12. From the *Tirannia paterna*, cited in Tarabotti, *Inferno monacale*, 112: "Non danno per ispose a Giesù le più belle e virtuose, ma le più sozze e diformi e se nelle lor famiglie se rittrovano zoppe, gobbe, sciancate o scempie, quasi ch'il difetto di natura sia difetto d'esse, vengono condennate a starsi prigione tutto il tempo della lor vita."

13. In 1602, a Venetian government decree sought to standardize the level of nuns' dowries, in all the city's convents, at one thousand ducats (a not inconsiderable sum). For a summary of legislation concerning conventual dowries from 1602 to 1620, see ASV, *Compilazioni Leggi*, busta 288, fol. 405; also Innocenzo Giuliani, "Genesi e primo secolo di vita del magistrato sopra monasteri, 1519–1620," *Le Venezie francescane: Rivista storica artistica letteraria illustrata* 28 (1961): 141–43. A systematic analysis of marital dowry levels in early modern Venice has yet to be undertaken. However, the indications are that the official ceilings on marriage dowries, imposed by the Senate, were continually exceeded. As early as 1532, when the law stated three thousand ducats as the maximum dowry, the diarist Marino Sanuto recorded that the contract for a high-society marriage alliance had been concluded with a dowry of eight thousand: *Diarii*, ed. Rinaldo Fulin, Federico Stefani, Nicolò Barozzi, et al., 58 vols. (Venice: Visentini, 1879–1903), vol. 56, col. 33. The inflationary trend continued throughout the century with noble dowries often exceeding twenty thousand ducats, according to David Chambers and Brian Pullan, *Venice: A Documentary History, 1450–1630* (Oxford: Blackwell, 1992), 223. Cowan supplies several examples of marriage dowries of forty thousand ducats being paid in the mid-seventeenth century: *Urban Patriciate*, chapter 6, esp. p. 136. For the case of fifteenth-century Florence, Trexler estimates that a conventual dowry of one hundred florins should be compared with marital dowries of three hundred to one thousand florins for a girl of the same class: "Le Célibat," 1340.

14. This argument recurs in several articles by Stanley Chojnacki. Concerning the dowry inflation of the fifteenth century, he claims that "once women started bringing larger dowries to their marriages, . . . they became more economically substantial persons, with a greater capacity to influence the economic fortunes of those around them": "Dowries and Kinsmen," 586. One way in which women could exercise their economic influence was through the provision of bequests, often to female relatives; see also Chojnacki, "Patrician Women in Early Renaissance Venice," *Studies in the Renaissance* 21 (1974): 176–203.

15. ASV, *Provveditori sopra monasteri* (henceforth *PSM*), busta 263, 1561 [more veneto], Spirito Santo, fol. 12v: "perche la voleva la sua parte di quel suo padre et di suo fratello et anco la dote di sua madre." Cox has pointed out that the Venetian feminist Moderata Fonte, writing toward the end of the sixteenth century, made a clear connection between financial independence and self-determination: Virginia Cox, "The Single Self: Feminist Thought and the Marriage Market in Early Modern Venice," *Renaissance Quarterly* 48 (1995): 560–61.

16. Tarabotti, *Inferno monacale*, 44: "Non si trova già legge per la quale habbiano più ragionevoli pretensioni le maritate che le monacate sopra le case de' loro parenti."

17. Stanley Chojnacki, "La posizione della donna a Venezia nel 500," in *Tiziano e Venezia: Convegno internazionale di studi, Venezia, 1976* (Vicenza: Pozza, 1980), 68; Robert C.

Davis, "The Geography of Gender in the Renaissance," in *Gender and Society in Renaissance Italy*, ed. Judith C. Brown and Robert C. Davis (London: Longman, 1998), 32–36.

18. Tarabotti, *Inferno monacale*, 46: "le più grosse e ruvide tele"; "che sovvente non riescono di bastevole longhezza e le maniche sono a tal'una diverse dal rimanente." On the sumptuous festivities of Venetian wedding ceremonies, see Cowan, who cites the example of one patrician wedding that cost two thousand ducats (twice the cost of a conventual dowry): *Urban Patriciate*, 131–32. See also Patricia Allerston, "Wedding Finery in Sixteenth-Century Venice," in Dean and Lowe, *Marriage in Italy*, 25–40.

19. ASV, *PSM*, busta 268, 1642, San Lorenzo: "[i] primi sangui e nascite di questa città."

20. Sanuto, *Diarii*, vol. 31, cols. 276–77: "bastarde greche e popolari."

21. Archivio Curia Patriarcale di Venezia (henceforth ACPV), *Visite pastorali*, misc. 1452–1730, 1593, SS. Biagio e Castaldo: "l'è vero ch'io non manco di amonirle, et di reprenderle, ma il penitentiarle non si usa a questi tempi, che le figliole sono messe qui dentro più tosto in salvo, che per monache."

22. Stella, *Chiesa e stato*, 191: "non potendole maritare a pari loro per non haver facultà bastanti, et non volendole maritare ad altri inferiori per non diminuire con questo lo splendore delle famiglie loro. Conciosiachè da questa radice nascono tutti i discordini."

23. Tarabotti, *Inferno monacale*, 71: "che sforzando le vostre figliuole ad entrar ne'monasteri, siete partecipi di tutte le loro attioni scandalose."

24. Girolamo Priuli, *I Diarii*, ed. Roberto Cessi, 4 vols. (Bologna: Zanichelli, 1912–38), 4:34: "queste monache meretrice erano fiole over sorelle, over parenti deli primi Senatori, quali gubernavano la Republica Veneta"; "publici bordelli et publici lupanari"; for similar comments, see ibid., 2:115 and 4:115.

25. Sanuto, *Diarii*, 1:836: "quando vien qualche signor in questa terra, li mostrate li monasterii di monache, non monasterii ma postriboli e bordelli publici."

26. Cited by Piero Tacchi-Venturi, *Storia della compagnia di Gesù in Italia*, 4 vols. (Rome: Civiltà cattolica, 1930), 1:81: "che molti monasteri di vergini, già dedicati a Dio, tengano le veci di bordelli."

27. ASV, *PSM*, busta 266, 1620, S. Servolo: "non parendo loco di religiose ma di vere meretrice."

28. Sebastiano Franco, H. Fory, and Henrico Dalmazzo, eds., *Bullarum diplomatum et privilegiorum sanctorum romanorum pontificum*, 25 vols. (Turin: Augustae Taurinorum, 1857–85), 7:447–50. For a discussion of the technical implications of this bull, see Raymond Creytens, "La riforma dei monasteri femminili dopo i decreti tridentini," in *Il Concilio di Trento e la riforma tridentina* (Rome: Herder, 1965), 45–84.

29. ACPV, *Visite pastorali*, Vendramin, 1609–18, 1609, SS. Rocco e Margherita.

30. Antonio Grimani, *Constitutioni et decreti approvati nella sinodo diocesana, sopra la retta disciplina monacale* (Venice: Meietti, 1592), cap. XLVI.

31. For regulations concerning nuns' musical activities, see ACPV, *Visite pastorali*, Trevisan, 1560–89, undated "Mandatum generale," fol. 48r; also, ibid., Vendramin, 1609–18, 1609, S. Anna. Two extensive studies of female monastic music in this period are Monson, *Disembodied Voices*, and Robert Kendrick, *Celestial Sirens: Nuns and their Music in Early Modern Milan* (Oxford: Clarendon Press, 1996).

32. ASV, *PSM*, busta 266, 1620, S. Marta, fol. 20r: "ho sempre generalmente persuaso à lasciar le amicitie particolari e dentro e fuori del monasterio: perche amicitia huius mundi est inimica Deo."

33. Codified versions of these regulations, so often reiterated in both secular and ecclesiastical legislation, may be found in Lorenzo Priuli, *Ordini & avvertimenti, che si devono osservare ne' Monasteri di Monache di Venetia, Sopra le visite et clausura* (Venice: Rampazetto, 1591); and Grimani, *Constitutioni et decreti.*

34. For discussion of the Counter-Reformation as a process of negotiation between reformers and reformed, see David Gentilcore, *From Bishop to Witch: The System of the Sacred in Early Modern Terra d'Otranto* (Manchester: Manchester University Press, 1992); and Marc Forster, *The Counter-Reformation in the Villages: Religion and Reform in the Bishopric of Speyer, 1560–1720* (Ithaca: Cornell University Press, 1992). Relating to nuns, the essays in Craig Monson, ed., *The Crannied Wall: Women, Religion, and the Arts in Early Modern Europe* (Ann Arbor: University of Michigan Press, 1992) are sensitive to the permeability of enclosure.

35. In 1558, Patriarch Vicenzo Diedo named the permitted "gradi di parenti" as "padre, fratelli, barbani . . . nepoti, cognati, et zermani": Venice, BMC, *Codice Cicogna* 2570, pp. 167–68. According to Patriarch Priuli's orders of 1591, fathers, brothers, and uncles were the only male relatives admitted to the *parlatorio*; he also specified that male ecclesiastics were banned from visiting nuns whatever the ties of blood: *Ordini & avvertimenti.*

36. ASV, *PSM*, busta 163, 1566 [m.v.] S. Andrea de Zirada, fol. 3r–v.

37. ACPV, *Visite pastorali*, Priuli, 1592–96, 1595, S. Croce di Giudecca, fol. 494r.

38. The custom was condemned in a patriarchal regulation of 26 Nov. 1554, "Novitie non accedant ad Monasteria Monialium," Venice, BMC, *Codice Cicogna* 2583. Patriarch Giovanni Trevisan reiterated the ban in a visitation order of 1560 to the nuns of Corpus Domini: "Che non si possi admetter, ne parenti, ne novizze alla porta maistra, ne vederle, ne manco tocarli la man" (ACPV, *Visite pastorali*, Trevisan, 1560–89, fol. 2v).

39. For example, at San Zaccaria in 1596, the complaint was made that suor Agata and suor Cipriana "hanno fatto gran presenti ad alcune sorelle sue, che si sono maridate": ibid., Priuli, 1592–96, 1596, S. Zaccaria, fol. 578r.

40. ASV, *PSM*, busta 263, 1566 [m.v.], S. Andrea di Zirada, fol. 2v: "ella tien le galine da otto o diese de madonna S. Gabriela a casa sua, et essa madonna S. Gabriela . . . la sustenta de pan et de vin et di ogni altra cosa accio la ge nutrissa queste galine."

41. Ibid., fol. 12r: "queste porta via [robba] et porta ciancie su et zozo."

42. Grimani, *Constiutioni et decreti*, cap. LXXX: "la prattica di molte feminette, che conversano continualmente alle porte, et fenestre, per servitio delle monache."

43. ASV, *PSM*, busta 267, 1621, S. Servolo: "puttane, ruffiane, e strighe."

44. Other festivities that evidently impinged on the convents were the feast of Saint Martin, 11 Nov. (ACPV, *Visite pastorali*, Trevisan, 1560–89, 1560, Corpus Christi, fol. 2v) and the feast of the Birth of the Virgin Mary, "la Madonna di Settembre," 8 Sept. (Ibid., Priuli, 1592–96, 1596, S. Maria delle Vergini, fol. 589r).

45. On the Venetian Carnival, see Edward Muir, *Civic Ritual in Renaissance Venice* (Princeton: Princeton University Press, 1981), 156–81; Peter Burke, *The Historical Anthropology of Early Modern Italy: Essays on Perception and Communication* (Cambridge: Cambridge

University Press, 1987), 183–90; Guido Ruggiero, *Binding Passions: Tales of Magic, Marriage and Power at the End of the Renaissance* (New York: Oxford University Press, 1993), 3–23.

46. ACPV, *Visite pastorali*, Trevisan, 1560–89, 1588, fol. 83v: "sopra li abusi, et eccessi, che si fanno nelle chiese, e parlatorii delle Monache massimamente in questi tempi di Carnevale con collationi, mangiar, et bever, sonar, cantar, e ballar, o in maschera entrarvi in dishonor de Dio, et della nostra questa Religione."

47. Ibid., Priuli, 1592–96, 1595, Miracoli, fol 369r: "Che alcune volte le monache cantano cose profane, che li suona di citara, e liuto, e si vestono tal volta da huom per far dimostrationi . . . che non si doveria lasciar pigliar robbe da secolari per adoperar nelle dimostrationi."

48. Elissa Weaver, "Spiritual Fun: A Study of Sixteenth-Century Tuscan Convent Theater," in *Women in the Middle Ages and the Renaissance,* ed. Mary Beth Rose (Syracuse: Syracuse University Press, 1986), 179–80.

49. Elissa Weaver, "The Convent Wall in Tuscan Convent Drama," in Monson, *Crannied Wall,* 76.

50. ASV, *PSM,* busta 265, 1614, S. Zaccara, fol. 10v: "le monache in quel tempo da Carnevale sogliono vestire da huomo, et da donna, et caminar la notte per il Monasterio."

51. ASV, *PSM,* busta 264, 1612, Spirito Santo.

52. Ibid., *PSM,* busta 267, S. Maria dell' Orazione di Malamocco, fol 4r: "sto carneval tre over quatro giorni particolarmente el giorno di Sant'Apolonia sie vestita in habito secolar da gentildona con beleto sul viso e anda a balar nei parlatorii alla presentia dele sue petegole e de un homo che sonava de violin."

53. One nun, suor Marietta Dolfin, was singled out for comment by the patriarchal visitor in 1595: "che à detta Dolfin sono stati trovati belletti, zoccoli alti, e porte da calze di seda con merletti d'oro": Venice, ACPV, *Visite pastorali,* Priuli, 1592–96, 1595, S. Iseppo, fol. 516r. For references to Stanley Chojnacki and Robert C. Davis, see note 17 above.

54. Dennis Romano, *Patricians and Popolani: The Social Foundations of the Venetian Renaissance State* (Baltimore: Johns Hopkins University Press, 1987), 120. Romano extends his discussion of the control of female access to city space in his article "Gender and the Urban Geography of Renaissance Venice," *Journal of Social History* 23 (1989): 339–53.

From *Putte* to *Puttane*

Female Foundlings and Charitable Institutions in Northern Italy, 1530–1630

Philip Gavitt

Honor and Savonarolan Reform

Well after the death of Savonarola, Lorenzo Polizzotto has shown, Savonarolan piety continued to influence lay devotion and lay religious organization until Grand Duke Cosimo's so-called dissolution of the monastery at San Marco in 1545. Savonarolan reformers knit together a system of charitable institutions that by 1530 already suggested that care of vulnerable females—young girls, adolescent girls, and widows, especially— was to be the major focus of charitable concern. This chapter will examine the proliferation of charitable institutions for girls and women and the origins of this concern in terms of family strategy, inheritance practice, and preventive approaches to the problems of prostitution. In addition to the abundant evidence from Florence's Ospedale degli Innocenti, this chapter will also examine institutions for wayward girls in Rome and throughout the north of Italy as a means of understanding sixteenth-century perceptions of marginalization as well as the material realities of a group of women who, though marginalized, represented a problem that drove straight to the heart of the central values and gender constructs of premodern Mediterranean systems of honor and shame.

Gabriella Zarri's excellent work on female religious already shows a dynamic at work between family strategies and overcrowding of convents in Bologna as early as the last quarter of the fifteenth century. The later fifteenth century, with its accelerated dowry inflation and increased population, propelled the tendency to send daughters to convents (whose dowries were typically much lower than those required for a respectable marriage), but before 1500 the proliferation of new religious foundations sufficed to meet the demand. Only with the Italian wars of 1498–1530 did the nobility come under such pressure to preserve patrimony that some sons and daughters became an insuperable liability. As a mid-sixteenth-century Bolognese chronicler wrote:

> Thus those women, who for whatever praiseworthy reason cannot find a husband without having an immense dowry, are [almost as badly off] as foundlings, and sometimes forced by their fathers and brothers to enter with a pitiable fortune into convents, not to pray or bless the name of the Lord, but rather to blaspheme and curse the bodies and souls of their parents and relatives, and to bemoan to God that they had ever been born. And those holy houses built for the total devotion of chaste souls are used as dumps and rubbish heaps for the refuse of families.[1]

Just as during the republican period Florentine humanists linked civic wealth, moral reform, and Christian charity to the collective salvation of the *civitas,* so did Savonarolan piety, as Donald Weinstein has shown, place the practice of charity at the forefront of the Christian *renovatio* that would render Florence worthy of salvation. Savonarola's "new Jerusalem" would be one in which every citizen sacrificed his own interests to those of Christian community. The Savonarolan regime acted quickly to associate itself with the city's major charitable institutions, placing the foundlings of the Innocenti, in particular, at the very center of ritual devotion. Savonarolan-inspired processions of children dressed in white moving their elders to tears on Palm Sunday, as well as substituting for their usual Carnival pranks the distribution of alms to the poor, firmly fixed the association between radical Christian reform and charity.[2] The anti-Jewish flavor of many of these processions also found an echo in the Savonarolan intervention that led to the official foundation of the Florentine *Monte di Pietà* as a replacement for Jewish moneylending in 1495.[3]

Less publicly visible, but no less important, were the links that Savonarolan reformers already had to the Innocenti. Although Polizzotto describes both the Innocenti and Santa Maria Nuova as too com-

plex to fall completely under Savonarolan control, I would argue that
Polizzotto underestimates the hold that the prophet's followers had on
the foundling hospital. Indeed, a comparison of the families who occupied the consulate of Florence's prosperous silk guild, the Innocenti's
patrons and putative founders, with Polizzotto's list of families involved
with the *piagnoni* shows a truly remarkable correspondence.[4] The del
Pugliese family, for example, prominent Savonarolan sympathizers, were
also generous patrons of the hospital's church.

Piero del Francesco Pugliese in particular commissioned Piero di
Cosimo's painting of the *Madonna con Bambino e Santi,* which has formed
part of the Innocenti's artistic patrimony since 1493 and which is now
visible in the hospital's museum gallery. Another Piero di Cosimo tem-
pera and oil glazed panel, a *sacra conversazione* with the Madonna and
Saints John the Baptist, Peter, Dominic, and Nicholas (holding the traditional three balls that symbolize his association with dowries) hangs in
the St. Louis Art Museum and bears the del Pugliese family coat of arms.
Even the relationship among this seemingly odd assortment of saints
ties together Florence's patron saint, the founder of the Dominican order,
and Saint Nicholas's protection of girls, in which Saint Peter stands not
merely as the foundation of the church but also as holder of the keys to
communal salvation. Saints Nicholas and Dominic kneel in adoration
before the Madonna and Child, while Saints John the Baptist and Peter
place sponsoring hands on the shoulders of Dominic and Nicholas respectively. As further reinforcement of the Dominican connection to this
devotional piece, its predella illustrates scenes from the history of the
Dominican order.[5]

The Innocenti's Savonarolan identity became even more firmly consolidated with the appointment in the early sixteenth century of messer
Francesco Petrucci as superintendent. Petrucci was one of at least three
Florentine hospital superintendents to be actively involved in the Savonarolan movement during the first quarter of the sixteenth century. In
1503 Petrucci successfully negotiated an agreement between the youth
confraternity of San Zanobi and the Dominicans of San Marco to give
San Zanobi's members more meeting space. Another *piagnone* silk guilds-
man, ser Lorenzo Violi, whose family ran a flourishing firm of dyers that
had branches as far flung as Bruges and Alexandria, notarized the agreement, while the guarantors were two more prominent silk guildsmen,
Francesco del Pugliese, the son of Piero di Cosimo's patron, and Niccolò

del Nero. An astonishing proportion (94 percent) of members of San Zanobi who were already destined for the religious life between 1501 and 1530 were persuaded to join the Dominicans at San Marco.[6]

In addition to ser Lorenzo Violi, another notarial family, that of ser Andrea di Cristoforo Nacchianti, illustrates the ties between the Innocenti, the Savonarolans, and the youth confraternity of San Zanobi. In 1487, ser Andrea commissioned Cosimo di Lorenzo Rosselli to decorate his new family chapel in the church of San Simone, a chapel dedicated to Sant'Andrea. Rosselli also undertook several commissions for the youth confraternity of San Zanobi and was temporary guardian of the boys' confraternity of the Archangel Raphael.[7]

But the *ricordanze* of the Nacchianti family, memoirs housed in the archive of the Istituto degli Innocenti, do not merely illustrate the ties of Nacchianti to the Innocenti, but also reveal a number of family attitudes and crises that shed considerable light on what might push even a wealthy family to entrust a child to the care of an institution. The wills of ser Andrea Nacchianti and of his son Giovanbattista are an interesting case in point. Ser Andrea Nacchianti was a prosperous notary, one of three brothers in a large extended family. In his last will and testament, composed 19 February 1510, shortly before his death, he put his only son, Giovanbattista, seven years old, under the tutelage of three guardians and appointed him as universal heir. During the seven years that elapsed between his father's death and his own decision to join the Dominican order, Giovanbattista was resident at the Ospedale degli Innocenti.

The will of the elder Nacchianti, ser Andrea, makes quite clear that a dowry crisis in the Nacchianti family precipitated Giovanbattista's extended residence at the foundling hospital. The elder Nacchianti secured Giovanbattista's entrance into the Innocenti by leaving a deposit to the hospital of Santa Maria Nuova. Giovanbattista's will, drawn up when he was only fifteen so he could leave his estate to the Innocenti and join the Dominicans at San Marco, states that his father's will "left many obligations and debts," so many, in fact, that half the proceeds from the dowry of Giovanbattista's mother had to be earmarked for his sister Antonia's dowry.[8] Thus, only a very small portion of Andrea's estate benefited his wife and wife's daughter from the first marriage. Indeed, only by dividing his wife's dowry in half could Antonia be supported at all, and even then it was at the short-term expense of Giovanbattista.

Certainly a striking example of how Florentines had to provide for daughters from a first marriage, and how they viewed such arrangements, occurs in another act of family generosity undertaken by Andrea Nacchianti in May 1500:

> I record this day, 6 May 1500, Maddalena, my daughter and wife of Giovanni Guidacci, came to the villa with her daughter, Papera, from her husband, Lionardo Mazzei. She commended her daughter to me and I in turn commended her to Maddalena my wife. And seeing that she [Papera] is in need, I am happy to help the said girl as much as I can. And concerning what I spend on her, I want it understood that my heirs may never at any time try to extract anything from her, so that God might concede to me his grace that I stay healthy so I can help her and do her this favor that I recognize as a worthy charity.

The wording of this *ricordanze* entry is telling, underscoring as it does the homeless status even of granddaughters, and that the testator undertook the project out of charity and need rather than out of family obligation.

One easily imagines how less gladly the finances of less well-heeled families would have sustained such burdens, and Giovanbattista Nacchianti's major institutional bequest proves this point. After joining the Dominicans at San Marco, he became professor of philosophy at the Dominican College of the Minerva in Rome, and in 1544 was appointed by Pope Paul III as the bishop of Chioggia.[9] The donation he made inter vivos to the Innocenti when he joined the Dominican order quite clearly reflects the family anxieties and concerns generated by the collision of family strategy and family obligation. In particular, he donated two thousand florins for the Innocenti to build adjacent to the women's cloister a hospice for girls "who wish neither to unite themselves with a man nor to become nuns."[10]

PUTTE TO *PUTTANE* AT THE INNOCENTI: THE CIVILIZING PROCESS AND ITS DISCONTENTS

At some point in the first three decades of the sixteenth century, the hospital's scribes stopped using the terms *fanciulla* (singular) and *fanciulle* (plural) and began to refer to the hospital's boys as *putti* and the hospital's girls as *putte*. It is perhaps too crude an analysis to attribute this early shift to increases in infant mortality; nonetheless, the terms suggest not only the innocence associated with *putti* in Italian painting, but also the otherworldly fate that awaited most infants admitted to the Innocenti during the sixteenth century. Although this usage continued throughout the sixteenth century, by the last quarter of the sixteenth century the Ospedale degli Innocenti called up images of prostitution as readily as images of more ethereal beings. Francesco Settimani's court history, for example, charges that the Innocenti became so overcrowded and mismanaged during the last years of the tenure of its superintendent Vincenzio Borghini (1552–80) that hospital officials released hundreds of adolescent girls into the streets of Florence, "where out of necessity they became prostitutes *(puttane)*." Although Settimani's history is exaggerated, it is not without truth, since the Orbatello, the institution to whom the hospital's older women were discharged, aroused suspicions among those who saw young silk guildsmen frequenting it in 1585.[11]

A treatise written by Borghini, *Considerationi sopra l'allogare le donne delli Innocenti, fuora del maritare o monacare,* also took as its major assumption that without some sort of opportune remedy, the only alternative to marriage or becoming a nun was prostitution. Borghini's proposal that the Innocenti should reintroduce household service did not so much expand girls' occupational options as it provided a means for girls to finance meager dowries through the wages of their own work rather than from the hospital's coffers. Moreover, the increasing toll that the overwhelming presence of girls took on the resources of the Innocenti could be somewhat mitigated by sending them out to live as household servants. This was an option unavailable to girls between the end of the fifteenth century and Borghini's tenure; moreover, at comparable institutions for girls, such as that of the Santissima Annunziata della Minerva at Rome, founded by Torquemada in 1466, girls who had merely had a history of domestic service were already barred from entering.[12]

Thus women without familial or institutional ties were, by definition and regardless of their individual character traits, naturally in a state of disorder, which only paternal or ecclesiastical authority could properly confine. Remedying such disorder involved application of the monastic discipline of work, and in particular work suited to the demands of female honor. The notion that sewing and other occupations having to do with cloth was a proper occupation for young women was explicitly stated in treatises that outlined their upbringing and education. Torquato Tasso's 1582 dialogue, *Il Padre di Famiglia,* for example, devoted a long section to the virtues of the *madre di famiglia:*

> But her most principal care should be that of the linens, woven pieces, and of silk, with which she can provide not only for the needs and for the honor of the house, but also make some honest earnings.... Such particularly are the cloths and other works of art produced by weaving with which the good family matron can provide her daughter with a rich and honorable trousseau.[13]

Indeed, Tasso goes to great length to show that weaving is an occupation of noblewomen, and he cites Virgil in support of his view that "not without reason was this skill attributable to Minerva goddess of wisdom." In Homer and elsewhere Tasso found the precedents of Penelope and Circe, while from Roman antiquity, even though noblewomen were not allowed to cook, they were encouraged to weave. Thus the virtuous Lucretia was engaged in just such activity when Brutus and Tarquin found her at home. Within a less exalted context, Tasso praised weaving as one of the few legitimate ways women could contribute to the expenses of the family household and accumulate objects, if not capital, for their dowries.[14]

In 1581, Borghini's successor at the Innocenti, fra Niccolò Mazzi, pulled together a summary of "the duties and occupations of the women" of the Innocenti, a summary that clearly reflects the function that weaving would have had in Tasso's ideal household.[15] Noting that "there is no doubt to any who consider the matter that there is no greater work of piety and charity, or more pleasing to God or closer to the heart of the Republic, nor more necessary to this city, than this House of the Innocenti," Mazzi devoted the remainder of his summary to the successful efforts of the institution in placing out girls for household service, convents, and marriage.[16] Nonetheless, despite Borghini's efforts to reduce the number of women in the hospital (somewhat successful, since the hospital's census of women had declined from 980 to just under 700), they still, in Mazzi's view, represented too great a drain on the hospital's resources. He resolved, therefore, to "reorder" their supervision and care, and "to address [the problem] of how to instruct and encourage them in all those crafts and feminine manual work that can possibly be introduced."[17] Mazzi explicitly set out the financial rationale behind the scheme: "so that with their effort and skill, these women can contribute to their own upkeep." At the same time the work will "make them industrious so they can have better results when they wish to be placed."[18] Left unspoken was that this, too, would contribute to easing the hospital's financial burden. To this end Mazzi posted each worker's earnings weekly so she could understand her individual contribution to the hospital's efforts.[19] Moreover, a certain portion of each worker's weekly earnings was posted to her account to be spent on her clothing and other "comforts," with the most industrious worker to receive a bonus.[20] This was only one step shy of what Sandra Cavallo documented for the Casa del Soccorso in Torino beginning in 1682, where high productivity and earnings "were also essential to obtain a dowry."[21]

Not all of women's work, however, was dedicated to the *bottega*. The hospital's female staff included four sacristans "whose duties are ... to make sure that the girls pray for the remission of sins for all the benefactors as well as for the salvation of the city and its state."[22] The hospital also employed four female pharmacists and five female physicians, including two in training, who had to "order and keep track of the spices and medicine and to minister according to their craft."[23] At least some of these female physicians, moreover, were not hired from outside but rather were foundlings themselves, as is clear from a list of fourteen girls who were learning to read. One of the female physicians was from Bologna, which raises the possibility that she had been trained there. The office of physician was conceived differently from that of the six nurses, whose function was "to administer medication and to supervise the sick with charity and diligence."[24]

In addition to this phalanx of pharmacists, doctors, and nurses to treat the sick, women also participated in the administration of the women's convent and supervised some of the boys. Four *rottaie* could be pressed into service at the wheel where infants were admitted, as well as three porters to guard the door. Those women who addressed themselves directly to the care of children supervised either them or their clothes, including two women who were assigned to taking care of the hosiery. In addition, seven women were assigned to the storeroom and kitchen. Altogether, the statistical profile accounted for 586 women within the hospital in 1581, about 80 percent of whom were involved in the production of the hospital's *bottega*.

Table 1. Occupations of women in the Innocenti, 1581.

Occupation	Number of Women
Production workers	484
Administrators	57
Direct care of children	20
Students	14
Ill	11
Total	586

Source: AOIF, *Nota di ufizi e arti di donne di casa*, XLVI, 1, fol. 10r, Anno 1581.

HOMES FOR WAYWARD GIRLS AND ASYLUMS FOR WIDOWS

Italian city-states in the sixteenth century moved on several fronts to address the problem of the escalating cost of dowries, the modified female primogeniture that resulted, and the consequent danger to the honor of young girls. The Italian wars of the first three decades of the sixteenth century also clearly provoked crises of social and economic dislocation that made the problem of women one that crossed boundaries of status and geography. In Rome, new congregations to assist the poor proliferated. Giulio Folco's *Effetti mirabili della limosina*, published in 1586, detailed the foundation of the Compagnia delle Vergini Miserabili di Santa Caterina della Rota a half century earlier.

In this case, Folco was much more explicit about the dangers to which abandoned girls were exposed, perhaps because the company was founded in 1536, only nine years after the sack of Rome. The Roman Santa Caterina company "not only nourishes the bodies, but conserves the innocence of those bodies from wicked men; and who knows otherwise what wickedness, rapes, and almost infinite sacrilege would be committed if our company did not house and preserve the poor little virgins." The poor little virgins in question were "for the most part daughters of courtesans, of women of evil life, or persons of extreme poverty, who either through lack of concern on the part of their relatives, through the straits of necessity, or through the bad example set by their impure mothers, can easily fall away from the path of righteousness."[25]

Another Roman institution, Santa Maria del Rifugio, invited Silvio Antoniano to edit its statutes in 1595, which make clear that this institution admitted repentant prostitutes, provided they were not married: "Women of evil life are also accepted, and even public prostitutes who do not have a husband, but who do intend to renounce their past life and its sins, and to reduce themselves to leading a Christian life in God's grace. These will be kept in the novitiate for three months at the most, and then provided the safety of being received in the Convent of the Convertite, or in another convent, or some other honorable refuge."[26]

Santa Maria del Rifugio's admissions policies were more liberal than those of comparable institutions to be discussed below, but order within the institution was more strictly controlled. Two women in residence supervised the girls housed there, "so that [these two supervisors] may more easily work in the house where the dangerous girls stay. The women will have full and ample authority and power to enter into any residential unit whatsoever, and to remove any girl whom they suspect might be in danger of committing evil in order to put her in a safe place." Thus moral contagion required the same isolating measures as medical contagion, and the girls themselves easily slipped from being "endangered" to being "dangerous."[27]

In Genoa also, institutional solutions served the new needs of Genoese girls and women at the beginning of the sixteenth century. Thanks to the support of a wealthy benefactor, don Tommaso Doria, one of its hospitals for the poor extended its walls to house the abandoned girls who could not be so easily placed out as the boys. In 1551, Mariola de' Negri founded the Opera della Pietà di Gesù e Maria:

> to receive grown and adult women so they can raise themselves from sin and then to place them out to stay with their relatives or with others with whom they can live and work honestly, as well as for young adolescent girls to save them from the dangers of dishonesty and of doing evil. They are instructed in the Christian life and helped to get married or to make themselves nuns according to how the grace of the Holy Spirit shall manifest itself.[28]

In addition to institutional solutions, most Italian city-states by the early sixteenth century provided some form of dowry assistance, either through various congregations, or through more sophisticated methods such as communal dowry funds. In Florence, the *Monte delle doti* since 1425 had assisted patrician fathers in preserving their family interests and meeting the high cost of dowries by allowing them to invest in the fund and to retrieve their capital and interest if their daughters survived to a marriageable age.[29] Virtually from the first years the Ospedale degli Innocenti admitted foundlings, it put deposits for them in the communal dowry fund.[30] In the sixteenth century, especially during and after the reforms of the 1540s undertaken by Duke Cosimo, the activities of the communal dowry fund slowed considerably, no doubt partially because rulers of the early duchy singled out *Monte* investors to pay forced loans and gabelles or risk having parts of their deposits used instead. Not surprisingly, investors increasingly used charitable institutions as safer havens for their capital. If the return on their investments was an unexciting 5 percent, as opposed to the higher rates possible under the older communal schemes, most sixteenth-century investors in the funds of charitable institutions were likely to get their full deposit back with interest.[31] Honor and dowry were always tied, and such funds as the communal dowry funds in Florence, Rome, and other Italian cities appealed to all social levels. In the fourteenth and fifteenth centuries, providing dowries was an extremely popular form of giving. In the sixteenth century, donations for poor girls to receive dowries became increasingly wrapped up in the rhetoric of honor and in new institutions specifically created to save it, and this connection between institutions and dowries as mechanisms to preserve feminine honor persisted well into the eighteenth century. As one early eighteenth-century Bolognese commentator put it, "Marriage is not the end proposed by the testator but only the means most likely to attain that end. The goal, therefore, is to keep poor girls distant from proximate danger to their honor, either by marrying them, or putting them into a convent."[32]

Over the course of the sixteenth and seventeenth centuries, private dowry trusts either replaced, absorbed, or existed parallel to municipal dowry funds. In Rome, the confraternity of Santissima Annunziata, founded in 1460, administered 450 dowries per year in the mid-seventeenth century. Private individuals during the sixteenth century saw providing funds for dowry assistance even to friends and neighbors a worthwhile charity, and a number of prominent examples can be found in Florence in the fourteenth century as well, especially after the Black

Death. John Henderson has shown the increase in percentage of giving for dowries in the late fourteenth and early fifteenth century in Florence, and Samuel Cohn has noted similar patterns in Siena as well.[33] But the sixteenth century saw the establishment of dowry trusts by noble and even royal benefactors. In Florence in 1595, Grand Duke Ferdinand I, patron of the hospital of San Paolo de' Convalescenti, entrusted a confraternity that had its headquarters at the hospital with the administration of dowries.

Typical of such foundations was the institution of the dowry lottery. Most likely, the confraternity of Santissima Annunziata in Rome administered such a lottery, as did the Casa Santa di Santa Maria del Rifugio.[34] In Florence in 1606, the Captains of the Company of Santa Maria delle Laude and San Zanobi administered a city-wide dowry lottery in which the Ospedale degli Innocenti submitted five names and won three dowry subsidies of thirty lire each. The hospital could claim reimbursement for these sums on presentation of the marriage certificate for each of the three girls involved. A similar entry exactly a year later suggests that this lottery was an annual event.[35]

For those girls who did not win the dowry lottery, or who could not successfully find vocations in household service, employment, marriage, or a nunnery, the alternative was a lifetime of institutional care. When, in 1579, the bankruptcy of the hospital of the Innocenti forced its committee of reformers to find ways to reduce its expenditures, sending the older women to the so-called "widows' asylum" of the Orbatello became the strategy of last resort. Founded in 1377 by a member of the Alberti family, and ostensibly the beneficiary of the patronage of the Parte Guelfa, Santa Maria in Orbatello is the only foundation solely for Florentine laywomen that had its origins before the Savonarolan reform movement. It addressed the issues involved in gender and inheritance both innovatively and directly: when a male head of household died (or in some cases had merely abandoned his family), not only his widow but also her children could be admitted into the Orbatello's apartments, eventually to be supervised by elderly women who had become the matrons of the institution.

Thus, even the architecture of the Orbatello attempted to preserve what was left of the integrity of the household unit. During the fifteenth and sixteenth centuries, Orbatello was not merely a widow's asylum but also a shelter for *malmaritate,* a category that embraced both unruly and abused women. In this respect it seems to have anticipated the kind of institution that would become much more numerous during the six-teenth century.[36] Only with the sudden influx of girls from the Innocenti did the stabilization achieved in mid-century become compromised, and the overwhelming collision of family structures, gender roles, and demo-graphic realities made the *putte* of the Innocenti vulnerable to becoming the *puttane* of the Orbatello.[37]

By 1606 it was clear that the Orbatello was hardly the sheltered envi-ronment for which Innocenti officials had hoped, as the charges leveled by the inmates themselves indicate. In a letter to the grand duke, the inmates accused Prior Staccini of exploiting their labor as well as confis-cating such meager property as they might possess and keeping it after they had died:

> The poor Innocenti women living in Orbatello, most humble servants of Your Highness, explain to him with all due respect that for the past fourteen years or so they have been under the care of don Alessandro Staccini, chaplain in the said place. These poor women have been very badly mistreated both physically and spiritually. Worse, he has always attempted to cheat them, and has cheated them, and robbed them of the effort of their labors which they need to survive and by which they are fed, having no other support in this world than the sweat of their brow, sewing day and night. Even very young girls are at risk of some accident. Those who have not already broken their necks cannot at their death expect to have more than four pennies at their disposal for a decent funeral mass.[38]

The petitioners provided extremely specific evidence, naming some seven-teen women who had been victimized and enumerating how much the priest had taken from them. As if taking the very clothes off their backs were not sufficient, Staccini beat them publicly with sticks, and when these poor women died, they died "like animals, not even fed and nour-ished by those sacraments necessary for all good Christians, and without which their souls cannot even be recommended to heaven." The petition-ers begged "by the bowels of Christ Jesus" that the grand duke remedy the problem by removing don Staccini and placing the girls back under the care of Ruberto Antinori, superintendent at the Innocenti at the turn of the seventeenth century.[39]

CONCLUSION

Thus if this wide variety of institutions attempted to save the moral lives of young girls, placing the problematic of gender squarely within the context of the collective salvation of the city and the honor of successive grand dukes of Tuscany, one cannot with any great confidence proclaim their success at rescuing such girls from the margins of society. The monastic vision of discipline that would so successfully evolve into a self-disciplined society exacted a high toll as the workhouse model eclipsed the self-governing conventual model, leaving older women vulnerable to a much wider variety of exploitation than the mere dangers of "capitar male." Unfortunately, institutions that assisted various strategies of patrician family preservation were always double-edged. Preserving the ideological vision of the extended family sometimes required the sacrifice of its most vulnerable members. Clearly, as Daniela Lombardi's study of the Hospital of the Mendicanti in the seventeenth century has so eloquently argued, the norms of lineage, order, and decorum could only assume coherence through the visible identification and eventual isolation of those who visibly threatened them.[40]

NOTES

1. Gabriella Zarri, "Monasteri femminili e città (secoli XV–XVIII)," in *Storia d'Italia: Annali*, vol. 9, *La chiesa e il potere politico dal Medioevo all'età contemporanea*, ed. Giorgio Chittolini and Giovanni Miccoliof (Turin: Einaudi, 1986), 365, citing the anonymous mid-sixteenth-century *Ragionamento sopra le pompe della citta di Bologna*: "Le donne poi, che per qual si voglia laudabil parte, non trovano marito senza immensa dote, *quasi come esposte . . .* sono forsi alcuna volta sforzate da i padri et da i fratelli ad entrare con miserabil fortuna ne i monasteri, non per orare et benedire, ma talhor per bestemmiare et maledire il corpo et l'anima de' progenitori et attinenti suoi et accusare Iddio che le habbia destinate a nascere. Et quelle sante case fabricate per libera dedicazione d'animi casti, sono usate, che Dio no'l voglia, come per sentine di cose rifiutate dal mondo et spurgatoi et scaricamenti delle famiglie" (emphasis mine).

2. On Savonarolan reform, see Donald Weinstein, *Savonarola and Florence* (Princeton: Princeton University Press, 1970); and Lorenzo Polizzotto, *The Elect Nation: The Savonarolan Movement in Florence 1494–1545* (Oxford: Clarendon Press, 1994). On processions of children, see Luca Landucci, *Diario fiorentino dal 1450 al 1516, continuato da un Anonimo fino al 1542* (Florence: Sansoni, 1883), 53; Richard Trexler, "Ritual in Florence: Adolescence and Salvation in the Renaissance," in *The Pursuit of Holiness in Late Medieval and Renaissance Religion*, ed. Charles Trinkaus and Heiko Oberman, 200–264 (Leiden: Brill, 1974); Philip Gavitt, *Charity and Children in Renaissance Florence: The Ospedale degli Innocenti, 1410–1536* (Ann Arbor: University of Michigan Press, 1990), 296–97; Domenico di Agresti, *Sviluppi della riforma monastica Savonaroliana* (Florence: Olschki, 1980), 7.

3. On the foundation of the Florentine *Monte di Pietà*, see the excellent detailed study by Carol Bresnahan Menning, *Charity and State in Late Renaissance Italy: The Monte di Pietà of Florence* (Ithaca: Cornell University Press, 1993), 37–63.

4. Of the twenty-five surnames listed for the silk guild's consulate in 1474 and 1475 (the latest year for which I have an available list), only seven are missing from Polizzotto's list of families who numbered Savonarolan sympathizers among their kin. Moreover, a number of prominent silk guild families, including the del Benino, the Parenti, and the del Pugliese, were prominent among the *piagnoni*. For a list of the silk guild's consuls and the *operai* of the hospital of the Innocenti, see Archivio di Stato di Firenze (hereafter ASF), *Arte della Seta*, 246, passim.

5. Laura Cavazzini, "Dipinti e sculture nelle chiese dell'Ospedale," in *Gli Innocenti e Firenze nei secoli: Un ospedale, un'archivio, una città*, ed. Lucia Sandri (Florence: Studio per Edizioni Scelte, 1996), 119–20; and *The Saint Louis Art Museum Handbook of the Collections* (St. Louis: The Museum, 1991), 84.

6. On the Innocenti's priors (Petrucci and Buonafè) as Savonarolans, see Polizzotto, *Elect Nation*, 35. On Petrucci negotiating the agreement for more space for the youth confraternity of San Zanobi, and on San Marco's remarkable success in controlling this confraternity and recruiting its young members to the Dominican order, see ibid., 193–95.

7. On Cosimo Rosselli's commission for the chapel of Sant'Andrea, see Dario Covi, "A Documented Altarpiece by Cosimo Rosselli," *Art Bulletin* 53 (1971): 236–38. For Cosimo Rosselli's involvement with San Zanobi delle Laude and his temporary guardianship of the confraternity of the Archangel Raphael, see Konrad Eisenbichler, *The Boys of the Archangel Raphael: A Youth Confraternity in Florence, 1411–1785* (Toronto: University of Toronto Press, 1998), 258–59, 409.

8. ASF, *Diplomatico, Spedale degli Innocenti*, 19 Feb. 1509 [stile fiorentino (henceforth st. fior.)]: "Item attento quod ipse testator alimentauit et tenuit in eius domo Antoniam filiam olim Ser Bart' Laurentii not. flor [lacuna] Dianore eiusdem testatoris uxoris et filia olim Bardi de Gherardinis per annos otto *[sic]* vel circa. Et quod dicta de causa fratres dic[ti] eius patris tenererunt ad satisdationem dictorum alimentorum prestitorum et prestandorum dicte puelle dicto testatori et eius her[edibus] de causis animum dicti testatoris mouentibus omnia iura dictorum alimentorum dictus testator iure legati reliquit et legauit pro omn[ia] iure dicti testatoris dicte domine Dianore eius uxori et matri dicte Antonie et prohibuit infrascriptis eius herede et executoribus quod non poss[int] ab ea occaxione predicta petere vel exigere vel eam aliqualiter molestare." For the many debts and obligations

left by ser Andrea, see the will of Giovanbattista, ibid., 22 Feb. 1517 [st. fior.]: "Et considerans in hereditatem patris sui remansisse multa bona immobilia et multa nomina debitis et qualiter alique ex dictis debitis sunt tales a quibus ipse testator non intendit quod ab eis fiat exactio."

9. For a brief bibliography on Nacchianti, see Philip Gavitt, "Charity and State Building in Cinquecento Florence: Vincenzio Borghini as Administrator of the Ospedale degli Innocenti," *Journal of Modern History* 69 (1997): 249n.

10. Ibid., 255–56.

11. Francesco Settimani, "Memorie Fiorentine," ASF, *Manoscritti*, 129, p. 212v. For the 1585 charges, see ASF, *Parte Guelfa Nero*, fol. 75r, 17 Jan. 1584 [st. fior.], cited in Richard Trexler, "A Widow's Asylum of the Renaissance: The Orbatello of Florence," in *Old Age in Pre-Industrial Society*, ed. Peter Stearns (New York: Holmes and Meier, 1982), 149n.

12. Vincenzo Borghini, *Considerationi sopra l'allogare le donne delli Innocenti fuora del maritare o monacare*, ed. Gaetano Bruscoli (Florence: Ariani, 1904), 29; Vittorio Frajese, *Il popolo fanciullo: Silvio Antoniano e il sistema disciplinare della controriforma* (Milan: Franco Angeli, 1987), 93–94.

13. Torquato Tasso, "Il Padre di Famiglia," in *Dialoghi*, 3 vols., ed. Ezio Raimondi (Florence: Sansoni, 1958), 2:376: "Ma principilissima cura sua dee esser quella de' lini e delle tele e delle sete, con le quali ella potrà non solamente provedere a' bisogno e alla orrevolezza della casa, ma fare anco alcuno onesto guadagno ... e tali sono particolarmente le tele e l'altre opere d'arte del tessere con le quali la buona madre di famiglia può fare alla figliuola ricco e orrevol corredo."

14. Ibid., 376–77: "Né senza ragione quest'arte à Minerva, dea della sapienza, fu attribuita, sì che da lei prese il nome ... Ne' quali versi [of Vergil] si comprende ch'egli parla non delle vili feminelle ma delle madre di famiglia, la qual da molte serve suol esser servita; e tanto di nobiltà par che questa arte abbia recata seco che non solo alle privati madri di famiglia, ma anco delle donne di reale condizione è stata attribuita.... E se ben i Greci non osservano tanto il decoro quanto par convenevole, i Romani nondimeno, che ne furono maggiori osservatori, tutto ch'il cucinare e altre simili operazioni alla madre di famiglia proibissero, gli concedevano il tessere non senza molta laude della tessitrice: e in questa operazione fu ritrovata Lucrezia da Collalatino, da Bruto e da Tarquinio, quando se n'inamorò."

15. Archivio dell'Ospedale degl'Innocenti di Firenze (henceforth AOIF), *Nota di Uffizi e arte di donne di casa*, XLVI, 1, anno 1581.

16. Ibid., loose fol.: "El non à dubio a chi ben considera che l'opera di questa casa dell'Innocenti non sia delle maggiori e di pietà e carità acepta a Dioe grata e a cuore a lor' Altezze e a tutta la Republica necessaria che nessuna altra di questa città."

17. Ibid., fol. 1r–v: "Invigilando à così gran cura e gouerno di decto spedale trouandosi maxime di presente carico di gran' debito exausto di denari e di gran numero di creature e maxime di donne adulte in cosi sinistri temporali non si può senon dificilmente dar' recapito conueniente, ha pensato di riordinar' la cura e gouerno di dette creature e maxime delle donne che di presenete ascendono al numero di 700 e sempre crescono con indirizzarle à farle instruir' e exercitar' in tutte quelle arti e opere manuali femminili che possibil' sia introdursi."

18. Ibid., fol. ɪv: "acciò che con le fatiche e virtù loro possino in parte aiutare l'hospedale alla stessa lor' alimentatione. Et di poi fatte industriose possino anchora trouar' miglior partiti quando allogar' si volessino."

19. Ibid.: "che si riscuoterà e porle creditori guadagni dell'Arte di nostre donne in un conto à parte à ciò si possi veder' chiaramente quello che li guadagno, per far' poi che ciascuna secondo e guadagni e meriti loro partecipi e sia riconosciuta della sua fatiche e industria da dichiararsi dalli suddetti Reuerendo priore e Signori Operai à fine che le pouerelle possino più promptamente e habbino occasione di lauorare e sentir' commodo e benefitio delle loro fatiche."

20. Ibid., fol. ɪ2r: "Ciascuna settimana facesi o guadagnassi e tutte insieme e far' che ciascuna partecipassi dei suoi guadagni...che di loro guadagni...star' commodi e servirsene per vestirsi e altri loro bisogni parendo al Signor e Signor operai che douessi star bene che le partecipassino a ragione di 4 soldi per lire e di poi alla più industriosa dar' qualche vantaggio."

21. Sandra Cavallo, *Charity and Power in Early Modern Italy: Benefactors and Their Motives in Turin, 1541–1789* (Cambridge: Cambridge University Press, 1995), 113 (although the supporting archival reference mentions only that a confraternity of women gave out medals for especially noteworthy productivity).

22. AOIF, *Note di ufizi e arti di donne di casa*, XLVI, ɪ, fol. 2v, *anno* 1581: "L'offitio de' quali si è di tener cura de' panni e paramenti della chiesa e chiamar' e indur' le fanciulle e tutta l'altre alle messe e offitie alla deuotione e timor del Dio e preghar' per la remission' de' peccati per tutti i benefactori e saluationi della città e stato."

23. Ibid., fol. 2v: "l'offitio delle quali si è ordinar' e tener' conto della spetiera e medicina e medicare secondo l'arte loro."

24. Ibid.: "l'offitio delle quali sia di dar' la medicina e gouernar' l'infermi con carità e diligentia."

25. For these descriptions of the Roman institutions of Santa Caterina della Rota and Santa Maria del Rifugio, see Frajese, *Il popolo fanciullo*, 90, citing Giulio Folco, comp., *Effetti mirabili de la limosina: Le sentenze degne di memoria appartenenti ad essa* (Rome: Zanetti, 1586), 154: "non solamente nudrisce i corpi, ma conserva l'innocenza de' corpi e dell'anima dalli huomini tristi; et chi sa quante scelleratezze, stupri, et quasi infiniti sacrilegi, se commetteranno se la nostra compagnia non racogliesse et conservasse queste vergini giovanette." This company was founded for "figliuole per lo più di cortigiane o donne di mala vita, o persone di estrema poverta, le quali o per poca cura de' loro parenti o per l'angustia della povertà, o per malo esempio domestico delle loro madri impure, facilmente possono scapitare dell'onestà."

26. Rome, Biblioteca Vallicelliana, codex G43, *Regole et ordini che si haveranno da observare nella Santa Casa della Santissima Madonna del Rifugio nuovamente eretta di N. S. Clemente VIIII, e poi cardinale della S. R. Chiesa*, fol. 2v, cited by Frajese, *Il popolo fanciullo*, 93: "accetteran tutte le donne di mala vita, et meretrici etiam pubbliche che non haveranno marito, et haveranno animo di lasciare la vita passata, et il peccato e di ridursi à vivere christianamente in gratia di Dio, e queste di terranno per modo di novitiato per tre mesi al più, quando però preceda la sicurezza d'esser poi ricevute nel Monastero delle Convertite, o in altri monasterij, o altrimenti provistole d'honesto recapito."

27. Rome, Biblioteca Vallicelliana, codex G43, fol. 8v, cited by Frajese, *Il popolo fanciullo*, 96: "che più facilmente et destramente possono praticare nelle case dove stanno zitelle pericolose et quella haveranno piena et ampia autorità, et Potestà di potere entrare in qualsivoglia casa, et pigliare de facto qualsivoglia zitella sospetta che stesse in pericolo di far male per metterla in sicuro."

28. On the Genoese institutions, see Edoardo Grendi, "Ideologia della carità e società indisciplinata: La costruzione del sistema assistenziale genovese (1470–1670)," in *Timore e Carità: I poveri nell'Italia moderna, Atti del convegno "Pauperismo e assistenza negli antichi stati italiani,"* ed. Giorgio Politi, Mario Rosa, and Franco della Peruta (Cremona: Bibloteca Statale e Libreria Civica di Cremona, 1987), 66–67. The Opera della Pietà di Gesù e Maria was founded "di ricevere le donne grandi e adulte acciò si levino dal peccato e poi mandarle fuori dell'opera per stare con li suoi ovvero con altri per honestamente vivere ed esercitarsi, e le adolescente giovinette perchè si levino dal pericolo della honestà e dal far male e se istruiscono nella cristiana vita e aiutarle à maritarsi o farsi religiose segondo li mostrerà la gratia dello Spirito Santo."

29. On the foundation of the Florentine dowry fund, see Anthony Molho, *Marriage Alliance in Late Medieval Florence* (Cambridge: Harvard University Press, 1994), 30–38.

30. On the Innocenti's involvement in the dowry fund, see Molho, *Marriage Alliance*, 105–7; and Gavitt, *Charity and Children*, 78–83.

31. On hospitals as deposit banking institutions, see Richard Goldthwaite, "Banking in Florence at the End of the Sixteenth Century," *Journal of European Economic History* 27 (1998): 512–16; and Lucia Sandri, "L'attività di Banco di deposito dell'ospedale degli Innocenti di Firenze: Don Vincenzo Borghini e la 'bancarotta' del 1579," in *L'uso del denaro: Patrimoni e amministrazione nei luoghi pii e negli enti ecclesiastici in Italia: secoli XV–XVIII*, ed. Alessandro Pastore and Marina Garbellotti (Bologna: Il Mulino, 2001), 155–62. I wish to thank Lucia Sandri for kindly sending me a manuscript version of her article and to thank Richard Goldthwaite for much valuable information concerning the Innocenti's deposit banking operations.

32. Bologna, Archivio Storico della Banca di Monte di Bologna e Ravenna, *Opere Pie Dotali, Torfanini*, 8, fasc. 2, no date, cited in Isabelle Chabot and Massimo Fornasari, *L'economica della carità* (Bologna: Il Mulino, 1997), 20.

33. On the activities of the confraternity of Orsanmichele of Florence after the Black Death, see John Henderson, *Piety and Charity in Late Medieval Florence* (Oxford: Clarendon Press, 1994), 317–20. For Siena, see Samuel Kline Cohn, *Death and Property in Siena, 1200–1800: Strategies for the Afterlife*, The Johns Hopkins University Studies in Historical and Political Science, 106th series, 2 (Baltimore: Johns Hopkins University Press, 1988), 28–29.

34. Frajese, *Il popolo fanciullo*, 96–97, notes that the Casa di Santa Maria di Rifugio also was the "intermediary for the dowry lottery. Indeed, beginning in 1519, when Agostino Chigi himself provided a legacy to dower three poor girls for 100 scudi each, the Casa del Rifugio began to become increasingly involved in the business of providing dowries, participating in the Roman *Monte delle Doti* and every year on the feast of the Assumption dowering at least six girls and marrying them off" (my translation).

35. AOIF, *Filze d'Archivio*, LXII, 19, fol. 95r, 19 Nov. 1606: "Illustrissimo et reverendo priore: Li nostri capitani della compagnia di Santa Maria delle laude et Sancto Zanobi hanno

con loro partito vinto tre fanciulle delle cinque che sono state mandate in nota dalla Compagnia di Santa Caterina de' Barbieri per hauere da cotesto spedale per dote o, parte di dote, lire trenta per ciascuna quando saranno maritate ... Piaccia à Vostra farne fare ricordo acio quando produranno fede del matrimonio." For the following year, see fol. 573r, 18 Nov. 1607.

36. Trexler, "Widow's Asylum," 120–26. Admittedly, the Orbatello did not do much to solve gender and inheritance issues among the merchant elite, among whom in some respects such issues were the most pressing.

37. Ibid., 141.

38. AOIF, *Filze d'Archivio*, LXII, 25, fol. 764r, 21 Apr. 1606: "Serenissimo Gran Duca[:] Le pouere donne nocentine habitante in Orbatello, humilissime seruitrici di Vostra Altezza Serenissima con ogni debita reuerentia li espongano, come quattordici anni in circa sono state sotto il gouerno et custodia di Don Alessandro Staccini, cappellano in detto luogho doue che le pouerelle sono state dal detto capellano, molto male bistrattate sì del corpo loro come del' anime, oltre, che sempre ha cercato d'usurpalle, si come ha sempre usurpate, et tolto 'l loro la fatica delle loro braccia, della quale li conueniuano viuere, et con quella nutrirsi, non hauendo altro sussidio in questo mondo, che la fatica delle braccia loro, che giorno e notte stanno del continuo à incannare. Dando occasione ancora e di molte giouane di detto luogho, di farle capitare male, che da lui non è restato, che non hanno rotto il collo, si ancora, che alla morte loro, le pouerelle non possono pur disporre il quattro cratie per far' fare un' poco di bene per l'anime loro non essere signore di far dire pur una messa."

39. Ibid.: "son venute percosse malamente col bastone, oltre le parole brutte, et disoneste, che del continuo li vien dette loro, riceuendo, sempre dal detto cappellano catiuissimi esempli, che di questo pure inporterebbe poco male pouerelle ritrouandosi in su quel'ultimo punto della morte, moiano come bestie, che da detto prete non vengano à essere pasciute, et nutrite di quei santissimi sacramenti si come si conuiene a' buon' cristiani, senza pur riceuere le raccomandazione de' anima à tale, che le pouerelle ricorrono genuflesse à benigni piedi di Vostra Altezza Serenissima suplicandola per le viscere di Jesu Cristo, che ci gli ripare, à un tanto disordine, con rimuouere detto D.Alessandro, et mettere dette pouerelle sotto la buona cura, et custodia del Molto Reuerendo Signore Ruberto Antinori, spedalingo dell'Innocenti huomo molto esemplare, et di buoni costumi si per essere loro nocentine, et essere nutrite et alleuate sotto la custodia di detto Reuerendo spedale, e ancora per essere in detto luogho abondanza di sacerdoti, che in quel ultimo della loro morte veranno à essere nutrite e cenate di quei cibi sprituali, che si conuiene."

40. Daniela Lombardi, *Povertà maschile, povertà femminile: L'Ospedale dei Mendicanti nella Firenze dei Medici* (Bologna: Il Mulino, 1988), 183.

PART III

MARGINAL VOICES

8

LES LIVRES DES FLORENTINES

RECONSIDERING WOMEN'S LITERACY IN QUATTROCENTO FLORENCE

JUDITH BRYCE

Studies of literacy in later medieval and Renaissance Florence have traditionally tended to ignore, or to pay scant attention to, the question of female literacy, while the classic article that does address the subject directly is characterized by a predominantly negative or pessimistic tone. I have in mind Christiane Klapisch-Zuber's seminal study, "Le chiavi fiorentine di Barbablù: L'apprendimento della lettura a Firenze nel xv secolo," published in 1984.[1] Referring to the mercantile classes of the fifteenth century, she suggests that a young woman who could read was regarded as a rarity, whereas for boys the possession of such a skill was normal.[2] The situation is aggravated in the case of writing, which is viewed as an almost exclusively male monopoly.[3] The cases cited as examples of female literacy are therefore consistently presented as exceptions, and her conclusion, citing Leon Battista Alberti, is that in the Florentine version of Bluebeard's castle the forbidden key is the one to the door leading to the male domain of the *scrittoio*.[4] As in other writings by Klapisch-Zuber on women's experience, the study of female, as opposed to male, access to the skills relating to literacy is marked by recurring notions of surveillance, control, repression, limitation, enclosure, immobility, silence, and marginality.[5] While there is undoubtedly a considerable degree of truth in such a view, from the perspective of the early twenty-first century it may appear that the danger of being overly influenced by

contemporary male discourses on Quattrocento women's lives and behavior has not been entirely avoided. There is constant recourse to a
fairly homogeneous set of views from individuals otherwise as varied as
Paolo da Certaldo, Giovanni Dominici, and Leon Battista Alberti, all of
whom are regularly cited on the subject of women, rather than an attempt
to address the realities of women's experience, difficult and problematic
though these might be to fathom given the overwhelmingly patriarchal
bias of the sources.[6]

What I wish to do in the present study is to revisit the topic of female
literacy in Quattrocento Florence, not by challenging the idea of a quan-
titative or qualitative discrepancy between male and female competen-
cies in this area, something that is probably indisputable, but by adopting
a more positive approach to the existing evidence as well as by adding to
that evidence. What follows cannot be a statistical exercise. We remain
restricted to individual cases, mainly from within the Florentine mercantile elite, and too few from which to attempt any generalization as to
the extent of women's literacy, even within that class as a whole. I shall
not be dealing with exceptional literary (as opposed to literate) women
in Florence in this period, the creative writers—of whom there seem to
be just two, Lucrezia Tornabuoni de' Medici and Antonia Tanini Pulci—
nor shall I make more than a brief mention of the impact of print in the
last decades of the century with its significance, in turn, for women's access to the written word.[7] Instead, the emphasis will fall primarily on
devotional reading as central to women's culture and to their varied uses
of literacy, countering a tendency, common outside the realm of religious
history, to dismiss or undervalue this sphere of activity.

I have suggested that Klapisch-Zuber paints perhaps too negative a
picture. Her use of the later fourteenth-century case of Giovanni Morelli's
sisters exemplifies both this approach and, at the same time, some of
the wider problems relating to the whole matter of women's literacy.
The fact that Mea and Sandra Morelli can read and write "tanto bene
quanto alcun uomo" ("as well as any man"; here Klapisch-Zuber is citing
their brother) appears in a note underpinning the remark alluded to earlier, namely that a girl who can read is to be regarded as a rarity.[8] But does
Morelli's text necessarily support this interpretation? There has been
some conflation and, inevitably, omission. A similar phrase in fact occurs
with reference to Mea (b. 1365), while three pages further on Morelli's
pen portrait of Sandra (b. 1369) describes her thus: "She possessed all

the skills one would expect of a respectable woman: she could embroider, and read and write; she was very eloquent, a good speaker, knowing how to express herself confidently and well."[9] The opening phrase of this quotation, with its apparently normative (and positive) connotations, is not cited by Klapisch-Zuber, or indeed by Franco Cardini, both of whom prefer to interpret Morelli as viewing his sisters' literacy as exceptional.[10] Branca, too, tends in this direction. He refers in a footnote to Paolo da Certaldo for whom literacy, the third of five keys to wisdom, should be the virtually exclusive territory of men with only a nod in the direction of convent-taught literacy for nuns.[11] In the same note, however, he also refers to the clear "exceptions" present in Morelli's text, the writer's two sisters and another female relative, Lena, wife of Bartolomeo Morelli. In short, he, and we, are brought face-to-face with the discrepancies between morally prescriptive and more socially descriptive texts. But neither is this latter category unproblematic. There is probably an external model operating in Morelli's *Ricordi:* not the writings of churchmen or of secular moralists, but of Boccaccio (as Branca also notes), hence Morelli's seemingly untroubled reference in this context to Sandra's articulacy, a characteristic strikingly unmarked by that fear of women's speech that predominates in other contemporary male discourses.[12] In short, an idealizing process may well still be at work, and the fictional model could account for the fact that the personality and abilities of Sandra Morelli seem to leap from the page. Boccaccio may provide a more enabling vision for women who aspire to literacy than that proposed by men such as Paolo da Certaldo, but whether or not Morelli's remarks have an unproblematic relation to reality remains uncertain.

For the Quattrocento itself, on which the present study will focus, it is perhaps inevitable that one should begin with Alessandra Macinghi Strozzi, although she is in fact disappointing on the subject of female literacy despite being a notable example of it. There is no reference in any of the seventy-three surviving letters as to how or when or why she herself learned to read, or whether her own daughters could do so.[13] In a letter of 31 August 1465, however, in which she reports to her son Filippo, then still in exile in Naples, about a prospective Florentine bride, Alessandra relates a neighbor's judgment on the young woman, an unnamed daughter of Francesco di Messer Guglielmino Tanagli. According to the neighbor, Costanza, wife of Pandolfo Pandolfini, among the girl's other virtues is that "ella legge così bene."[14] Once again, it seems as dubious to interpret such a phrase as evidence of women's scarce literacy (it is not that the girl *can* read, as opposed to not knowing how to read, but that she reads *so well* and that this is a point in her favor as a prospective marriage partner) as to use it to claim universal female literacy among the Florentine mercantile classes.

An apparent paradox in the whole vexed issue of women and literacy is the association of women as teachers of reading in their capacity as mothers.[15] Klapisch-Zuber gives the example (again presented as an exception) of Bartolomea, wife of Bernardo Rinieri, using the *tavola* and the Psalter to teach her sons at home before sending them to school at the age of five or six.[16] Alessandra Strozzi claims to be teaching her grandson, Alfonso, to read at the age of not more than fifteen or sixteen months.[17] In the latter case, in particular, it seems clear that "leggere" is to be understood in its very first stage, the recognition of letters of the alphabet, perhaps by the method recommended by Giovanni Rucellai (who does not, however, mention the role of the mother), namely forming letters out of fruit or cake which are then earned by the child on correct identification of the letter represented.[18]

Recognition of the letters of the alphabet using the *tavola* or hornbook, the first step in the normal sequence of instruction, was followed by learning first syllables and then whole words in Latin, using the Psalter as a primer or first reader, and thereby providing access to standard prayers such as the Pater Noster and Ave Maria.[19] Reading at this second stage was, for both sexes, still perhaps largely a matter of repetition, memorization, and oral recitation, terms frequently used to describe the limited reading ability often specifically attributed to women by scholars who have tended to stress rote learning in connection with female religious training—"reading for the purposes of prayer"—rather than a training in reading per se, although, as we shall see later, this is altogether too narrow a view of women's uses of literacy.[20] After the initial process, middle- and upper-class Florentine boys would progress to a tutor or to a school to learn the Donatus, the rudiments of Latin grammar, and/or to the *abbaco*, the specialized school that taught commercial arithmetic.[21] For the majority, reading continued in the vernacular, whereas the sons of the well-off might proceed to a full-blown humanistic education and/ or university. The only young Florentine woman of the period, for whom we have information, who in any way approaches this level of education is Alessandra Scala, daughter of the Florentine chancellor.[22] The norm would seem to be that even in the topmost echelons of the Florentine mercantile elite, there is a divergence between male and female education as exemplified by the juvenile letters of Lucrezia and Piero di Lorenzo de' Medici, the pair openly competing with one another in writing to their elders, the former in the vernacular to her grandmother, the latter in Latin to his father, complaining that the greater difficulty should bring him greater reward.[23]

Who taught girls to read? Clearly, at least in some cases, the role of mothers in the early stages of reading must have benefited daughters as well as sons, but there is also limited evidence, albeit for the fourteenth century, of families willing to pay outsiders, both male and, occasionally, even female, for lessons. In the mid-fourteenth century, Tommasa di Francesco Delli, a niece and ward of the Niccolini family, was taught by the sister of a Latin master who was paid five soldi for three months' tuition.[24] Then there is the well-known case of Margherita Datini, taught by her husband's notary and friend, ser Lapo Mazzei. Margherita learned to read late in life, but what is also significant is that it was felt appropriate that Ginevra, her husband's illegitimate daughter by a slave girl, was taught by a *maestra* when she was nine. Did the experience of her stepmother as a late learner influence a family decision to begin much earlier with the child?[25]

Margherita Datini, Alessandra Strozzi, and the nine-year-old Lucrezia de' Medici could also write, but we have no knowledge as to whether the daughter of Francesco Tanagli or Ginevra Datini could do so, for, as Roger Chartier says, reading and writing were "dissociated and successive," and in the case of many individuals with a degree of reading ability, both women and men, writing was a skill that was not acquired at all.[26] Alessandra Strozzi relates the saga of her youngest son, Matteo, still struggling with the pen at the age of eleven *after* he has attended an *abbaco*.[27] One current of contemporary male opinion certainly seems to have been that women were less suited to writing than men, lacking manual dexterity and concentration, although the case of Matteo Strozzi and the acknowledged skills of the nuns of the Florentine convent of Le Murate, in both book production and needlework, point up the contradiction inherent in such a view and, in general, the unsafe nature of much received wisdom in this area.[28] Alessandra's own much-quoted lamentations about writing ("writing wears me out," "these wretched letters," "the discomfort of writing") surely owe less to her sex's "natural" incapacity than to issues of sheer quantity, of the quality of the materials involved, and of health, including the problems with her eyesight that forced her to invest in spectacles shortly after having been involved in acquiring a pair to send to Filippo in Naples.[29] Furthermore, in interpreting Alessandra's letters, one must also take into account the various emotional and psychological factors in play, including all sorts of subtle accommodations and manipulations of her sons that still await critical analysis.

One of the problems when considering the writing skills of individual women is that, just as letters addressed to them could have been read out by others, so letters apparently written by them could have been dictated to others, unless, that is, we have concrete internal evidence such as the formulaic "scritto di mia mano" ("written by my hand"), which we will find later in the case of Margherita Soderini. But even the use of scribes hides a diverse reality: Alessandra Strozzi using her son Matteo to write for his own practice as well as to save her the effort, the doubtful literacy of Contessina de' Bardi, wife of Cosimo de' Medici, not writing till a scribe is available, or the case of her daughter-in-law, Lucrezia Tornabuoni, fully literate but also using scribes, as indeed, it would be as well to remember, did their literate male relatives.[30]

Physical distance between male and female members of a family may well have been a powerful motivating force as regards female literacy among the Florentine middle and upper classes. Exile, as recognized by Fulvio Pezzarossa, was a potentially crucial factor, with Alessandra Strozzi poignantly aware of the power of her literacy to maintain emotional ties during long periods of separation: "it seems as though I am with you," "I have almost lost hope of any consolation, except through your letters," and "I see that you are writing more to give me the satisfaction of receiving your letters than from any real necessity. This has given me great pleasure since I can't have you with me in person."[31] In the Florentine context, however, other reasons for absence were also extremely common: on business (Margherita to Francesco Datini; Fiammetta, and then Selvaggia, to Filippo Strozzi), in the service of the Florentine state (Bartolomea to Otto Niccolini in Rome on a diplomatic mission; Guglielmina della Stufa to her husband, Luigi, commissioner in Arezzo), on grounds of health (Lucrezia di Lorenzo de' Medici to her grandmother,

Lucrezia Tornabuoni, at the Bagno a Morba), or simply due to frequent moves to and fro between villas and town houses with all the associated domestic complications.[32] The practical advantages of this could not have been lost, even on those husbands who listened to the reservations expressed by preachers and moralists. In spite of Alberti's vision of the passive, presumably uneducated wife, the management and preservation of property in all its forms (food, clothes, household textiles, furnishings, etc.), which constituted the core of the wifely role, and particularly the role of wives of the mercantile elite, is facilitated by some degree of skill in reading, writing, and basic numeracy, particularly in the absence of the male householder for whatever reason. The issue of women's numeracy skills (recognition of Roman and Arabic numerals, prices, weights and measures, dates) is still to be researched. Alessandra Strozzi had to ask for help with more difficult accounts, but it seems she could handle day-to-day ones.[33] Her *libro di ricordi*, her account book, is in the Archivio di Stato (as is the one belonging to a daughter-in-law, Filippo's second wife, Selvaggia Gianfigliazzi). Klapisch-Zuber comments that Filippo took over the family's financial affairs in Florence after his return from exile in 1466, but Alessandra had begun her *quadernuccio*, as she usually calls it, some thirteen years earlier in 1453: "this book...in which I shall write down some of my affairs."[34]

How often, then, did pragmatism and self-interest triumph over any male fear of, or prejudice against, female entry into literacy and the excuse that, for women, literacy was in any case "funzionalmente inutile" ("functionally useless")?[35] Functional literacy skills sufficient for women's practical, religious, and even entertainment requirements, a literacy often not based on, or supported by, an extensive book culture linked to personal study and/or formal schooling, and heavily imbued with the forms and practices of oral culture, may have been more widespread among women of the Florentine mercantile classes than scholars have allowed. That Florentine women who could write did not tend to become women writers, far less women humanists, is not at issue. What should perhaps interest us more are the uses to which women put the literacy they possessed, bearing in mind that the plural, "literacies," is probably more appropriate, namely a diversity of reading skills and practices achieved by men as well as women in Quattrocento Florence, each case varying according to a combination of factors ranging from age, social class, and wealth to individual intelligence, opportunity, and degree of formal or informal education, and from virtual memorization to a virtually modern concept of reading.[36]

It is now time to ask the following question: what were "les livres des Florentines"? What was "read" by women who remained at the stage of memorization and recitation, and what by those who could read in a fuller sense of the word (whether or not they could write)? Christian Bec's classic study, *Les Livres des Florentins*, offers a statistical survey of books mentioned in inventories made by the Magistero de' Pupilli, the government office that looked after the interests of orphans, or at least of children whose fathers had died intestate or whose wills had so instructed.[37] Given that the death of the father is the trigger, it is not surprising that women figure very little in the records. Of the names of many hundreds of recently deceased book owners listed by Bec, only one or two seem to be women, as far as the fifteenth century is concerned: for example, Monna Sandra, widow of Domenicho del Vaglia, owning two devotional books, a Book of Hours and one of Psalms.[38] An element of gender blindness or of active discrimination would appear to have affected Bec's findings, however, and Armando F. Verde's fuller version of the same material reveals other women, including four belonging to the Inghirami family, Checa della Volta and her fifteen-year-old daughter, Bartolomea, and the daughters of Piero Carnesecchi, all owning Books of Hours.[39] In some cases there is ambiguity: Margherita d'Angnolo Sichuro dal Borgho "has" a book concerning Dante, while suora Sandra, sister of the late Antonio di Goro Dati, "has" a Virgil.[40] "Having," or even owning, however, does not necessarily imply reading, and similarly with the case of a woman cited by Klapisch-Zuber as having bequeathed books in her will.[41]

The cases cited above include ten Books of Hours of the hundreds referred to in a range of "library" inventories from the poorest to the most substantial, but Bec chooses to omit them from his statistical enquiry in that they are, in his opinion, to be regarded more as precious objects than as books properly speaking.[42] This is the text that Roger Wieck describes as "*the* medieval best-seller, number one for nearly 250 years," containing a simplified form of the Divine Office of the Breviary arranged according to the canonical hours of the Office, and a variety of other material, some of it personalized, including a liturgical calendar, Hours of the Cross, of the Holy Spirit, and of the Dead, the Seven Penitential

Psalms, and prayers.[43] The text will usually be in Latin, although in Bec's lists some of them are described as "in volghare."[44]

The Book of Hours was intimately associated with the beginnings of literacy, being read after the *salteruzzo* or itself used as a primer. As Michael Clanchy suggests, "through the Books of Hours, ladies introduced their families and children to prayer—and hence to literacy—in their own homes. This domestication of the liturgical book was the foundation on which the growing literacy of the later Middle Ages was built."[45] Christian Bec may not count them as books, but these "libriccini di donna" are ubiquitous, both in his sources and in other fifteenth-century documents, notably lists of marriage gifts or inventories of bridal trousseaux. Clearly, women's domestic religious practices were viewed as beneficial, not only to themselves but to the newly constituted family unit with its potential for future increase, hence the association of Books of Hours with weddings and with women, even if men could, and did, own them too. Alessandra Strozzi's elder daughter, Caterina, married to Marco Parenti in 1448, has "un libriccino di donna" listed among her other possessions[46] while Maria, widow of Bernardo Portinari, and going as a second wife to Paolo Niccolini in 1457, has an "Office of Our Lady, and seven psalms all painted in miniature and gold, ornaments and clasps of silver, with a crimson cover."[47] Nannina di Piero de' Medici, marrying Bernardo di Giovanni Rucellai in 1466, has an illuminated "libriccino di Nostra Donna" with silver clasps and another covered in brocade.[48] Gentile Becchi gifted one to Clarice Orsini for her wedding to Lorenzo de' Medici in 1469, while for the marriages of three of their daughters, sumptuous illuminated manuscripts were prepared that figured in the 1992 quincentenary exhibitions.[49] The skeptical will continue to say that many such books were merely precious objects, but Bec's inventories also record well-worn copies as well as the presence of "libriccini di donna" in decidedly modest households.[50] The story of the prostitute Giannetta di Gherardo of Flanders, forced to return her Book of Hours to her pimp after entering a community of penitents, is a case in point: for her, it must surely have had a primarily spiritual significance and use, whereas his primary concern would presumably have been with its monetary value.[51]

How, in practice, women utilized their Books of Hours remains less than fully understood. Was it in conjunction with domestic religious images such as the gilt Virgin Mary listed in Nannina de' Medici's *donora*,[52] or the sort of items listed by Alessandra Strozzi in an inventory: a Virgin Mary made of wood in a ground-floor room, and another set in the wall in the large chamber?[53] For some, perhaps many, it may have been a case of a visual literacy based on the illuminated pictures, as opposed to an alphabetic literacy,[54] or combined with learning the much-repeated Latin texts by heart, with varying degrees of understanding, rather than reading them in any modern sense. But a pervasive skepticism among earlier scholars has been challenged by recent generations of historians operating in the field of women and religious history, who caution against "mechanically repeating that women's religious communication and devotional expression tended to be exclusively oral."[55] Evidence in Florentine sources for contemporary expectations as regards women's reading habits tends to suggest a mixed ability group comprising literate, semi-literate, and nonliterate individuals. For example, Vespasiano da Bisticci advises mothers on the upbringing of their daughters: "Train them to say the Office of Our Lady, if they know how to read."[56] This may imply that some do not know (or do not yet know, depending on age), but also that the Book of Hours requires being read or, at the very least, that memorization might require prompting by the presence of the written text before one.

Although there are examples to the contrary, as we have seen, and in spite of a degree of residual ambivalence, some of the most influential religious figures in Quattrocento Florence, Giovanni Dominici, Archbishop Antonino Pierozzi, and San Bernardino, whether orally through sermons and other teaching or pastoral work, or in writing through letters and tracts, followed the authoritative lead of Saint Jerome, encouraging women's access to devotional literature. Such authorization, it has been suggested, was supported by images such as the Virgin Mary with her book on her lap or on a lectern, the standard iconography of the Annunciation, which appeared in many accessible locations, not least as the first illustration in many Books of Hours.[57] One of Poliziano's *detti piacevoli*, incidentally, pokes fun at the anachronism of Mary herself reading this particular book: "A preacher, speaking about the Annunciation, said, among other silly things: 'Now then, you women, what do you think the Virgin Mary was doing at the time—dying her hair? Of course not. In fact she was standing before a Crucifix reading her Book of Hours!' "[58]

The question then arises, is it an increasing familiarity of women with books that leads to more frequent artistic representations of this kind? Although Michael Clanchy reminds us that "religious icons are stereotypes which do not depict reality,"[59] it is always possible that the Quattrocento female viewer might have interpreted them otherwise, as Susan Groag Bell has suggested—a case of an iconographic trend encouraging women readers by suggesting a *possible* reality.[60]

Vespasiano, perhaps influenced by the views of the churchmen cited above, or more pragmatically, by virtue of the fact of his professional involvement in the Florentine book trade, gives cautious approval to laywomen reading devotional texts. In the *Vita dell'Alexandra de' Bardi,* his only large-scale biography of a woman, he praises Alessandra's mother for teaching her to read (the Book of Hours in the first instance), so that she could perform, in her own domestic environment, an imitation of the daily ritual of the clergy as regards the canonical hours punctuating the devotional day.[61] In a digression, however, he introduces Caterina di Albertaccio Alberti, the widow of Piero di Filippo Corsini, whose reading clearly went beyond that: "she had read about famous women of the Old Testament, and about Anne the Prophetess in the New, and had their example before her eyes."[62] According to Vespasiano, Caterina had a Breviary, a Bible (reminding us of the fact that Florence was an important center for biblical translation into the vernacular), collections of homilies arranged according to the ecclesiastical calendar, and texts of biblical exegesis.[63] He also specifically says that she had a knowledge of Latin.[64] In this case at least, there can be little doubt about a substantial level of reading ability.

The downside of women's reading skills from the point of view of ecclesiastics and lay moralists alike was, of course, the possibility of straying beyond the comparatively, if not wholly, safe territory (as we shall see shortly) of devotional literature. We are back in the arena of male prescriptiveness about women's behavior when we reach Vespasiano's conclusion to his biography of Alessandra and his advice that Florentine women should take note of her exemplary life:

> learning not to allow their daughters to read the *Cento Novelle,* or the works of Boccaccio, or Petrarch's sonnets that, although they are not immoral, are not a good idea for innocent young

girls who should learn to love God and their husbands. Instead they should read religious works, lives of saints or sacred histories, so that they learn to temper their own lives and habits, and turn to serious rather than frivolous things.[65]

Similarly, we have Archbishop Antonino's admonition to Diodata degli Adimari: "Spend part of the day in prayer, and read often, not about the paladins and suchlike frivolities but holy doctrine."[66] For both writers, it seems, the existence of women readers of secular material is not unthinkable (except in the moral sense). Are Diodata, Alessandra, and the female audience that Vespasiano felt he was addressing (whether directly or indirectly) all then to be termed "donne singolari" ("exceptional women") in terms of their literacy, or is his standpoint determined by that totalizing discourse of female inferiority that in fact sits uncomfortably with a more complex reality?[67] The question of fifteenth-century Florentine women as readers of secular texts such as Boccaccio or the vernacular romances is one that remains to be explored. Instead, I shall conclude this study with two individual cases of women's uses of literacy, both in the field of personal piety, first that of Diodata (Dada) degli Adimari, who corresponded with Archbishop Antonino, possibly on a fairly regular basis, for about a decade from the later 1440s to his death in 1459, and second, that of Margherita Soderini, who made personal notes of the sermons of fra Mariano da Genazzano during the 1480s.

As his mentor Giovanni Dominici had done before him (and their common patristic model, Saint Jerome), Antonino directed letters and other writings on spiritual matters to Florentine women. Ginevra de' Cavalcanti, widow of Cosimo de' Medici's brother, Lorenzo, is the dedicatee of his *Regola di vita cristiana (Dello stato vedovile)* of 1441, while *La nave spirituale* of 1450 was for Annalena Malatesta, widow of Baldaccio da Anghiari (her husband's checkered career as a sometime *condottiero* for Florence ending in defenestration and the public display of his head in 1441), and the *Opera a ben vivere* of 1455 for the Tornabuoni sisters, Dianora, married to Tommaso Soderini, and Lucrezia, married to Piero de' Medici.[68] Lucrezia may indeed be deemed to be exceptional in her role as a creative writer, but much remains unknown about the precise nature of her range as a reader. What, for instance, are we to make of Gentile Becchi's remarks in a letter to her of 1473, suggesting that she might be consulted over the choice of staff for the Studio Pisano: "you who have always read so much, with a study full of books"?[69] Books belonging to her were lent to members of the Medici circle in 1481: a Ptolemy to Braccio Martelli, a Sallust to her son-in-law, Bernardo Rucellai, and to Poliziano, Aristotle's *Logic,* all "de' libri di madonna Lucretia."[70] Was this apparently personal library one that had been enriched along the way by classical manuscripts belonging to her late husband and that she now owned but did not herself use?

Dada degli Adimari is a much more shadowy figure. According to one source, she was the daughter of ser Paolo di Ser Lando (possibly a notary whose home would be a significant site of literacy if Bec's lists are anything to go by), married Baldinaccio degli Adimari, a member of one of Florence's magnate families whose ancestral territory lay just to the south of Santa Maria del Fiore and the archbishop's palace, and was left a widow with young children in 1449.[71] The Catasto records of 1457 complicate matters somewhat, listing a Mona Dada, aged fifty, as the widow of Baldinaccio di Buonaccorso Baldinacci.[72] Clearly, more biographical research remains to be done. Her own letters to Antonino have not survived (unsurprisingly), but his to her were preserved by one of her sons, Paolo, who became a monk of the Badia Fiorentina.[73] Only two of the letters are dated, one 26 March 1449, the other 21 November 1457. Some are clearly addressed "alla divota sua figliuola Dada" ("to his devout daughter, Dada"), but internal evidence suggests that she was also in fact the recipient of most of the others. They are often consolatory—on the recent death of her husband, on the death of a son, and of a daughter (1457)—and may well have begun with her widowhood when it seems clear that she sought spiritual guidance, not only taking the lead in initiating such a correspondence, utilizing what connections were available to her, whether from among her marital or her natal family, but maintaining it for a decade. His replies are usually in response to particular questions of a spiritual nature; his tone is often slightly weary, long-suffering, revealing that it is Dada who is the active agent rather than the passive recipient of a communication initiated by him: "I have been so busy that I haven't had time to reply to your little note *(letteruzza)* and I can't remember the question you asked except that it was generally about Saint Mary Magdalene."[74] The form "letteruzza," with its diminutive, may refer to the quality of expression, style, orthography, or content, for example the limited degree of theological understanding revealed by her questions, but it is also in keeping with his own style that is, at times, brisk, abrupt, or peremptory, discouraging emotional dependence, urging her to make her point succinctly with no superfluous material such as recommendations on behalf of others or expressions of reverence or affection.[75] He seems caught between two conflicting reactions. There is the desire, and indeed the duty, to offer guidance in the truths of religion to Dada the individual and to Dada the mother with young children to instruct (his sense of her educative role as a mother emerges clearly), and the niggling feeling that she is being importunate, overassertive, lacking humility, that her questions might arise out of what he calls "la vana curiosità" ("vain curiosity") on her part.

This same fear of intellectual or spiritual vanity or presumption is particularly clear in Letter 14, from which it emerges that she has been asking for guidance about reading and, in particular, about the possibility of reading the Breviary, in other words the liturgical mainstay of the professionals, the regular clergy and the monastic orders, both male and female.[76] It was a not uncommon aspiration of the laity over the centuries to imitate the devotional practices of the clergy, hence the scaled down Little Office of the Blessed Virgin Mary, the Book of Hours, but Dada's particular aspiration recalls Caterina di Albertaccio Alberti as described by Vespasiano: "she used to say the whole Office from the Breviary, as priests and monks do."[77] Antonino's response is intended to be off-putting. It is a text he uses every day, but it is written in such a small hand and with so many abbreviations that he thinks she would have difficulty reading it. (It is noteworthy that he does not raise the objection that it is in Latin, indeed he freely quotes the Scriptures in Latin in his letters to her, as does the priest Christofano d'Antonio di Maso in his letter to Lucrezia Tornabuoni.[78]) Copies of the Breviary are not readily available; they are in short supply. Prayer is perfectly acceptable; "non riprendo però di dire l'ufficio" ("I don't object to you saying the Office"), which I take, therefore, to mean the Little Office of the Virgin, the Book of Hours.[79] Prayer and meditation are recommended in between household duties, but also reading, which is clearly viewed as spiritually beneficial. The suggestion, "read, therefore, or else listen to holy scriptures and the church fathers, for the living voice is more effective than the dead one. Store in your memory what you have absorbed, reading or hearing the word of God," may mark his preference for oral communication, with the written word safely in the hands of men, and with women as receptive listeners.[80] Elsewhere, however, he says he may send her a Psalter, not the *salteruzzo da fanciulli* but the full liturgical text, and that he will try to borrow a copy of Saint Gregory's commentary on the book of Job or another similar vernacular book to give to her.[81] These quotations not only shed light on, but also offer concrete evidence of the uses of literacy and the reading habits of pious Florentine women of the middle of the century (for I think we must presume Dada was not unique), with spiritual advisors actively involved in the circulation of religious books, in response, at times, to the active solicitation of women.[82]

The equivocal nature of such activities is usefully exemplified in the correspondence by the archbishop's warning against a book which he judges dangerous: "And if you happened to obtain a book called 'On the Simple Soul,' which may be in the possession of some people who are reputed to be spiritual, take care not to read it, because it is dangerous, and has been the ruination of many."[83] This is interesting, first because he takes it for granted that she might acquire, or have access to, books from sources other than himself, and second because this particular book is identifiable as the *Specchio delle anime semplici* by Marguerite Porete, burned at the stake for heresy in Paris in 1310.[84] Although the authorship of this text remained shrouded in mystery for some part of its early history, that the writer was a woman was known by churchmen in Florence in 1435, and the text continued to be attractive to women readers, trying consciously or unconsciously to bypass a male-dominated religious hierarchy in order to achieve a more direct, unmediated relationship with the divine.[85]

Also of keen interest for our present purposes is Antonino's permission for Dada to consort with other devout women, "donne spirituali,"[86] although he accompanies it with a warning against heedlessly divulging personal family matters, in keeping with that habitual male fear of women's uncontrolled speech that we see in Alberti or Vespasiano. The notion of the existence of groups or networks of devout laywomen, perhaps principally widows like Dada, finds encouragement in the work done by scholars such as Katherine Gill in an Italian context, or Carol Meale and Felicity Riddy in relation to fifteenth-century England, directing their researches, for example, into identifying reading or textual communities of women.[87] Such a reading community may have existed, for instance, among the married women of the Medici, divided into their separate *brigate* but potentially circulating texts such as the writings of Sant'Antonino (including those works dedicated to individuals in the group), the abbreviated Psalter attributed to Saint Jerome translated by Marsilio Ficino for Clarice de' Medici, and the poetic compositions of Lucrezia Tornabuoni herself, mentioned as being enjoyed by the Medici women in July 1479.[88] Then there is the case of the heavily pregnant Bianca de' Medici who, in a letter to her mother written that same month, refers to having sent for, and received, a life of Saint Margaret, her interest probably centered on the fact that Margaret was one of the many female saints associated with childbirth, with the text perhaps assuming an additional talismanic aspect.[89]

But there is also the shadowy existence of women's lay religious associations operating outside the family unit, notably the group founded in 1460 under the name of Santa Maria del Popolo, with a meeting place in the Carmine church and a particular focus on the Brancacci Chapel. This group consisted of about eighty devout women belonging to the best families in Florence, led initially by Mona Lisa, widow of Niccolò Serragli.[90] It is an example of extra-familial, female sociability and devotional life, of a Florentine female subculture, about which we still know very little, not least because of the traditional assumptions that have blocked what Katherine Gill refers to as "a recognition of the possibility of female collaboration and agency."[91] Dada degli Adimari, as we have seen, was not a passive correspondent, but in many ways a demanding one. Like Alessandra de' Bardi or Caterina di Albertaccio Alberti, she was eager to enhance her own spiritual life in ways that involved a degree of literacy. One can only speculate about such women's individual or collective textual practices, basing oneself on the fragmentary evidence cited above for the Medici women—reading a text, or hearing someone else read it aloud, learning it, or portions of it, by heart, perhaps entering into informal discussions on the basis of such texts, whether read privately or read out loud—an oral culture primarily, perhaps, but one that was to some extent, perhaps to some considerable extent, text-based.

If we think of the circulation of pious works that might come into women's hands, the possibilities are, in fact, legion. A very few individuals might have accumulated personal libraries like that of Lucrezia Tornabuoni. Both new and secondhand manuscripts were available from booksellers or *cartolai*, but also from the friars, peddlers, *canterini*, *ciechi*, and such-like individuals identified by Susan Noakes as continuing to be active on into the new era of the printed book from the 1470s.[92] Texts possessed by male members of the family—husbands, sons, brothers— whether in the Florentine town house or in the more casual surroundings of the villa (Bec's lists offer examples), could not always have been guarded from female use. Husbands were urged by contemporary churchmen to read aloud to their wives and families, but a literate woman in the family could also perform this function. The home might even be a site of book production in terms of the transcription of texts or parts of texts, whether in connection with a husband's cultural or religious interests or a son's education. Of the many female scribes who might exist under a cloak of anonymity, two examples can be offered here: BNCF, *Magliabechiano*, VII, 702, described by Antonio Lanza as "autografo della Filomena di Giovanni da Prato," and a manuscript of Belcari's mid-century *sacra rappresentazione*, Florence, Biblioteca Riccardiana, *Abramo e Isacco*, Riccardiano 1429, copied by Benedetta, wife of Piero d'Antonio Nicholi in 1464–65.[93] Women might also commission manuscripts such as the illuminated Breviary ordered by Tommasa Gianfigliazzi in 1470 for two of her daughters, suora Marietta and suora Perpetua, nuns in Le Murate, and the fascinating case recorded by Carlo Delcorno of BNCF II II 89 containing extracts from the *Fior di virtù*, Cavalca's *Vite dei santi padri*, and Petrarch's *Trionfo d'Amore*, commissioned by Costanza, widow of Benedetto Cicciaporci, for herself and her daughters, one of whom, Lucrezia, later inherited the manuscript.[94]

As regards borrowing, the case of Dada reveals the active involvement of male spiritual advisers, confessors, or other clergy, but what of the Florentine female religious communities who were, after all, as Felicity Riddy suggests, "part of the same textual community" as regards religious literature?[95] The convent walls need not be viewed as a barrier to the circulation of texts that might arise out of a multiplicity of contacts between nuns and laywomen, the latter being either blood relations or individuals who had married into the nuns' natal families.[96] The Benedictines of Le Murate, with their tradition of book production, are known to have transcribed devotional texts, at least for laywomen of the social elite such as Clarice de' Medici in 1474, and the printing press of the Dominican nuns of San Jacopo di Ripoli, as well as producing secular works (famously Pulci's *Morgante*), was also responsible for large numbers of books of popular piety such as the *Legenda di Sancta Caterina* and the story of Saint Margaret mentioned earlier, copies of which must surely have found their way into the hands of women readers.[97]

My second individual case is that of Margherita di Tommaso Soderini, whose notes of sermons survive in manuscript in the Biblioteca Nazionale in Florence.[98] Margherita is almost certainly to be identified as the daughter of Maria di Giuliano Torrigiani, who was the first of four wives of Tommaso di Lorenzo Soderini (1403–85). Maria died in 1440 when her daughter was very young, and she was succeeded by a stepmother, Dianora Tornabuoni, sister of Lucrezia and dedicatee, as we have seen earlier, of Archbishop Antonino's *Opera a ben vivere* in the mid-1450s. Margherita was married twice, first to Francesco di Jacopo Baroncelli in 1451 and then to Gerozzo Pigli around 1462.[99] By the mid-1480s, she was probably a widow once more when she transcribed a number of sermons, all by the same preacher, "fra Mariano Romano," the Augustinian fra Mariano da Genazzano (later a rival and enemy of Savonarola). These include his Lenten sermons of 1484 delivered in Santa Maria del Fiore, and sermons delivered in 1488 to the nuns of San Gaggio and of Le Murate, the latter an institution with which the Soderini had particular connections.[100]

> If there are any imperfections, it is the fault of my memory. I, Margherita, daughter of Messer Tommaso Soderini, have written this with my own hand. Whoever reads it, pray God for me. If it is written well, it is a gift from God and I give thanks to him. All good comes from God, and all error is mine alone.[101]

The circumstances surrounding such a transcription by a woman are particularly fascinating from the point of view of the technical difficulties involved. Rather than the Magliabechiano manuscript representing a fair copy of notes made during the event, it seems in fact to be the result of a feat of memory ("non arei tenuto bene a mente"), a step beyond the contemporary practice of retelling sermons orally, and one that would permit Margherita and her family a more long-term use of the sermon material.[102] Certainly, the opening paragraph cited above seems to exclude a transcription either from a text provided by the preacher himself or from notes *(reportationes)* by another scribe.[103] Some entries are a mere seven to ten lines in length; others are more substantial, the gaps covered by phrases such as "here he said many fine things."[104] The notes cover a range of topics—good and evil, the Resurrection, conscience, angels, and the excellence of San Giovanni Battista, patron saint of Florence— but Margherita was clearly struck by the personal appropriateness of certain parts of these sermons, returning on more than one occasion to the subject of the conduct of widows, and also recording (or, for personal reasons, slightly altering?) a reference to a father away on business in Bruges or London: her second husband, Gerozzo Pigli, had managed the Medici bank in both cities.[105]

Were literate Florentine women such as Margherita Soderini, Dada degli Adimari, Caterina Alberti, or Costanza Cicciaporci so "exceptional"? Perhaps not. Were they locked in a purely passive or submissive relationship to men's texts, helpless before powerful patriarchal discourses continuously absorbed through the medium of both the spoken and the written word? Or should we rather envisage a more complex reality in which there was a potential for the appropriation of texts, whether through memorization, listening, reading, or writing, in response to their own needs, thereby resisting the imposition of an only apparently hegemonic norm and never completely imprisoned within the restricted spaces allotted to them by patriarchy? De Certeau's image of readers as voyagers moving across "lands belonging to someone else, like nomads poaching their way across fields they did not write, despoiling the wealth of Egypt to enjoy it themselves" is striking from women's perspective, for female readers could be said to be doubly removed from the site of male writing, suffering a double illegitimacy.[106] On the other hand, reading could offer particularly fruitful possibilities for travel in lands either alien or familiar, from within the enclosed space to which patriarchy attempted to consign them by virtue of their gender. San Bernardino's image cited earlier (note 58) of the "càmara serrata" as the sanctioned site of controlled female reading contrasts with the unambiguously positive and liberating one of the male *scrittoio*. It was, nevertheless, a possible starting place for a journey upon which some women in fifteenth-century Florence were eager to embark, not least in relation to the exploration of religious texts and the question of personal salvation. Their access to such texts may have been intensive rather than extensive, untutored rather than learned, hindered in its understanding by an absence of formal education, confronted at every turn by the male guardians of written and oral religious discourses. Viewed within the terms of her own contemporary culture, however, the woman reader or, more broadly, the woman consumer of the written word, while apparently marginal and marginalized, was nevertheless able to find constant confirmation both of the centrality of women through the presence of powerful female mediators such as the Virgin Mary, Mary Magdalene, Saint Catherine, and Saint Margaret and, above all, of the spiritual equality of women and of men before their God, an assurance that Dada degli Adimari was able, on more than one occasion, to wrest, in writing, from her sometimes reluctant archbishop.[107]

NOTES

1. Christiane Klapisch-Zuber, "Le chiavi fiorentine di Barbablù: L'apprendimento della lettura a Firenze nel xv secolo," *Quaderni storici* 57 (1984): 765–92. Other useful contributions on the question of women's education, both in Renaissance Florence and beyond, include Franco Cardini, "Alfabetismo e cultura scritta nell'età comunale: Alcuni problemi," in *Alfabetismo e cultura scritta nella storia della società italiana* (Perugia: Università degli Studi di Perugia, 1978), 147–86; Maria Ludovica Lenzi, *Donne e madonne: L'educazione femminile nel primo Rinascimento italiano* (Turin: Loescher, 1982); Isabella Chabot, "'Sola, donna, non gir mai': Le solitudini femminili nel Tre–Quattrocento," *Memoria: Rivista di storia delle donne* 18 (1986): 7–24; and Paul F. Grendler, *Schooling in Renaissance Italy: Literacy and Learning, 1300–1600* (Baltimore: Johns Hopkins University Press, 1989). See, too, Sharon Strocchia, "Learning the Virtues: Convent Schools and Female Culture in Renaissance Florence," in *Women's Education in Early Modern Europe: A History, 1500–1800*, ed. Barbara J. Whitehead, 3–46 (New York: Garland, 1999). This excellent article came to my attention too late to be integrated into the present study, for which it provides valuable support. On women's social education, see Judith Bryce, "Performing for Strangers: Women, Dance, and Music in Quattrocento Florence," *Renaissance Quarterly* 54 (2001): 1074–1107.

2. Klapisch-Zuber, "Le chiavi fiorentine," 776.

3. Ibid., 782.

4. Ibid., 784.

5. For instance, the groundbreaking essays in Christiane Klapisch-Zuber, *Women, Family, and Ritual in Renaissance Italy*, trans. Lydia G. Cochrane (Chicago: University of Chicago Press, 1985).

6. Among a number of voices insisting on the importance of acknowledging a discrepancy between contemporary discourses and "la réalité du vécu," see, for example, the preface by Georges Ulysse to *Les Femmes écrivains en Italie au Moyen Âge et à la Renaissance*, ed. Georges Ulysse (Aix-en-Provence: Publications de l'Université de Provence, 1994), 8–9.

7. For Tornabuoni, see Fulvio Pezzarossa, *I poemetti sacri di Lucrezia Tornabuoni* (Florence: Olschki, 1978); and Mario Martelli, "Lucrezia Tornabuoni," in Ulysse, *Les Femmes écrivains*, 51–86. For Pulci, see Antonia Pulci, *Florentine Drama for Convent and Festival:*

Seven Sacred Plays, annotated and trans. James Wyatt Cook, ed. James Wyatt Cook and Barbara Collier Cook (Chicago: University of Chicago Press, 1996); Georges Ulysse, "Un Couple d'écrivains: Les *sacre rappresentazioni* de Bernardo et Antonia Pulci," in Ulysse, *Les Femmes écrivains,* 177–96; Judith Bryce, "Adjusting the Canon for Later Fifteenth-Century Florence: The Case of Antonia Pulci," in *The Renaissance Theatre: Texts, Performance, Design,* ed. Christopher Cairns, 2 vols., 1:133–45 (Aldershot: Ashgate, 1999); and Bryce, "Vernacular Poetry and Mystery Plays," in *A History of Women's Writing in Italy,* ed. Letizia Panizza and Sharon Wood, 31–36 (Cambridge: Cambridge University Press, 2000).

8. Klapisch-Zuber, "Le chiavi fiorentine," 790 n. 74.

9. Vittore Branca, ed., *Mercanti scrittori: Ricordi nella Firenze tra Medioevo e Rinascimento* (Milan: Rusconi, 1986), 156, and cf. p. 153. All translations are mine unless otherwise indicated.

10. Cardini, "Alfabetismo e cultura scritta," 169 n. 37. Of Florentine women in general he writes (p. 168): "there was a tendency not to teach them to read, far less to write, considering that to do so would have been pointless and perhaps even morally harmful."

11. See Branca, *Mercanti scrittori,* p. 153 n. 5, p. 4, and p. 36 respectively.

12. Ibid., 153 n. 5.

13. Cesare Guasti, ed., *Lettere di una gentildonna fiorentina del secolo XV ai figliuoli esuli* (Florence: Sansoni, 1877). All references will be to this edition unless otherwise stated. Alessandra's encouragement to Filippo to write to his sister Caterina, the wife of Marco Parenti, obviously does not constitute hard evidence of the latter's literacy. See ibid., 294, 21 Apr. 1464. Parenti's letters to Filippo, however, offer some clues: "I have just had a letter of yours for Caterina [announcing the death of their brother, Matteo]. . . . I haven't had the heart to give it to her yet," and "I'll leave it to Caterina to reply." See Marco Parenti, *Lettere,* ed. Maria Marrese (Florence: Olschki, 1996), 47, 1 Sept. 1459, and 219, 23 July 1470. On Alessandra Strozzi, see Maria L. Doglio, "Scrivere come donna: Fenomenologia delle *Lettere familiari* di Alessandra Macinghi Strozzi," *Lettere italiane* 36 (1984): 484–97; Fulvio Pezzarossa, "'Non mi peserà la penna': A proposito di alcuni contributi su scrittura e mondo femminile nel Quattrocento fiorentino," *Lettere italiane* 41 (1989): 250–60; Ottavia Niccoli, "Forme di cultura e condizioni di vita in due epistolari femminili del Rinascimento," in Ulysse, *Les Femmes écrivains,* 13–32; and Georges Ulysse, "De la séparation et de l'exil: Les Lettres d'Alessandra Macinghi Strozzi," in *L'Exil et l'exclusion dans la culture italienne: Actes du colloque franco-italien, Aix-en-Provence, 19–21 octobre 1989,* ed. Georges Ulysse, 89–112 (Aix-en-Provence: Publications de l'Université de Provence, 1991).

14. Guasti, *Lettere,* 464.

15. "The 'domestication' of ecclesiastical books by great ladies, together with the ambitions of mothers of all social classes for their children, were the foundations on which the growth of literacy in fourteenth- and fifteenth-century Europe were constructed." See Michael T. Clanchy, *From Memory to Written Record: England 1066–1307,* 2nd ed. (Oxford: Blackwell, 1993), 252. See, too, Michael T. Clanchy, "Learning to Read in the Middle Ages and the Role of Mothers," in *Studies in the History of Reading,* ed. Greg Brooks and Anthony K. Pugh, 33–39 (Reading: Centre for the Teaching of Reading, University of Reading School of Education with the United Kingdom Reading Association, 1984); and Susan Groag Bell, "Medieval Women Book Owners: Arbiters of Lay Piety and Ambassadors of

Culture," in *Sisters and Workers in the Middle Ages*, ed. Judith Bennett, Elizabeth A. Clark, Jean O'Barr, B. Anne Vilen, and Sarah Westphal-Wihl (Chicago: University of Chicago Press, 1989), 148–51.

16. Klapisch-Zuber, "Le chiavi fiorentine," 771–72.

17. Guasti, *Lettere*, 587, 4 Mar. 1468 [stile fiorentino (henceforth st. fior.)].

18. Giovanni Rucellai, *Il Zibaldone quaresimale*, vol. 1 of *Giovanni Rucellai ed il suo Zibaldone*, ed. Alessandro Perosa (London: Warburg Institute, University of London, 1960), 14. For the distinction between the recognition of letters and reading, see, for example, Piero Lucchi, "La Santacroce, il Salterio e il Babuino: Libri per imparare a leggere nel primo secolo della stampa," *Quaderni storici* 38 (1978): 599–600. Signs of women having a clear sense of responsibility for the education of male, if not female, children, is evident in a variety of sources, for example in a letter to Lucrezia Tornabuoni, dated 25 Sept. 1473, from a priest, Christofano d'Antonio di Maso, who reports her grandson, Cosimo Rucellai, as protesting, "I didn't come on vacation to read," and his great-grandmother Contessina's displeasure. See Lucrezia Tornabuoni, *Lettere*, ed. Patrizia Salvadori (Florence: Olschki, 1993), 124. Another example is in a letter by Bartolomea Niccolini of 7 Apr. 1470 to her husband, Otto di Lapo Niccolini, in Ginevra Niccolini di Camugliano, *The Chronicles of a Florentine Family, 1200–1470* (London: Jonathan Cape, 1933), 330–31.

19. On phonetic literacy in Latin in combination (or not) with comprehension literacy in the vernacular, see Paul Saenger, "Books of Hours and the Reading Habits of the Later Middle Ages," *Scrittura e civiltà* 9 (1985): 241.

20. It is interesting in this context to juxtapose Lucrezia di Lorenzo de' Medici, aged six and three quarters, with a servant, Galasso, referred to in the letter from Christofano d'Antonio di Maso to Lucrezia Tornabuoni already cited in note 18 above. For Lucrezia di Lorenzo we have evidence of a fuller literacy achieved early in life (as we shall shortly see), writing (or using a scribe or tutor to write on her behalf?) to her grandmother about saying her daily prayers for the former's safe return. See Lucrezia Tornabuoni, *Lettere*, 145, 24 May 1477. Galasso, according to Christofano, "comes with me every morning to read . . . and I have much more trouble with him than with the others . . . nevertheless, with God's help, little by little I have got him to learn by heart the Salve Regina, and part of the preparatory prayers for Mass, and part of the Psalter." See ibid., 124, 25 Sept. 1473. Class and individual ability rather than gender are factors here. Clanchy, *From Memory to Written Record*, 37, writes about the unstable meaning of verbs associated with literacy, pointing out that learning by heart was the standard medieval and early modern learning procedure, with an inevitable blurring of the distinction between recitation and reading.

21. Grendler, *Schooling in Renaissance Italy*, gives an excellent overview of these options.

22. See Giovanni Pesenti, "Alessandra Scala, una figurina della Rinascenza fiorentina," *Giornale storico della letteratura italiana* 85 (1925): 241–67; and Alison Brown, *Bartolomeo Scala 1430–1497, Chancellor of Florence: The Humanist as Bureaucrat* (Princeton: Princeton University Press, 1979), 210–12 and 246–47.

23. Isidoro Del Lungo, *Letterine di un bambino fiorentino* (Florence, 1887), letter of 26 May 1479.

24. Niccolini di Camugliano, *Chronicles of a Florentine Family*, 41.

25. Iris Origo, *The Merchant of Prato: Daily Life in a Medieval Italian City* (Harmondsworth: Penguin, 1986; first published London: Jonathan Cape, 1957), 190–91; and see Valeria Rosati, ed., *Le lettere di Margherita Datini a Francesco di Marco (1384–1410)* (Prato: Archivio storico pratese, 1977). After citing the familiar strictures on female literacy issued by Paolo da Certaldo and Giovanni Dominici (the latter much admired by Francesco Datini and his wife), Origo sensibly points out the discrepancy that may exist between these and reality (*Merchant of Prato*, 190): "Just as Monna Margherita and her friends appear to have led a freer, more amusing life than the conventional picture of young women of their time, so Ginevra was brought up more indulgently than most children."

26. Roger Chartier, "Laborers and Voyagers: From the Text to the Reader," *Diacritics* 22 (1992): 58.

27. Guasti, *Lettere*, 6, 7, 24, 33.

28. See Kate Lowe, "Female Strategies for Success in a Male-Ordered World: The Benedictine Convent of Le Murate in Florence in the Fifteenth and Early Sixteenth Centuries," in *Women in the Church: Papers Read at the 1989 Summer Meeting and the 1990 Winter Meeting of the Ecclesiastical History Society*, ed. William J. Sheils and Diana Wood (Oxford: Blackwell, 1990), 216–17.

29. "Fatica mi pare lo scrivere" (Guasti, *Lettere*, 85, 22 Oct. 1450), "queste letteracce" (ibid., 309, 11 May 1464), "quel disagio delle lettere" (ibid., 533, 28 Dec. 1465). The spectacle references are in ibid., 347, 3 Jan. 1464, and 277, 22 Mar. 1463 [both st. fior.].

30. For Alessandra and Matteo, see the letter of 8 Nov. 1448 in Alessandra Macinghi Strozzi, *Tempo di affetti e di mercanti: Lettere ai figli esuli*, ed. Angela Bianchini (Milan: Garzanti, 1987), 71–73. For Contessina de' Bardi, see Gaetano Pieraccini, *La stirpe de' Medici di Cafaggiolo*, 2 vols. (Florence: Vallecchi Editore, 1924), 1:35. For Contessina's daughter-in-law, see Patrizia Salvadori's introduction to her edition of Lucrezia's *Lettere*, p. 36. Salvadori also makes useful points about the varying degrees of sophistication in women's literacy, style, orthography, etc.

31. Respectively Guasti, *Lettere*, 166, 27 July 1459; 394, 20 Apr. 1465; and 547, 11 Jan. 1465 [st. fior.]. For Pezzarossa's view, see "'Non mi peserà la penna,'" 251.

32. For Margherita Datini, see Origo, *Merchant of Prato*, 213; and Rosati, *Le lettere di Margherita Datini;* for Fiammetta di Donato Adimari, see Alessandra Strozzi to Filippo, 8 May 1469 (Guasti, *Lettere*, 592): "since I can't write often, you'll be compensated by Fiammetta," and Guasti also publishes a letter by her, clearly part of a series of which very little has survived (ibid., 598–99, 29 July 1469). For Selvaggia di Bartolomeo Gianfigliazzi, see Archivio di Stato di Firenze (henceforth ASF), *Carte Strozziane*, Serie III, CXXXI, fol. 11r and fol. 188r, referring to her dowry and to her mother's will. For Bartolomea Niccolini's letters, see Niccolini di Camugliano, *Chronicles of a Florentine Family*, 328–32, and for Guglielmina della Stufa's letter of 25 May 1495 to her husband, Luigi, see Alessandro Gherardi, *Nuovi documenti e studi intorno a Girolamo Savonarola*, 2nd ed. (Florence: Sansoni, 1887), 128–29: "My dear Luigi, we commend ourselves to you. I think you have forgotten about us because it has been three or four days since we had a letter from you. So, in order to prove that we have not gone completely from your mind, when it is convenient and you

are not too busy, write us a line. Since we are to be sustained by letters, don't let us go short."
For Lucrezia di Lorenzo to her grandmother on 24 May 1477, see Lucrezia Tornabuoni,
Lettere, 144–45.

33. "I haven't done Isabella's account because I find it difficult although it is a
small matter. There are various entries and I can't do so many calculations," in Guasti, *Lettere*, 160, 21 July 1459, to Lorenzo Strozzi in Bruges. See, too, pp. 151, 166, and 388.
Klapisch-Zuber, "Le chiavi fiorentine," 779, suggests that for girls time does not constitute
the structuring element of the personality that it does for boys. Again, there is an element
of truth in this, but one would have to say that in Alessandra Strozzi's household, she was
the custodian and guarantor of notably precise personal data, for instance as regards the
ages of her children. See Guasti, *Lettere*, 127, 27 Feb. 1452 [st. fior.], to Lorenzo Strozzi in
Bruges. She was also keenly aware of the official, two-month cycle of the Florentine governmental calendar. In this, she was presumably like other women of the office-holding
classes and perhaps, in particular, like other wives and mothers of exiles.

34. ASF, *Carte Strozziane*, Serie V, XV, fol. 1r. For Selvaggia Gianfigliazzi's account
book, see *Carte Strozziane*, Serie V, LXI; and Richard Goldthwaite, *Private Wealth in Renaissance Florence: A Study of Four Families* (Princeton: Princeton University Press, 1968), 78.

35. Cardini, "Alfabetismo e cultura scritta," 168.

36. Harvey J. Graff, "On Literacy in the Renaissance: Review and Reflections," in *The
Labyrinths of Literacy: Reflections on Literacy Past and Present* (London: Falmer, 1987), 147.
Yet another complication is revealed in the case of Margherita Datini, demonstrating how
the ability to read could be restricted in the age before print. It seems she was ambitious to
read her husband's business letters, but found the script too hard: "I do not wonder . . . that
she belongs to the same race as the priest who could not say the Office, except from his
own book. . . . But if Monna Margherita would indeed read merchants' letters, tell her to
study a month to do so, even as she has already studied her own book for six months." See
letter of Domenico di Cambio in Origo, *Merchant of Prato*, 214.

37. Christian Bec, *Les Livres des Florentins (1413–1608)* (Florence: Olschki, 1984);
and see, too, Armando F. Verde's remarks on Bec's use of this source in his "Libri tra le
pareti domestiche: Una necessaria appendice a *Lo Studio Fiorentino 1473–1503*," *Memorie
Domenicane* 18 (1987): 6–8. The subject is also discussed in Giovanni Ciappelli, "Libri e
letture a Firenze nel XV secolo," *Rinascimento* 29 (1989): 268–71.

38. Bec, *Livres des Florentins*, 183, 1452.

39. Verde, "Libri tra le pareti domestiche," 45, 77, 83.

40. Bec, *Livres des Florentins*, 50, 1472, and 95, 1480.

41. Klapisch-Zuber, "Le chiavi fiorentine," 789 n. 72.

42. Bec, *Livres des Florentins*, 25.

43. Roger S. Wieck, *The Book of Hours in Medieval Art and Life* (London: Sotheby's
Publications, 1988), 27.

44. For example Bec, *Livres des Florentins*, 153, 1420; 157, 1424.

45. Clanchy, *From Memory to Written Record*, 12.

46. Guasti, *Lettere*, 16.

47. Niccolini di Camugliano, *Chronicles of a Florentine Family*, 141.

48. Rucellai, *Zibaldone*, 33.

49. For Becchi's gift, see "Informazione delle noze di Lorenzo di Piero di Cosimo," in Parenti, *Lettere*, 249. For the books given to Lucrezia, Maddalena, and Luisa de' Medici, see Anna Lenzuni, "Tre libri d'ore per le figlie di Lorenzo," in *All'ombra del lauro: Documenti librari della cultura in età laurenziana*, ed. Anna Lenzuni, 166–68 (Florence: Amilcare Pizzi Editore, 1992).

50. Bec, *Livres des Florentins*, 195: "j libriciuolo, usato, di donna."

51. Gene Brucker, ed., *The Society of Renaissance Florence: A Documentary Study* (New York: Harper and Row, 1971), 211–12, cited by Katherine Gill, "Women and the Production of Religious Literature in the Vernacular," in *Creative Women in Medieval and Early Modern Italy: A Religious and Artistic Renaissance*, ed. E. Ann Matter and John Coakley (Philadelphia: University of Pennsylvania Press, 1994), 69–70.

52. Rucellai, *Zibaldone*, 33.

53. ASF, *Carte Strozziane*, Serie V, XV, fol. 80r. In a letter to her son Lorenzo in Bruges, Alessandra also alludes to devotional pictures from the Low Countries. See Guasti, *Lettere*, 230, 6 Mar. 1460. See too, Klapisch-Zuber, *Women, Family and Ritual*, 320–23, and Diana M. Webb, "Women and Home: The Domestic Setting of Late Medieval Spirituality," in Sheils and Wood, *Women in the Church*, 159–73.

54. Graff, "On Literacy," 147.

55. Roberto Rusconi, "Women Religious in Late Medieval Italy: New Sources and Directions," in *Women and Religion in Medieval and Renaissance Italy*, ed. Daniel Bornstein and Roberto Rusconi (Chicago: University of Chicago Press, 1996), 312. On the use of the Book of Hours, see Saenger, "Books of Hours"; Groag Bell, "Medieval Women Book Owners," 146–48; and, in general, Wieck, *Book of Hours*.

56. "Libro de le lode e comendazione de le donne," in Vespasiano da Bisticci, *Vite di uomini illustri*, ed. Ludovico Frati, 3 vols. (Bologna: Romagnoli, Dall'Acqua, 1892–93), 3:305.

57. See Groag Bell, "Medieval Women Book Owners," 154–55; and Webb, "Woman and Home," 163.

58. See Tiziano Zanato, ed., *Detti piacevoli* (Rome: Istituto della Enciclopedia Italiana, 1983), p. 98, no. 316. The "sciocchezze" may originate with San Bernardino whom Zanato cites in a note (p. 175): "But let's say where the Angel found her. Where do you think she was? Standing at the window or doing something equally vain? No, no! She was shut away in her room, reading, in order to set an example to you, young woman . . . learn the Office of Our Lady, and find delight in that."

59. Clanchy, "Learning to Read in the Middle Ages," 36.

60. Groag Bell, "Medieval Women Book Owners," 153–56; and Webb, "Woman and Home," 163.

61. See Aulo Greco, ed., *Le vite*, 2 vols. (Florence: Istituto nazionale di studi sul Rinascimento, 1970–76), 2:473–74.

62. Ibid., 495.

63. Ibid., 496. See Kenelm Foster, "Vernacular Scriptures in Italy," in *The Cambridge History of the Bible*, vol. 2, *The West from the Fathers to the Reformation*, ed. Geoffrey W. H. Lampe (Cambridge: Cambridge University Press, 1969), 458; and Samuel Berger, "La Bible italienne au Moyen Âge," *Romania* 23 (1894): 406. For Bible ownership in Bec's samples, see *Livres des Florentins*, 24 and 40.

64. "Avendo notitia delle lettere" (Greco, *Le vite*, 2:496), and compare: "aveva notizia delle lettere latine" ("Caterina Alberti Corsini" in Parte IV, "Donne illustri," in Vespasiano da Bisticci, *Vite*, 3:298).

65. See, Greco, *Le vite*, 2:499.

66. Tommaso Corsetti O. P. and Domenico Marchese O. P., eds., *Lettere di Sant'Antonino Arcivescovo di Firenze precedute dalla sua vita scritta da Vespasiano fiorentino* (Florence: Barbèra, Bianchi, 1859), 126. Susan Noakes, "The Development of the Book Market in Late Quattrocento Italy: Printers' Failures and the Role of the Middleman," *Journal of Medieval and Renaissance Studies* 11 (1981): 45 n. 82, comments on the considerable number of *cantari* surviving in written form.

67. In this sense Vespasiano's description of the two daughters of Checca (Francesca) and Donato Acciaiuoli as "two exceptional girls, more like boys" (see Vespasiano da Bisticci, *Vite*, 3:300) is the inevitable outcome of rigid Renaissance gender stereotyping.

68. For Dominici's letters or spiritual treatises addressed to women such as Bartolomea degli Obizi, wife of Antonio degli Alberti, see his *Lettere spirituali*, ed. Maria Teresa Casella and Giovanni Pozzi (Freiburg: Éditions Universitaires Fribourg, 1969); and the useful extracts from Dominici and Antonino in Lenzi, *Donne e madonne*, Part I, pp. 35–63. For Antonino and the Medici wives, see Peter Francis Howard, *Beyond the Written Word: Preaching and Theology in the Florence of Archbishop Antonino, 1427–1459* (Florence: Olschki, 1995), 20–21.

69. See Pezzarossa, *I poemetti sacri*, 38.

70. Ibid., 38 n. 6.

71. Biblioteca Nazionale Centrale di Firenze (henceforth BNCF), *Poligrafo Gargani, Adimari*, no. 22. The year of her husband's death can be ascertained from one of Antonino's letters. See Corsetti and Marchese, *Lettere di Sant'Antonino*, 121, 26 Mar. 1449: "Having been begged by others on your behalf to write to console you on your recent bereavement."

72. ASF, *Catasto*, 833, fol. 9v. Two of the children listed here, Francesco and Paolo, match the evidence of the published letters while another member of the household, Piero, aged thirty, may be the illegitimate son of Baldinaccio mentioned back in 1427. See ASF, *Catasto*, 81, fol. 481r.

73. For the manuscripts of the letters, BNCF, *Magliabechiano*, XXXV, 238, and XXXVIII, 124, see the introduction to Corsetti and Marchese, *Lettere di Sant'Antonino*.

74. Ibid., 112.

75. Ibid., 53.

76. Ibid., 145.

77. See *Vita dell'Alexandra de' Bardi*: Greco, *Le vite*, 2:496.

78. Corsetti and Marchese, *Lettere di Sant'Antonino*, 123, and see note 20 above.

79. Vespasiano describes Antonino taking steps to ensure that the clergy used their Breviaries and did not sell or otherwise dispose of them. See "Vita di Arcivescovo Antonino, Fiorentino," in Greco, *Le vite*, 1:229.

80. Corsetti and Marchese, *Lettere di Sant'Antonino*, 81.

81. Ibid., 148 and 98. According to Vespasiano, Antonino owned no books apart from his Breviary: "He got the books he needed on a day-to-day basis, either from San

Marco or San Domenico." See Greco, *Le vite*, 1:241. For Saint Gregory in Florentine libraries see, for example, Bec, *Livres des Florentins*, 24–25, and 182.

82. In her discussion of women's access to hagiographic literature, Anna Benvenuti Papi makes the point that it is not just a question of manipulation from above but a complex exchange, partly driven by a demand from below; see "Penitenza e penitenti in Toscana: Stato della questione e prospettive della ricerca," *Ricerche di storia sociale e religiosa* 17–18 (1980): 115.

83. Corsetti and Marchese, *Lettere di Sant'Antonino*, 147.

84. See Romana Guarnieri, *Il movimento del libero spirito: Testi e documenti* (Rome: Edizioni di storia e letteratura, 1965), 477. On Porete, see, for example, Peter Dronke, *Women Writers of the Middle Ages: A Critical Study of Texts from Perpetua (†203) to Marguerite Porete (†1310)* (Cambridge: Cambridge University Press, 1984); and Emilie Zum Brunn and Georgette Epiney-Burgard, eds., *Women Mystics in Medieval Europe* (New York: Paragon House, 1989).

85. Guarnieri, *Il movimento del libero spirito*, 469, cites a letter to Cecilia Gonzaga from Protonotary Gregorio Correr in Florence with the Papal Curia. See Guarnieri, too, for the wide-ranging influence of Porete's work in Italy.

86. Corsetti and Marchese, *Lettere di Sant'Antonino*, 147.

87. Gill, "Women and the Production of Religious Literature in the Vernacular" (for instance, p. 65); Carol M. Meale, "'...alle the bokes that I haue of latyn, englisch, and frensch': Laywomen and Their Books in Late Medieval England," Felicity Riddy, "'Women Talking about the Things of God': A Late Medieval Sub-Culture," and also Julia Boffey, "Women Authors and Women's Literacy in Fourteenth- and Fifteenth-Century England," in *Women and Literature in Britain, 1150–1500*, ed. Carol M. Meale, 128–58, 104–27, and 159–82 (Cambridge: Cambridge University Press, 1993).

88. For the Ficino translation, see Eugene F. Rice Jr., *Saint Jerome in the Renaissance* (Baltimore: Johns Hopkins University Press, 1985), 193. For the circulation, between written and oral, of Tornabuoni's poetry, see the letter of Angelo Poliziano to Lucrezia of July 1479, the date suggesting a search for forms of individual and collective consolation in the aftermath of the Pazzi conspiracy and the murder of Giuliano de' Medici: "Magnifica Madonna mia, I am sending back with Tommaso those hymns, sonnets, and poems in *terza rima* which you lent me when I was there. Those women took much pleasure in them and Madonna Lucrezia, or rather Lucrezia [di Lorenzo] learned the whole of Lucrezia by heart, and many sonnets." Cited by Martelli, "Lucrezia Tornabuoni," 65–66.

89. "I have often sent to your house to Marco for malmsey, and similarly for the book of Saint Margaret, and have received everything." See Lucrezia Tornabuoni, *Lettere*, 160, letter of 15 July 1479, Alla Torre. According to the *Golden Legend*, "if any woman who was in danger during childbirth called upon her, she would bring the baby out of the womb without harm." See Arrigo Levasti, ed., *Leggenda aurea: Volgarizzamento toscano del Trecento*, 3 vols. (Florence: Libreria Editrice Fiorentina, 1925), 2:779. Peter Burke, *The Historical Anthropology of Early Modern Italy: Essays on Perception and Communication* (Cambridge: Cambridge University Press, 1987), 112 and 211, mentions the legend of Saint Margaret being read aloud in childbirth in sixteenth-century Italy. For Florentine manuscripts of Cavalca's lives of the saints, including Margaret, see Carlo Delcorno, "Per l'edizione

delle *Vite dei Santi Padri* del Cavalca," *Lettere italiane* 29 (1977): 265–89, 30 (1978): 47–87 and 480–524. See, too, Bec, *Livres des Florentins,* for example, pp. 169–71. Printing brought the possibility of mass production, with two thousand single-folio "Saint Margarets" printed by the Ripoli press in December 1481, many of which must have been destined for women's use. See Mary A. Rouse and Richard H. Rouse, *Cartolai, Illuminators, and Printers in Fifteenth-Century Italy: The Evidence of the Ripoli Press* (Los Angeles: Department of Special Collections, University Research Library, University of California, 1988), 84–85. In a personal communication, however, Anabel Thomas has suggested to me that these may be images rather than texts.

90. See Anthony Molho, "The Brancacci Chapel: Studies in its Iconography and History," *Journal of the Warburg and Courtauld Institutes* 40 (1977): 83. Molho terms it "a lay women's religious company." See, too, John Henderson, *Piety and Charity in Late Medieval Florence* (Oxford: Clarendon Press, 1994), 465. For groups of "good Christian women" in Pisa in the late fourteenth and early fifteenth centuries, see Mary Martin McLaughlin, "Creating and Recreating Communities of Women: The Case of Corpus Domini, Ferrara, 1406–1452," *Signs: Journal of Women in Culture and Society* 14 (1989): 308.

91. Gill, "Women and the Production of Religious Literature," 66.

92. Noakes, "Development of the Book Market," 45, 52. According to Foster, "Vernacular Scriptures in Italy," 458 and 462, friars, especially Dominicans (Antonino's own order) and Franciscans, were the most active copiers and propagators of biblical texts. He also speaks (p. 463) of friars using texts such as the vernacular Bible for community reading. Women must surely have figured in such an audience.

93. Antonio Lanza, ed., *Lirici toscani del Quattrocento,* 2 vols. (Rome: Bulzoni, 1973), 1:19; and Nerida Newbigin, "Politics in the *Sacre Rappresentazioni* of Lorenzo's Florence," in *Lorenzo the Magnificent: Culture and Politics,* ed. Michael Mallett and Nicholas Mann (London: Warburg Institute, University of London, 1996), 119 n. 5.

94. For the Gianfigliazzi commission, see Mirella Levi D'Ancona, *Miniatura e miniatori a Firenze dal XIV al XVI secolo: Documenti per la storia della miniatura* (Florence: Olschki, 1962), 34–35. For Costanza Cicciaporci, see Delcorno, "Per l'edizione delle *Vite dei Santi Padri,*" 55–57: "This book was caused to be written by Mona Costanza, widow of Benedetto Cicciaporci, for the consolation of her own soul and, secondly, of those of her daughters." I owe this reference to Katherine Gill, "Women and the Production of Religious Literature," 97 n. 61. Costanza (daughter of Giovanni di Giovanni Bellacci) and Lucrezia are mentioned in the sketchy genealogical information provided in ASF, *Carte Dei,* Manoscritti 384.

95. Riddy, " 'Women Talking about the Things of God,' " 111.

96. For examples of convent book production, for instance Santa Lucia at Foligno, Monteluce at Perugia, Corpus Domini in Bologna, and in Florence, San Jacopo di Ripoli and also the Paradiso, see Gill's excellent study, "Women and the Production of Religious Literature," 67–70 and notes. Although she deals primarily with religious communities themselves, she also highlights laywomen's use of patronal and familial networks.

97. For Clarice's commission, see Francis W. Kent, "Lorenzo de' Medici, Madonna Scolastica Rondinelli e la politica di mecenatismo architettonico nel convento delle Murate a Firenze (1471–72)," in *Arte, committenza ed economia a Roma e nelle corti del Rinascimento*

(1420–1530), ed. Arnold Esch and Christoph Luitpold Frommel (Turin: Einaudi, 1995), 365 and n. 61, "Lucas abbas" to Clarice: "the transcription of your book is almost completed." For Ripoli, see Emilia Nesi, *Il diario della stamperia di Ripoli* (Florence: Seeber, 1903). Suora Marietta was paid (p. 52), "fiorini due larghi per parte della componitura del Morgante." My thanks to Anabel Thomas and Melissa Conway for their information on the numerous Caterina references in the original Ripoli manuscript. Women were involved with the new printed books as readers, but also as participants in the business of printing and bookselling. Noakes, "Development of the Book Market," 48, offers the suggestive detail of the mother-in-law of Bernardino "canterino," who picked up books from the Ripoli press on his behalf. For a more substantial involvement, see also Deborah Parker, "Women in the Book Trade in Italy, 1475–1620," *Renaissance Quarterly* 49 (1996): 509–41.

98. BNCF, *Magliabechiano*, XXXV, 98. I owe this reference to Lenzi, *Donne e madonne*, 186–87.

99. This biographical information is culled from Paula C. Clarke, *The Soderini and the Medici: Power and Patronage in Fifteenth-Century Florence* (Oxford: Clarendon Press, 1994), 137 and 140; and K. J. P. Lowe, *Church and Politics in Renaissance Italy: The Life and Career of Cardinal Francesco Soderini (1453–1524)* (Cambridge: Cambridge University Press, 1993), genealogical table, p. xiii.

100. For Soderini links with Le Murate, see Lowe, "Female Strategies for Success," 210 and 219. For fra Mariano, see Davide A. Perini, *Un emulo di Fra Girolamo Savonarola: Fra Mariano da Genazzano* (Rome, 1917).

101. BNCF, *Magliabechiano*, XXXV, 98, fol. 3v. See Lenzi, *Donne e madonne*, 186. For another collection of sermon notes and a reference to Margherita's, see Zelina Zafarana, "Per la storia religiosa di Firenze nel Quattrocento: Una raccolta privata di prediche," *Studi medievali*, 3rd series, 9 (1968): 1017–1113.

102. An example of the suggestion that men might recount sermons to their wives and children is in Cherubino da Siena's mid-fifteenth-century *Regole di vita matrimoniale:* "or else you go, and then relate, or have someone else relate the sermon at home, so that those who were not there will learn something—if not all, then a part" (cited by Lenzi, *Donne e madonne*, 185).

103. For the transcription of Savonarola's sermons in the 1490s by ser Lorenzo Violi and related difficulties, see Roberto Ridolfi, *Life of Girolamo Savonarola*, trans. Cecil Grayson (London: Routledge and Kegan Paul, 1959), 111–12.

104. BNCF, *Magliabechiano*, XXXV, 98, fol. 61r.

105. See ibid., fol. 58r; Clarke, *The Soderini and the Medici*, 140; and Raymond de Roover, *The Rise and Decline of the Medici Bank, 1397–1494* (New York: Norton, 1966), 324–25, 328–30, 379.

106. Cited by Chartier, "Laborers and Voyagers," 49.

107. Corsetti and Marchese, *Lettere di Sant'Antonino*, 72, 115 ("Christ makes no distinction between male or female"), 122, and 162.

9

EXILE, RHETORIC, AND THE

LIMITS OF CIVIC

REPUBLICAN DISCOURSE

STEPHEN J. MILNER

REPUBLICS AND EXILE

One of the foremost experiences of marginalization in late medieval and Renaissance Italy was undoubtedly that of exile. The list of its most famous victims reads like a Who's Who of the literary and political history of the period, from Brunetto Latini, Cino da Pistoia, and Dante to Leon Battista Alberti, Cosimo de' Medici, and, although self-imposed, Niccolò Machiavelli. Not surprisingly the subject has been the focus of considerable critical attention and the theme of several conferences, with the majority of studies falling into two main areas: exile as a sociopolitical phenomenon and exile as a literary trope.[1] Although the dividing line between these two fields is by no means clear-cut, the first has predominantly focused on the institutional practice, procedures, and political management of exile while the second has analyzed its literary consequences, from exile lyric poetry to the consolation literature of formal tracts and personal letters. While such literatures clearly originated from the experience of exile, their fusion of political with affective isolation often saw exile deployed in a metaphorical sense—a psychological alienation from the self rather than a physical distancing, especially in lyric with its Provençale and troubadour antecedents.[2]

As physical displacement, however, exile, as described by Edward Said, is a violent act of separation "produced by human beings for other human beings."[3] That this process was so widespread in late medieval and Renaissance Italy was a direct consequence of the peninsula's fractured political geography and a function of the contentious process whereby communities struggled internally between alternative visions of social ordering. As the majority of self-determining communes gave way to the signorial rule of the great dynasties such as the Sforza, Visconti, D'Este, Gonzaga, Montefeltre, Malatesta, and Carrara, the nature of exile changed, becoming more a consequence of splits within the ruling family over succession or the wholesale appropriation of their territory by an invading power.[4]

Yet for those obdurate communities that insisted on maintaining their self-determining status as republics, exile continued to characterize their attempts at self-definition as civic associations. In this context, exile as displacement was a consequence of the spatial and ideological struggle for preeminence. Indeed, it could be argued that to write a history of political exile in Florence, for example, would be to write a history of political conflict by default, charting successive alterations in the social ordering of the commune through an examination of those excluded, from the Guelf/Ghibelline conflicts and dynastic vendettas of the great aristocratic families of the Duecento, to the establishment of the Medicean Duchy in the sixteenth century. Along the way, the list of those expelled would provide an index of political change, from the *Primo popolo* to the exiled Magnates and Black Guelfs, and from the Ciompi and the victims of the arch-Guelf purges to the patrician rivalries between such families as the Albizzi, Medici, Pitti, and Soderini.[5]

Such a narrative, however, would be clearly at odds with the prevailing accounts of late medieval and Renaissance political thought, which repeatedly stress the centrality of inclusivity and consensus as the core values of so-called "civic republicanism." In highlighting the importance of civic participation and consensus in securing the liberty of its citizens, the discourse of civic republicanism is premised on a political tradition of unity and inclusion that is seen to stretch from the Bolognese *artes dictandi* treatises and the *ars aringandi* tracts of the

Due- and Trecento to the humanistic orations and school curricula of the Quattrocento.[6]

The purpose of the current study, therefore, is to begin questioning the seeming incompatibility between social studies of exile on the one hand and a history of late medieval political thought that charts an increasingly articulate republican rhetoric of inclusion and consensus on the other. In the process, it will be suggested that the rhetoric of civic republicanism was as much a discourse of exclusion and dissensus as of inclusion and consensus due to its intolerance of opposition, and that current interpretations of civic republicanism have failed to acknowledge this exclusive aspect of its character. In viewing rhetoric as a component part of political struggle, the aim is to reemphasize the symbiosis between social and linguistic conflict, between rhetorical changes and successive alterations in governmental forms.[7] Although there is little doubt that a Ciceronian form of rhetorical humanism eventually established civic republicanism as the hegemonic political discourse, especially within Florence, the process was far from a foregone conclusion.

It is axiomatic that for any civic association to be formed there have to be both material and symbolic limits, for identities are necessarily constructed through differentiation and the identification of the Other.[8] The binaries of citizen/exile, insider/outsider, center/periphery were crucial in defining the limits of republican inclusivity, in imagining republican communal identity, and in maintaining its moral integrity.[9] In this context it is necessary to acknowledge the recent recognition of shared concerns by those working in the respective fields of rhetorical and cultural studies. For both, rhetoric is understood as a practice that is primarily concerned with issues of representation and persuasion, and how language and other symbolic systems both render experience meaningful and construct identities with a view to effecting action in the world. Defined in these terms, rhetoric is seen less as a repertory of stylistic figures or the province of opinion than as a discipline with both a political and purposive function in which there exists a tangible relationship between its status as an expressive form and the construction of social order.[10] Such a reading of rhetoric places its affective potency firmly in a performative context as an exercise of power whereby a particular vision of social ordering seeks to establish legitimacy and secure consent.[11] Once rhetoric is acknowledged, in the wake of this "interpretative turn,"

as the medium through which communal identities are generated, secured, and contested, an examination of political conflict can take place
that focuses on the dynamic intersection between language, space, and
power in the quest for legitimation.[12]

From the ritual exiles of the ancient Athenian *demos* to the *Legge de'
discoli* described by Machiavelli in his 1520 assessment of the constitution
of Lucca, republics have provided for the ostracism of individuals considered disruptive of communal life.[13] Yet in late medieval Italy, such was
the scale of displacements that questions concerning the nature of legitimate community were addressed in both juridical and political writings. What these discussions reveal is the tensions that existed between
community understood as a symbolic entity and community understood
as a physical place. The Roman law glossators of the Trecento, for example, were not wholly consistent when debating the question of where
the symbolic sovereignty of the commune resided when the numerical
majority of the commune was exiled. For Baldus de Ubaldis, the expelled majority constituted a legitimate corporation while the minority
left in the city were a sect, presenting the possibility of a legitimate exile
community formed by a displaced citizenry.[14] Yet elsewhere he states
quite clearly that when exiled, those ousted had no jurisdictional powers
relative to those who remained within the city walls: "I concede that
jurisdiction remains with the inhabitants [literally "those inside who
hold the territory"], because jurisdiction attaches to a territory and the
inhabitants are in possession of the territory. Moreover, the inhabitants
represent a whole and exiles are individuals."[15] It was exile as physical
displacement and symbolic alienation, therefore, that focused attention
on the relation between the commune understood in a material sense,
city as place, and in an imagined sense, city as body politic or *corpus
mysticum*.[16]

While the walls of the city might define the commune's material
boundaries, rhetoric was one of the foremost media through which communal identity was imagined and sustained. Significantly, Brunetto Latini
in his *Rettorica* asked, "What is a city? A city is a coming together of people organized to live rationally; hence they are called citizens of the same
commune because they have come together in order to live according
to a shared rationale, not because they are gathered together within a
circle of walls."[17] For Latini, reasoned speech was the basis of a virtuous

community. Yet who was to judge whether such speech was reasoned and virtuous or dissembling and devoid of any sense of moral import?

IN OR OUT: THE TWO FACES OF CICERONIAN RHETORIC

In this context it is important to identify the two faces of the Ciceronian rhetorical paradigm that exercised such an influence over late medieval rhetorical writings. What medieval writers knew of Roman rhetoric was almost wholly mediated through the *De Inventione* and later the pseudo-Ciceronian *Rhetorica ad Herennium* with both enjoying an extensive commentary tradition in their guise as the *Rhetorica Vetus* and *Rhetorica Nova*.[18] While the latter is far more perfunctory in its treatment of the parts of rhetoric and markedly more nebulous and amoral in character, it is in the more discursive *De Inventione* that Cicero's civic morality is unambiguously tied to the art of virtuous speech. According to the fictional account of the origins of civic communities, men were drawn together by the persuasive speech of a mythical man whose words were combined with reason and wisdom. Consent was therefore secured through reasoned speech.[19] The implicit assumption made in all later readings of the text was that Cicero himself was coterminous with this good man, the *vir bonus*, whose virtuous words reflected his virtuous nature.

This is not to say that Ciceronian rhetoric precluded contestation.[20] All three genres of rhetoric as defined by Cicero, namely judicial, deliberative, and epideictic, depended on controversial issues that he termed *quaestiones* or *constitutiones:* to prosecute or defend, to do or not to do, to praise or to blame.[21] The same controversial framework is also found in the *Ad Herennium*.[22] Yet the underlying assumption, given the moralizing nature of the *De Inventione*, was that the ability to argue either side of a dispute, "in utramque partem disputare," guaranteed that all issues would be fully and vigorously debated in a process that saw consensus reached through reasoned deliberation or legitimate contestation, what political theorists today refer to as deliberative democracy.[23] All Cicero's heirs were to varying degrees affected by what can be defined as the controversial nature of his rhetoric, the centrality of *controversia*, or what Italians referred to as *lite*, arguments.[24] However, by focusing on the cohesive

and inclusive dimension of Ciceronian rhetoric, most subsequent readings have neglected its exclusive dimension.

In describing the position of the virtuous orator, Cicero simultaneously prescribed the position of any possible opponents. By definition
they must be men whose speech was devoid of wisdom and virtue, men
who were unable to govern their passions, men who pursued their own
interests rather than those of the community, and men who sought to
gain access to public offices in order to exercise power.[25] According to this
binary configuration, therefore, a man was either virtuous or corrupt,
and his rhetoric either conducive to civic unity or a simulacrum that
masked his true intentions. It is precisely the absence of a legitimate contrary voice in Cicero's rhetoric that reveals the exclusive violence of the
Ciceronian rhetorical paradigm. For the "other side" is conspicuous in
its absence in Cicero's own rhetorical writings except when described in
pejorative terms as hostile to community. It is the silencing of this other
voice that reveals the subjectivity of Cicero's narrative, its one-sided and
agonistic character.

This becomes clear when the definition of "parte" is widened to encompass its other meanings as place and political party as well as an
argumentative position. For in relation to these three senses of "parte,"
Cicero assumes a clearly defined argumentative position, *his* oratory as
beneficial to the well-being of the community; a clearly defined political
point of view, *his* opposition to those *he* deemed inimical to the health of
the republic; and a clearly defined physical position at the center of power.
According to the Ciceronian paradigm, therefore, the orator might well
be able to argue "in utramque partem," but the moral dimension of his
rhetoric placed him rhetorically, politically, and physically in clearly
defined positions that differentiated him from his opponents. There is
some irony in the fact that at the very heart of Cicero's republican rhetoric of freedom and consent lies an inescapable intolerance of any form of
opposition that threatens the status quo. What becomes clear from
Cicero's agonistic paradigm is that legitimacy is mostly derived from
position. The speaker who occupies the public offices, who speaks the
normative discourse of republican values from the privileged sites of government, who represents his opponents as self-seeking enemies of the
republic enjoys a distinct advantage relative to any dissenting group that
lacks the lexis, sites, and authority that such occupation confers. For the
orator speaking from this privileged position enjoys complete control of

the republic's symbolic repertory in his self-representation and is consequently far more persuasive.

The partiality of civic republican rhetoric and its consequent subjectivity are neatly illustrated by the figure of *subiectio* found in Book IV of the *Ad Herennium* and known by the Greeks as *hypophora*. Although cited as a figure of diction by the author of the *Ad Herennium,* Quintilian classified it as a figure of thought in his *Institutio Oratoria*.[26] In effect the orator who deploys this figure assumes both sides in a dispute and effectively denies his opponent a voice. For by speaking both parts the orator can effectively foreclose opposition by seemingly representing his adversary's point of view to his own advantage. This figure is commented upon in a number of the late medieval rhetorical texts, the definition found in the *Trattatello di colori rettorici* of the late 1320s being particularly concise: "Subiectio: this figure is used when you challenge an adversary and then assume his voice in anticipating his possible reply. Then without delay you supply your reasoned response in such a way that it supports your case and prejudices your adversary's."[27] This figure describes precisely the dynamics of the Ciceronian rhetorical paradigm. For it neatly embodies the ambivalence of subjectivity as not only self-referential, but also repressive discourse in the etymological sense of "sub iectio," meaning "to be thrown under." This is suitably illustrated in an early printed translation of the *Ad Herennium:* "*Subiectione* is when we ask our adversaries what they can say against us, and then put down and break *(sottomettendo e rompando)* the reply to our advantage."[28] Subjection, therefore, is premised on such rhetorical questions, properly understood, that foreclose the possibility of reply.

Conceived in these terms, Cicero's civic republican rhetoric was as exclusive as it was inclusive, for in defining the rational basis of republican community it simultaneously defines its limits and differentiation from the dissident Other as described by Cicero himself. As such it is fair to characterize the rhetoric of the *De Inventione* as simultaneously a rhetoric of dissensus and consensus, for it sought to stigmatize its opponents through vilification and displace them as inimical to the common good. It is no coincidence that it is in the *De Inventione* that the figure of the rhetorical tyrant makes its first appearance in classical Roman writing.[29]

The means whereby the rhetoric of civic republicanism secured its hegemonic status, therefore, could not be clearer, illustrating the crucial interrelationship between rhetoric, power, and place in the establishment of legitimacy. For although Ciceronian rhetoric was by definition controversial and adversarial, all three genres were designed for deployment within the legitimating structures of the state apparatus, from the law courts to the civic councils and the communal piazza.[30] In this respect the position of the exile was wholly other, for he was rhetorically silenced, politically stigmatized, and positionally displaced.

ADDRESSING EXILE: THE *ARS DICTAMINIS* AND MEDIEVAL CICERONIANISM

The influence of Ciceronian rhetoric on the precepts contained within the medieval instruction manuals concerning the composition of letters, the so-called *Ars dictaminis*, has long been acknowledged. Not surprisingly, therefore, such texts, and the collections of model letters often added as appendices, are largely silent concerning the political reality of exile.[31] This absence can be explained by the orientation of such instruction manuals, for they were overwhelmingly intended to address the needs of functionaries in the papal and imperial chanceries of medieval Italy and the executive arms of the increasingly bureaucratic civic communes. Directed toward those officials serving the commune's offices as clerks and communal officials, the intention was not to educate dissident voices to speak from beyond the confines of the commune but rather to ensure the eloquence of the communal voice in its dialogue with other powers and to maintain the security of the community as a whole. This perspective is confirmed in one of Guido Fava's dictaminal tracts of the mid-thirteenth century, the *Gemma purpurea,* in which the author states his intention to provide rhetorical instruction in order to "lift up the subjected, condemn the presumptuous, send the arrogant into exile, and belittle the lying sycophants."[32] Amongst rhetoric's functions, therefore, is the power to expel. Such a brief is apparent in one of the earliest *artes dictandi,* Hugh of Bologna's *Rationes dictandi* of 1119–24, which notes how Decretals, as an epistolary form, "expel beyond the limits of our empire rebels and infidels who disturb the peace."[33]

That exiles stood beyond the bounds of reasoned speech is also apparent from the discussions of the salutation found in many dictaminal works. The formal greeting with which a letter began was one of the most extensively glossed parts of the *Ars dictaminis* and subject of several tracts in its own right, for it not only set the tone of the subsequent letter through the decorous address of the recipient, but also maintained the rigid hierarchies of medieval social differentiation. In the *Candelabrum*, a dictaminal treatise by Bene da Firenze of the 1220s, the author defines the salutation as "the threshold of a letter" the word "salutatio" itself being a compound of "salutis" and "optatio," the infinitive "salutare" meaning "to wish the best of health."[34] Yet the address of those considered enemies was normally dealt with under a generic heading such as that found in Hugh of Bologna's *Rationes dictandi:* "In the eventuality that we should surrender to an enemy." Similarly, both Guido Fava's later *Summa dictaminis* and *Rota Nova* and Bene's *Candelabrum* contain sections dedicated to the address of Others, for example: "Concerning those persons who should not be addressed: note that excommunicates, Saracens, Jews or heretics, and those who belong to any sect whatsoever that does not recognize Catholic purity should not be greeted with respect."[35]

The identification of those excommunicated as outside the parameters of normal civil discourse assumes particular significance in the context of the bitter epistolary dispute between Frederick II and successive popes during the 1220s. For although the disputes lacked a territorial dimension, the ultimate sanction that resided with the pope was that of excommunicating the emperor, a symbolic form of exile from the spiritual community of Christians, an act of deselection from the elect. In this instance, it actually took place when Gregory IX excommunicated Frederick II in 1227. In fact it was in the course of the rhetorical jousting that characterized the epistolary conflict of the 1220s between the imperial and papal chanceries over jurisdictional sovereignty in Italy that the framework for the controversial communal rhetoric of the mid-Duecento onward was laid. During that decade, the oppositional nature of the disputes became far more accentuated as jurists replaced ecclesiastical officials in composing imperial correspondence, shifting the emphasis of their writings from the traditional dictaminal concerns with "dispositio," "elocutio," and the salutation to the more persuasive vehicles of "inventio," the narration, and the exordium.[36] In fact, it was in the 1220s that Bene da Firenze concluded the section on the salutation in his *Candelabrum* by noting that it had no place in Cicero's analysis of the parts of rhetoric, as the greeting was incompatible with the controversial nature of the Ciceronian rhetorical paradigm.[37]

The correlation between speech and exile articulated by Buoncompagno da Signa in his quixotic, but remarkable, *Rhetorica Novissima* of 1235 was based wholly on a Christian view of controversy as the destiny of the damned. The title playfully announced Boncompagno's intention to supplant Cicero's *Rhetorica Nova* with a more authoritative text of rhetorical instruction that he delivered to the bishop of Bologna and assembled clerics.[38] The author's utilitarian reduction of the parts of rhetoric to three, namely "causa," "persuasio," and "dissuasio," emphasized its applicability to the fractious arena of communal politics. In terms of our threefold definition of "parte," however, the locational sense is found in heaven and hell, the sense of "parte" as group embodied by the differentiation between the elect and the damned, and the argumentative "parte" by the litigious state of fallen man prior to the Day of Judgment, which Buoncompagno evocatively describes as the "final meeting" or "last discussion."[39] In condemning Satan to hell, the author notes, God will bring an end to contention and controversy as judge of all. Christianity, therefore, like Ciceronianism, is also presented as a discourse of exile with the redemptive hope of peace in the Kingdom of God. Prior to salvation, however, man was subject to Satan's persuasive skills, skills that secured him a following in his revolt against God and convinced Eve to taste the forbidden fruit. While the first resulted in the creation of law, the second saw the exile of mankind from the Garden of Eden.

It is in the early Italian commentaries of the *De Inventione* and the *Rhetorica ad Herennium*, however, that the agonistic and exclusive dimensions of the Ciceronian paradigm become fully apparent. In Bono Giamboni's redaction and partial translation of the *Rhetorica ad Herennium*, which went under the name *Fiore di Rettorica*, rhetorical precepts are entirely directed toward those within the legitimate discourse community. The only intimation of the political fact of exile arises in the section on the types of conclusion to a speech, where the citation of exile is recommended as a means of arousing the pity of an audience.[40] Yet it is in the writings of Brunetto Latini, communal chancellor during the ascendancy of the *Primo popolo* in Florence between 1250 and 1260, that the classical Ciceronian paradigm was most fully adopted and applied, in an elaborated form, to the political context of late medieval Florence.

LATINI'S ELABORATION OF THE
CICERONIAN PARADIGM

Both of Latini's classic texts were not only written during a period of enforced exile from Florence in the 1260s but also heavily dependent on
the Ciceronian rhetoric of the De Inventione. The two texts were the en-
cyclopedic Li Livres dou Tresor, which he almost immediately translated
into the volgare, and the Rettorica, a partial commentary of Cicero's De
Inventione based on a twelfth-century Latin gloss by Victorinus.[41] The
experience of exile was central to the production of both texts, for not
only did it provide the time to reflect and write, but it also provided an
opportunity for Latini to articulate a particular vision of the political life
that placed the effective regulation of language, both spoken and written,
at its very heart.[42] In both the Rettorica and the Tresor, Latini addresses
the controversial dimension of the Ciceronian paradigm and notes that
all the confrontational forms of rhetoric should be characterized by what
he terms tencione or tençon, translatable as dispute—as in the troubadour Tenso or debate poem.[43]

Yet the assumption is always that the speakers are inside, are members of the rhetorical community, and are using all the tools at their disposal to try and persuade their follow citizens of the rectitude of their
advice. The health of the collective can only be served by the vigor of its
verbal exchanges that ensured the moral probity and security of the material and linguistic commune. There is no sense in either the Tresor or
the Rettorica that rhetoric is a tool for use in arguing one's way back into
the city as place, especially when those occupying the city clearly do not
subscribe to the same vision of how it should be institutionally and ver-
bally constituted. This is borne out by Latini's definition of what he describes as the "material of the art of rhetoric" in the Rettorica, when he
illustrates its contestatory nature by considering the question of whether
or not Cicero should be exiled as a result of his actions during the time
of the Catiline conspiracy. Significantly, Latini's own partiality is demonstrated by his more fulsome exposition of the answer in the negative:
"He should not be exiled, for the citation of his name alone suggests
goodness while condemnation and exile are synonymous with badness
and it is not credible that a good man should act in a way that requires
he be condemned and sent into exile."[44] From the outset of the tract,
therefore, the differentiation is made between those who are worthy

of exclusion and those who are worthy of inclusion. Not surprisingly, Cicero's inclusion is secured on account of his ethos as virtuous citizen in the face of self-interested conspirators.

That the contestatory nature of the Ciceronian paradigm had no place for the exile is apparent from Latini's inability to successfully graft it onto the epistolary model of the *Ars dictaminis* in his *Rettorica*. Indeed, it has been argued that the noncompletion of the commentary was a consequence of his inability to reconcile the exclusively contestational Ciceronian model with the more broad-ranging *Ars dictaminis* tradition that encompassed the private realm of personal correspondence and friendship.[45] As a civic discourse, it had no place for the composition of the kind of consolation literature that exile itself provoked. Latini's rhetorical writings were solely addressed to those involved in the contestatory realm of communal politics rather than those removed from it.

For Latini, the symbolic construction of community, therefore, involved the marshaling of rhetoric, which was necessarily contentious, as a central part of the imagination of communal government as the preferred from of social ordering. This becomes clear when Latini, following Cicero, repeatedly asserts, in both the *Rettorica* and the *Tresor,* that the political life requires the management, "il reggimento," of words as well as deeds at both the individual and communal level. This privileging of speech by Latini's saw the promotion, following Victorinus, of rhetoric from an element of politics, according to Cicero, to its most important element.[46] For Latini's definition of politics was fundamentally premised upon the interdependence of social and linguistic composition, the "arte" understood as guilds combining with the rhetorical "arte" in the composition of communal government. As a result, the mercantile and verbal economies of his particular political vision were as one, bound into a process of exchange that was simultaneously linguistic and financial: "It is a natural thing for man to be a citizen and converse with other men and with other guildsmen."[47]

The commune, therefore, was envisaged as much as a speech community as a mercantile one, for in making the distinction between "detti" and "fatti" Latini accords the same importance to the social fabrication of community as he does to its linguistic imagination. In this sense verbal order was not just analogous to social order but homologous, as the designation of community actually constructed what it claimed to describe. Latini's belief in the transformative powers of rhetoric, therefore, clearly lay behind his rhetorical teachings, for by providing instruction in rhetoric as an "arte," or skill, he was seeking to make civil, or civilize, those whose speech was unruly, in the literal sense of without rules. That he achieved some success is witnessed by Villani's comments later in the Trecento that Latini "was the one who began to teach Florentines to be less coarse."[48]

Yet his originality lay in the elaboration of the preclusive and marginalizing dimension of the model. For, through the wholesale importation of Sallust into both the *Rettorica* and the *Tresor*, specifically the *Bellum Catilinae*, and through the translation into the *volgare* of Cicero's orations against Catiline, Latini found the immoral type to Cicero figured as the moral antitype. The Catiline described by Latini was noble, haughty, and proud, and supported by a circle of decadent young men resentful of the preeminence of Rome's new men as embodied by Cicero himself.[49] The applicability of the political conflict between Cicero and Catiline in Republican Rome to the cultural habitus of late medieval Florence allowed Latini to identify himself with Cicero the orator-statesman in an unprecedented manner, even acknowledging him as coauthor of his *Rettorica:* "This work has two authors."[50] His opponents, the recalcitrant noble families, on the other hand, clearly conformed in his eyes with Catiline and his circle.

The parallels with Catiline, therefore, furnished Latini with a classical example of the threat posed to republican liberty by would-be rhetorical tyrants. At the same time, in his guise as Other, Catiline was instrumental in Cicero's, and by default Latini's, self-fashioning as a virtuous patriot.[51] Where the Cicero of the *De Inventione* had no interlocutor to speak the "other part," in Catiline Latini found an eloquent opponent to assume the morally corrupt argumentative position. Not only was Catiline cast in this role in both the *Rettorica* and the *Tresor*, but by translating all of the set-piece speeches connected with the Catiline revolt, Latini established a rhetorical tradition that evolved from the late Trecento onward in the city's schoolrooms and saw students learning to argue "in utramque partem" through the assumption of the opposing positions of Cicero and Catiline or the contrasting advice of Caesar and Cato on how to proceed against the conspirators.[52] The morality of civic republicanism was thereby inculcated in the rhetorical pedagogy of young patrician Florentines, further implanting the polarizing Ciceronian paradigm into the collective subconscious of the ruling elite, for the teaching of ordered syntax and grammar simultaneously furnished education in the syntax of government thereby strengthening the reciprocal relationship between ordered speech and ordered life.

Latini's fascination with Catiline, therefore, constructed him as the dissident Other who was both a source of fascination and a danger, and revealed more concerning the fears and anxieties of Florentines than it did about the figure himself.[53] By clarifying the boundaries of the Ciceronian paradigm, Latini provided no instruction in arguing one's way back into the city as place, especially when those occupying the city did not subscribe to the same political vision. Rather he enhanced the agonistic dimension of the model.

In terms of the Ciceronian paradigm, therefore, Latini assumed the morally virtuous "parte" in terms of his argumentative position. He too saw himself as addressing the damage caused to the commune by "men who speak at length without wisdom."[54] Yet in terms of the remaining two senses of "parte," Latini's was an exile voice, distanced from the legitimating structures of communal government that he had previously occupied, while politically, his particular vision of social ordering was a manifesto of the *Primo popolo* whose political program was far from hegemonic in a city plagued by the dynastic violence of the Florentine aristocratic consular class. Latini's hopes of persuading a fractious aristocracy to subordinate their familial identities to that of a popular commune and join the debates of a guild-based deliberative form of republican government reflect the consensual and cohesive dimension of the Ciceronian paradigm, while retaining its marginalizing dimension. Significantly, with the Ordinances of Justice first promulgated in 1293 by the popular Priorate, many Florentine knights designated as Magnates were indeed exiled.[55]

SEEKING REENTRY:
INTERNAL AND EXTERNAL VOICES

It would be untrue to suggest that those exiled were wholly silenced. While the Ciceronian paradigm outlined in the *De Inventione* was effective in stigmatizing the excluded as factious Catilines, there was nothing stopping the excluded from seeking to persuade possible arbitrators to intercede on their behalf. They themselves might be silenced, but other legitimate interlocutors could assume their voice in pleading for their repatriation, usually a higher power such as the pope, Holy Roman Emperor, or podestà.[56] In the collections of exemplary set-piece speeches that constituted the *ars aringandi* of the Trecento, there are several models that granted a voice to the excluded. What is striking, however, is the amoral nature of the rhetorical models provided and their lack of specificity regarding the ethical status of the relative interlocutors. While clearly political in seeking to effect a return to the polis for those who had been driven out or banned, there is no judgment made concerning the virtue or otherwise of either the exiles or the exilers. One set-piece oration in Matteo dei Libri's *Arringhe,* which is also found in modified form in both Giovanni da Vignano's *Flore de Parlare* and the *Dicerie* of Filippo Ceffi, involves a petition to the pope for help and advice on the part of a faction driven from their homes by the treachery and duplicity of their fellow citizens. In a telling addition to the introductory rubric, the author adds: "And a prudent orator is also able to speak in the same way when addressing the emperor or a king, subject to a few minor changes as the situation demands."[57] In adapted form, the refashioned speech could serve any excluded constituency irrespective of allegiance. The anxiety generated by an upheaval in a neighboring power is apparent in another of the model orations entitled: "How one should reply when a commune complains about internal division or being driven from an ally's territory."[58] In this instance rhetoric is deployed as an instrument of pacification and reconciliation, although the offer by the neighboring power to act as arbiter is clearly self-interested.

While the *ars aringandi* tracts bear testimony to the perceived efficacy of rhetoric, none of the models addresses a scenario whereby the excluded can petition those responsible for the initial ban, namely the civic councils of the home city. For one of the rhetorical consequences of the transition from podestaral communes to self-determining popular government was the reconfiguration of the relative positions of addresser and addressee as the podestà's role was downgraded from judge and arbitrator in all matters concerning the peace and tranquility of the commune to a more narrowly defined judicial role. The kind of petitioning speeches found in the *ars aringandi* collations were no longer appropriate to the political situation of Florence in the latter part of the Trecento. For there was no process or place within governmental procedures whereby those excluded could formally appeal and argue their way back to the center. They were dependent upon petitioners who remained within the legitimating structures of the commune.

This is dramatically illustrated in a mid-fourteenth-century *volgare* paraphrase of the more ethically indeterminate pseudo-Ciceronian *Rhetorica ad Herennium*. In the section dedicated to the genre of deliberative rhetoric, the anonymous translator illustrates the opposing positions that can be assumed in addressing the issue of the right action to take according to the dictates of virtue by supplying two complete model orations under the heading: "Concerning the making of peace with rebels and their reintegration into the city." The orations themselves are entitled "The person not desirous of peace with the rebels could speak as follows" and "As for the person who desires peace, he could respond as follows."[59] Both speeches move through the four cardinal virtues in espousing their opposing views regarding the right course of action to take for the good of the commune. Neither position is granted moral superiority, and the eventual decision was clearly a matter for the civic council in which the imaginary interlocutors spoke.

As the Florentine elite secured its hegemonic status in the latter part of the Trecento, however, mass exile was increasingly rare, and the marginalization of specific families, or parts thereof, reflected struggles within the elite itself. In this context the Ciceronian paradigm assumed renewed significance. Whereas for Latini the threat came from overbearing aristocrats and knights, some hundred years later the paradigm helped stigmatize those who generated suspicion on account of their perceived signorial tendencies. The clearest example of this phenomenon, and the continued significance of the three meanings of "parte" as place, party, and argumentative position, is found in the controversial exile of the Florentine patrician Donato Acciaiuoli in 1396 for conspiracy to overthrow the republic.

What is remarkable in this instance is that the arguments of both sides are still extant and contained in the correspondence between Acciaiuoli as exile in Puglia, and the signoria in Florence as transcribed into an anonymous diary of 1382–1401.[60] Although letters rather than speeches, the epistolary dispute harks back to the *Ars dictaminis* tradition in seeing letters as the speeches of those unable to be present.[61] Indeed, the epistolary form of the dispute can be seen as a function of the physical distancing enforced by exile as Acciaiuoli by definition was unable to be present. While the letter allowed him to petition from a distance, it

was precisely that distance that put him at a distinct disadvantage in seeking to establish the legitimacy of his case. A comparative reading illustrates perfectly the threefold meaning of the term "parte," Acciaiuoli's
status as a man of considerable learning and a powerful orator figuring
him as a dangerous adversary for the incumbent priors and communal
officials of the Florentine Chancery.

Those who had initially sought his execution were argued down in a
communal meeting, or *pratica*, of 11 January 1396 on account of the credentials of his family, "given that his ancestors had been ardent Guelfs
and lovers of this city." When Donato himself appeared before the *pratica*
he reportedly bowed before the priors, "and with this gesture he delivered
a fine speech, citing certain Psalms of David and referring to his father
and grandfather who had been champions of the city of Florence and the
Parte Guelfa."[62] In the correspondence he subsequently sent from Puglia
after his exile, Acciaiuoli claimed that the confession he made to the priors
before being exiled was forced upon him by circumstance. Threatened
with the possibility of death, he claimed, he accepted exile as the lesser of
two evils, a classic example of the deliberative form of (self-)counseling:
"What is the best course of action?"[63] His own preoccupation, however,
and the reason for the letter, was that any form of redress for the wrong
done to him would be impossible given that his friends and fellow citizens would be circumspect in speaking out in favor of an exile, however
worthy his case:

> Signori, if it were possible for somebody to come before you
> and present my case without fear of being suspected, many peo-
> ple would present themselves to you with the most just petitions.
> However, fear and previous examples render this wholly incon-
> ceivable. As a result, I am forced to write this long letter to you
> concerning my case.[64]

He continued by reasserting his credentials as a "citizen most faithful to
the *Popolo* and Guelf cause, and desirous of both the commune's well-
being and liberty." In the concluding paragraph he emphasizes his allegiance to the commune, depicting himself as one of many true citizens
who were suffering at the hands of a self-interested clique: "For I am not
offended by either the Commune or the opinions of the people, but I am
offended, like many others, by the self-interest of those who hold sway

and power through their dissembling lies and slanderous falsehoods, their jealous thoughts conceived in hard hearts, and their dishonest ways."[65]

The signoria's response illustrated their proprietorship of the civic and moral high ground as they deployed arguments drawn from the virtue of temperance ("Come si può consigliare per via di misura") to condemn Donato's actions as destabilizing of the established order and manifesting excessive greed for power.[66] This is described in spatial terms that clearly illustrate the correlation between morality and visibility. He held discussions in private to achieve his ends, while publicly he had confessed his errors. He sought to "destroy the Guelf constitution... with private and clandestine discussions" and "change everything secretly, not publicly." In an attack on his oratorical prowess, they stated that his desire to secure himself "a larger share of public government than had been instituted and agreed" was never the act of a good citizen, "no matter how great his eloquence." Finally they cite Donato's own words in his confession, "we use his own words," to conclude their case. The veracity of his confession is secured through its inscription by the senior civil servant of the *res pubblica,*

> And maybe he [Acciaiuoli] has also forgotten that he himself freely confessed everything to both our Chancellor, who makes a written record of all things, and to the judge of the Capitano del popolo. Similarly, his procurator, who was specifically appointed according to the standard procedures, confessed all when appearing before the court.[67]

What these testimonies illustrate is the threefold sense of "parte" as discussed above. Both sides seemingly considered themselves as operating in the public interest, while their opponents were factious, self-seeking, and subversive. Both deployed the normative discourse of civic republicanism and the terminology of citizenship and liberty to legitimate their actions. Yet it was Acciaiuoli who had to refrain from overtly describing the incumbent regime as factious, preferring to characterize his persecutors as a nameless and mysterious group. In terms of "parte" understood as place, it was Acciaiuoli's status as exile, displaced citizen, that prejudiced his chances of receiving a fair hearing. The Republic, personified by the priors, granted legitimacy, and with occupancy of the moral high ground came control over the reading of others' actions and words. Accordingly, it would seem, the "reggimento" always enjoyed a distinct advantage in defining the limits of community and controlling its representation.

Conclusion

To date, the discourse of civic republicanism has chosen to concentrate its attention almost exclusively on the consensual. This was clearly the orientation of Hans Baron nearly fifty years ago when developing his thesis concerning the emergence of what he termed "civic humanism."[68] Yet his contention that the threat posed to Florentine liberty by the duke of Milan at the end of the fourteenth and early fifteenth centuries was the catalyst for the production of an unprecedented quantity of patriotic literature by the Florentine humanists identifies the rhetoric of "civic humanism" solely as a response to a threatened breach of its physical boundaries from outside. Baron's thesis, therefore, stressed the rhetorical reinforcing of the commune's symbolic boundaries through the restating of the values of communal government aided by a more extensive exploitation of the ancient sources then available. Deploying these authoritative voices, Florentine humanists were able to more clearly identify the moral rectitude of their own governmental form through the stigmatization of the Milanese "tyrants" and the launching of invectives against their mendacious humanist apologists.

Yet where Baron's humanists were inside looking out, the current study assumes the subject position of those former citizens on the outside looking back in. From this perspective, exile functions as a heuristic device in focusing attention on both the commune's material boundaries and the limits of its rhetorical imaginings. In focusing on who it was deemed necessary to throw out, rather than keep out, it demonstrates how the imagined commune was also defined through difference in identifying the enemy within. In the terms of the body politic analogy those parts not considered to be working "in comune" were to be cut off and removed, or in the words of the Trecento chronicles, "scomunato." Whether inside looking out or outside looking in, both viewpoints were fundamentally concerned with describing and maintaining the symbolic boundaries that defined the republican body politic and ensured it remained unmolested and free of infection.[69]

One of the aims of the present study, therefore, has been to suggest that there was always an oppressive dimension to civic republicanism, for the establishment of hegemony necessarily entails both persuasion and coercion. In this respect, exile was a violent act of separation that involved both a spatial and a verbal displacement. In the process of suppressing dissident voices, exile simultaneously revealed aspects of the cultural geography of rhetoric and its privileging of certain sites of authoritative discourse and the manner in which the exile remained without a legitimate platform from which to challenge the prevailing vision of social order or challenge the legitimacy of those occupying the center.[70]

The voices of exile found in both exile lyric and the literature of consolation, therefore, can be read as a function of the limits of the Ciceronian paradigm described above as simultaneously an inclusive and exclusive rhetoric. Excluded from their homes, exiles became citizens of the world; deprived of political involvement, they enjoyed the peace of the *vita contemplativa;* victims of adverse fortune, they learned the lessons of Stoic patience. Rhetorically, however, there was no model to imitate that would secure their repatriation and political re-placement. While invective presented them with the chance to vent their frustration, it also reduced the chances of possible return. It was no coincidence that the best chance of repatriation lay in private diplomacy and clientage, the very practices derided by civic republican discourse as inimical to the well-being of the republic. The only other hope lay in the mutability of fortune, a subject that remained a continuing preoccupation of the period.[71]

It was only toward the end of the Florentine republican experience, when Machiavelli wrote his *Discourses on Livy,* that civic republican discourse found a spokesperson that espoused a more optimistic reading of difference as a celebration of diversity and pluralism. For Machiavelli, Republican Rome provided the ideal model of an expanding political form that embraced difference and the inevitable political conflict that came with it. Machiavelli contrasts this vision of Rome with the static, and racially exclusive, Spartan republic, whose glory never matched that of the Romans' on account of their exclusive constitution. In his view, Rome the mongrel nation was far greater than Sparta the pedigree state. In his own day, Venice may well have been serene but she could never be as glorious as a community that expanded and embraced difference with all its concomitant tensions.[72] That such arguments were themselves a product of his self-imposed exile and the failure of his attempt to write his way back to the center through the agency of *The Prince* would have been an irony not lost on the "quondam" secretary.[73] It should be noted, however, that it was in the very process of accommodating diversity that the Roman republic contained cultural difference.[74]

It is my contention, therefore, that exile was a precondition of the formation of popular communal identity, especially in republican Florence. While those positively identified as threats to the established order were expelled, those negatively identified remained citizens in the broadest sense. In place of discussions of positive and negative liberty, therefore, I propose a typological model of citizenship that configures the exile as type to the citizen as antitype. The question is no longer who is active and who is passive in the governmental process, but who is inside and who is outside the linguistic and ritual community. Citizenship understood in this broader sense opens up the possibility of moving away from a historiography that concentrates on the exclusivity of the legal terms of citizenship or the precise identification of the patrician elite to a celebration of the multiple identities such communes accommodated and the manner in which civic participation encompasses far more activities than mere office holding.[75]

In the context of continuing debates concerning the durability of civic republicanism, such a reading might also identify the cultural source of the "grammar of hostility" and "impulse towards polarization" that has become such a concern in debates over the fragmentation of community in contemporary America.[76] Similarly, it might also focus renewed attention on the means whereby the stereotyping of a threatening Other, whether it be a dissident Catiline, a serpentine duke of Milan, or dark forces from the East, serve to reinforce the boundaries of republican polities and thereby imagine them as communities.

NOTES

1. The bibliography is vast, but the following major studies may serve as a point of departure for further reading. On the politics of exile, see Christine Shaw, *The Politics of Exile in Renaissance Italy* (Cambridge: Cambridge University Press, 2000); Jacques Heers and Christian Bec, *Exil et civilisation en Italie (XIIe–XVIe siècles)* (Nancy: Presses Universitaires de Nancy, 1990); Jacques Heers, *L'esilio, la vita politica e la società nel medioevo* (Naples: Liguori, 1997); and Randolph Starn, *Contrary Commonwealth: The Theme of Exile in Medieval and Renaissance Italy* (Berkeley: University of California Press, 1982). The pro-

ceedings of a conferences held in Aix-en-Provence in 1989 were published as Georges Ulysse, ed., *L'Exil et l'exclusion dans la culture italienne: Actes du colloque franco-italien, Aix-en-Provence, 19–21 octobre 1989* (Aix-en-Provence: Publications de l'Université de Provence, 1991), and exile was the theme of the International Medieval Congress 2002 at the University of Leeds, some of the papers of which will be published as Laura Napran and Elisabeth van Houts, eds., *Exile in the Middle Ages: Selected Proceedings from the International Medieval Congress, University of Leeds 8–11 July 2002*, International Medieval Research 13 (Turnhout: Brepols, forthcoming). On the literature of exile, see Jo-Marie Claassen, *Displaced Persons: The Literature of Exile from Cicero to Boethius* (London: Duckworth, 1999); Marià-Inés Lagos-Pope, ed., *Exile in Literature* (Lewisburg: Bucknell University Press, 1988); and Angelo Bartlett Giamatti, *Exile and Change in Renaissance Literature* (New Haven: Yale University Press, 1984). On exile literature from a postmodern perspective, see the essays in Elazar Barkan and Marie-Denise Shelton, eds., *Borders, Exiles, Diasporas* (Stanford: Stanford University Press, 1998).

2. María Rosa Menocal, *Shards of Love: Exile and the Origin of the Lyric* (Durham: Duke University Press, 1994); Catherine Keen, "Images of Exile: Distance and Memory in the Poetry of Cino da Pistoia," *Italian Studies* 55 (2000): 21–36; and Corrado Calenda, "'Esilio' ed 'esclusione' tra biografismo e mentalità collettiva: Brunetto Latini, Guittone d'Arezzo, Guido Cavalcanti," in Ulysse, *L'Exil et l'exclusion*, 41–47.

3. Edward Said, "The Mind of Winter," *Harper's*, September 1985, 50.

4. Philip Jones, *The Italian City-State: From Commune to Signoria* (Oxford: Clarendon Press, 1997); and Daniel Waley, *The Italian City-Republics*, 3rd ed. (Harlow: Longman, 1988).

5. Although a history of Florentine exiles remains to be written, the studies of Gene Brucker, *Florentine Politics and Society 1343–1378* (Princeton: Princeton University Press, 1962), *The Civic World of Early Renaissance Florence* (Princeton: Princeton University Press, 1977), and, together with Dale V. Kent, *The Rise of the Medici: Faction in Florence 1426–1434* (Oxford: Oxford University Press, 1978), contain extensive treatment of exile in their respective periods. Since the writing of this chapter Alison Brown has charted the exits and entrances of Florentine Republican exiles in graphic form in her piece "Insiders and Outsiders: The Changing Boundaries of Exile," in *Society and the Individual in Renaissance Florence*, ed. William J. Connell, 337–83 (Berkeley: University of California Press, 2002). Numerous studies have appeared relative to the exile experience of particular Florentine patrician households, especially in the Quattrocento. See, for example, Susan F. Baxendale, "Exile in Practice: The Alberti Family In and Out of Florence 1401–1428," *Renaissance Quarterly* 44 (1991): 720–56; and Dale V. Kent, "I Medici in esilio: Una vittoria di famiglia ed una disfatta personale," *Archivio storico italiano* 132 (1974): 3–63.

6. This tradition stretches from the classic study of Hans Baron, *The Crisis of the Early Italian Renaissance: Civic Humanism and Republican Liberty in an Age of Classicism and Tyranny*, 2 vols. (Princeton: Princeton University Press, 1955), via the work of Felix Gilbert, Charles Davies, John G. A. Pocock, and more recently Quentin Skinner. Given the latter's influence on the republican thesis, see Quentin Skinner, "The Vocabulary of Renaissance Republicanism: A Cultural longue durée?" in *Language and Images of Renaissance Italy*, ed. Alison Brown, 87–110 (Oxford: Blackwells, 1995), and Skinner, "Machiavelli's *Discorsi* and the Pre-humanist Origins of Republican Ideas," in *Machiavelli and Republi-*

canism, ed. Gisela Bock, Quentin Skinner, and Maurizio Viroli, 121–41 (Cambridge: Cambridge University Press, 1990). Recent assessments of Baron's thesis have remained largely within the same analytical framework. See Arthur Rabil Jr., "The Significance of 'Civic Humanism' in the Interpretation of the Italian Renaissance," in Renaissance Humanism: Foundations, Forms, and Legacy, ed. Arthur Rabil Jr., 3 vols., 1:141–74 (Philadelphia: University of Pennsylvania Press, 1988); and Ronald Witt, "The Crisis after Forty Years," American Historical Review 101 (1996): 110–18. Unease with this prevailing model is apparent in the various contributions contained in James Hankins, ed., Renaissance Civic Humanism: Reappraisals and Reflections (Cambridge: Cambridge University Press, 2000), although no alternative model is proposed. In the context of the current study, however, see especially Alison Brown, "De-masking Renaissance Republicanism," 179–99. For the endurance of the civic republican thesis, see Adrian Oldfield, Citizenship and Community: Civic Republicanism and the Modern World (London: Routledge, 1990).

   7. See Stephen J. Milner, "Communication, Consensus and Conflict: Rhetorical Principles, the ars concionandi and Social Ordering in Late Medieval Italy," in The Rhetoric of Cicero in its Medieval and Renaissance Commentary Tradition, ed. Virginia Cox and John O. Ward (Leiden: Brill, forthcoming).

   8. For theoretical discussions of identity and the Other, see the essays collected in Jonathan Rutherford, ed., Identity: Community, Culture, Difference (London: Lawrence & Wishart, 1990); Stuart Hall, "The Spectacle of the 'Other,'" in Representation: Cultural Representation and Signifying Practices, ed. Stuart Hall, 223–79 (London: Sage, 1997); and Kathryn Woodward, ed., Identity and Difference (London: Sage, 1997). On the centrality of boundary to any conceptualization of community, see Anthony P. Cohen, The Symbolic Construction of Community (London: Routledge, 1985).

   9. The concept of the "imagined community" is borrowed from Benedict Anderson, Imagined Communities: Reflections on the Origin and Spread of Nationalism (London: Verso, 1983). Anderson states (p. 15) that a political community "is imagined because the members of even the smallest nation will never know most of their fellow-members, meet them, or even hear of them, yet in the minds of each lives the image of their communion." The current chapter can be seen as an extension of his analysis to a consideration of the role of rhetoric in the process of imagining premodern states. The "limits" in the chapter's title refer to Anderson's contention (p. 16) that all nations are inherently limited "because even the largest of them . . . has finite, if elastic boundaries, beyond which lie other nations. No nation imagines itself coterminous with mankind." While his observations are applicable to the premodern Florentine republic intolerant of difference, they have themselves been seen as overly prescriptive in describing the limits of the modern Western nation. See Homi K. Bhabha, "DissemiNation: Time, Narrative and the Margins of the Modern Nation," in Nation and Narration, ed. Homi K. Bhabha, 291–322 (London: Routledge, 1990). On the continuing debate amongst political philosophers concerning the limits of contemporary democratic states, see the essays collected in Ian Shapiro and Casiano Hacker-Cordón, eds., Democracy's Edges (Cambridge: Cambridge University Press, 1999).

   10. The renaissance of rhetoric in this period has been the subject of considerable study, although the majority of attention has been focused on its revival as a stylistic pro-

gram that saw its apotheosis in the pure Ciceronian style of Leonardo Bruni. See Ronald Witt, *In the Footsteps of the Ancients: The Origins of Humanism from Lovato to Bruni* (Leiden: Brill, 2000); and Witt, "Medieval Italian Culture and the Origins of Humanism as a Stylistic Ideal," in Rabil, *Renaissance Humanism*, 1:29–70. The predominantly philosophical orientation of scholars of humanism has resulted in the pejorative description of "mere rhetoric" as the medium of opinion that, in its insincerity, has no regard for truth. For example, see Paul O. Kristeller, *Renaissance Thought and Its Sources* (New York: Columbia University Press, 1979), 258: "Rhetoric in all its forms is based on mere opinion, and therefore it should be subordinated to philosophy."

    11. See the essays collected in Thomas Rosteck, ed., *At the Intersection: Cultural Studies and Rhetorical Studies* (New York: Guilford Press, 1999); and Walter Jost and Michael Hyde, eds., *Rhetoric and Hermeneutics in Our Time* (New Haven: Yale University Press, 1997); and see also John Hartley, "Rhetoric," in *Key Concepts in Communication and Cultural Studies*, ed. Tim O' Sullivan, John Hartley, Danny Saunders, Martin Montgomery, and John Fisk, 2nd ed. (New York: Routledge, 1994), 266–67.

    12. For a case study, see Stephen J. Milner, "The Florentine *Piazza della Signoria* as Practiced Place," in *Florence: the Dynamics of Space in the Renaissance City*, ed. Roger J. Crum and John Paoletti (Cambridge: Cambridge University Press, forthcoming).

    13. On Athens and Lucca, see Richard Sennett, *Flesh and Stone: The Body and the City in Western Civilization* (London: Routledge, 1994), 55; and Niccolò Machiavelli, "Sommario del governo della città di Lucca," in *Opere minori di Niccolò Machiavelli*, ed. Filippo Polidori (Florence, 1852), 231–37. The first use of the law seems to date back to 1482 when four individuals were expelled. See Archivio di Stato di Lucca, *Consiglio Generale: Riformagioni pubbliche*, 21, fols. 186r–187v, 31 July 1482. For a discussion of the anxiety of contamination as a function of cultural identity, see Mary Douglas, *Purity and Danger: An Analysis of Concepts of Pollution and Taboo* (repr. London: Routledge, 1995 [1966]), 30–41.

    14. See the discussion concerning the legal status of the so-called "maior pars" in Joseph Canning, *The Political Thought of Baldus de Ubaldis* (Cambridge: Cambridge University Press, 1987), 153–54. More generally, see Diego Quaglioni, "'Civitas': Appunti per una riflessione sull'idea di città nel pensiero politico dei giuristi medievali," in *Le ideologie della città europea: Dall'Umanesimo al Romanticismo*, ed. Vittorio Conti, 59–76 (Florence: Olschki, 1993).

    15. Cited in Joseph Canning, "The Corporation in the Political Thought of the Italian Jurists of the Thirteenth and Fourteenth Centuries," *History of Political Thought* 1 (1980): 23: "Et concedo quod iurisdictio remanet penes intrinsecos, quia coheret territorio, et intrinseci possident territorium. Item intrinseci sunt universi, et expulsi sunt singuli." See also Canning, *Political Thought of Baldus*, 127–31.

    16. For a discussion of the differentiation between the symbolic and material body of the *Corpus reipublicae mysticum*, see Ernst H. Kantorowicz, *The King's Two Bodies: A Study in Medieval Political Theology* (Princeton: Princeton University Press, 1957), 207–32. Isidore of Seville in his *Etymologiae*, ed. Friedrich Lindemann (Lipsiae: B. G. Teubner and F. Claudii, 1833), Bk. 15, 2, 1, defined the city as follows: "civitas non saxa sed habitatores vocantur."

    17. See Brunetto Latini, *La Rettorica*, ed. Francesco Maggini (Florence: Le Monnier,

1968), 13: "Che è cittade.—Cittade èe uno raunamento di gente fatto per vivere a ragione; onde non sono detti cittadini d'uno medesimo comune perché siano insieme accolti dentro ad uno muro, ma quelli che insieme sono acolti a vivere ad una ragione."

18. See John O. Ward, "From Antiquity to the Renaissance: Glosses and Commentaries on Cicero's *Rhetorica,*" in *Medieval Eloquence: Studies in the Theory and Practice of Medieval Rhetoric,* ed. James J. Murphy, 25–68 (Berkeley: University of California Press, 1978); and Ward, *Ciceronian Rhetoric in Treatise, Scholion and Commentary,* Typologie des sources du Moyen Âge occidental 58 (Turnhout: Brepols, 1995). See also Karin Margareta Fredborg, "Twelfth-Century Ciceronian Rhetoric: Its Doctrinal Development and Influences," in *Rhetoric Revalued,* ed. Brian Vickers, 87–97 (Binghamton: Medieval and Renaissance Texts and Studies, 1982); and Mary Dickey, "Some Commentaries on the *De Inventione* and *Ad Herennium* of the Eleventh and Early Twelfth Centuries," *Medieval and Renaissance Studies* 6 (1968): 1–41. A comprehensive examination of the tradition is planned in the forthcoming volume edited by Cox and Ward, *Rhetoric of Cicero.* On the centrality of the *De Inventione* in the medieval curriculum, see Martin Camargo, "Rhetoric," in *The Seven Liberal Arts in the Middle Ages,* ed. David L. Wagner, 96–124 (Bloomington: Indiana University Press, 1983).

19. Cicero, *De Inventione,* ed. and trans. Harry M. Hubbell (Cambridge: Harvard University Press, 1949), Bk. I, i.2–3, pp. 4–8.

20. On the contestational dimension of medieval Ciceronian rhetoric, see Virginia Cox, "Ciceronian Rhetoric in Italy, 1260–1350," *Rhetorica* 17 (1999): 239–88.

21. Cicero, *De Inventione,* Bk. I, viii.10, p. 20.

22. [Cicero], *Ad C. Herennium: De Ratione Dicendi,* ed. and trans. Harry Caplan (Cambridge: Harvard University Press, 1964), Bk. I, ii.2, p. 4.

23. This is the principal thesis of Victoria Kahn, *Rhetoric, Prudence and Skepticism in the Renaissance* (Ithaca: Cornell University Press, 1985). On deliberative democracy, see, for example, Joshua Cohen, "Deliberation and Democratic Legitimacy," in *The Good Polity: Normative Analysis of the State,* ed. Alan Hamlin and Philip Pettit, 17–34 (Oxford: Blackwell, 1989).

24. See Sarah Spence, "Rhetoric and Hermeneutics," in *The Troubadours: An Introduction,* ed. Simon Gaunt and Sarah Kay, 164–80 (Cambridge: Cambridge University Press, 1999); Linda M. Paterson, *Troubadours and Eloquence* (Oxford: Clarendon Press, 1975); and Nathaniel Smith, "Rhetoric," in *A Handbook of the Troubadours,* ed. F. R. P. Akehurst and Judith Davies (Berkeley: University of California Press, 1995). On the *Ars dictaminis,* see the survey of Martin Camargo, *Ars dictaminis Ars dictandi,* Typologie des sources du Moyen Âge occidental 60 (Turnhout: Brepols, 1991).

25. Cicero, *De Inventione,* Bk. I, iii.4–5, pp. 8–11.

26. [Cicero], *Ad C. Herennium,* Bk. IV, xxiii.33, pp. 310–15, and Quintilian, *Institutio Oratoria,* ed. and trans. Harold E. Butler, 4 vols. (Cambridge: Harvard University Press, 1920–22), 3:502.

27. See Antonio Scolari, "Un volgarizzamento trecentesco della *Rhetorica ad Herennium:* Il *Trattatello di colori rettorici,*" *Medioevo romanzo* 9 (1984), 249: "Subiectio: questo colore si manifesta quando tu domandi l'aversario e di' quello aállui ch' elli ti potrebe rispon-

dere, poi tu sanza indugio rispondendo rendi ragione, la quale conseguita la tua causa e pregiudica alla sua." For another discussion of this figure, see Bene Florentini, *Candelabrum*, ed. Gian Carlo Alessio (Padua: Antenore, 1983), Bk. II, 20, pp. 52–53.

28. See *Rhetorica Nova de Marcho Tullio Cicerone vulgarizata novamente* (Venice: Iacobo di Penci da Lecco, 1502), Bk. IV, 20, p. 55: "Subiectione e quando noi domandemo li adversarii quello che loro possano dire contra noi sottomettendo e rompando quello e redugando in nostro favore."

29. See J. Roger Dunkle, "The Rhetorical Tyrant in Roman Historiography: Sallust, Livy and Tacitus," *Classical World* 65 (1971): 12–20.

30. For a consideration of forms of resistance to oligarchic representational practices, including rhetorical ones, as exercised in the piazza, see Milner, "The Florentine *Piazza*."

31. Of the 220 model *exordia* contained in Guido Faba's *Dictamina rhetorica*, none provides a model address for an exile. A model opening for a letter of consolation upon a death is included, but none for exile. See "Guidonis Fabe, *Dictamina Rhetorica*," ed. Augusto Gaudenzi, *Il Propugnatore*, n.s., 5 (1892): i, 86–129, and ii, 58–109. The same is true for the 355 epistolary *exordia* furnished in Matteo de' Libri's *Summa artis dictaminis* of the later Duecento. See Paul O. Kristeller, "Matteo de' Libri, Bolognese Notary of the Thirteenth Century and His *Artes Dictaminis*," *Fontes Ambrosiani* 26 (1951): 283–320.

32. Arrigo Castellani, "Le formule volgari di Guido Faba," *Studi di filologia italiana* 13 (1955): 24: "Volens quidem facilem prebere assensum peticionibus equitatis, confracta consolido, abiecta sublevo et omnes presumptores condempno, arrogantes mitto in exilium, adulatores falsitatis relego et omnes proscribo inanis glorie amatores, litteratis artius iniungendo."

33. Hugh of Bologna, *Rationes dictandi*, in *Briefsteller und Formelbücher des eilften bis vierzehnten Jahrhunderts*, ed. Ludwig Rockinger, 9 vols., Quellen und Erörterungen zur bayerischen und deutschen Geschichte (Munich: Scientia Verlag Aalen, 1863–64; repr. 1969), 1:77: "rebelles et infideles pacem inquietantes a nostri finibus imperii expellant."

34. Bene Florentini, *Candelabrum*, Bk. III, 6–9, p. 95: "Salutatio est limen epistole."

35. See Hugh of Bologna, *Rationes dictandi*, 67–68. On Faba, see "Guidonis Fabe, *Summa dictamini*," ed. Augusto Gaudenzi, *Il Propugnatore*, n.s., 3 (1890), 327: "Que persone non debeant salutari: Item nota quod non salutantur excommunicati, Saraceni, Iudei, vel Patareni, cuiuscumque secte fuerint dum tamen Catholicam non sapiant puritatem." The *Rota Nova* reference is quoted in A. P. Campbell, "The Perfection of Ars Dictaminis in Guido Faba," *Revue de l'Université d'Ottawa* 39 (1969): 316: "Qui non debeant salutari: Item, nota quod non salutantur excommunicati, Saraceni, patareni, Iudei, sed dicitur 'spem consilii sanioris.'" Bene da Firenze furnishes a number of sample openings for letters destined to those unworthy of our affections in *Candelabrum*, Bk. III, 45: "De indignis, hostibus et excommunicatis," 121–22.

36. See Laurie Shepherd, *Courting Power: Persuasion and Politics in the Early Thirteenth Century* (New York: Garland, 1999), 137–56; and Nicolai Rubinstein, "Political Rhetoric in the Imperial Chancery during the Twelfth and Thirteenth Centuries," *Medium Aevum* 14 (1945): 22–43.

37. Bene Florentini, *Candelabrum*, Bk. III, 55, p. 128: "Ipse [Tullius] autem de solis perfectis partibus orationis tractabat vel ideo fecit quia salutatio locum in controversiis non habet ad quas ipse totam rethoricam reducebat."

38. Boncompagni da Signa, *Rhetorica Novissima*, ed. Augusto Gaudenzi, in *Bibliotheca Iuridica Medii Aevi*, 3 vols., 2:249–97 (Bologna: Piero Virano, 1892). Delivered (p. 259) "in presentia venerabilis patris Henrici Bononiensis episcopi," the religious orientation of elements of the tract were clearly a function of the audience.

39. Ibid., 297: "Postmodum vero ipse Dei filius in ultimi iudicii contione terribilis apparebit."

40. Bono Giamboni, *Fiore di Rettorica*, ed. Giambattista Speroni (Pavia: Università di Pavia, 1994), 73–74: "Come si fa conclusione per via di misericordia . . . Il sesto, quando si duole in ciò ch'è povero, o infermo, o cacciato di suo paese."

41. For mentions of his exile in the works themselves, see Brunetto Latini, *Li Livres dou Tresor de Brunetto Latini*, ed. Francis J. Charmody (Berkeley: University of California Press, 1948), Bk. I, xxxvii, p. 45, and Latini, *La Rettorica*, 7. Latini also provides a poetic account of how he learned of the exile of the Florentine Guelfs on return from his embassy to Spain. See Brunetto Latini, *Il Tesoretto*, ed. Marcello Ciccuto (Milan: Rizzoli, 1985), vv. 152–62, p. 61. On Brunetto as the probable translator of the *volgare* version of the *Tresor*, see Marcello Ciccuto, "Tresor di Brunetto Latini," in *Letteratura italiana: Le Opere*, ed. Alberto Rosa, 4 vols. (Turin: Einaudi, 1992), vol. 1, *Dalle origini al Cinquecento*, 46. Julia Bolton Holloway, *Brunetto Latini: An Analytic Bibliography* (London: Grant and Cutler, 1986), 26–30, is more assertive concerning the identification of Latini as the translator on the basis of the manuscripts listed.

42. That such a vision was implicit, rather than explicit, can itself be considered a function of his exile. For if Latini, as has been suggested, was dependent upon the repatriation of the exiled Guelfs under the protection of Charles of Anjou to effect his own return to Florence, an overt espousal of the values of the *Primo popolo* he supported might well have alienated the returning Guelfs who were themselves scions of the ancient Florentine dynastic families. See Julia Bolton Holloway, *Twice-Told Tales: Brunetto Latino and Dante Alighieri* (New York: Peter Lang, 1993), 63–65.

43. On the four conflictual forms, see J. R. East, "Book III of Latini's *Tresor*: An English Translation and Assessment of Its Contribution to Rhetorical Theory" (Ph.D. dissertation, Stanford University, 1960), 114–17. On the *Tenso* as genre and the troubadour involvement in intercommunal conflict of the Due- and Trecento, see Maria Luisa Meneghetti, "Intertextuality and Dialogism in the Troubadours," and Miriam Cabré, "Italian and Catalan Troubadours," in Gaunt and Kay, *The Troubadours*, 127–40 and 181–96; and Martin Aurell, "Chanson et propagande politique: Les Troubadours gibelins (1255–1285)," in *Le Forme della propaganda politica nel Due e nel Trecento*, ed. Paolo Cammarosano, 183–202 (Rome: École Française de Rome, 1994). This more technical rhetorical sense of *tencione* is to be differentiated from Latini's use of the word *tençon* as one of the cluster of words associated with the sin of anger. See Petrus A. Messelaar, *Le Vocabulaire des idées dans le "Tresor" de Brunet Latin* (Assen: Van Gorcum, 1963), 149.

44. Latini, *La Rettorica*, 55–56: "Non è da sbandire, ché ricordando pure lo nome sig-

niffica buona cosa et isbandire et exilio signiffica mala cosa, e non è da credere che buono uomo faccia quello che ssia da sbandire degno né de exilio."

45. See Ronald G. Witt, "Brunetto Latini and the Italian Tradition of *Ars Dictaminis*," *Stanford Italian Review* 2 (1983): 15.

46. Latini, *La Rettorica*, 50: "Alla fine conclude Tulio e dice che Rettorica è parte della civile scienza. Ma Vittorino sponendo quella parola dice che rettorica è la maggiore parte della civile scienza; e dice 'maggiore' per lo grande effetto di lei, ché certo per rettorica potemo noi muovere tutto 'l popolo, tutto 'l consiglio, il padre contra 'l figliuolo, l'amico contra l'amico, e poi li rega in pace e benevoglienza."

47. Latini, *Livres dou Tresor*, Bk. II, v, p. 178: "Naturele chose est a l'home k'il soit citeins et k'il se converse entre les homes et entre les artiers." John M. Najemy, "Brunetto Latini's 'Politica,'" *Dante Studies* 112 (1994): 41, translates "se converse" as "to live," which misses the double sense of "conversation" and "exchange" implicit in the term. The *volgare* version renders "k'il se converse" as "e che ei costumi" in the broadest sense of "to associate with," and elsewhere "conversazione" is used to denote speech. See Pietro Chabaille, ed., *Il Tesoro di Brunetto Latini volgarizzato*, 4 vols. (Bologna: Romagnoli, 1878), Bk. VII, iii, 3:19, and xxii, 3:80–82.

48. Giovanni Villani, *Nuova Cronica*, ed. Giovanni Porta, 3 vols. (Parma: Ugo Guanda Editore, 1990–91), Bk. IX, 10, 2:28: "egli fue cominciatore e maestro in digrossare i Fiorentini, e farli scorti in bene parlare."

49. As notary of the Anziani of the *Primo popolo* at a time when the city was expanding rapidly with the influx of new citizens, Latini too was an orator seeking to curb aristocratic excesses and he too underwent the experience of exile. For Latini's political career, see Holloway, *Twice-Told Tales*, 3–175; and Bianca Ceva, *Brunetto Latini: L'uomo e l'opera* (Milan: Ricciardi, 1965), 9–58.

50. Latini, *La Rettorica*, 6: "L'autore di questa opera è doppio." In this context I have difficulty understanding the assertion made by Davis that, "Even more unusual was Brunetto's admiration for Cicero the man." See Charles T. Davis, "Brunetto Latini and Dante," in *Dante's Italy and Other Essays* (Philadelphia: University of Pennsylvania Press, 1984), 173.

51. Two-thirds of the rhetorical material in the *Tresor* is derived from the *De Inventione*. Of the remaining third, Sallust provides the largest portion in tandem with material derived from the *Ars dictaminis* tradition. See East, "Book III of Latini's *Tresor*," 86–95.

52. For an excellent treatment of Catiline's *fortuna* in Florentine historiography, see Patricia J. Osmond, "Catiline in Fiesole and Florence: The After-life of a Roman Conspirator," *International Journal of the Classical Tradition* 7 (2000): 3–38. I would like to thank Prof. Osmond for her generous correspondence on the subject of Sallust and Catiline in the Renaissance.

53. The dynamics are exactly the same as those outlined by Edward Said, *Orientalism* (London: Routledge, 1978), in relation to the West's construction of the East as simultaneously exotic and threatening.

54. Latini, *La Rettorica*, p. 3: "uomini molto parlanti senza sapienza."

55. See Carol Lansing, *The Florentine Magnates: Lineage and Faction in a Medieval Commune* (Princeton: Princeton University Press, 1991), 192–211.

56. For examples of judicial officials speaking on behalf of exiles seeking repatriation in the late Duecento, see Alessandro Gherardi, ed., *Le Consulte della Repubblica Fiorentina dall'anno MCCLXXX al MCCXCVIII*, 2 vols. (Florence: Sansoni, 1896), 1:98–99 and 135.

57. Matteo dei Libri, *Arringhe*, ed. Eleonora Vincenti [with the edited text of Giovanni da Vignano's *Flore de Parlare* added as an appendix, pp. 231–325] (Milan: Ricciardi Editore, 1974), 134–36: XLVII, *Cum aliqua pars:* "Et providus arengator potest dicere coram imperatore vel rege, mutatis aliquibus, secundum quod ad conditionem cuiuslibet pertinet"; and 304–5: 62, *Como se po' dire.* See also Giuliana Ginnardi, ed., *"Le Dicerie di Filippo Ceffi," Studi di filologia italiana* 6 (1942): 55–56: XXXIII, *Come li cacciati.*

58. Ibid., 36–37: X, *Come si de' dire:* "Come si de' dire quando alcuno comune si duole d' alcuna divisione o cacciata di terra amica."

59. Biblioteca Nazionale Centrale di Firenze, *Fondo principale* II. I. 68, fols. 54v–57r: *Avvenga che Dio.* The rubrics run: "Di far pacie cho' ribelli rimettergli nella ciptà," "Per chi non vuole pacie cho' ribelli si può dire così," and "Per lo parte di chi vuole pacie si può rispondere." Since the completion of this chapter, the two speeches concerned have been transcribed and translated in Virginia Cox, "Ciceronian Rhetorical Theory in the *Volgare:* A Fourteenth-Century Text and Its Fifteenth-Century Readers," in *Rhetoric and Renewal in the Latin West 1100–1540: Essays in Honour of John O. Ward*, ed. Constant J. Mews, Cary J. Nederman, and Rodney M. Thomson (Turnhout: Brepols, 2003), 216–25. See also Milner, "Communication, Consensus and Conflict."

60. The relevant letters are found in Anthony Molho and Franco Sznura, eds., *Alle bocche della piazza: Diario di un Anonimo Fiorentino* (Florence: Olschki, 1986), 185–203. See also Brucker, *Civic World*, 97 n. 200.

61. Camargo, *Ars dictaminis*, 18.

62. Molho and Sznura, *Alle bocche*, 187: "ch' e suoi erano stati molti ghuelfi e amatori di questa città . . . E con questo fecie uno bello parlamentare, aleghando certi salmi di Davit e aleghando il padre e l'avolo suo, che erano stati canpioni per la città di Firenze e per Parte Guelfa."

63. Giamboni, *Fiore di Rettorica*, 117: "Il modo del consigliare che s'apella 'che è da fare magiormente': catun partito che si può pigliar è buono, ma l'uno è via miglior che l'altro; overo è catuno partito reo, ma l'uno è men rio."

64. Molho and Sznura, *Alle bocche*, 198: "Signori, se io avessi chi per me avesse a dire le mie ragioni dinanzi a voi e non temesse essere fatto sospetto, verebono molti dinanzi da voi con giustissimi prieghi. Ma non è lecito a nullo, per la paura e per lo esenpro di molti: il perché con lungheza di lettera mi costrignie a dovervi scrivere queste cose."

65. Ibid., 199: "fedelissimo cittadino popolano e ghuelfo, e al bene comune e libertà desideroso . . . E non sono ofeso dal Chomune né dalla ragione del popolo, ma sono ofeso, chome molti altri, dalla voluntà propria di chi n'ebe voluntà e forza, chon bugiardi colori e chalionose falsità e gelosi pensieri di crudeli animi, con disonesto modo."

66. Giamboni, *Fiore di Rettorica*, 93.

67. Molho and Sznura, *Alle bocche*, 202–03: "tòr via gli ordinamenti di ghuelfi . . . con privati e segreti coloqui"; "mutare ogni cosa ochultamente, non *publice*"; "più dello stato piuvicho che egli cogli altri abia ordinato e volute"; "di quantunque grande eloquenzia si

sia"; "noi usiamo le sue parole"; and "E anche forse à dimentichato che per sé medesimo al chancelieri nostro, il quale ridusse ogni cosa in iscrittur, e personalmente al coletterale del Capitano nel palagio nostro, liberamente confessò ogni cosa e che per lo suo prochuratore ispetialmente a queste cose ligittimamente chostituto, quello medesimo pro tribunali sedendo ogni cosa confessò."

68. Baron, *Crisis of the Early Italian Renaissance*.

69. Douglas, *Purity and Danger*, 30–41.

70. These issues are addressed in Stephen J. Milner, "Citing the *Ringhiera:* The Politics of Place and Public Address in Trecento Florence," *Italian Studies* 55 (2000): 53–82.

71. See Letizia A. Panizza, "Stoic Psychotherapy in the Middle Ages and Renaissance: Petrarch's *De remediis,*" in *Atoms, Pneuma, and Tranquillity: Epicurean and Stoic Themes in European Thought,* ed. Margeret J. Osler, 39–65 (Cambridge: Cambridge University Press, 1991).

72. Niccolò Machiavelli, *Discorsi sopra la prima Deca di Tito Livio,* ed. Giorgio Inglese (Milan: Rizzoli, 1984), Bk. I, ii, iv–vi, and Bk. II, iii.

73. After Soderini's exile in September of 1512, Machiavelli remained in Florence. In November, as part of the purge of the chancery, he was banned from entering the Palazzo della Signoria and required to remain in Florentine territory under a surety of a thousand florins to prevent him contacting his former patron. Destitute, he retreated to his small-holding at Sant'Andrea in Percussina in April 1513 from whence he wrote *The Prince*. See J. R. Hale, *Machiavelli and Renaissance Italy* (Harmondsworth: Penguin, 1961), 100–106; and John M. Najemy, *Between Friends: Discourses of Power and Desire in the Machiavelli-Vettori Letters of 1513–1515* (Princeton: Princeton University Press, 1993), 95–117.

74. For this crucial distinction, see Homi K. Bhabha, "The Third Space," in Rutherford, *Identity: Community, Culture, Difference,* 207–9.

75. In this sense, I am proposing a rhetorically orientated companion piece to Trexler's classic study of Florentine ritual in which he demonstrated how ritual transcended particular interests, tied individuals to the commune, and involved groups in the collective celebration of something greater than its constitutive parts, thereby transforming the republic as abstract entity into a concrete form. In the place of Weber's disenchanted impersonal city, Trexler proposed a heavily personalized entity that encouraged participation and involvement, and conditioned behavior through the ordering of symbolic space. Richard C. Trexler, *Public Life in Renaissance Florence* (New York: Academic Press, 1980). The discourse of civic republicanism performed exactly the same function through its rhetorical imagining of the commune.

76. See James D Hunter, *Culture Wars: The Struggle to Define America* (New York: Basic Books, 1991); and Arthur M. Schlesinger Jr., *The Disuniting of America: Reflections on a Multicultural Society* (New York: Norton, 1992).

10

DOMINICAN MARGINALIA

THE LATE FIFTEENTH-CENTURY PRINTING PRESS
OF SAN JACOPO DI RIPOLI IN FLORENCE

ANABEL THOMAS

This chapter is concerned with the business activities of printing presses and associated religious and lay groups in late fifteenth-century Florence. Attention focuses on the roles assumed by members of the Dominican community of San Jacopo di Ripoli on what is now the Via della Scala, when one of the first Florentine printing presses was established inside that conventual complex in 1477.[1] Consideration is given, also, to the numerous tradesmen and other individuals in the city who contributed to the production and distribution of merchandise at the Stamperia di San Jacopo. A variety of workshops were called upon to oversee the individual stages necessary to the completion of each printed book or broadsheet. Representatives ranging from street peddlers to itinerant clerics contributed then to the dissemination of the finished merchandise. At the same time, the women of San Jacopo assumed a number of roles in maintaining and supporting the business itself. While the central force was the press, "marginal" activities within the conventual complex and in the lay community fueled its success.

It is widely believed that women in female religious communities during the Renaissance period played little part in the world of practical affairs.[2] Such women, it is argued, could neither stimulate nor control the mundane activities of craftsmen, whether printers, painters, manu-

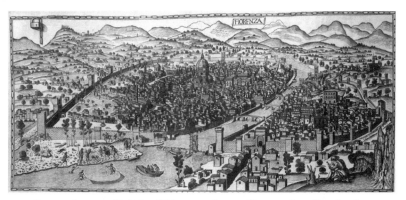

Figure 1. *Catena woodblock view of Florence*, woodcut, attr. Francesco Rosselli, early 1480s. Copyright Staatliche Museen zu Berlin–Preussischer Kulturbesitz, Kupferstichkabinett. Photograph Joerg P. Anders.

script illuminators, or paper merchants. Enclosed behind their conventual walls, they were beyond reach, their daily existence measured only by prayers for their own souls and for those of the lay community, with whom they had little, if any, contact. Yet evidence exists to suggest that religious women could control the production of artistic merchandise. In addition, they often provided important channels through which such work could be distributed. Consideration of the Stamperia di San Jacopo and the nature of printed matter produced there throws significant light on a hitherto little considered business activity and network of communication in late fifteenth-century Florence.[3]

Although somewhat marginalized, being established toward the western boundaries of the city (Figure 1), the community of Third Order women at San Jacopo di Ripoli was associated with the male community of Santa Maria Novella very early in its history.[4] It thus not only acquired well-established protectors, but also found itself securely imbedded within the Dominican community in Florence by the end of the thirteenth century. This was no doubt a significant factor in determining relationships with other female houses within the same order. Surviving records in the form of a workshop ledger show that the women of San Jacopo established webs of contact both across the city and in the broader Dominican community beyond.[5] At the same time it clarifies the relationships established between lay and religious workers, revealing the complex processes whereby printed pages and single images were produced, assembled, decorated, and subsequently circulated and sold.

In the course of its comparatively short lifetime of six or so years
the San Jacopo press published over seventy major works, as well as a
large number of broadsheets and single images.[6] Analysis of printed
material associated with the press prompts consideration of the extent
to which small-scale woodcut or metal-engraved prints produced for the
private devotions of women in Dominican communities and congregations reflected the iconography and design of decorations displayed in
the more central spaces of Dominican churches and chapels.[7] Records
concerning the mass production and distribution of broadsheets and
devotional images in the San Jacopo ledger reveal that many of the cus-
tomers were individual members of female communities and companies.
Surviving metal engravings (some of which may be directly associated
with the San Jacopo di Ripoli press) suggest that in purchasing such merchandise these women often acquired miniature versions of large-scale
pieces of decoration displayed in their own conventual church or set up
on the altar of the motherhouse in which devotions were offered on their
behalf. These mass-produced prints of the late fifteenth century must
have contributed to a broader sense of institutional membership, drawing the furthest edges of the Dominican community together.

Magliabechiano, X, 143 is apparently all that has survived to chart the
production and distribution of printed books in the Stamperia di San
Jacopo. Individual entries reveal that the press produced a variety of
texts, some plain, others illustrated. Such entries also indicate a concentration initially on the production of religious tracts, with a later expansion into the printing of humanist tracts and reproductions of ancient
authors. The ledger also covers such diverse matters as production lines
and the number of individual tracts or texts published; transactions with
cartolaio (paper merchant) and *miniatore* (illuminated manuscript painter)
shops for the binding and decoration of the printed pages; payment for
such work; costing of finished merchandise; sales policy and distribution patterns; as well as details about the financial and practical support
offered by the women of San Jacopo themselves in the day-to-day running of the business.

While clearly not assuming the central practical role suggested in
some earlier considerations of the Stamperia di San Jacopo, there is much
evidence to suggest that the women's financial support was crucial to
the success of the business. Numerous entries record monetary loans
from the nuns for the purchase of typeface and other necessary equip-

ment during the setting up of the press and the early days of its business. Thus, in April 1477 twelve gold florins were returned to the prioress of San Jacopo in part repayment of the twenty she had previously lent in connection with the printing of the Legend of Saint Catherine during that year.[8] And in August 1477 reference is made to a loan of six florins from suora Constanza.[9] In the same year also there are references to loans from suora Betta and suora Angela.[10] Such evidence should alert us to the fact that it was not only the nominal head of a female conventual complex who might assume some significance in business affairs. Clearly, several women at San Jacopo di Ripoli were in a position to make loans of some substance in support of the new business venture. This managerial or "financial backer" role is significant. On occasion the women of San Jacopo seem even to have assumed responsibility for workshop expenses such as assistants' salaries and upkeep. Thus, in an entry of 1478 there is a reference to an assistant Lorenzo ("garzone allo sta[m]pare") who owes seven florins to the nuns for expenses offered him during seven months' work in printing books at the press.[11] Such entries indicate that the women of San Jacopo played a considerable role in financing this new enterprise. The surviving ledger thus not only provides a unique insight to the working practice of a printing press set up in a conventual complex in Florence during the early period of development of this new technology, but also reveals much about the role assumed by the women of that community in promoting that venture.

The surviving ledger also reveals that the women were on occasion involved in the everyday running of the business itself. Several entries record activity within the printing shop in setting up type. Thus, in 1478 there is a reference to ten florins being set aside for the "salary of our nuns" who were typesetting ("co[m]ponghano allo sta[m]pare") in the company of ser Bartolo (probably the paper merchant referred to in an initial inscription in *Magliabechiano*, X, 143).[12] And in 1480 reference is made again to the involvement of the nuns in typesetting, and to a monthly wage of fifteen lire.[13] Such work must have brought the women in close contact not only with the texts generated by the press, but also with the illustrations set within them. While there is no evidence in the ledger to support claims concerning the role of these nuns as illustrators, it seems quite possible that other activities practiced by them may have influenced the workings of the press. San Jacopo, like many other female religious communities, assumed a significant role as a center of embroidery.[14] The women there must have established close personal relationships with drawings furnished for their needlework by some of the leading artists of the day. They may thus have played an advisory part in the illustration of printed matter produced by the press. Some drawings used for the working of cloth may even have been adopted for the decoration of the printed page.

Officially, the San Jacopo printing press was managed by men, the frontispiece of *Magliabechiano*, X, 143 informing us that the business was set up by the community's *vicario*, or procurator, Dominican fra Domenico da Pistoia of Santa Maria Novella, and the women's confessor, fra Piero da Pisa. The essential business of typesetting and printing was run centrally by these two individuals, but many parts of the process (such as binding and decorating) were subcontracted out to paper workers and illuminators and decorators. The frontispiece inscription explains that fra Domenico and fra Piero initially formed a company with the *cartolaio* Bartolo and his companions "to produce books in compact form" ("affarre libri i[n] forma ca[m]pacte"). A partnership was also formed in May 1477 with a German printmaker called Giovanni.[15]

A number of paper merchants were enlisted to help with the production of books printed by the new press. *Magliabechiano*, X, 143 reveals that both loose printed pages and bound books were delivered to paper merchants, who then made arrangements for their decoration. The term most frequently used in the context of decoration is *miniare*, indicating hand painting with brush and paint rather than woodcut or metal-engraving printing. Some doubt has therefore been expressed about the extent of such "illumination," the suggestion being that these outside decorators were on the whole involved in the painting of initials and marginal marking up of individual parts of the text.[16] But variations in the prices quoted for completed merchandise suggest that decoration of the printed pages often went beyond the touching up of initial letters in red or blue. In addition, records quoting sums at the lower level of the price scale often contain no reference to decoration. On this basis, alone, one could argue that those selling at the higher level were distinguished by having extra embellishment.

Individual entries in *Magliabechiano*, X, 143 offer further support for this hypothesis. In 1480 the paper merchant Chimenti is described as receiving two company books, one of which was "sciolto et no(n) miniato" ("in loose leaves and undecorated"), and the other of which was "leghato a mezo chuoio e comi(n)ciato a miniare" ("bound in half leather and partially [or initially] decorated").[17] It seems likely from this that the decoration of the latter related to the filling in or painting of capital letters, or the marking up of individual parts of the text. Other entries reveal distinctions concerning workshop expertise and subcontracting in *cartolaio* workshops. In many cases, paper merchants commissioned directly by the press established further production levels, where decorating and binding were seen as quite separate activities. Books were often initially delivered to a paper merchant and then sent on elsewhere to be finished. The two "libri di compagnia" delivered to the paper merchant Chimenti were subsequently delivered to the paper merchant Zanobi for binding.[18] On this occasion Chimenti emerges principally as a decorator. Such subcontracting was no doubt eased by the fact that many of these paper merchants and illuminators set up business in close proximity to each other and, like many other trades, established a monopoly in one part of the city.[19] *Magliabechiano*, X, 143 contains the information that Zanobi was established next door to the paper merchant Domenico di Piero,[20] while the paper merchant Antonio is described as working in the workshop where Bartolo "used to work."[21] Elsewhere, what is probably the same individual Zanobi is described as working "nel gharbo," and, at roughly the same period, two other paper merchants (Francesco and Nardo) are described as working in the same area.[22]

It seems clear that the late fifteenth-century *cartolaio* trade combined a variety of skills. Many illuminators either worked in close proximity to paper merchants or practiced alongside them. Thus, ser Niccolò is described in 1480 as working as an illuminator in the workshop of the paper merchant Domenico.[23] Yet what is apparently the same individual (Domenico) is described as both binding and illustrating, and on occasion is even recompensed for demonstrating his own expertise to others.[24] Moreover, although Niccolò is clearly defined as illustrating in the shop of Domenico, Domenico did not rely on him alone: on at least one occasion he put illumination work out to tender. Thus one entry in *Magliabechiano*, X, 143 records that Domenico has arranged for a number of Legends of Saint Catherine to be decorated ("miniati") in the shop of Gherardo di Monte.[25] Elsewhere, work was specifically subcontracted to miniaturists working as "assistants" (albeit apparently on an almost equal basis from the evidence of individual payments) in another master's illuminating business. Thus, in 1477 there are references to payments for decoration work to Bernardino, who is described as "minia in bottega di Monte."[26] Another individual, fra Michele da Pistoia, while on some occasions clearly doing his own miniature decoration, at other times contracted out both binding and illuminating.[27] Such variations suggest not only a great flexibility in workshop practice, but also the possibility that distinctions were made between different kinds of work.

A large number of individuals were drawn into the new enterprise. This was not a situation where one workshop organization established a monopoly in the trade. *Magliabechiano*, X, 143 notes a number of transactions with several different illuminators or miniaturists. The new technology thus created a new market niche amongst the workshops of Florence. At least four different miniature painters are recorded working alongside each other in the comparatively short period of time during which the press operated at San Jacopo. In one year alone, the miniaturist Niccolò is credited with two Legends of Saint Catherine, Francesco in the workshop of Francesco at Santa Felicità was allotted five, Bernardino (elsewhere described as working in the shop of Monte di Monte) was given six, and Gherardino di Monte engaged in the illustration of fourteen.[28] Gherardino di Monte's shop seems to have been particularly favored by the San Jacopo press for illumination work. It was also popular with individual paper merchant shops eager to subcontract illustration of the pages they themselves were apparently on occasion only competent (or willing) to bind.

It is clear from *Magliabechiano*, X, 143 that the San Jacopo press concentrated on the production of Legends of Saint Catherine during the first few years of its existence. Clearly, such matter would have been of specific interest to religious women attached to Dominican houses. This tract remained a mainstay of the business at San Jacopo. Individual entries in the San Jacopo di Ripoli account book show that different editions of the Legend of Saint Catherine sold at varying prices. Basic, undecorated texts sold for as little as two lire (or forty soldi). Many copies sold for even less. Other versions sold for as much as four lire and ten soldi, which (on the assumption that the text itself and the size of the paper remained constant) must indicate some distinction in terms of the decoration.[29] Comparison between these sums and the salaries paid to those responsible for their decoration is illuminating. On one occasion in May 1477 ser Niccolò in the shop of the paper merchant Domenico was paid eleven soldi for his work on a Legend of Saint Catherine; on another, Gherardino di Monte and Bernardino working in his workshop received only ten soldi for apparently producing very similar work.[30] Where legends were sold for two lire such compensation would have accounted for about 25 percent of the selling cost.

Far higher sums were paid (comparatively) for individual frontispiece decorations. The illuminator Bernardino received five and a half soldi for a "principio," half as much as the payment to ser Niccolò for the "complete" decoration of another book.[31] In this respect, it is significant to note the way in which frontispieces are recorded separately in *Magliabechiano*, X, 143. Thus, in November 1480, the illuminator Bartolo delle Selve is paid not for unspecified "decoration" but for "i principii."[32] This indicates that such work involved a different kind of expertise or process. Such variations in price presumably related to both the extent of work and the detail of individual illustrations. In this context, it may be significant to note that on one occasion (in August 1477) the sum of eighteen soldi was recorded in reference to the entire decoration ("miniatura") of a Psalter.[33] It is significant also to note how such sums compared to payments made for binding. On one occasion eighteen soldi is recorded in respect of decoration for a Psalter, while twenty-two soldi was paid for the binding.[34] If such divisions in payment remained constant and applied also to texts such as Legends of Saint Catherine, such figures would suggest that binding and decorating accounted for over 50 percent of the selling price. Other expenses, including paper, ink, and the running costs of the press itself, must have contributed further to a narrow margin of profit, unless, as is argued here, some production lines altered the balance.

There are comparatively few references to frontispieces in *Magliabechiano*, X, 143. This may indicate that elaborate decoration was rare in the books printed by the press. However, there could be some covert reference to such work in the several references to the "reillustration" of books. Although such "reillustration" might only have involved touching up of initials and repairing minor damage caused in binding, it is possible that this part of the process involved more elaborate decoration involving the insertion of frontispieces. Evidence for this lies in descriptions of how the paper merchant Chimenti received a bound text in which the decoration had only been begun ("cominciato a miniare"), and another recording that a text was first decorated by the paper merchant

Domenico and then taken to another illuminator named Francesco for further decoration.[35] This latter individual was established at the Benedictine community of Santa Felicita, and apparently received quite competitive payment for work from the San Jacopo press. In 1479 he was paid the handsome sum of thirty soldi for illuminating or decorating a *libricino*, or little book, *delle monache* (of the nuns).[36] At almost three times the payment for decorating a complete Legend of Saint Catherine, and nearly six times the payment of an illuminated or decorated frontispiece, this "little book of the nuns" must have been a fairly elaborate production.

While such entries offer detailed information about production costs and payments to individual workers, others reveal how finished work was distributed through what appears to have been a comparatively complex network of sales outlets. The San Jacopo press had a number of outlets both within the city and far beyond. *Magliabechiano, X, 143* contains references to places as far apart as San Gimignano, Siena, Pistoia, and Venice. Moreover, for each of these centers different individuals contributed to the distribution and sale of the merchandise. In Florence, there are references to retailers varying in trade from builders to cloth workers who accepted copies of the Legend of Saint Catherine for onward sale. Itinerant preaching friars also played an important role. A large number of sales were directed toward and managed by the Dominican community within Florence. But this was not an exclusive outlet.

During March 1477/8 Friar Domenico Guerrucci, who is described as preaching in Santa Felicita, not only is recorded as selling San Jacopo merchandise there,[37] but also seems to have acted as a middleman in delivering merchandise to Santa Felicita so that it could be decorated by the illuminator Francesco, who was attached to that community.[38] From these entries it is clear that Francesco was reilluminating work that had previously been decorated by the paper merchant Domenico. The fact that Francesco is specifically mentioned also in the context of reilluminating Legends of Saint Catherine may also be relevant in terms of identifying the artistic style of surviving prints depicting that saint. There is clear evidence, also, of transactions with Dominican houses outside Florence. Thus, in 1480 a Dominican "maestro Michele" from Pisa is recorded as receiving ten volumes of penitential Psalms, ten volumes of the Art of Dying Well, two Legends of Saint Catherine, and other merchandise from fra Domenico da Pistoia (with in each case an agreed minimum price at which each volume should be sold), including an un-decorated Legend of Saint Catherine, which Michele had acquired sepa-rately from fra Pietro "che stava a Ripoli" ("who was resident in Ripoli").[39]

Success in targeting a female Dominican clientele depended upon the aggressive sales policies of friars servicing individual communities, or direct requests from male advisers and protectors of such women.[40] *Magliabechiano*, X, 143 includes at least two references to the "friar" of the nuns of San Domenico (presumably San Domenico del Maglio) pur-chasing on their behalf a copy of the Legend of Saint Catherine.[41] There are also references to the nuns of San Jacopo themselves selling the press's merchandise.[42] Religious women in other Dominican communi-ties were likewise involved in sales promotion. In an entry dated March 1477/8 there is a reference to two Legends of Saint Catherine being sent to the prioress of San Vincenzo so that she could sell them on behalf of the press.[43] In the event, one was sold for three lire. There are several other references to San Vincenzo in *Magliabechiano*, X, 143 that suggest that it may have served as a regular outlet for the sale of merchandise from the press.[44] Other Dominican communities operated in a similar capacity. Thus, during March 1477/8 reference is made to Legends of Saint Catherine being sent to the prioresses of Santa Lucia and of San Giuliano.[45] In May of the same year reference is made to Santa Lucia in Pistoia, indicating sales transactions in female communities both inside and outside Florence.[46] In fact, such entries reveal that merchandise often circulated from one community to another before being sold. Moreover, copies were frequently returned to San Jacopo after being loaned to in-dividual communities as demonstration copies or on spec. Illustrated Leg-ends of Saint Catherine must thus have been significant transmitters of Dominican imagery. In addition, the very act of circulating such goods may independently have contributed to their greater embellishment. On several occasions there are references to books being reillustrated or decorated after such circulation. Perhaps such "restoration" followed minor damage. Perhaps it was also seen as an efficient way of "revamp-ing" rejected items, or of making them more attractive to other prospec-tive purchasers.

Other entries in *Magliabechiano*, X, 143 reveal the vast quantities in which such merchandise was manufactured, highlighting the lacunae in our understanding of the trade in religious images and books distrib-uted by such presses as the Stamperia di San Jacopo in late fifteenth-

century Florence. The disparity between the surviving merchandise and
the recorded scale of printing activity is startling. In December 1481 an
entry in the San Jacopo di Ripoli account book notes the commission
from Giovanni Francesco cermatore (cimatore?) of not one, but one thousand images of Saint Margaret at the cost of thirteen lire and ten soldi.[47]
Although the financial outlay was comparatively small, the sheer number of pieces of paper that Giovanni Francesco was prepared to handle is
impressive. That he was confident he could dispose of such merchandise raises interesting questions, also, about the Renaissance art market
and laws of supply and demand. There is little doubt that print runs of
what would now be described as "marginal" artistic merchandise were
catering to a mass market.

No specific reference is made to the identity of the Saint Margaret
mentioned in the 1481 entry, but it seems likely (given the Dominican
associations of the San Jacopo press) that the prints in question depicted
either the ancient Margaret of Antioch or Margaret, daughter of the king
of Hungary, or Margaret of Città di Castello (both born during the thirteenth century, and both members of the Dominican community).[48]
Saint Margaret of Città di Castello joined the Third Order. Saint Margaret
of Hungary, by comparison, assumed the Dominican habit and rules and
regulations of the enclosed Second Order. She is clearly depicted and labeled in this guise (her royal status indicated by the crown and coat of
arms at her feet) standing next to Saint Catherine of Siena (who, by comparison, wears the white veil of the Third Order) in the late fifteenth-
century German woodcut print of The Genealogical Tree of the Dominicans
dated to ca. 1473 (Figure 2).[49] She is probably also included in the first
row of female figures kneeling at the left-hand side of Saint Dominic in
the fifteenth-century Tractatus de Paenitentia manuscript illumination of
Saint Dominic and members of his order (Figure 3).[50]

Surviving depictions of both Margaret of Città di Castello and of
Saint Margaret of Hungary in Italian panel paintings are comparatively
rare. In those that do exist of Saint Margaret of Hungary, the saint is frequently depicted wearing a crown. One such example is that found in
the diminutive figure of the saint inserted amongst the ranks of Dominicans surrounding the enthroned figures of Christ and the Virgin in
a panel attributed to Orcagna and painted for Santa Maria Novella. This
standing figure wearing a crown and holding several stems of lilies is
clearly identifiable by the inscription in her halo, and by the fact that she

Figure 2. *The Genealogical Tree of the Dominicans,* German woodcut print, dated ca. 1473.
Copyright The British Museum.

Figure 3. *Tractatus de Paenitentia*, fifteenth century. MS C 57 VI M.
Copyright Biblioteca degli Intronati, Siena.

is wearing the habit of the Second Order. Margaret of Città di Castello is
apparently not shown. Although there can be no certainty regarding the
specific identity of the Saint Margaret images printed by the San Jacopo
press in 1481, the painting attributed to Orcagna in the mother church
may have offered some guidance for the depiction of the regal Hungar-

ian saint. It is perhaps also significant that a couple of months prior to the order for images of Saint Margaret, the press recorded the printing of a similar number of images depicting the Madonna of the Rosary, a design that, like Margaret of Hungary, required the depiction of a queenly figure.[51] In that case the record reveals that the press was persuaded to produce these images of the Madonna of the Rosary by the friars of San Marco. Clearly, that order was an "in-house" Dominican initiative. The *Magliabechiano, X, 143* entry indicates that there was some concern about the outcome of such a large-scale venture, since an additional note seems to query how the project would fare.[52] Subsequent entries note that the friars of San Marco were purchasing these Virgin of the Rosary images in comparatively small batches of only tens and fifties, and that individual prints were selling for about one and a half soldi. Compared with the sums quoted elsewhere in the Stamperia ledger in respect of Orations of the Cross (which sold for about one denaro each),[53] these images of the Virgin of the Rosary clearly fell into the category of "luxury" goods. This is significant, not only in terms of the doubt apparently expressed by the press concerning the financial wisdom of such bulk printing, but also for what it may indicate about the complexity of design of such images.

The first Company of the Rosary to be established in Florence was associated with the Dominican community of San Marco.[54] It was here, between 1480 and 1481, that the Compagnia del Rosario was offered the altar of the Annunciation to the immediate right of the entrance to the church for the celebration of their devotions.[55] It was no doubt in celebration of this foundation that the friars of San Marco persuaded the San Jacopo di Ripoli press to produce one thousand images of the Virgin of the Rosary. But this was not the only work commissioned by the friars of San Marco at that time. In August 1481, the press was also asked to produce the "libri di compagnia" of the newly established Company of the Rosary.[56] It was further entrusted in November 1481 with running off the "bolle" or papal bulls associated with the confirmation of that community.[57] It seems clear from this that there were particularly close links between San Marco and San Jacopo di Ripoli during the early 1480s.

The role played by the San Jacopo press in establishing new imagery such as the Virgin of the Rosary invites further analysis.[58] It may not be coincidental, for example, that the mandorla garland of roses encircling the standing figure of an early sixteenth-century French woodcut of the Virgin, now at Basle, is strongly reminiscent of that surrounding the

Quefto/ e /elfegno della cōpagnia del Rofario
della Vergine Maria.

*Est Marij S. Eugenÿ Senarum
Ad usum D. Benedicti Abbatis*

Figure 4. *Symbols of the Compagnia del Rosario*, frontispiece, *Statuti della Compagnia del Rosario*, published by Antonio Miscomini, after May 1485. MS M VI 57 (previously C 57. VI. M). Copyright Biblioteca degli Intronati, Siena.

symbols of the Compagnia del Rosario on the frontispiece of a printed book closely associated with the San Jacopo di Ripoli press that survives in the Biblioteca degli Intronati in Siena (Figure 4).[59]

This book, which consists of five separately printed sections, contains in its first part the statutes of the Company of the Rosary. These (like the Imitatio Christi that follows) were apparently printed in Florence by Antonio Miscomini, some time after May 1485. The following two sections, an *Oratio de Chantata* by Francesco Bonaccorsi and an *Ars Moriendi* by Francesco di Dino, were likewise printed in the second half of the 1480s, while the fifth section, a Book of Confessions by Paolo Fiorentino, was printed by Niccolò di Lorenzo about 1477. Only the last section, therefore, falls within the precise period of activity of the San Jacopo di Ripoli press. However, given the association with Florence and the connection with the Company of the Rosary, one can at least argue that Antonio Miscomini's publication was influenced by the San Jacopo press and thus presents us with some of its characteristics.

The frontispiece decoration, which combines a crown and hanging bead rosary in the middle of a hexagonal-shaped outline encircling the garland of roses and rose leaves, provides us with a unique example of decoration associated with the newly established company. Its basic design is simple, with no shading or hatching, definition being given through the repetition of short, stumpy incised lines. Although partially colored with green, pink, and red, it is possible that it was originally intended as a monochrome decoration. Regardless of these finer details, there seems little doubt that this design served as a kind of stamped bookplate. It identifies and authorizes the text that follows. It may even have been printed or stamped separately from the rest of the book. Certainly, it seems quite different in style from the Annunciation on the opposite page. There the fine line technique relates to the incisions of an engraved plate or the template for embroidery (Figure 5). Moreover, the design and iconography, although comparatively crude, seem to have their roots in contemporary depictions of the Annunciation in painted panels and frescoes, rather than developing from the characteristically flat and spatially nonspecific renderings of the same subject on woodcut blocks. Such evidence may reflect a contribution on the part of religious women in presenting designs they used for needlework for appropriation in the new technology of the printing press. In the case of the *Libro della Compagnia del Rosario,* it is almost as if two quite separate traditions are deliberately combined with reference to two quite separate functions in the same book—one concerned with officialdom, and the other with a more private world of personal devotion. Such distinctions are in some measure reflected in the accompanying lines of red text under each image. Beneath the sign of the company is the simple identifying inscription

Figure 5. *Annunciation*, first page, *Statuti della Compagnia del Rosario*, published by
Antonio Miscomini, after May 1485. MS M VI 57 (previously C 57. VI. M).
Copyright Biblioteca degli Intronati, Siena.

"Questo e elsegno della co(m)pagnia del Rosario della Vergine Maria" ("This is the sign of the Company of the Rosary of the Virgin Mary"). Beneath the Annunciation image, however, is a longer passage that does not refer specifically to the decoration above, but explains instead that the book contains the ordinations, institutions, chapter rulings, regulations, privileges, and indulgences associated with the membership of the Company of the Rosary.

The following text includes directions concerning the number of times members of the company were obliged to say the rosary each week, and the way in which this should be done. Thus, they must recite the entire "psalterio" or "rosario" consisting of 150 Ave Marias and 15 Pater Nosters at least once a week. This procedure involved first reciting a Pater Noster and then ten Ave Marias. Other instructions relate how the Psalms should be recited, and the number of Pater Nosters and Ave Marias appropriate to the contemplation of each of the three mysteries.[60] Beginning with the Annunciation, members were required to recite one Pater Noster and ten Ave Marias for each mystery. It seems clear from this that the image of the Annunciation on the first page of the *Libro della Compagnia del Rosario,* while marking the beginning of the book itself, also provided a vehicle for the recitation of the rosary itself. Evidence of this kind prompts consideration of the changing role of drawings circulating in female religious communities. If the hypothesis holds that drawings first used in embroidery were subsequently adopted for printed matter, what was initially transmitted through cloth for external consumption and display must subsequently have been harnessed to much more private devotions.

That the *Libro della Compagnia del Rosario* book was well loved, yet passed through several different hands early in its history, is reflected in the series of inscriptions adorning both the frontispiece and the first page. Although carefully cancelled when passed on to a new owner, variations in the type of script indicate the passage of time and allow some reconstruction of the identity of individual owners. Probably the most recent inscription is that written in a large and confident hand directly beneath the sign of the Compagnia del Rosario and its explanatory red inscription. This informs us that the book belongs to the Sienese monastery of Sant'Eugenio and that it was used by the abbot, don Benedetto. The inscriptions on the opposite page indicate, however, that the book may first have been commissioned, not for Siena, but for a religious community in Prato. At the bottom of the page, in what appears to be the labored work of one or two hands little used to the production of elegant text, are two lines of writing that, although partially cancelled, are decipherable as "Questo 1 libro rosaio S(uo)ra ?madalena" and "de...in Sa(nc)ta V(er)diana." Immediately above this are the words "di S(uor)a cherubina" in a different and more confident hand, but, like that below, appearing through its italic script to predate a third inscription on the base of the same page that, in the rounded script of a more modern period, reads "Q(u)esto libro e di pierfranc(esc)o di choredi (?)pechori." At the top of the page, immediately above the illustration of the Annunciation and in the neat script of what appears to be a fifteenth-century hand, runs one long and carefully positioned sentence, stretching from left to right and reading "conve(n)to S(ant'). An(n)a de P(ra)to ad usu(m) fr(atr)is B(ern) d... (?Bernardo) Flor(enti)a fri (fieri?) Arch S(an)cta A(?N). gf."

These marginal additions indicate that the book, although published in Florence, began life in a religious community outside Florence, albeit in the possession of a Florentine friar. It seems subsequently to have belonged to a nun in a different community and to have then been passed on by her to one of her sisters. Thereafter, it fell into the hands of the lay man Pier Francesco, and only at a comparatively late date found its way back into a religious community in Siena. Clearly, such patterns of ownership might depend purely on individual circumstances. Yet it is worth noting how these marginal additions reflect the networks of distribution recorded in the San Jacopo di Ripoli account book. The friar at Sant'Anna, like the priest Domenico Guerrucci, could well have acted as a middleman in acquiring the company book and subsequently passing it on to a female community.

The *Libro della Compagnia del Rosario* and its subsequent parts contain variations in levels of decoration that bear comparison with several of the entries in *Magliabechiano*, X, 143. The text of the *Libro della Compagnia del Rosario* contains very few touches of color, consisting in the main of large blue capital letters and occasional red signs that signal the beginning of paragraphs. These are interspersed at times with smaller red capitals and occasional red lines of type. In many instances, a lowercase letter in black print was left as a guideline for the differently colored capital letter, which was apparently stamped in later. In the *Libro della Compagnia del Rosario* all these appear to be "set" or printed, rather

than painted, but in other sections such additions are painted in. Perhaps this minimal embellishment is what was meant by "partial decoration" in various entries in *Magliabechiano, X, 143*. Further evidence that
may usefully be compared with entries concerning decoration in the
San Jacopo ledger is found in the images on the frontispiece and first
page of the *Libro della Compagnia del Rosario*. These are quite clearly em-
bellished with a thin wash of green and pink on part of the garland of the
company sign, and with thicker touches of green, red, and yellow paint
on the inset crown and rosary beads. Similar, bolder areas of color (including red, green, yellow, and brown) embellish the Annunciation image.
Although it is possible that the first owner, "fra ?Bernardo," or "suora
Madalena" or "suora Cherubina," added these rudimentary touches of
color to the rosary garland and the scene of the Annunciation, it seems
more likely that they are original. Indeed, such fragments would seem
to offer evidence in respect of references to "partial decoration" or "decoration only just begun" in *Magliabechiano, X, 143*. Where a Legend of
Saint Catherine is recorded as selling at the lowest end of the price scale,
one could argue that not even the capital initials were distinguished in
color from the surrounding text. Where merchandise is described as
"partially decorated" or appeared to sell in the middle price range at
about three lire a copy, it seems more likely that the text was marked in
part with blue and red and that it contained some further embellishment.
In those cases where a Legend was sold at the highest end of the price
scale, for four or more lire, the probability is that it included woodblock
stamps or metal engravings, or a combination of both, comparable to
those in the Miscomini edition of the *Libro della Compagnia del Rosario*.
At the highest level, one could expect decoration of an even more complex kind.

The *Libro della Compagnia del Rosario* also offers clear evidence of
the links established between the layout and embellishment of the metal-
printed page and that of earlier book production practice. Variations in
the color and embellishment of the text, paragraph openings, initial letters, and inset illustrations are closely related to the conventions and
traditions of illuminated manuscripts, a clear example being the page
from the *Tractatus de Paenitentia* illustrated here. The simple outlining
in red and in-filling with the restricted palette of blue, red, white, black,
and gold of the Saint Dominic image in the *Tractatus de Paenitentia* bears

direct comparison also with the *Libro della Compagnia del Rosario* Annunciation, which, likewise, has a thick painted border (originally brown rather than red, and now much faded). Under the frontispiece decoration of the standing Saint Dominic, four lines of red text with a blue opening marker are followed by a lengthier piece of text in black ink and ornamented with a decorated initial "I." The text immediately below the image of Saint Dominic explains that the manuscript is a "copy of the privileges, full powers, approval, and confirmation of the state and order of penitential brothers and sisters of Saint Dominic, the order to which the venerable and blessed virgin Catherine of Siena belonged." Catherine herself is probably depicted (in the white veil and habit of the Third Order) in the initial "I" decoration. Here, a kneeling figure (presumably Dominic) offers (or, more likely, takes) a tract to (or from) the standing figure of Pope Innocent III, while at the same time reaching back with another tract to the male and female figures kneeling behind him.

The image of Saint Dominic in the *Tractatus de Paenitentia*, standing with mantle raised by angels in reflection of the Madonna della Misericordia, and surrounded by the kneeling and segregated figures of Dominican monks and nuns, may likewise have set a visual precedent for contemporary and later woodcut prints and metal engravings produced for insertion in similar tracts. In this context, it is relevant to note the prices quoted in reference to frontispieces in the San Jacopo press account book. By their price, these were clearly quite elaborate. Like the *Tractatus de Paenitentia* image of Saint Dominic, they also clearly served as introductions to the text. If produced for a Legend or history of Saint Catherine, one could also argue that such frontispieces, like the *Tractatus de Paenitentia* image, contained not only an image of the saint, but also included depictions of Catherine's own followers, or references to her life and miracles.[61]

In conclusion, there can be little doubt that the individual illustrations and text in this little book of the Company of the Rosary, produced so close in time to the main period of activity of the San Jacopo di Ripoli press, offers concrete evidence of the "look" of merchandise produced on the Via della Scala premises. Although the initial printing press set up at San Jacopo di Ripoli was a comparatively short-lived venture, the survival of its workshop account book provides us with a unique insight to printing activity on the margins of Dominican society in late fifteenth-century Florence. At the same time, analysis of the individual records contained in *Magliabechiano, X, 143* encourages a reevaluation of the role and function of religious women and laymen in supporting such ventures, as well as contributing to the practical day-to-day business.

NOTES

1. For the foundation and history of this printing press, see Padre Vincenzio dal Fineschi, *Notizie storiche sopra la stamperia di Ripoli* (Florence: Moucke, 1781). See also B. Camisasca, "La stamperia di san Jacopo di Ripoli" (Ph.d. thesis, Università del Sacro Cuore, Milan, typescript photocopy, 1968); Helen M. Latham, "Dominican Nuns and the Book Arts in Renaissance Florence: The Convent of San Jacopo di Ripoli, 1224–1633" (Ph.D. thesis, Texas Woman's University, 1986); Melissa C. Flannery, "San Jacopo di Ripoli: Imprints at Yale Beineke Library," *Yale University Gazette* 63 (1989): 115; and Mary A. Rouse and Richard H. Rouse, *Cartolai, Illuminators, and Printers in Fifteenth-Century Italy: The Evidence of the Ripoli Press* (Los Angeles: Department of Special Collections, University Research Library, University of California, 1988).

2. The role assumed by religious women in business transactions, and in particular in the patronage of conventual art, is considered in my *Art and Piety in the Female Religious Communities of Renaissance Italy: Iconography, Space and the Religious Woman's Perspective* (Cambridge: Cambridge University Press, 2003).

3. The original company folded after the death of its founder, fra Domenico, in August 1484.

4. For the early history of San Jacopo di Ripoli and its relationship with San Domenico del Maglio in Florence, see Anabel Thomas, "Conventual Imagery in Context: New Light on the Rosselli Family and the Dominican Convent of S. Domenico del Maglio in Florence," *Fifteenth Century Studies* 26 (2001): 200–14; and Thomas, *Art and Piety*, 77–78.

5. Biblioteca Nazionale Centrale di Firenze (henceforth BNCF), MS *Magliabechiano, X, 143* (hereafter *Maglia., X, 143*). The ledger bears an inscription dated 11 Jan. 1477 (1478) on its frontispiece. For bibliographical references and a complete transcription of the ledger, see Melissa Conway, *The Diario of the Printing Press of San Jacopo di Ripoli (1476–1484)* (Florence: Olschki, 1999).

6. Flannery cites Curtius Rufus, Aurelius Victor, Sallust, Suetonius, Statius Valerius Flaccus, Aesop, and Plato amongst the ancient authors; the writing of Donatus, Giovanni Baptista Guarino, and Niccolò Perotti amongst grammatical works; and Bartolommeo della Fonte, Donato Acciaiuoli, Luigi Pulci, and Marsilio Ficino amongst contemporary works.

7. Such considerations are included in Thomas, *Art and Piety*.

8. BNCF, *Maglia., X, 143*, fol. 6v.

9. Ibid., fol. 10v.

10. Ibid., fols. 11r and 12r.

11. Ibid., fol. 2r. There is also a reference in July 1477 to "Lorenzo nostro composi-tore" (fol. 9v) indicating that he was involved in typesetting. This may well be the same in-dividual who in 1484 is described as "Lore(n)zo venitiano nostro gharzone": see ibid., fol. 130r. This might indicate that Venetian expertise was offered to the press early in its exis-tence. The press certainly established business links with Venice, several references being made in BNCF, *Maglia.*, X, 143 (fols. 16r and 16v) to Legends of Saint Catherine being sent there in 1477. Some legends were sent to Venice via frate Girolamo at San Marco, others through the agency of the paper merchant Benedetto.

12. Ibid., fol. 43r.

13. Ibid., fol. 77r. This was equivalent to about ten soldi a day.

14. Annarosa Garzelli, *Il ricamo nella attività artistica di Pollaiolo, Botticelli, Bartolomeo di Giovanni* (Florence: Edam, 1973).

15. BNCF, *Maglia.*, X, 143, fol. 8r.

16. Rouse and Rouse, *Cartolai, Illuminators, and Printers,* 49.

17. BNCF, *Maglia.*, X, 143, fol. 53r.

18. Ibid.

19. For a recent consideration of such monopolies and a survey of associated bibliog-raphy, see Anabel Thomas, *The Painter's Practice in Renaissance Tuscany* (Cambridge: Cam-bridge University Press, 1995).

20. BNCF, *Maglia.*, X, 143, fol. 71r. What was possibly the same Zanobi is also recorded as working in the workshop of the paper merchant Chimenti; see ibid., fols. 81v and 121r. He may also be identifiable as the Zanobi di Mariano mentioned in October 1477 (fol. 26r).

21. Ibid., fol. 78v.

22. Ibid., fols. 81v, 93r, and 94r. Elsewhere (fol. 100v) Francesco is referred to as "detto macino."

23. Ibid., fols. 71r and 72v.

24. Ibid., fol. 14v (13 May 1477), where Domenico is paid fifty soldi for binding and decorating a Legend of Saint Catherine.

25. Ibid., fol. 17r. For the relationship between the workshop of Monte and Gherardi di Monte and the printing press at San Jacopo di Ripoli, see Giuseppe S. Martini, *La bottega di un cartolaio fiorentino della seconda metà del Quattrocento: Nuovi contributi biografici intorno a Gherardo e Monte di Giovanni* (Florence: Olschki, 1956).

26. BNCF, *Maglia.*, X, 143, fol. 16v. Gherardino and Monte are mentioned separately in the same year (fol. 16v) as decorating Legends of Saint Catherine and receiving pay-ments of ten soldi for each book.

27. Ibid., fol. 6r.

28. Ibid., fols. 13r, 13v, 12v and 16v, and 16v respectively.

29. For varying sale prices, see ibid., fols. 6r, 6v, 7v, 8v, and 9r.

30. Ibid., fols. 7r and 12v.

31. Ibid., fol. 16v.

32. Ibid., fol. 77r.

33. Ibid., fol. 10r.

34. Ibid., fol. 17v.

35. Ibid., fols. 53r and 13v. Francesco is recorded as an assistant or worker in the workshop organization of Francesco the miniaturist. There are also references to him illuminating Books of Death; see ibid., fol. 18r.

36. Ibid., fol. 59r.

37. Ibid., fols. 13r and 6r.

38. Ibid., fol. 13v.

39. Ibid., fol. 43r.

40. There are several references in this respect in BNCF, *Maglia.*, X, 143 to the priest Domenico Guerrucci. See also Susan Noakes, "The Development of the Book Market in Late Quattrocento Italy: Printers' Failures and the Role of the Middleman," *Journal of Medieval and Renaissance Studies* 11 (1981): 23–55.

41. BNCF, *Maglia.*, X, 143, fols. 6v and 13r. The price of the Legend is recorded as two lire and ten soldi, indicating that it may have been quite simply decorated.

42. Ibid., fol. 16r, for a reference in July 1477 to a Legend of Saint Catherine being sold by "le monache" for three lire.

43. Ibid., fol. 13r.

44. Ibid., fol. 15v.

45. Ibid., fol. 13r.

46. Ibid., fol. 14v.

47. Ibid., fol. 90r.

48. For Saint Margaret of Hungary, see George Kaftal, *Iconography of the Saints in Tuscan Painting* (Florence: Sansoni, 1952), 201. For Margaret of Città di Castello, see ibid., 199.

49. London, British Museum, A111. See Campbell Dodgson, *Catalogue of Early German and Flemish Woodcuts preserved in the Department of Prints and Drawings in the British Museum*, 2 vols. (London: Quarto Press in association with British Museum Publications, 1903), 1:107–8.

50. Siena, Biblioteca degli Intronati, C 57 VI M.

51. BNCF, *Maglia.*, X, 43, fol. 20v.

52. Ibid.

53. Ibid., fol. 29r, where record is made on 14 Nov. 1477 of the sale of one thousand Orations of the Cross for the sum of four lire (ninety-six denari). Orations of Saint Julian were apparently even cheaper. On 27 Dec. 1477 an entry (fol. 32r) notes that a thousand of these were sold for exactly half the price. Other entries (fols. 42r and 49r) record similar rates.

54. For a discussion of the development of the Rosary, see Roberta J. M. Olson, "The Rosary and Its Iconography, Part I: Background for Devotional Tondi," *Arte Cristiana* 86 (1998): 263–76, and "The Rosary and Its Iconography, Part II: Devotional Tondi," *Arte Cristiana* 86 (1998): 334–42. See also Anna Padoa Rizzo, "Firenze e l'Europa nel Quattrocento: La 'Vergine del Rosario' di Cosimo Rosselli," in *Studi di Storia dell'Arte in Onore di Mina Gregori*, ed. Miklós Boskovits, 64–69 (Milan: Silvana, 1994).

55. See Olson, "The Rosary, Part I," 266.

56. BNCF, *Maglia.*, X, 143, fol. 84v.

57. Ibid, fol. 87v.

58. See Anabel Thomas, "Images of Saint Catherine: A Re-evaluation of Cosimo Rosselli and the Influence of His Art on the Woodcut and Metal Engraving Images of the Dominican Third Order," in *Revaluing Renaissance Art,* ed. Gabrielle Neher and Rupert Shepherd, 165–86 (Aldershot: Ashgate, 2000), for an investigation into one aspect of this.

59. Siena, Biblioteca degli Intronati, M VI 57 (previously C 57. VI. M).

60. For further explanation of the use of the rosary, see Olson, "The Rosary, Part I," 263–64.

61. This argument is explored further in Thomas, "Images of Saint Catherine."

PART IV

MINORITY GROUPS

11

SLAVES IN ITALY, 1350–1550

STEVEN A. EPSTEIN

The themes of ethnicity and marginality are complex when applied to the circumstances of slaves in Italy from the mid-fourteenth to the mid-sixteenth centuries. As David Nirenberg has observed for late medieval Spain, "the study of minorities and attitudes toward them is not the study of society's margins, and the terms 'margin' and 'center' are of little relevance in the effort to understand the place of minorities in medieval society," an observation that applies with equal force to the Italian later Middle Ages.[1] The point is that slaves, a legally defined minority, were not Italian in origin (at least in the first generation). Slaves began life as outsiders, but only in that limited sense did they live at the margins of Italian society. Slaves in Italy constituted a small minority of the population, but a large part of the ethnic diversity of the peninsula and islands. At the center was the free population of Italy, itself containing a small number of ex-slaves. The existence of slaves, even in tiny numbers, permitted all Italians, regardless of their own class and regional differences, a way to define themselves in contrast to these "dishonored" chattel.[2] Hence slaves from places as distant as Nigeria and the Caucasus played a major role in shaping Italian attitudes about people of color and also the way law codes defined what liberty meant. These influences on Italian society should not be seen as marginal.

Italian slaves in these centuries came from almost every known ethnic group, from Tartars, Circassians, Georgians, and Abkhazians from the Black Sea region, to North African Moors and sub-Saharan blacks, to Slavs and Greeks from the Balkans, Jews and Saracens from Spain, and people from the Canaries and Cape Verde islands. Even a few Indians from the Americas appeared in Italy. These slaves covered the spectrum of human colors from light to dark, spoke a bewildering (to Italians) number of languages, and made Italian slavery perhaps the most ethnically diverse slavery that has ever been practiced anywhere on the planet, with the possible exception of ancient Rome.[3]

A central question about slavery is how this unique experience affected the ways Italians saw the world, and how their culture and society differentiated itself in the presence of so many "others." It must be emphasized that in large parts of Italy slaves were rare or nonexistent, and where they were most numerous—in Venice, Genoa, and Sicily—their numbers amounted to a small percentage of the population. No parts of Italy conform to standard models of slave society, usually based on the New World variants.[4] Also, the seventeenth century witnessed the virtual withering away of Italian slavery, though it lingered into the Napoleonic period. The fate of these slaves and their descendants was to be absorbed into the Italian population, and no group in Italy (apart from Italian Jews) can plausibly claim to descend from slaves. This eventual complete assimilation seems to close the book on Italian slavery (and again provides a sharp contrast to the Americas), but in fact its legacies endure in Italian society. The presence of slaves from many ethnic backgrounds in Italy helped to define ideas about what it meant to be an Italian when Italy itself was just a geographic expression.

In order to understand the place of slaves after the plague of 1348, it is necessary to summarize some of the fundamental historical facts about slavery in Italy. Ancient Roman society, a genuine and complex slave culture, left behind as one of its main bequests the most sophisticated law on slavery ever conceived by the human mind. On every part of slavery, from buying and selling to beating to the most arcane aspects of the institution, Roman law provided authoritative answers to the problems of slavery. Since Roman law, even in its vulgar forms, remained everywhere the common law of Italy unless supervened by new legislation, the normative assumption was that slavery was a traditional, legal, and moral aspect of society.[5] The durable prestige of Roman law guaranteed this conclusion, and even the Christian emperors did not condemn the practice of slavery. Even though by the year 1000 the kind of rural slavery the Romans practiced had completely disappeared from Italy, except perhaps on Muslim Sicily, the rules on slavery still existed in the great Code and Digest, awaiting any new situation that might require them.[6]

Similarly, in the thirteenth century the papacy had fully accommodated the practices of the Christian church to slavery by making it clear that it was legal for Christians to own Christian slaves, and of course Muslim or Jewish ones.[7] These rulings, intended initially to bolster the crusading and Iberian states, also ratified practices in Italy, especially the lucrative business of slave trading, an impossible one if slaves might free themselves by converting. The combined prestigious weight of Roman and canon law raised no doubts about the practice and morality of slavery in Italy. Italian merchants, mainly the Venetians and Genoese, had been actively trading in slaves since the twelfth century if not earlier. By the fourteenth century entrepots like Caffa in the Crimea and Tana near the mouth of the Don in the Black Sea served as major sites for importing slaves from Asia and the Caucasus. The words *schiavo* and *schiava* in Italian for slave point to the Slavic Adriatic coast and the Balkans as one of the oldest and most reliable sources of slaves for Italy.[8] Sardinia too was an early victim of slave raiding from the mainland. Finally, the legacy of Muslim rule left behind some special features of Sicilian slavery. Even though by 1350 the island's Muslim population was practically gone, the Jews still survived, and the acceptance of slavery by these two religions made slavery on Sicily both more durable and ethnically more complex than on the mainland. Also, nearness to North African supplies of slaves meant that slavery on Sicily extended beyond the urban areas into the countryside. Finally, slaves were becoming more expensive even before the plague, and afterward they were increasingly luxury items.

With this background in mind, we can turn to the sources on Italian slavery, almost invariably from the masters, reflecting their needs and hypocrisies. Slave owners, and the notaries they employed, produced all the written evidence on slavery. Only rarely does the direct voice of a slave enter the historical record, usually in a legal declaration filtered by the notary's control of language. For example, the slave Giacomo was freed on 16 October 1504, and a little later that day, now a free man, he made a series of promises to his former owner, the Genoese nobleman Teramo Centurione.[9] Giacomo obligated himself to pay his former owner the substantial sum of 125 lire and to continue to work for him for three years. The words are those of a man who was a slave in the morning and a free man by evening, but they are set in a legal Latin far from his own speech. Sometimes a slave received notice in the private correspondence or diaries of free people. Alessandra Macinghi Strozzi, writing on 7 April 1464 to her son Filippo in his exile in Naples, was pleased to hear that his slave Marina was taking such good care of him, though she tied this solicitude directly to her son's slow progress toward marriage.[10] This Florentine mother, who was herself a slave owner, understood that sexual relations between wealthy men and their slaves were common enough and sometimes an impediment to marriage. Marina's own plight, as a slave who could not lawfully resist the sexual advances of her master, receives no notice in the correspondence.

Several fifteenth-century Florentine poets wrote short poems making fun of the way slaves spoke the Tuscan dialect.[11] It would be a mistake to read into these condescending attempts at humor the real voices of slaves, but we need to remember what a formidable barrier the local dialects were to the slaves imported into Italy. The slaves mentioned in these poems are nameless characters, as in many other types of documents. The slaves in the notarial records, at least usually named, appeared as property to be bought and sold, with no right to object to the transaction. As late as 1594, the English merchant Robert Richman had brought to Venice a cargo of black Moorish slaves to sell to local merchants and nobles.[12] Simon Castellano purchased a twelve-year-old girl named Antonia for the ostensible purpose of freeing her; Giovanni Maria Canevalli acquired seven slaves between the ages of ten and twenty—a lot sale of nameless souls destined for an uncertain fate. All these contracts, executed in strict legal form, portray the slaves as voiceless objects. Contracts and legislation controlled the place slaves occupied in Italian societies. These legal, notarial, and literary sources from all over Italy are not well known or everywhere good, so the best approach is to examine those places and periods that have the best evidence.[13]

FLORENTINE SLAVERY IN THE LATE TRECENTO

In 1363 the Florentine commune decided to foster the security of owning slaves by making it easier to pursue and identify runaways, so it began to keep records on transfers of slaves. This register also included the price

and a very detailed physical description of slaves.[14] The descriptions included skin color, moles, scars, pierced ears, and other features that
would be useful in tracking slaves in the city, as well as those who dared
to flee. From 1366 to 1397 there is good evidence on about 357 slaves
(some changed hands more than once). Many startling facts emerge
about this population; the first is that the numbers include 328 women
and only 25 men. With a few exceptions, mostly concerning the special
cases of male slaves as rowers in the sixteenth-century galleys, what we
can call Renaissance slavery remained overwhelmingly female. At the
time of the *catasto* of 1427 there were apparently no male slaves in Florence.[15] Prices of course varied enormously by age, appearance, and other
factors, but most slaves cost between thirty and fifty florins, well beyond
the reach of most Florentines. Most slaves, especially in northern Italy,
were expensive females working as domestic servants in the houses of
the rich. The imbalance in sexes implies that breeding slaves was not a
priority, which is a curious result given how costly slaves were. The general rule that status followed the mother's condition meant, however, that
free men could father new slaves on these women. But there was some
reluctance to seeing one's own flesh become a slave, and such children
were often an embarrassment to the household, to be dumped in the public orphanage, the Ospedale degli Innocenti.[16] Sometimes freedom for the
mother and child might be the reward from a kind-hearted father/owner.
Iris Origo explored this problem and the many other consequences to
family life, for free people and slaves, that resulted from the presence of
these "domestic enemies," the female slaves.[17] The rape of a slave was
no crime except a kind of trespass on the owner, and the masters had
free, if not always easy, sexual access to their slaves, if they chose. For all
these complicated reasons, the Italian slave population was not a self-
reproducing *slave* population, and so constant imports were required to
maintain numbers—one of the reasons slaves were so expensive. Venetian and Genoese merchants were the main importers of slaves into Italy,
but foreigners like the Catalans also were active in the trade.

The ethnic composition of the Florentine slave population is also
remarkable. For the female slaves the breakdown is as follows: 242 Tartars, 24 Greeks, 9 Russians, 7 Turks, and 17 others from the eastern Mediterranean and Black Sea regions. The Tartars brought to Italy by the
Venetians and Genoese comprise the overwhelming majority of slaves,
but a closer look at the ethnic label reveals a more complex picture. The

Florentine records also noted skin color as a key identifier, and for the Tartar women this is the pattern: 45 white, 16 reddish or fair, 161 olive, 18 brown, 2 black. The core of this group consisted of olive-complexioned Mongol women with distinctive oval eyes and a face that struck the Florentines as flat. The Tartar homelands in Ukraine and southern Russia had clearly incorporated much ethnic diversity, in terms of color and appearance. Some other ethnic groups were in effect becoming Tartars, and ended up as slaves in Italy. Italy itself no longer supplied slaves, and even the western Mediterranean and North Africa, original suppliers of slaves, no longer furnished Florence with slaves. Slavery had a strong ethnic base in Florence, largely confined to Tartars, at least some of whom resembled Italians in color if not in all facial features. Hence Italian slavery had a strong but not absolute basis in color and ethnicity.

SICILY AND GENOA

Another view of slavery emerges from Sicily in the thirteenth and four-teenth centuries. Henri Bresc discovered that for Palermo, in the period 1290–1460, slaves were less than 12 percent of the population.[18] Slaves were hence more numerous in Palermo than they ever were in Venice or Genoa. Around 1350 slaves on Sicily were mostly "Saracens," Muslims imported from North Africa. By then the indigenous Muslim population of medieval Sicily had disappeared, through either expulsion, conversion, or migration. Women were about two-thirds of the Sicilian slave popula-tion, suggesting, as in the northern cities, that they were primarily em-ployed as domestic servants in the houses of masters wealthy enough to afford them. Male slaves, more likely perhaps to be killed than captured, and more in demand elsewhere in the Mediterranean (the slave-based armies of Mamluk Egypt come to mind), were not yet needed in the gal-leys and seem to have been less desirable as domestic servants. Greek slaves, caught up in the Ottoman advances through the southern Balkans, arrived in increasing numbers in the early Trecento. These slaves, all Greek Christians, were treated with less severity than Muslim slaves.[19]

After the first onslaught of the bubonic plague and its recurring rav-ages after 1350, both free and slave labor was in short supply. Highly priced slaves, the Tartars, arrived in increasing numbers in Sicily, as in the northern cities like Florence. The gendered aspect of slavery was also similar: the Tartar slaves were overwhelmingly women and commanded a high price, 7.16 ounces of gold in Palermo.[20] In the early fifteenth century Bresc describes a Sicilian style of slavery in which Tartar and Saracen slaves were coming into balance, as were the sex ratios.[21] Over the course of the Quattrocento, sub-Saharan African slaves, called Ethiopians, became more common in Sicily. The Catalans supplied these slaves and became increasingly dominant in the slave trade. As more of southern Italy fell into Aragonese control, new attitudes about slaves and peoples of color came into Italy from the west. This cultural exchange is usually seen the other way, at least from the Italian perspective, as their growing influence on elite culture in Spain. At the same time, merchants from Iberia were altering the ethnic mix of peoples in the Mezzogiorno, especially in Sicily.

From the point of view of Catalan merchants, or indeed of explorers like Columbus, Sicily might appear at first glance to be part of a chain of islands, stretching from Cyprus to Hispaniola, where slaves might be profitably employed in agriculture—in sugar. Sicily was not well suited to become a sugar island because of its climate—generally too dry, though small amounts of cane were raised there. Sub-Saharan African slaves continued to be imported into Sicily, where they were put to work in the cities as well as the countryside. What Sicily has in common with the Atlantic sugar islands is that a large number of slaves were easily identified because they were darker than most of the free population. In complex ways that demand further research, the Mezzogiorno's place on the geographical "margins" of the Spanish world empire introduced even more vivid ideas of color, blood, and race into Italian culture. Naturally the concept of "razza" remained hazy in these centuries, but Italians discriminated among potential supplies of slaves according to their color. In some cases ethnicity was a proxy for color; "Ethiopian" always meant "black," but the Tartar slaves came in a bewildering array of colors.

A few pieces of later evidence from Sicily indicate how complicated this nexus between slavery and race was becoming. San Benedetto Il Moro (Saint Benedict the Moor, 1524–89), born at Sanfradello, was the son of sub-Saharan freed slaves.[22] Benedetto led a pious life as a Franciscan hermit and later as a Capuchin monk at the order's house in Palermo, where he acquired a reputation for saintliness. Canonized in 1807 and one of the patron saints of Palermo, San Benedetto was an object of devotion in Sicily and in the New World for centuries before he became an official saint. Spanish missionaries found a good use for a saintly Sicilian monk who also happened to be black. His life supports the conclusion that Sicily was, in this period, a relatively tolerant society in which the child of former black slaves was accepted into society and eventually revered—by no means marginal to anything. Not all ex-slaves had as easy a time as San Benedetto, but most of them seem to have remained in Italy even when freed. It may be that these slaves, many brought to Italy as children and emancipated many years later with little or no wealth, had little choice, but Italian societies allowed them to remain. Gradually a small class of Tartar and black ex-slaves in parts of Italy in the fifteenth and sixteenth centuries complicated any neat identification of race or ethnicity with slavery.

A census of slaves taken in Palermo in 1565 reveals that there were 645 male slaves in a city containing 56,785 men, so a little more than 1 percent of the population, a big decline from the previous century.[23] Blacks were the largest category among the slaves, but by now many slaves had been born on the island and it seems that the trade was diminishing. Tax records from Trapani in 1593/4, whose population was about 16,500, reveal precisely 323 slaves, 120 men, 199 women, and 4 uncertain, about 2 percent of the population.[24] In this town slavery was more a fixture of rural agriculture than a prestigious luxury item. The same tax records from 1682 showed only four slaves left in Trapani, so the end of slavery in Sicily is basically a seventeenth-century story, for reasons we will consider below.[25]

Genoa's rich notarial records provide wonderful portraits of the actual practice of slavery in the Trecento, admittedly drawn by notaries and not the slaves themselves. For example, emancipations occurred and reduced the number of slaves as these people entered free society. The realities of emancipation could be complex. On 10 December 1362 the draper maestro Antoniolo de Calana freed his slave Giovanna, of North African stock from Tripoli.[26] He did this for the good of his soul, as inserted in a marginal note in the contract, and for the twenty-four florins he received from the slave's mother, Benedetta de Tripoli. Giovanna also had to continue working for her master for the next twenty months. But Giovanna became completely free with the right to be the head of a family and bear free children. Her master also renounced any rights of patronage that Roman law conferred over ex-slaves. Benedetta de Tripoli, who was also certainly an ex-slave and kept as a last name a remembrance of her ethnic origin, bought her daughter out of slavery. This emancipation reminds us that a steady stream of ex-slaves became Genoese. In 1381 a master carpenter freed his slave Niccolò, ostensibly for the benefit of his soul.[27] The next notarial act laid out the terms: Niccolò had to pay his ex-master twelve and a half florins a year for the next eight years to make up the sum of a hundred florins, or else the emancipation was cancelled. This huge sum, far more than the price of any slave, shows the economic as well as the spiritual calculations that entered into the decision to free a slave. Still, this Niccolò took his master's name and became Niccolò Vairolo da Camogli, to all appearances a Genoese. Giovanna, Benedetta, and Niccolò, by ethnicity not Italians, could now choose their names, occupations, and residences, and were lucky not to die as slaves. It is impossible to say what percentage of Genoese slaves were freed, except to note that such contracts were a small fraction of slave sales.

Jacques Heers has observed that slaves were an important part of the population in northern and central Italy, and in Genoa they were perhaps as much as 4 percent of the population in the middle of the fifteenth century.[28] Genoa offers good evidence on slaves, and Domenico Gioffré's exhaustive search of the archives yielded about 1,600 notarial acts concerning slaves, and more important, the records of the head tax on slaves for 1458.[29] In that year there were 2,059 slaves in a city of perhaps 60,000, but even more revealing are these numbers: 2,005 women and 54 men. Notices from other cities confirm these startling figures; there were apparently no male slaves at all in Lucca and Florence at this time.[30] By 1472, the number of slaves in Genoa had fallen to about eight hundred, and by the end of the century there were probably even fewer.[31] The two fundamental facts about slavery in Genoa were that it was overwhelmingly female and that by the late fifteenth century it was waning. Accounting for these two features of slavery will help to explain the place of slaves in Genoese society. Also, Genoa's laws reveal a sophisticated attempt to regularize the buying and selling of human beings in a Christian community.

Between the tax and notarial records we have a very good sense of Genoese slavery and its economics, from the point of view of the buyers and sellers. As expected, slaves from the east—Tartars, Circassians, Abkhazians, and Russians—predominated in Genoa, and these women tended to be the most expensive on the market, often costing as much

as a hundred lire, the price of a small house.[32] Only the rich could afford
the luxury of owning these slaves. Yet the prices of slaves varied considerably by the age and ethnicity of the women, so there was supply at the
bottom of the market for the middling group of Genoese consumers to
purchase older and darker slaves at lower prices. Black slaves were rare
in Genoa in this century, so the darker slaves came from the Moors of
Spain and North Africa; there was a last burst of supplies of the former
when Granada fell in 1492.[33] Spain also supplied the few Jewish slaves
who appeared in the 1490s. These sources of supply from the western
Mediterranean reiterate the major problem for the Genoese: that after
the Ottoman conquest of Constantinople in 1453 it became much harder
to import white slaves from the Black Sea regions, and after the fall of
Caffa in 1475 it was practically impossible. The Ottoman state, with its
own extensive slavery, absorbed these traditional supplies of slaves, both
the men and the women. As we have seen, the Catalans were able to
supply increasing numbers of Africans to Sicily to make up for the collapse of eastern supplies. This solution did not work for Genoa and
Venice, probably because the cities were usually on bad terms with the
Catalans, but also because their sources of supply before 1500 were modest. In the sixteenth century the growing demand for slaves in the New
World would draw the Africans in that direction, at prices the Italians
were unwilling to pay.

Where male slaves existed in large numbers, they were likely to be
rowers in galleys and not likely to live long. Male slaves in domestic service or in agricultural work fared better. In Genoa the large numbers of
women slaves again suggest that domestic service in the houses of the
wealthy was the work the slaves performed.[34] Some slave women also
served as wet nurses. A lucrative side business for slave owners was the
renting out of lactating slaves to families needing them. The price data
on Genoese slaves contain a lot of variability, with the clear trend that
slaves were more expensive as their numbers decreased by century's
end. Gioffré's price data suggest that women slaves were most costly in
their late twenties, cheaper in adolescence and as they aged.[35] As in Sicily,
the darker women were less expensive. By the 1490s, when the average
price of a slave had reached 132 lire, women from the east cost 203 lire,
and one of the rare black women, from Guinea, cost 90 lire. These figures
indicate that the average price is less meaningful than price, age, and
color together. Age was significant because without doubt many of the

women were purchased by the male owners for sexual reasons, and as we will see, the law cases show how sexually active slave women complicated the owners' domestic lives. Supplies of darker slaves were becoming available just as the price of Circassians, always the most expensive white slaves, was going through the roof. Market substitution might have occurred as Genoese consumers shifted to African slaves, but they never really did. In Genoa as in Venice there was always the alternative of employing local women or migrants as servants. As Dennis Romano has shown, there was always a tension in these choices, and certainly both cities continued to demand large numbers of servants, most of whom were wage laborers.[36] Revealed preferences demonstrate a hierarchy in which a few exotic Africans might grace the odd noble household in the north, but in general they were not wanted. Potential owners would rather abandon slavery and hire servants instead. One obvious consequence is that the status of servants grew perilously close to that of slaves, most clear in the right to beat servants. These choices also show that racist attitudes, already strong in northern Italy, were drawing distinctions between the Tartars, exotic and light-skinned enough to be acceptable, and the darker, more threatening Africans. It is impossible to imagine San Benedetto of Palermo's career taking place in sixteenth-century Venice or Genoa. Hence attitudes about color in Italy may have their origins in this experience of slavery, another sign that small numbers do not translate into marginal people or influences.

THE LAW

Being a slave was a legal fact, and there were some interesting cases in which a slave disputed his or her status.[37] The law, whether canon, Roman, or civil law particular to a city or state, needed to define who was slave and free. The law also exemplified the values and fears of a slave-owning society. Besides the statutes that provide an idealized portrait of slavery, we can also look at a legal case to see how in practice society dealt with slavery. Again, though slaves were a small percentage of the population, their legal status affected broader issues like labor and punishment, and so they are hardly marginal.

The Genoese law code, revised in 1407, provides a detailed look at slavery and the law.[38] This municipal code does not contain a slave code;

instead, rules on slavery permeate the law at almost every turn. This itself is useful evidence for how ordinary and accepted the practice of
slavery was in Venice and Genoa as well as on Sicily. Fear of slaves is one
of the themes of this code. No money changer, goldsmith, or any other
person was allowed to buy silver, pearls, precious stones, or gold from
any slave, servant, or boy or girl less than fifteen years of age.[39] This
telling set of slaves, servants, and minors, the legally powerless, raises
the question of whether having slaves in a society debases the status of
those free persons at the bottom of the social hierarchy. The law shows
that at times some free people's status came very close to that of slaves.
On the same theme, dealers in used keys were prohibited from selling
keys to any servant, slave, or any person except the master of the house.[40]
If fear of theft and housebreaking were not enough, the law also revealed that the more somber threat of poisoning was on owners' minds.
It made sense that only the master of an apothecary shop should be allowed to sell arsenic, and the law permitted his son to act in his place, but
never an apprentice or slave.[41] More explicitly, the law prohibited any
apothecary from training any Tartar or Turkish slave at all. Since the law
allowed for the possibility that slaves from other ethnic groups might be
so trained, we have evidence that the Genoese especially feared these
people. Turks and Tartars were formidable enemies to Christian powers
in Europe, and perhaps these slaves struck Italians as threatening because
of their fierce, aggressive traditions. The subtle violence of poisoning was
disconcerting because the slaves in domestic service had ready access to
the owners' food and drink. There is a revealing poison case from Venice
in 1410, in which a female Tartar slave bought arsenic and in revenge
murdered her master.[42] This episode resulted in new laws on poisons in
Venice, and it highlights both the issue of fear as well as slave resistance to inhumane treatment.

Another sign of fear is the Genoese law, derived from an older code,
stating that owners could not free their slaves by will lest the slaves pro-
cure or hasten their masters' deaths in order to obtain their liberty.[43]
Genoa was harsh on manumission by testament, and most slave-owning
societies permitted it. But the reasoning makes sense in light of suspicions about slave loyalty. Even when free, ex-slaves were not equal to
the rest of society. Manumitted male or female slaves who became involved in or were suspected of prostitution, adultery, or thefts or who
aided other badly behaved people, and therefore earned the hatred and

contempt of their neighbors, could be expelled from their residences if three-quarters or more of the neighbors agreed.[44] Ex-slaves were in the unique legal status of having to be on their best behavior and please their neighbors or else be kicked out. Ethnicity may play a part here too; most of these slaves were not like the Genoese, and they may have seemed, even at their best, to be undesirable neighbors. Legislation by Frederick III of Sicily provided Muslim and Jewish slaves with incentives to convert, and this, along with the lenient terms afforded Greek slaves, suggest that both ethnicity and religion shaped how the law treated present and former slaves.[45]

The criminal law in Genoa contained two special provisions about slaves. First, though the law imposed the death penalty on rapists, it punished the rape of a slave or "dishonest woman" with a fine of fifty to one hundred lire, and in the slave's case half the fine went to the owner.[46] Free women whom society considered unworthy lost protection, as did all slaves, whose rape might become a financial benefit to the owner, surely a moral and legal morass. Similarly, if anyone made a female slave pregnant, he had to pay the master twenty-five lire, and fifty lire if the slave died in pregnancy, and for twenty-five lire more he got to keep the baby.[47] The law conceded that a female slave might have voluntary sex outside the household, and the masters benefited, and of course enjoyed free sexual access to slaves. Second, the law allowed that people needed to control what it called the malices and excesses of slaves.[48] It imposed a curfew on all slaves and gave the masters a virtually unlimited right to beat slaves even to the point of death, provided that they did not use a weapon. The law itself stated that it was necessary to beat slaves; everyone recognized the fundamental violence that maintained obedience. This law protected servants by stating that anyone killing them faced the regular legal penalties. But if a servant raised a hand against his or her master, there was no crime committed no matter what the employer did in self-defense. Slavery muddled the difference between slave and free doing the same work, and it placed in the hands of slave owners a right to correction certain to be abused.

The legal opinions or *consilia* of Bartolomeo de Bosco, a Genoese lawyer active in the early fifteenth century, provide a glimpse of how individual slaves fared in the courts, albeit as objects.[49] Battista de' Gogio bought a nameless slave and now claimed that she was diseased when sold and in fact died shortly thereafter, and so he wanted his money back.

This seems like an ordinary commercial case on defective merchandise, but when the commodity was a person, things were not so simple. Bosco, brought in by the seller, raised other issues. He pointed out that Battista had not returned the slave in thirty days (the reasonable period), or asked if she had ever been treated by doctors, so he bore responsibility for the outcome. More important, he had purchased the slave for sex, and when he was unable to be potent with her because of his own grave illness, only then did he try to return her. Second, he treated the slave for a case of skin mites with an unguent that might have killed her. By placing the base motives, impotence, and possible poisoning in the judges' minds, Bosco earned his fee and gives us an unintended glimpse into the realities of this nameless girl in Renaissance Italy.

CONCLUSION

Slaves, although a small percentage of the Italian population, helped to shape the meaning of liberty, morality in the marketplace, as well as the treatment of wage laborers. Slavery also brought to Italy a diverse ethnic population that raised questions about what it meant to be Genoese, or Florentine, or eventually an Italian. Especially after the plague of 1348, slavery seemed to be a potentially vibrant part of trade and urban society. The vast majority of Italians, who never ventured beyond their peninsula, saw exotic peoples on their city streets—as distinguished ambassadors from foreign realms, or as slaves.

Why then did slavery wane in sixteenth-century Italy? No moral outcry occurred to produce this result. Charles Verlinden concluded his massive collection of data on slavery by observing that the high price of slaves made them into luxury items hard to employ profitably in either agriculture or other endeavors.[50] When considerations of profit were secondary, as in the galleys, states continued to use captive men (alongside convicts) as slave rowers provided that they could be obtained at little or no cost through warfare with North African corsairs. The profitable use of slaves in the New World, the unsuitability of most of Italy to plantation-style agriculture for world markets, and the increase of the free population that started by the century's end probably all doomed Italian slavery to a slow death. Using slaves was one point on a spectrum of ways to exploit labor. When supplies of free labor increased and were available at no capital costs to employers, it made sense to employ wage laborers rather than compete in international markets for increasingly expensive African slave labor. The moral consequences to Italy for failing to reject slavery for any other reasons remain incalculable.

NOTES

1. David Nirenberg, *Communities of Violence: Persecution of Minorities in the Middle Ages* (Princeton: Princeton University Press, 1996), 16.

2. The theme of slaves as dishonored persons is the point of the book by Orlando Patterson, *Slavery and Social Death* (Cambridge: Harvard University Press, 1982). His *Freedom: Freedom in the Making of Western Culture* (New York: Basic Books, 1991) provides a good background to medieval slavery. William D. Phillips Jr., *Slavery from Roman Times to the Early Transatlantic Trade* (Minneapolis: University of Minnesota Press, 1985) is the best general work on medieval slavery. For a general study of slavery in Italy, see Steven Epstein, *Speaking of Slavery: Color, Ethnicity, and Human Bondage in Italy* (Ithaca: Cornell University Press, 2001).

3. The best survey on Roman slavery is Keith Bradley, *Slavery and Society at Rome* (Cambridge: Cambridge University Press, 1994).

4. The best synthesis on the rise of the Atlantic slavery system is by Robert Blackburn, *The Making of New World Slavery: From the Baroque to the Modern 1492–1800* (London: Verso, 1997). This book suggests that Mediterranean slavery had a very minor role in the rise of plantation slavery in the New World. For a recent study that stresses the similarities between early modern slavery in Italy and the rest of the world, see Salvatore Bono, *Schiavi musulmani nell'Italia moderna* (Naples: Edizioni scientifiche italiane, 1999).

5. For more on this idea of a common law in Europe based on Roman principles, see Manlio Bellomo, *The Common Legal Past of Europe 1000–1800*, trans. Lydia Cochrane (Washington: Catholic University of America Press, 1995).

6. On the disappearance of rural slavery in Italy, see Pierre Toubert, *Les Structures du latium médiéval* (Rome: École française de Rome, 1973), 507–16.

7. Benjamin Z. Kedar, *Crusade and Mission* (Princeton: Princeton University Press, 1984).

8. Daniel Evans, "Slave Coast of Europe," *Slavery and Abolition* 6 (1985): 41–58.

9. Luigi Tria, "La schiavitù in Liguria," *Atti della società ligure di storia patria* 70 (1947): 1–253 (manumission document no. 93, pp. 225–26, promises no. 94, pp. 226–27).

10. Heather Gregory, trans., *Selected Letters of Alessandra Strozzi: Bilingual Edition* (Berkeley: University of California Press, 1997), 110–11.

11. Mario Ferrara, "Linguaggio di schiave del Quattrocento," *Studi di filologia italiana* 8 (1950): 320–28.

12. For examples of these contracts, see Alberto Tenenti, "Gli schiavi di Venezia alla fine del Cinquecento," *Rivista storica italiana* 67 (1955): 52–69.

13. Special notice should be given to Iris Origo, "The Domestic Enemy: The Eastern Slaves in Tuscany in the Fourteenth and Fifteenth Centuries," *Speculum* 30 (1955): 321–66, an

outstanding article that I need not summarize here. Piero Guardacci and Valeria Ottanelli, *I servitori domestici della casa borghese toscana nel basso medioevo* (Florence: Salimbeni, 1982) depends on Origo's work but has fresh insights on slaves in Tuscany (pp. 77–94).

14. The original decree and register are in Ridolfo Livi, *La schiavitù domestica nei tempi di mezzo e nei moderni* (Padua: CEDAM., 1928), 141–217, also a major source for Origo.

15. David Herlihy and Christiane Klapisch-Zuber, *Les Toscans et leur familles: Une étude du "catasto" florentin de 1427* (Paris: Fondation nationale des sciences politiques: École des hautes études en sciences sociales, 1978), 142 (p. 294 women).

16. For notices of abandoned slave children, see Philip Gavitt, *Charity and Children in Renaissance Florence: The Ospedale degli Innocenti, 1410–1536* (Ann Arbor: University of Michigan Press, 1990).

17. Origo, "Domestic Enemy."

18. Henri Bresc, *Un monde méditerranéen: Économie et société en Sicile 1300–1450*, 2 vols. (Rome: École française de Rome, 1986), 1:439 (pp. 439–63 for what follows).

19. Ibid., 443.

20. Ibid., 444.

21. Ibid., 447.

22. Giuseppe Carletti, *Vita di S. Benedetto da S. Filadelfo detto il moro* (Rome: Presso Antonio Fulgoni, 1805), 1–7 for biographical details.

23. Antonio Franchina, "Un censimento di schiavi nel 1565," *Archivio storico siciliano* 32 (1907): 374–89.

24. Giovanni Marrone, *La schiavitù nella società siciliana dell'età moderna* (Caltanissetta: S. Sciascia, 1972), 56–57.

25. Ibid., 159.

26. Archivio di Stato di Genova, *Cartolari Notarili*, Cart. N. 289, fol. 131r–v, Benvenuto de Bracelli notary.

27. Ibid., fol. 92r–v, Benvenuto de Bracelli notary.

28. Jacques Heers, *Gênes au XVe siècle* (Paris: SEVPEN, 1961), 555.

29. Domenico Gioffrè, *Il mercato degli schiavi a Genova nel secolo xv* (Genoa: Fratelli Bozzi, 1971), 79.

30. For Florence, see note 15 above; for Lucca, see Michael E. Bratchel, *Lucca 1430–1494: The Reconstruction of an Italian City Republic* (Oxford: Oxford University Press, 1995), 148–49.

31. Gioffrè, *Il mercato*, 70.

32. For the house, see ibid., 142, and my own observations. As Gioffrè notes, a sailor made fifty-eight lire a year, a well-paid trade.

33. Ibid., 31–38, for this and what follows.

34. For some general comments on the work of women slaves, see Franco Angiolini, "Schiave," in *Il lavoro delle donne*, ed. Angela Groppi (Roma-Bari: Laterza, 1996), 105–11.

35. Gioffrè, *Il mercato*, 130–42.

36. Dennis Romano, *Housecraft and Statecraft: Domestic Service in Renaissance Venice, 1400–1600* (Baltimore: Johns Hopkins University Press, 1996), 25–48.

37. See for example a petition from Giorgio da Caffa, living in Siena and claiming to be a free runaway slave, in Giulio Prunai, "Notizie e documenti sulla servitù domestica nel territorio senese," *Bulletino senese di storia patria* 7 (1936): 415.

38. *Leges Genuenses* (henceforth *LG*), in *Historiae Patriae Monumenta*, 22 vols. (Turin: Officina regia, 1901), vol. 18, cited by column. For background, see Robert Delort, "Quelques précisions sur le commerce des esclaves à Gênes vers la fin du XIVe siècle," *Mélanges d'archaeologie et d'histoire* 77 (1966): 215–50; Steven A. Epstein, *Genoa and the Genoese 958–1528* (Chapel Hill: University of North Carolina Press, 1996), 266–70.

39. *LG,* 564.

40. Ibid., 643.

41. Ibid., 675.

42. Romano, *Housecraft and Statecraft,* 52.

43. *LG,* 822.

44. Ibid., 645.

45. Clifford R. Backman, *The Decline and Fall of Medieval Sicily* (Cambridge: Cambridge University Press, 1995), 259.

46. *LG,* 922.

47. Ibid., 951–52.

48. Ibid., 959–62.

49. Bartolomeo de Bosco, *Consilia* (Lodano: Franciscum Castellum, 1620), no 301, p. 493. For more details on this lawyer's work on slavery, see Steven Epstein, "A Late Medieval Lawyer Confronts Slavery: The Cases of Bartolomeo de Bosco," *Slavery and Abolition* 20 (1999): 49–68.

50. Charles Verlinden, *L'Esclavage dans l'Europe médiévale*, vol. 2, *Italie–Colonies italiennes du Levant – Levant latin – Empire byzantin* (Bruges: De Tempel, 1977), 1027–28. This book is a compendium of notices of slaves in Italian documents and is most informative on slave prices.

12

THE MARGINALITY OF
MOUNTAINEERS IN
RENAISSANCE FLORENCE

SAMUEL K. COHN JR.

The social order of the Middle Ages was not so firmly set in stone as medieval philosophers such as John of Salisbury may have wished or as stable as modern historians sometimes have imagined.[1] For ritual space, Richard Trexler's examination of processions in late medieval and Renaissance Florence has shown the dramatic repositioning in times of crisis of "liminal groups" from the margins to the center, such as when boys and women assumed center stage in processions at the end of the Florentine republic. Hierarchical and gender shifts were not restricted to a ritual moment of the "world turned upside down"; the relation between center and periphery could change also in social and geographic space and over longer periods than that embraced in a procession.[2]

The history of Florence's mountain communities along the Apennine ridges shows such changes in the marginality of mountain dwellers from the Black Death of 1348 to the end of the fifteenth century. Traditionally, historians have seen the mountains in the Mediterranean as fixed on the margins of urban civilization. With near-poetic verve, Fernand Braudel has described these mountain peasants as backward and their dwellings as the patriarchal refuge of outlaws, harboring "rough men, clumsy, stocky, and close-fisted." Along with other niceties of urban culture, religion was slow here to penetrate. It was "a world of sorcerers, witchcraft, and primitive magic; black masses were the flowerings of an ancient cultural subconscious."[3] However, he also speculated that pre-biblical civilizations might have arisen first in the mountains before spreading irreversibly to the plains.[4] Later, the Florentine historian Elio Conti showed that this mountain dominance as seats of culture persisted into the twelfth century.[5] Indeed, the Carolingian monastery of Badia di San Salvatore in the Monte Amiata (at 822 m) retained its centrality as a place of culture, wealth, and authority vis-à-vis the plains until the draining of its malaria-ridden lowlands in the eighteenth century.[6]

But according to the latest historiography—principally that from Giovanni Cherubini[7]—mountain communities in Tuscany had assumed the characteristics Braudel attached to them by the beginning of the fourteenth century, if not before, and would retain them through the early modern period. To his credit, Cherubini went beyond the sources relied upon mostly by Braudel—literary scraps from prejudiced urban writers. Instead, from the tax records of Florence Cherubini argued that the social structure of the mountains was categorically different from the plains. With the fourteenth-century spread of the *mezzadria* system (sharecropping), the city had "proletarized" the agriculture of the plains and nearby hills. By contrast, the mountains lay outside this urban influence and, according to Cherubini, remained steeped in an "egalitarianism" founded in poverty. Yet Cherubini failed to compare the social structure of the mountains with the hills or plains, or to investigate change over time.

The richness of the Florentine archival sources makes possible further evaluation of the mountains' social structure. From 1355 to 1487 twelve separate tax registers survive for the countryside. Indeed, because of the city's desire and power to place direct taxation on the shoulders of residents of the surrounding countryside, the *contado,* we now know more about the economic, demographic, and social structure of the countryside than about the city of Florence at least until 1427.

From samples of twenty-eight villages and one neighborhood *(porta)* of Prato, I have found that the social structure of the mountains was hardly static over the long term, and in relation to the plains, I find no mountain egalitarianism founded in poverty, even though the *mezzadria* system rarely penetrated lands above five hundred meters and urban investment in these highlands was virtually unknown from the pre–Black Death castles of the Bardi to the hunting lodges of Lorenzo *il Magnifico*

at the end of the fifteenth century. Instead of "egalitarian poverty," the
richest peasants in the countryside hailed from the mountains, such as
a 104-year-old Bartolo di Bartolo from Monte Morello who ruled over a
four-generational family with seventeen members and whose property
value in 1393 exceeded five hundred lire. It is not accidental that when
the late fourteenth-century storyteller Franco Sacchetti wanted to satirize
a peasant for having too much money as opposed to casting the usual
barbs against rural poverty and idiocy, he chose a peasant family living
on the Apennine borders of Florence and Bologna.[8] Yet alongside Bartolo, 46 percent of the household heads of his parish (S. Maria Morello)
possessed no taxable wealth; and further up, in the Mugello village of
Mangona two-thirds of the households were *miserabili* in 1393. Indeed,
in that tax year, the average wealth of mountain households was slightly
greater than that of villages in the plains. In that tax year no significant
difference in the distribution of wealth distinguished any of these geographical zones — plains, hills, or mountains.[9]

But can one generalize from a single point in time? In the earliest
tax records to estimate property (1365), Apennine highlanders were more
than one-and-a-half times wealthier than plainsmen. But by 1371 the highlanders' well-being began to deteriorate, and by the beginning of the
next century they had assumed the social characteristics attributed to
them by Braudel and Cherubini. In 1402, propertied highlanders possessed half as much as plainsmen. Further, the demographic paralleled
the economic. In the aftermath of the plague (the earliest surviving of
the *capi di famiglia* drawn up in 1355), the mountain hamlet of Mangona
was among the largest villages in the Florentine countryside. Counting
220 families with possibly as many as a thousand individuals, it was
larger than the market town of Sesto in the plains near the city of Florence. Before the plague Mangona may have been more than double its
postplague size. Far from being absent from the mountains, because
supposedly they were more salubrious, the plague may have hit some
mountain areas even more severely than cities or plains. At least, this is
the impression given from peasant pleas in the latter half of the fourteenth century. In 1348, for example, Mangona was the only commune
to petition successfully to Florence for the cancellation of fiscal penalties
because of the havoc wrought by the plague. It pleaded that it had missed
payments due to Florence because three-quarters of its population had
been swept away by the plague, and no villager remained who could re-

member Mangona's rental payments due to the city of Florence.[10] However, even if Mangona's ambassadors had not exaggerated the demographic damages of the plague of 1348, their post-1348 demographic experience was even more disastrous than that caused by pestilence in
1348. The community declined steeply through the fourteenth century.
By 1412 fewer than seventy families remained. The demographic history
of other villages along the Apennine ridges followed a similar pattern.
Nearby Montecarello's decline was even steeper than Mangona's; it lost
over 70 percent of its population in the half century after the onslaught
of 1348. On the other hand, the demographic experience of the plains
was markedly different. After 1348, their village populations remained
relatively stable before turning upward in the fifteenth century.

So why did wealth and population decline in the mountains both
absolutely and relative to the plains? While natural disasters may have
played some role, there is little evidence for it after 1348. Instead, the
reasons turn more on man-made causes—taxation and war.[11] By linking
the tax records called *estimi* (the assessments of property values of both
land and movables) with the *lire* (the final tax base calculated in the city),
it is possible to compare tax rates over time and space. This record link-
age reveals that the villages of the countryside, even within the traditional *contado* of Florence, were not taxed at the same rates. Indeed, the
differences could be extraordinary. In 1393 Mangona was taxed thirty
times more than San Lorenzo outside the walls of Florence, and in 1402
the tax inequalities worsened. On average, mountain villages were taxed
more than four times more than lowland communities. But such fiscal
prejudice against the mountain dwellers had not been a constant of Florentine policy. In 1365 both zones had been taxed at roughly the same
rates; their rates began to diverge in 1371, reaching an apex in 1402, which
led to the demographic and economic consequences sketched above.

Further, these inequalities must be seen against the backdrop of increasing warfare in northern Italy after the Black Death and the resulting acceleration of public indebtedness. Direct taxes placed on the *contado* mounted, while its population tumbled. To meet growing military
demands, the Florentine government increased the coefficients (on which
the tax rates were multiplied) by twelve times from the 1370s to 1401.
Given the tax-rate inequalities between mountains and plains, this meant
that highlanders had to shoulder disproportionately these increases. As
a result, a community such as Mangona was forced from 1396 to 1401 to

turn over 66 percent of its wealth annually to the Florentine tax collector. In addition, these mountain communities were the theaters of military activity and thus paid even more than the treasury records reveal. Over and beyond their taxes, they were forced to provision castles, requisition troops, and pay as the objects of warfare with torched fields and their houses burned to the ground, ransoms to free their neighbors, brigandage by enemy as well as Florentine troops, and diminished populations from mortality and migration.

You may well ask how the mountain communities could have possibly met such demands even in the best of times. As tax petitions and demands of the opening years of the fifteenth century attest, Mangona, along with other mountain communes along the Florentine Apennines, simply could not and did not pay, at least in full. Instead, their first means of protest was with their feet. From 1383 to 1402 emigration climbed from 10 to over 40 percent of the standing population. Moreover, these highlanders did not leave for greener pastures lower down the valleys with lower tax rates as Florentine oligarchs may have wished or as historians usually assume;[12] instead, they moved upward and across the borders into the higher mountains of Pistoia, Bologna, and the Romagna, fleeing Florentine direct taxes and other impositions altogether.

Why had Florence turned against their highlanders, transforming them from the wealthiest peasants in the *contado* into the most impoverished in less than a generation? I have yet to uncover any documents that spell out the government's rationale, but the context of economic and demographic factors mixed with the politics of patronage suggests an answer. Just as Florence pushed its direct taxes on its *contadini*, it also wished to protect those peasants in the plains, close to the city, who worked on their citizens' farms. In economic terms, high taxes here would have cut into these peasants' ability to work their farms and pay their rents to Florentine landlords. Thus excessive taxation would have become in effect a tax on citizens. But more was at stake than pure economics as numerous diaries *(ricordanze* and *zibaldoni)* attest. The accounts of patricians such as Bernardo Machiavelli[13] and Lapo di Giovanni Niccolini[14] often interspersed the affairs of their *mezzadri* with those of their own families. The myriad of *mezzadria* contracts from the late fourteenth century also shows the revival of near-feudal obligations between *mezzadri* and their *osti*. Sharecroppers were obliged to present gifts ceremoniously at the gates of their landlords' urban residences at Christ-

mas and at other feast days,[15] while the last wills and testaments of Florentine patricians show that gift exchanges ran in both directions: citizens gave their *mezzadri* clothing, animals, and tools and established
dowry funds to marry off their village girls.[16] Despite increasing surveillance over the affairs of sharecroppers, patrician diaries of the fifteenth
century reinforce the sense that affective ties bonded urban landlords
and their lowland peasants. According to Giovanni Rucellai, the forty-
three men of the lowland parish of San Piero Quaracchi gathered "of
their own free will" to maintain the Rucellai gardens from their own expenses. According to Rucellai, they did so because of the "many benefits"
received from him and because the "beauty and gentility of the gardens"
bestowed as much fame on them as they did on him.[17] By contrast, few
patricians owned any land in the upper Mugello and none (according to
the fourteenth- and early fifteenth-century tax records) further north in
the Alpi Fiorentine.

Further, the ties between urban landlords and villages near the city
increased rapidly from the 1370s through the early fifteenth century as
the pace of urban investment in land and the transformation of property
from small independent plots to farms *(poderi)* worked by sharecropping
quickened. In the villages around Sesto, these investors ranged from
great families such as the Strozzi to doublet-makers and dyers.[18] This agricultural expansion, moreover, was occurring at the very moment when
manpower shortages were being felt most acutely in the countryside as
reflected by increasing legislation after 1364 to lure agricultural workers
into Florence's valleys.[19] But Florence's policies toward its hinterland in
the last decades of the fourteenth century were contradictory: while the
councils addressed the problems of their desperately shrinking rural
population by issuing more favorable tax exemptions to newcomers,
taxes on those who stayed behind soared, leading more peasants and especially mountaineers into exile.

With the war still raging between Florence and Milan, the years at the
beginning of the fifteenth century marked a turning point for the Florentine *contado* in terms of peasant wealth, population, migration, taxation, and other Florentine policies toward its hinterland. In 1402, peasant household wealth in the mountains had reached its nadir both
absolutely and relative to peasants in the hills and plains.[20] Afterward
and for most of the fifteenth century, mountain peasants' taxable wealth

reversed directions: it climbed steadily to the Laurentian period. By the *catasto* of 1487 mountaineers were seven times wealthier than they had been in 1402, and, relative to plainsmen, their property values increased from three-quarters of the plainsmen's worth to more than double it. The demographic, again, paralleled the economic: the mountain dweller's average household size hit its low point in 1402, resting at three and a half members, and climbed steadily through most of the fifteenth century, touching five and a half members. Furthermore, with the better times, migration out of the Florentine territory eased after 1402.

While economic factors, such as the relative values of meat versus wheat, may have played a role in the mountaineers' absolute and relative prosperity, political factors, principally war and Florentine taxation, were the levers in the transformation of the Florentine rural ecology. The year 1402 marked not only the high point in Florence's fiscal burden on its *contado*, it also witnessed the widest gap in tax rates between the mountains and the plains. The gap narrowed dramatically by the next tax survey of 1412, and in 1427 Florence eliminated altogether the old medieval mosaic of unequal community taxes in the countryside, so that peasants from parishes next to Florence's city walls now paid the same rates and were taxed by the same principles as those from communes on the distant Apennine borders.

Why did the urban elites change their minds about fiscality and the plight of their highlanders around 1402? From the day-to-day decisions of Florence's upper councils it is clear that the Florentine ruling class had realized for some time that its tax policy not only was affecting adversely the economy of mountaineers, but also was creating grave military consequences for the Florentine state. Nonetheless, as we have seen, Florence continued to hammer those in the mountains with higher and more inequitable taxes through the opening years of the fifteenth century. Florence's change of heart appears to have come less from the military threat of Milan than from another source obscured or not reported at all in the Florentine narratives. Between 1401 and 1404 waves of peasant insurrections swept across the mountain communities from the Montagna di Pistoia to the Alpi and Podere Fiorentino and eastward along the mountains of the Aretine Casentino.[21]

Except for Ricciardo Cancellieri's revolt in Pistoia and guerrilla warfare from his mountain base at Sambuca, these insurrections came after the so-called crisis of 1402, that is, after the death of Giangaleazzo Visconti, when, according to contemporaries and traditional Florentine historiography, the threat from Milan had subsided. While the presence of Bolognese and Milanese troops certainly made these insurrections possible, the revolts were not simply feudal uprisings of the old magnates, the Ubaldini, Guidi, Ubertini, or Pazzi clans, as the few references in contemporary narratives made them out to be.[22] In contrast to the chronicles, the judicial records detail these insurrections from cattle raids and kidnappings to the building of new bastions in the Alps, the use of the cannon as an offensive weapon, the takeover of old Alpine castles, and the siege of Florence's frontier town, Firenzuola. From the summer of 1402 to April 1403, the Florentine courts sentenced more insurgents with charges of conspiracy and rebellion in the Alpi Fiorentine and Podere alone than they had for the much better remembered urban revolt of the Ciompi a generation earlier.[23] The insurgents listed in the criminal cases in 1402 and 1403 were mostly peasants identified by name, patronymic, and village. Moreover, they figured as more than canon fodder for the duke of Milan or the Ubaldini lords. Instead, the criminal cases highlight indigenous villagers as the ringleaders, who prepared strategy for the siege of Florence's frontier town, Firenzuola, and even gave orders to men as exalted as the Lord Jacopo del Verme, the visconti's lieutenant stationed at Bologna.

Even more extraordinary than the criminal descriptions of these "rebellions" was their reckoning in the Florentine decrees or *provvisioni* registers in 1403, a year after the start of the insurrections. In normal years these records pertained largely to urban matters, from settling citizens' bankruptcies to deciding on how much to feed the town's lions,[24] but in 1403 they were transformed to negotiate a flood of demands from the countryside, mostly from the highlands. These petitions record the negotiations between mountain ambassadors and the Florentine elites and list the remarkable concessions peasants won from the hands of the Florentine state. Those condemned to death a year earlier for acts of rebellion were absolved, and in the place of condemnations, they gained licenses to carry weapons anywhere within the city and territory of Florence, lifetime exemptions from all taxes, and in some cases hereditary rights to pass these fiscal exemptions down their male lines. In addition, in some of the Alpine communities, the villagers won sinecures as officers of the Florentine state with lifetime salaries and privileges to decide who could or could not immigrate to their villages with tax exemptions. The mountain ringleaders won privileges for their rebel villages as well, which included ten- to fifteen-year exemptions from all taxes and the cancellation of numerous village debts to the Florentine commune. In the years 1403 to 1405, the Florentine councils answered favorably pleas from 282 rural parishes and communes with tax exemptions, adjustments of tax assessments, and the cancellation of public debts. Ninety percent of these villages were in the mountains. For the moment, the mountain communities were certainly no longer on the margins of Florentine policy and the preoccupations of the Florentine lawmakers. Nor were these peasants simply acted upon. Instead, they had become actors in furthering Florentine expansion into Bologna in the early years of the fifteenth century.

Moreover, their actions in 1402 to 1404 had changed the thinking of the Florentine rulers toward their governance of their territory. In the following decades of the early fifteenth century, the number of successful petitions from the countryside increased, especially in peacetime, and the distribution of these petitions that addressed the day-to-day welfare of peasants and lowered fiscal and other monetary burdens flowed down from the mountains and into the hills and plains nearer the city of Florence. A change in the rhetoric of these peasant pleas followed as well. From pleas of humility and filial supplication poured at the feet of their urban lords, post-1402 peasant ambassadors increasingly framed their pleas as threats, often closing their concrete demands with the logic that if the Priors, *Gonfalonieri*, and Twelve Good Men of Florence should decide not to grant the peasant community its reasonable demands, the peasants would have no other choice than to flee their villages, which would further undermine Florence's tax base and the military support of its peasantry.[25]

But was this change, like medieval and early modern rituals of the "world turned upside down" only of the moment, even if in the case of these mountain dwellers a moment that lasted for at least three years? In fact, a simple counting of successful petitions from the countryside suggests that business may have returned more or less to usual by 1406, when the average number of successful petitions from the countryside shrank from a high of forty-four petitions in the insurrectionary year of 1403 to just over thirteen per annum from 1406 to the end of my analysis in 1434.[26] A more in-depth analysis shows, however, longer-term consequences of the insurrections of 1403—a change in government attitudes toward its *contado* and its mountain communities. First, after 1406, the number of successful peasant petitions increased, even if not dramatically, from 8.2 (in the period 1347 to 1402) to 13.4 per annum.

More importantly, the reasons behind the government's decisions to grant welfare and reprieves from its taxation to its rural dependencies changed: from the Black Death to 1402 successful petitions from the countryside came mostly in wartime and correlated strongly with Florence's military needs to defend its territory by refurbishing or building new fortifications. By contrast, after 1402, the cycles of successful petitions changed with greater numbers coming in peacetime as opposed to war years. Before 1402 even the plague itself barely registered as a cause that aroused government clemency. Remarkably, in 1348 and 1349 only two petitions approved from the countryside mentioned the plague, and in one case it was not to gain fiscal concessions but to ask the government to accept as legally binding last wills and testaments redacted during the plague by nonmatriculated notaries. (The petition argued that all the notaries in their community, Montevarchi, had perished in the plague.) By contrast, after 1402, plague emerged as the most important cause for granting tax relief, even though the post-1402 plagues were far less virulent and thus less crippling to the tax base of individual villages than had been those of the latter half of the fourteenth century. In addition, other natural disasters—floods, crop failures, and, for the first time, hailstorms—figure boldly in the post-1402 cries for tax relief, whereas earlier, if they had arisen at all, the Florentine legislative bodies allowed only for studies of the damages as opposed to more beneficial exemptions of taxes or other monetary allotments to assist the damaged communities. Instead of a sudden climactic change in Florentine Tuscany, what had changed was the mindset of the Florentine ruling elites. Before 1402, only petitions from villages with large populations and a direct bearing on Florentine military and economic concerns made their way through the thicket of Florentine bureaucracy; afterward villages with as few as four families and of no immediate military interest to Florentine defenses succeeded.

Parallel to this shift, villagers won more favorable fiscal settlements. Before 1402, the most common grant to peasants was not the cancellation of public debts or the lowering of community taxes. Instead, rural communes hard hit by warfare were allowed to convert certain taxes into payments for castle repairs and fortifications, leaving their overall fiscal commitments to the Florentine state unchanged. The villagers' payments were thus merely transferred from one government account to another. After 1402, these parsimonious grants declined to less than 5 percent of all awards. In their place, communities won outright tax exemptions, the lowering of payments to public officials, such as the podestà, and the cancellation of long tallies of public debts, sometimes amounting to thousands of florins. In the case of communes like Foiano on the war-torn borders of the Valdichiana and the Isle of Giglio, whose ambassadors described continuous raids from Genoa and Barbary pirates, the exemptions and debt cancellations were renewed at five-year intervals through the early fifteenth century.[27]

These changes reflect a transformation in Florence's perceptions of its state. Previously, its *contado* had served as a reservoir to be tapped for fiscal and military benefits and as a buffer against invading armies. By 1409 Florence's humanist bureaucrats began to use a new word, *imperium*, to refer to its territory—city, *contado*, and *districtus*.[28] The word embraced a new sense of the state that differed from the city's older tributary relation to its *contado* that had structured taxation and decisions on tax relief before the 1402 insurrections. With a new noblesse oblige toward the fiscal plight of its *contadini*, Florentine bureaucrats increasingly saw their own fate as intertwined with that of the countryside, no matter whether the village touched the city walls, possessed lands owned by citizens, or lay at distant mountain outposts along the Apennines.

Perhaps Florence's new sense of territorial incorporation is best reflected in the settlement that became most prominent after 1402. In over 30 percent of successful peasant petitions, the Florentine councils cancelled villagers' public debts by passing them on to Florence's funded debt or *Monte*. Thus, in effect, they made *contadini* shareholders in the Florentine funded debt. These allocations of debts fundamentally reversed the role peasants played in the financial structure of the Florentine state. Previously, the peasants' direct taxes had provided part of the revenues to pay off the forced loans and *Monte* investments awarded at high interest rates to the privileged citizens of Florence. After 1402, although still paying direct taxes, peasants could also move to the receiving end of the *Monte*'s seemingly limitless largesse. Like citizens, they too could benefit from Florence's surging deficit financing and skyrocketing debt. *Contadini* and more so Florence's highlanders were no longer on the margins, at least not to the extent they had been at the beginning of the fifteenth century. With the next financial crisis of the Florentine state in 1424 to 1433, the Alpi Fiorentine as well as the *contado* as a whole remained remarkably quiet. This time around the previously privileged subject cities—Volterra, Arezzo, and Pisa and their former *contadi*—would feel the pinch of Florentine fiscal oppression and, as a result, would revolt.[29] The notion of who was in and who was out had changed.

NOTES

1. John of Salisbury, *Policraticus: Books I–IV* (Turnholt: Brepols, 1993); and Georges Duby, *The Three Orders: Feudal Society Imagined* (Chicago: University of Chicago Press, 1980).

2. See Richard C. Trexler, *Public Life in Renaissance Florence* (New York: Academic Press, 1980); and Trexler, "Ritual in Florence: Adolescence and Salvation in the Renaissance," in *The Pursuit of Holiness in Late Medieval and Renaissance Religion*, ed. Charles Trinkaus and Heiko Oberman, 200–264 (Leiden: Brill, 1974).

3. For my criticisms of the common assumptions about the religious piety of highlanders in late medieval and Renaissance Tuscany, see "Piety and Religious Practice in the Rural Dependencies of Renaissance Florence," *English Historical Review* 114 (1999): 1121–42.

4. Fernand Braudel, *The Mediterranean and the Mediterranean World in the Age of Philip II*, trans. Sîan Reynolds, 2nd ed., 2 vols. (London: Collins, 1973), 1:25–53.

5. Elio Conti, *La formazione della struttura agraria moderna nel contado fiorentino*, 3 vols. (Rome: Istituto per il Medio Evo, 1965), 2:211.

6. Giovanni Cherubini, "Risorse, paesaggio ed utilizzazione agricola del territorio della Toscana sud-occidentale nei secoli XIV–XV," in *Civiltà ed economia agricola in Toscana nei secc. XIII–XV: Problemi della vita delle compagne nel tardo medioevo (Pistoia, 21–24 aprile 1977)*, 91–115 (Pistoia: Il Centro, 1981).

7. Cherubini has written numerous articles on the Tuscan mountains; among these, see "Appunti sul brigantaggio in Italia alla fine del medioevo," in *Studi di storia medieval e moderna per Ernesto Sestan*, 2 vols., 1:103–33 (Florence: Olschki, 1980); "La 'civiltà' del castagno in Italia alla fine del Medioevo," *Archeologia medievale* 8 (1981): 247–80; *Una comunità dell'Appennino dal XIII al XV secolo: Montecoronaro dalla signoria dell'abbazia del Trivio al Dominio di Firenze* (Florence: Olschki, 1972); "Paesaggio agrario, insediamenti e attività silo-pastorali sulla montagna tosco-romagnola alla fine del medioevo," in *Fra Tevere, Arno e Appennino: Valli, comunità, signori* (Florence: Tosca, 1992), 39–69; "Risorse, paesaggio ed utilizzazzione"; "La società dell'Appennino settentrionale (secoli XIII–XV)," in *Signori, contadini, borghesi: Ricerche sulla società italiana del basso medioevo* (Florence: La nuova Italia, 1974), 130–31.

8. Franco Sacchetti, *Il Trecentonovelle*, ed. Antonio Lanza (Florence: Sansoni, 1984), no. CLXXIII, pp. 383–86.

9. For these statistics and those that follow on the social and economic structure of the hills and plains, see Samuel K. Cohn, Jr., *Creating the Florentine State: Peasants and Rebellion, 1348–1434* (Cambridge: Cambridge University Press, 1999), 55–109.

10. Archivio di Stato di Firenze (hereafter ASF), *Provvisioni, Registri,* 36, fols. 8v–10v (12 Sept. 1348).

11. I explored this theme more fully in "Insurrezioni contadine e demografia: Il mito della povertà nelle montagne toscane (1348–1460)," *Studi Storici* 36 (1995): 1023–49.

12. On migration within the countryside, see most recently, David Herlihy and Christiane Klapisch-Zuber, *Les Toscans et leurs familles: Une étude du "catasto" florentin de 1427* (Paris: Fondation nationale des sciences politiques: École des hautes études en sciences sociales, 1978), 301–26; and Charles de la Roncière, *Prix et salaires à Florence au XIVe siècle (1280–1380)* (Rome: École française de Rome, 1987), 661–80.

13. Bernardo Machiavelli, *Libro di ricordi,* ed. Cesare Olschki (Florence: Olschki, 1954).

14. Lapo di Giovanni Niccolini, *Il libro degli affari proprii di casa de Lapo di Giovanni Niccolini de' Sirigatti,* ed. Christian Bec (Paris: SEVPEN, 1969).

15. See for instance the thousands of notarial contracts redacted by the Mazzetti family of notaries in the area of Sesto from 1348 to 1426; ASF, *Notarile antecosimano,* 13521–13531 (M 352 to M 359 old style).

16. See Samuel K. Cohn Jr., *The Cult of Remembrance and the Black Death: Six Renaissance Cities in Central Italy* (Baltimore: Johns Hopkins University Press, 1992); and Giovanni Rucellai, *Il Zibaldone quaresimale,* vol. 1 of *Giovanni Rucellai ed il suo Zibaldone,* ed. Alessandro Perosa (London: Warburg Institute, University of London, 1960), 26.

17. Rucellai, *Zibaldone,* 23.

18. These conclusions are based on a statistical analysis of the land contracts taken by the Mazzetti family of notaries; see my *Creating the Florentine State,* 101–7.

19. Ibid., 229–31.

20. For the following statistics, see ibid., 80–109.

21. On the description and analysis of these riots, see ibid., 113–94.

22. For a survey of this literature, see ibid., 113–37.

23. On the lists of insurgents in these urban revolts, see Samuel K. Cohn Jr., *The Laboring Classes in Renaissance Florence* (New York: Academic Press, 1980), 172–94.

24. On the *provvisioni* and the legislative procedures of the Florentine councils, see my *Creating the Florentine State,* 197–209.

25. See ibid., 172–94.

26. Before 1403, the average number of successful petitions from the countryside had been 8.2 per annum.

27. For these statistics, see my *Creating the Florentine State,* 197–243.

28. See Riccardo Fubini, "La rivendicazioni di Firenze della sovranità e il contribuito delle 'Historiae' di Leonardo Bruni," in *Leonardo Bruni cancelliere della repubblica di Firenze,* ed. Paolo Viti (Florence: Olschki, 1990), 51.

29. On these revolts, see Samuel K. Cohn Jr., *Women in the Streets: Essays on Sex and Power in Renaissance Italy* (Baltimore: Johns Hopkins University Press, 1996), 98–136.

13

Vecchi, Poveri, e Impotenti

The Elderly in Renaissance Venice

Dennis Romano

Since its very inception the Italian Renaissance has been associated with youth, novelty, and vigor. From Vasari's *rinascità* of art to Burckhardt's origins of the modern state, the concept of the Renaissance has suggested beginnings rather than endings, possibilities rather than fulfillment, energy rather than lethargy and has been juxtaposed to the waning clerical and chivalric culture associated with northern Europe. Scholars have found evidence for this youthful Renaissance culture in everything from Petrarch's sonnets and Lorenzo de' Medici's carnival songs to Michelangelo's heroic male nudes and Titian's sumptuous Venuses.[1]

During the last three decades, social historians have inadvertently reinforced this image through their own studies of the young in Renaissance Italy. Numerous works have appeared that examine the rites of passage associated with the early stages of life (birth, childhood, and marriage) and add to our knowledge of institutions both formal, such as orphanages, and informal, such as youth brigades, geared to the young.[2] In his study of the Ospedale degli Innocenti, Philip Gavitt has even argued that a "cult of childhood" developed in Renaissance Florence.[3]

By contrast the number of studies that consider old age and the end of life in Renaissance Italy remains small. Among them is Creighton Gilbert's essay "When Did a Man in the Renaissance Grow Old?" which explores Renaissance notions of old age and its chronological markers.[4]

Literary scholars have examined the theme of the "ages of man" in Renaissance literature, while art historians have shown considerable interest in the problem of artists' "old age styles."[5] Important contributions have been made as well in the field of demographics, most notably by David Herlihy and Christiane Klapisch-Zuber.[6] And one significant work of synthesis has appeared, Georges Minois's *History of Old Age from Antiquity to the Renaissance*.[7] According to Minois, the Renaissance emphasis on physical beauty (which he argues was also characteristic of classical Greece) led to a devaluation of old age and in many instances outright contempt for the elderly.[8] At the same time, Minois detects an important shift over the course of the Renaissance: during the fourteenth and fifteenth centuries, the position of the elderly improved in response to their increase as a percentage of the population; however, in the sixteenth century with renewed population growth, the situation of the elderly deteriorated once again.[9]

For Venice, the sole contribution to the literature is Robert Finlay's 1978 essay "The Venetian Republic as a Gerontocracy: Age and Politics in the Renaissance."[10] Finlay contends that the Republic of Venice stood apart from other early modern states as a gerontocracy. In his view, Venetian republicanism and rule by the elderly were linked in two important and complementary ways. First, members of the Great Council, the set of politically enfranchised adult males, agreed on a tacit set of rules that generally precluded men from embarking on political careers before the age of forty and then made them ineligible for the city's highest offices, such as procurator of San Marco or doge, until age sixty or beyond. Venice was able to indulge this preference for rule by the elderly while in most other states dynastic imperatives "precluded any political expression of deference to the old."[11] Second, Finlay suggests that informal age qualifications and the slow moving cursus honorum served Venetian republicanism well by molding the character of the political class. Those patrician males who wished to advance politically had "to subordinate themselves—their personalities, ambitions, and resources—to making their way in service to the Republic."[12] Preference for the old bred a political elite that was conservative by nature and wary of innovation. Finlay accordingly posits gerontocracy as yet another reason for the Venetian republic's much vaunted stability and longevity and places the elderly (at least elderly elite males) at the very center of Venetian society.

At the same time, Finlay is careful to note that this "political" conception of old age differed from "conventional standards." In his view, "the
political definition...was identical with modern conventional notions
which assign the advent of old age to the mid-sixties, [whereas] outside a
Venetian political context...a man of 40 was thought to be entering the
winter of his years."[13] Finlay recognizes then that two different constructions of old age operated simultaneously in Venice, one that applied to
elite males and assigned them a central place in society, the other that
encompassed the rest of the populace and served to marginalize them
from the political sphere.

Drawing on Finlay's important insights, this essay seeks to further
our understanding of the place and role of the elderly in Renaissance
Venice. To do this, it investigates how biological factors and family strategies conjoined in the creation of these conceptions of old age and how
the weight of these constructs fell differently upon men and women, patricians and *popolani*. Too, it examines how the attributes of old age were
ascribed and considers the strategies by which Venetian men and women
of different social ranks navigated the final stages of life.[14] It suggests
that both the elite and nonelite elderly occupied a position between centrality and marginality in Renaissance Venetian society.

DEFINING OLD AGE

A number of sources shed light on how old age was biologically, chrono-
logically, or in Finlay's formulation, conventionally defined during the
Renaissance. Literary works with a wide circulation throughout Italy including Venice followed various schemes for reckoning the ages of man.
Dante divided the ideal human life span into four stages: adolescence,
which lasts to age twenty-five, youth, defined as ages twenty-five to forty-
five, old age from forty-five to seventy, and senility *(senio)* to age eighty.[15]
Petrarch was unsure when old age commenced, noting that Cicero placed
the onset at forty-six, other writers at age fifty, and Saint Augustine at
sixty.[16] In her treatise *Il merito delle donne*, the writer Moderata Fonte suggested that old age starts for males between forty-five and fifty.[17]

According to governmental statutes and regulations, the sixth or seventh decade of life marked the beginning of old age. In the fourteenth

century, for example, the Venetian government set the period of active militia service for all males between twenty and sixty.[18] In the same century, the Republic instituted a special tax on pepper and other commodities in order to support aged mariners known as the *poveri al pevere*. A Great Council law of 1362 restricted eligibility for this charity to native Venetians age sixty and above.[19] However, by the early seventeenth century, official definitions of old age for men had declined to fifty. According to instructions given to census takers in 1607, males were to be counted in one of three categories: "boys" *(putti)* to age eighteen, "men" *(huomini)* to age fifty, and "old men" *(vecchi)* fifty and above. In contrast, there were only two categories for females: "girls" *(putte)* to age eighteen, and "women" *(donne)* over eighteen.[20]

Private charities established in wills provide still other indications of how society viewed the beginning of old age. In his testament registered in 1417, nobleman Giovanni Contarini left houses for the maintenance of women age fifty or above, the same age doge Cristoforo Moro recommended for retired sailors who were to receive quarters he left for their use.[21] Pietro Regla, on the other hand, set the minimum age for sailor beneficiaries of his charity at age sixty.[22] A further piece of evidence comes from the 1564 witchcraft trial of a woman named Giovanna known by her nickname "the Astrologer." One thirty-year-old witness described her as "rather old," estimating her to be between fifty and sixty.[23] Generally speaking, literary, official, and private sources agreed that old age commenced somewhere between those ages.

The vocabulary used to describe old age is more revealing than the chronological markers of its commencement. A variety of words in Latin and Italian were employed to indicate the elderly and old age itself. These include (for elderly) *senex, vecchio, antiquus,* and *antico,* and (for old age) *senectus, vecchiezza,* and even *età decrepita.* However, writers often coupled these terms with more descriptive ones that reveal an understanding of what it meant to be elderly. By far the most frequent coupling was *vecchio* with *impotente.* For example, the chronicler and diarist Marino Sanuto described Marino Caravello, one of the candidates for the dogeship in 1423, as "most aged and impotent."[24] Impotence could encompass several different senses of powerlessness (economic, political, physical, or reproductive) but was most commonly used to describe someone who could no longer perform his or her normal activities, as its less frequently employed synonym *inabile* suggests. For example, a certain donna

Angelica da Cologna was described as "sixty years old, infirm and unable to perform service."[25] Illness and poverty too were often linked with old age. Giovanna "the Astrologer" described herself as a "poor old woman in ill health," while the grammar teacher Corbacino was characterized as "impotent, old, and in greatest need and poverty."[26] Procurator of San Marco and future doge Leonardo Donà described his former servant Pascha di Rossi as "poor and around seventy years of age."[27] Indeed, old age, poverty, and impotence became nearly synonymous, as in the case of Paola Manfredi, who described herself in a supplication to the procurators of San Marco as "old, impotent, and most impoverished."[28] These conditions were so tightly conjoined they suggest that society's understanding of old age actually had less to do with chronology than with notions of productivity and potential, qualities the conventional old clearly lacked.

At the same time an alternative vision or construction of old age existed, namely, of the elderly as keepers of knowledge and possessors of wisdom. This view circulated in learned tracts on government and in legislation and applied most commonly to the political elite.[29] In his *De bene istituta re publica*, for example, Domenico Morosini wrote, "There are no wise men who are not old, and even then, very few."[30] Such views served to justify and reinforce Venice's gerontocratic regime. Yet this image of the elderly had some resonance outside learned circles and was occasionally applied to nonelites. When in the early fourteenth century, for example, the *giudici del piovego*, officials in charge of public facilities, were investigating whether properties such as canals and embankments were publicly or privately owned, they relied not only on written evidence, such as deeds, but also on the witness of old men who testified about the condition of the properties when they were young.[31] Generally speaking, however, this view of the elderly as wise was socially circumscribed and infrequently employed. It was much more common to view the old as sick and impoverished, and thus a distinct category included within the worthy poor.[32] And as such, the elderly constituted a problem requiring a response.

Both the government and a variety of institutions, including confraternities and guilds, reacted with charitable efforts designed to assist the elderly. The government directed much of its charity for the aged at the succoring of destitute old men who had spent their lives in service to the Republic aboard its ships, or as a 1368 law governing the *poveri al pevere* described them, "good and old poor veteran sailors."[33] The institution of the *poveri al pevere* changed over time as the number of men designated as *poveri* increased and the government modified the eligibility requirements for enlistment among their ranks. A 1416 law added ship carpenters and caulkers to the list of those eligible since without them, as the law stated, "our ships would not be able to sail."[34] But as a 1403 law makes clear, the government had other motives besides simple gratitude and charity; it wished to strengthen the navy. Officials believed the favorable treatment of ancient mariners would serve as an "example to others" and encourage loyalty and service in the fleet. Additionally, the state hoped to venerate God and earn his continuing favor.[35] The latter impulse led the Republic in 1474 to begin plans for a hospital for aged sailors, as thanksgiving for the victorious defense of Scutari in Albania from the Turks.[36] Private individuals also endowed hospices for the maintenance of elderly sailors. According to data compiled by Franca Semi, two such institutions were established in the fourteenth century, three in the fifteenth, and two more in the sixteenth. But these figures do not convey the full extent of this kind of charity since they do not include almshouses that were bequeathed for the use of sailors, but not established as hospices per se.[37]

While elderly sailors received help either from the government or from privately endowed institutions, other men received assistance through their guilds. The tailors, fruit sellers, and bakers all had hospices for elderly members of their trades, and other guilds had less formal means of assisting aged brothers.[38] Generally speaking, institutional assistance for old men was tied to the professions they had practiced during their productive years. There were, however, no institutional charities geared to the maintenance of elderly male patricians. As we will see below, this was due in part to the nature of patrician family life but just as importantly to the very incompatibility of the concept of male nobility with this view of old age.

By contrast, hospices existed to serve noble as well as nonnoble elderly women. Eligibility was determined by a woman's social standing or marital status. Calculating the number of hospices created for elderly women is more difficult than establishing the number for men since many served widows, not all of whom were considered old. Some widows were still of childbearing age and thus did not meet the criterion of impotence (in this case reproductive) associated with old age.[39] Status and moral distinctions also played a far more conspicuous role in women's institutions than men's. When, for instance, in the late fourteenth century Bonafemina Aleti endowed a hospice in her will, she specified that it benefit "eleven poor and impotent widows, who are of good condition and reputation and who have led a good and decent life in this world."[40] Two centuries later the famous courtesan Veronica Franco saw the need to aid aging and indigent prostitutes and helped organize the Ospizio del Soccorso.[41] Benefactors expressed concern with the reputation of female inmates and the danger of mixing between women of sound and unsound character. Such preoccupations were less urgent in men's institutions since they were both professionally and socially more homogeneous.

Altogether a number of state-sponsored and privately endowed charities assisted the poor and impotent elderly in Renaissance Venice. These institutions tried to recreate what society viewed as the appropriate spheres for the sexes. Thus while men's institutions usually had a professional focus and perhaps retained some of the trappings of the world of work, women's institutions, some of which allowed for children and pets, maintained and even promoted, as has been demonstrated for another kind of women's hospital, that of the Zitelle, a familial atmosphere and attended to notions of status and rank.[42] Unfortunately, without good census data it is impossible to know what percentage of the elderly population these institutional charities served. At the same time, as the absence of hospitals for aged noblemen indicates, the situation of the elderly and indeed the very likelihood of being perceived as old varied markedly for different groups in society.[43]

ELDERLY PATRICIANS

During the Renaissance, as today, one of the most important determinants of a person's condition in old age was his or her family situation. The structure of the household, control of resources, inheritance customs, and affective ties all shaped the place of the elderly within family life and kinship networks. At the same time, these factors varied considerably across social classes. The state of their health was another element determining the condition of the elderly; yet this too varied widely since some professions required physical strength whereas others demanded mental acuity.

For many Venetian patricians, the *fraterna*, a form of household structure particularly well adapted to Venice's commercial economy, shaped their family life. According to Venetian law, brothers who did not go to court to be emancipated from one another were treated as a financial and legal unit, a *fraterna*. Frederic Lane viewed this arrangement as ideally adapted to the elite's business needs since undivided patrimonies provided the capital required during Venice's period of commercial expansion.[44] Beyond its narrow legal definition, however, *fraterna* also referred to household living arrangements characteristic of some patrician families. Even when legally separated, brothers often continued to live under the same roof *in fraterna*. By so doing they were able to save money on food, fuel, and other living expenses. For this reason, James C. Davis argues that the *fraterna* was also well suited to periods of commercial contraction since it served as a wealth-conserving family arrangement.[45]

The *fraterna* clearly benefited older elite males in Venice since it mitigated the need for fathers to make early distributions of capital to their sons in order for them to make their own fortune.[46] Instead fathers often retained control of the patrimony, knowing that it would eventually devolve undivided to their sons. For this reason patrician fathers were less likely to fall into destitution than in some other city-states and more importantly retained a degree of control over other family members. Another consequence of living *in fraterna* was that male patricians were deeply embedded in networks of overlapping households that cared for their needs as they aged. This was the case for nobleman Lorenzo Priuli, who had three sons who lived into adulthood. Father and sons lived together off and on in a house that Lorenzo rented in the parish of Santa Fosca, and in a household that at times included as many as thirteen kin and eleven domestic servants. We know that at least one son, the diarist Girolamo Priuli, was legally separated from his father and brothers; nevertheless all continued to live together, providing mutual support and assistance.[47]

Another characteristic of Venetian patrician families was the restriction of marriage to only one or two brothers as a way of conserving family wealth.[48] In this arrangement the brother or brothers who married (and their sons in turn) bore some responsibility to look after those who did not. Davis cites an example from the early seventeenth century in which Leonardo Donà, who was married, agreed to provide food, lodging, and servants for his unmarried brothers and widowed mother.[49] According to Stanley Chojnacki these bachelor brothers or "subaltern patriarchs" tended to name as the beneficiaries of their wills not only their brothers' children (both male and female) but those of their sisters as well.[50] While the primary motive for such bequests was almost certainly, as Chojnacki argues, a concern for the patriline tinged by affective ties for sisters, another may well have been a desire to shore up a supportive network of kin (both men and women) as insurance for old age.

To be sure, there were destitute elderly noblemen in Venice; but they did not, as the absence of hospitals geared to their care suggests, figure prominently in the social landscape. Rather, charity was accorded to them on an individual basis through *grazie* or special favors.[51] Generally speaking, elderly patrician males continued to enjoy their privileged status in Venetian society; and the financial security provided by the *fraterna* allowed for the particularly lengthy and leisurely cursus honorum characteristic of Venetian politics.[52] In turn, they used the classically inspired discourse on the wisdom of the elderly to justify their monopoly of political power. Indeed, except for the idea of the sagacity of the aged, notions of male nobility and old age were essentially incompatible. And in practice elderly patrician males seldom relinquished their role as patriarchs and governors, but when they did so, they were no longer portrayed as wise (according to the governmental standard) but were subsumed into the more conventional categorization of the elderly as ill and impotent.[53] In 1416, for example, future doge Francesco Foscari was able to get himself elected procurator of San Marco when he convinced members of the Great Council that Procurator Giovanni Barbo was no longer able to carry out his duties on account of "infirmity and illness."[54] Ironically, forty years later Foscari was himself removed from the dogeship when the Council of Ten declared him "ineffective" on account of "old age and decrepitude."[55] Only when severely incapacitated (or so described by others) were noblemen recognized as old according to its more common definition and thereby rendered politically impotent.

The position of elderly noblewomen was more uncertain than that of noblemen since they were much more likely to meet the criteria conventionally ascribed to old age, namely to fall into poverty and once past childbearing years to be perceived as both literally and figuratively un-productive. Married women enjoyed the most favorable situation among elite females since they could, in theory at least, reclaim their dowries in widowhood.[56] Even so the situation of widows was precarious if they were not accepted by their affinal kin or reintegrated into their biological kin network.[57] Some patrician men acknowledged these possibilities by including financial incentives in their wills for their brothers and sons to look after their sisters and mothers.[58] When patrician widows were able to reclaim their dowries, they gained a degree of financial security, and some wielded power as matriarchs overseeing the family. This was the case with Cristina Barbarigo, widow of the merchant Andrea, who acted to secure her sons' future and protect her deceased husband's as-sets and who enjoyed position and precedence within the household until her death. It was true as well of former dogaressa Marina Foscari, who helped supervise the upbringing of her fatherless grandson Niccolò.[59]

Old age was much less secure for unmarried patrician women since they had far fewer financial resources at their disposal. Some became nuns and enjoyed the support of monastic communities; but increasingly in the sixteenth century the number of women forced into spinsterhood grew, as marriage portions increased and fathers, who were concerned with the conservation of family wealth, denied their daughters the funds to marry or enter a convent.[60] Both the writer Moderata Fonte and Agos-tino Valier, bishop of Verona, paint a bleak picture of the lives of these spinsters, forced to live as virtual servants to their brothers. They ad-vised them, unlike their married sisters, to be content with plain food and simple clothes.[61] The situation for unmarried women may have grown even worse in old age when they were no longer useful even as servants and became a further drain on household finances.[62] At the same time, the expansive networks of female friends and relations so well documented in women's wills likely served as a safeguard against complete abandonment in old age.[63]

On the whole, old age was a riskier time for patrician women than men since their finances depended on so many variables that were only partially under their control: the size of the dowry and the ability to re-claim it in widowhood, the receptivity and hospitality of natal and affinal kin, and (for spinsters) an almost total dependence on the largesse of their brothers and female kin and friends. At the same time women suf-

fered a further disability in that they were excluded from the highly gendered discourse on the wisdom of the elderly generated by humanist
writers.

THE POPOLANO AGED

Among the *popolani,* those who worked with their hands and bodies,
health took its place alongside family relations as another factor powerfully shaping the situation of the elderly. Men and women of the lower
classes relied on manual dexterity (for example for weaving) or sheer
physical strength (as in the case of stevedores) in order to earn a living,
and old age could be a truly desperate time if their bodies gave out and
they were no longer able to work. Such was the case for boatman Giacomo Poleto, who was forced in 1540 to give up his *traghetto* or ferry post
because he had become "old and impotent."[64] In another heart-rending
example, in March 1546 the painter Lorenzo Lotto had to dismiss sixty-
year-old servant donna Lucia, whom he had hired just a month earlier to
do housekeeping and spinning, when he discovered that she could not
perform her duties on account of age.[65] Blindness was especially dis-
abling. A servant by the name of donna Angela was fortunate in that her
master continued to feed and shelter her even though he received no
service from her since she had been "rendered impotent" and lost her
sight, while another servant named Stella left service when she became
"old and blind."[66]

One measure of the dependency of the working classes on their
bodies is the price of slaves. Data compiled by Charles Verlinden show
that prices peaked for slaves in their teens and twenties and then tended
to drop after age thirty-five. In 1417, for example, a fifty-five-year-old Tartar
slave sold for a mere 11 ducats, whereas the purchase price for twenty-
year-old Tartars in the same period averaged 54.6 ducats.[67] Some hospitals
recognized the problem created by the physical disability of the elderly
and made it their special mission to serve those who could no longer
work.[68]

In some highly skilled trades, the elderly gradually gave up more
physically demanding tasks to concentrate in areas where their expertise
and experience counted more than their bodily strength. Many painters,

including Titian and Tintoretto, worked into advanced old age aided by assistants.[69] The glassmakers of Murano with their special knowledge of the formulae for various kinds of glass are another example of workers in a trade in which the knowledge and skill generated by years of experience were valued and may actually have favored the elderly. The physically demanding shipbuilding guilds, apparently at the prompting of the government, made special provision for the hiring of elderly workers known as veterans. The statutes of the caulkers' and carpenters' guilds contained clauses requiring foremen to hire at least one master over age fifty-five every time they employed six masters or more. However, in 1440 the obligation was dropped in favor of a tax to support these veterans. The system was designed to guarantee a livelihood to older men in these physically taxing professions and further reflects the special consideration accorded those associated with the navy.[70]

While infirmity forced some workers to quit work altogether and others to make a gradual transition into retirement, declining health caused still others to shift livelihoods and take up less rigorous and remunerative tasks. Old women prepared and hawked food, work they could perform with limited physical or capital expense.[71] Both old women and old men found employment performing tasks associated with the Catholic cult of the dead, such as washing corpses, keeping vigil, and participating in funeral processions. In his will dated 1539, nobleman Antonio Capello left money for twelve "old, dispossessed, and poor" sailors to accompany his body to the grave. Each was to receive a candle as well as a small payment for his service.[72] Care of the dead continued after burial as the elderly were commissioned to say prayers and seek indulgences for the souls of the deceased. Masters and mistresses often assigned the job of collecting indulgences to aged servants, especially nurses. The modest payments associated with this labor and the routine of visiting specific churches on set days (for example, San Lorenzo on Wednesdays and Santa Croce on Fridays) provided the elderly with income as well as opportunities to socialize.[73]

Old women of higher social status also found work at jobs with a spiritual dimension. The aged female humanist Cassandra Fedele was awarded the position of prioress of the Hospital of San Domenico di Castello, while the Hospital of the Zitelle required that its in-house administrator, the *Madre* or *Madonna*, be at least forty years of age.[74] Such positions allowed women of high but not exalted rank to earn a modest living while maintaining their respectability. At the opposite extreme in terms of reputation, aging prostitutes followed, according to Pietro Aretino, a downward spiral, a kind of *cursus impudorum*, that began with prostitution, descended to innkeeping, procuring, and laundering, and ended with begging.[75] In fact, a fine line existed between outright begging and receiving payment for tasks such as participating in funerals. The aged certainly were to be found among the city's beggars and shared with them a reputation for illness. Mendicancy itself was a form of work, one well suited to the physical limitations of the elderly. The prostitute then is emblematic of the dependency of the working classes on the earning power of their bodies and the poverty that often awaited them when their strength gave out.

At the same time, the lower-class elderly displayed extraordinary ingenuity in trying to avoid just such an end. Like their patrician counterparts, many *popolani* looked to their kin for assistance and sought to make it financially advantageous for relatives to care for them. For example, minor officials with government sinecures as well as guildsmen and ferry operators with shops or licenses for restricted trades sought to install their kinsmen, usually their sons, in their place, in return for care in old age. The case of the wine measurer Zaneto di Antivari is illustrative. In April 1517 he got permission from the Great Council to pass the position on to his son.[76] When Giacomo Poleto renounced his ferry post on account of old age, he was able to transfer it to his son Matteo, who agreed in turn to care for his parents for the rest of their lives, as well as pay his father's debt of fourteen ducats to the *traghetto's scuola*.[77] Some working-class parents transferred assets to their children at the time of emancipation in return for the children's agreement to support them with annuities.[78] Such transfers helped children establish themselves at the same time that they guaranteed care for aging parents.

The expectation among both patricians and *popolani* was that wives would look after their elderly husbands, and some provision was made for those for whom this was not the case. When, for example, nobleman Ludovico Priuli left funds for a hospital for the aged in 1569, he specified that the inmates were to be elderly men with neither children nor wives.[79] Likewise, when the government reformed the old sailors' hospital of Messer Gesù Cristo in 1589, it limited admission to men over sixty without wives.[80] But demographics worked against the lower classes since their families were often smaller and less extended than elite ones.

Consequently many working-class elderly had few kin or no kin at all on whom to rely and had to pursue other strategies.[81] In one case, a cutler left his shop to a young man with the proviso that the youth practice the trade for ten years and share half the profit with the cutler's widow.[82] A number of elderly employees in the Fondaco dei Tedeschi arranged to transfer their posts to persons who were not related to them in return for a one-time fee or a percentage of their future earnings.[83] Many working-class elderly relied on friends or charitable institutions for assistance.[84] And single women sometimes took up residence together in order to share expenses and provide support, while others sought refuge in the church as *converse*.[85] In his last years the painter Lorenzo Lotto became an oblate at the Santa Casa di Loreto where he was guaranteed care. As a younger man he had relied on friends and relatives for aid.[86]

Personal patrons also provided assistance such as annuities for the working-class elderly. Doge Andrea Gritti, for example, arranged for his servant Marta to receive housing, as well as a yearly allotment of grain and wine for as long as she lived.[87] Others placed clients in hospitals or made them the beneficiaries of other established charities. While procurator of San Marco, Leonardo Donà arranged for his former servant Pascha to receive a small almshouse administered by his office.[88] Some masters continued to maintain servants in their homes, even when they could no longer provide any work. Notary Domenico Baldagara, for instance, recorded in his will that his servant of twenty years, donna Anzola, had gone blind. Nevertheless, he continued to house her and enjoined his sister to do the same after his death, "out of charity and out of love of the Lord and of me."[89] Laura Trevisan forbade her husband and sons "to abandon in old age or sickness" her servant Angela Bonzanina; and nobleman Piero Soranzo arranged not only for the maintenance of his aged servant Fior, but for her burial as well.[90] Masters and mistresses sometimes treated servants as part of the family who were entitled to care in old age.

In return elderly retainers, especially former nurses, continued to serve the families of their patrons. In addition to performing such practical tasks as knitting and watching children, they played a pedagogical role, recounting stories of the past and keeping family memories alive.[91] Most important of all, these aged employees bestowed spiritual benefits that, as we have seen, often continued after death. When Alvise Macipo wrote his will, he stated that he wanted his servant Menega to be maintained in his house and not forced to perform any labor. Instead she was to be free to go about her devotions and prayers.[92] By performing this good deed for Menega, Alvise hoped to gain spiritual benefits for himself in return. In cases such as this, masters and servants effectively reversed roles, with servants taking on the position of patrons as they advocated with the saints for the souls of their masters.[93]

The predominance of elderly women assigned tasks such as these indicates that Venetians, like their counterparts elsewhere, viewed old women, especially poor old women, as possessors of special powers, which could be used either for good or for ill. Some of the women tried for witchcraft in Venice were elderly, although the percentage was not as high as in some other cities.[94] The tasks that old women commonly performed—food preparation, care of the infirm, and prayers for the dead—easily blended into the work of witches: mixing potions, healing the sick, and summoning spirits.[95] Venice was home to a number of lower-class women who claimed spiritual authority and exercised a special hold on their followers. Among the best known is madre Giovanna, a woman about fifty years of age who inspired Giullaume Postel and others at the Ospedaletto of San Zanipolo.[96] The most economically disadvantaged and vulnerable members of society, namely elderly *popolano* women, simultaneously enjoyed a reputation for special access to supernatural power.

Limited in their family resources and dependent on their bodies, *popolano* men and women were especially vulnerable to the vagaries of old age. Most continued to work for as long as their bodies held up. But once struck by illness or sheer physical exhaustion, they were forced to seek assistance wherever they could find it. At the same time, some elderly women enjoyed a reputation for sagacity, although the realms in which they were perceived to be expert differed markedly from those of the city's male elite.

CONCLUSION

In Renaissance Venice old age was not understood simply in chronological terms, as a measure of age against average life expectancies, but also with highly marked status and gender valences. For an elite few, namely patrician males, it was seen as a time of wisdom and experience, while for the vast majority old age was associated with poverty, illness, and impotence. By law and custom, married patrician males continued to enjoy significant control over family resources and performed work that required mental acuity and experience rather than physical strength. This largely accounts for the disproportionate share of power old men wielded in government, and explains why a man such as forty-three-year-old fleet commander Vicenzo Capello was described as "zovene" (although he was the same age as Lorenzo il Magnifico at the time of his death) and why fifty-eight-year-old Domenico Trevisan was, in Sanuto's words, "too young" to be a viable ducal candidate.[97] When noblemen were labeled as old, it carried different meanings, according to a privileged vision of the elderly as sagacious rulers.

By contrast, others in society, including patrician women and the working classes, were often categorized as the miserable old. In the case of elite women, their reproductive capability and financial insecurity made them susceptible to both poverty and impotence, as were working men and women, who were likely to become destitute when their bodies wore out. These same elderly, however, figured as particularly worthy recipients of assistance and were the beneficiaries of significant charitable endowments. What is more, they were important to the religious view that aid to the poor was crucial to the salvation of the rich. Those who were marginal according to one standard of old age were central according to another.

NOTES

This is a revised version of a paper presented at Villa I Tatti, the Harvard University Center for Italian Renaissance Studies in November 1998. I wish to thank the former Director, Walter Kaiser, as well as Michael Rocke for the opportunity to present my research there. I also want to thank Konrad Eisenbichler for his reading of a later version of the essay.

1. See, for example, Robert S. Lopez, The Three Ages of the Italian Renaissance (Boston: Little, Brown, 1970), which divides the Renaissance into stages of youth, maturity, and decline.

2. A few examples will have to suffice: James B. Ross, "The Middle-Class Child in Urban Italy, Fourteenth to Early Sixteenth Centuries," in The History of Childhood, ed. Lloyd de Mause, 183–228 (New York: Psychohistory Press, 1974); Philip Gavitt, Charity and Children in Renaissance Florence: The Ospedale degli Innocenti, 1410–1536 (Ann Arbor: University of Michigan Press, 1990); Richard C. Trexler, Power and Dependence in Renaissance Flo-

rence, 3 vols. (Binghamton, NY: Medieval and Renaissance Texts and Studies, 1993), vol. 1, *The Children of Renaissance Florence;* and Konrad Eisenbichler, *The Boys of the Archangel Raphael: A Youth Confraternity in Florence, 1411–1785* (Toronto: University of Toronto Press, 1998).

3. Gavitt, *Charity and Children,* 284.

4. Creighton Gilbert, "When Did a Man in the Renaissance Grow Old?" *Studies in the Renaissance* 14 (1967): 7–32.

5. Elizabeth Sears, *The Ages of Man: Medieval Interpretations of the Life Cycle* (Princeton: Princeton University Press, 1986); James D. Folts, "Senescence and Renascence: Petrarch's Thoughts on Growing Old," *Journal of Medieval and Renaissance Studies* 10 (1980): 207–37; Kenneth McKenzie, "Antonio Pucci on Old Age," *Speculum* 15 (1940): 160–85; Erin J. Campbell, "The Art of Aging Gracefully: The Elderly Artist as Courtier in Early Modern Art Theory and Criticism," *Sixteenth Century Journal* 33 (2002): 321–31.

6. David Herlihy and Christiane Klapisch-Zuber, *Tuscans and Their Families: A Study of the Florentine Catasto of 1427* (New Haven: Yale University Press, 1985), chapter 6. See also the brief remarks on old age in James S. Grubb, *Provincial Families of the Renaissance: Private and Public Life in the Veneto* (Baltimore: Johns Hopkins University Press, 1996), 59–60 and 97; and Richard C. Trexler's essay on the Florentine widows' asylum, the Orbatello, in his *Dependence in Context in Renaissance Florence* (Binghamton, NY: Medieval and Renaissance Texts and Studies, 1994), 415–48.

7. Georges Minois, *History of Old Age from Antiquity to the Renaissance,* trans. Sarah Hanbury Tenison (Chicago: University of Chicago Press, 1989).

8. Ibid., 305.

9. Ibid., chapters 8–10.

10. Robert Finlay, "The Venetian Republic as a Gerontocracy: Age and Politics in the Renaissance," *Journal of Medieval and Renaissance Studies* 8 (1978), 157–79. Brian Pullan was the first to call attention to this aspect of Venetian governance. See his *Rich and Poor in Renaissance Venice: The Social Institutions of a Catholic State to 1620* (Cambridge: Harvard University Press, 1971), 116.

11. Finlay, "Venetian Republic," 165.

12. Ibid., 174.

13. Ibid., 164.

14. In a recent essay Hugh Cunningham argues that the history of childhood has been divided into discourses "on the cultural construction of ideas about childhood, on biological factors in the growing up of children, or on the roles of children in family economies," and that these discourses need to be integrated with one another. The same is true for the history of old age. See Hugh Cunningham, "Review Essay: Histories of Childhood," *American Historical Review* 103 (1998): 1196.

15. Sears, *Ages of Man,* 103–4.

16. Folts, "Senescence and Renascence," 223.

17. Moderata Fonte (Modesta Pozza), *The Worth of Women, Wherein Is Clearly Revealed Their Nobility and Their Superiority to Men,* trans. Virginia Cox (Chicago: University of Chicago Press, 1997), 78.

18. Frederic C. Lane, *Venice: A Maritime Republic* (Baltimore: Johns Hopkins University Press, 1973), 49.

19. Archivio di Stato di Venezia (henceforth ASV), *Compilazione Leggi*, busta 309, fascicle "Poveri al Pevere," fol. 386r.

20. Venice, Biblioteca Museo Correr (henceforth BMC), Donà dalle Rose 351, "Anagrafi," first page of notebook entitled "S. Polo 1607."

21. ASV, *Scuole Piccole*, busta 57 bis, Mariegola of the Scuola of SS. Apostoli, pp. 140–43; for Moro, see Franca Semi, *Gli "Ospizi" di Venezia* (Venice: Helvetia, 1983), 204.

22. ASV, *Notarile Testamenti* (hereafter *NT*), busta 572, notary Giorgio di Gibellino, unbound testament 224, 8 Jan. 1403 [more veneto].

23. Marisa Milani, ed., *Streghe e diavoli nei processi del S. Uffizio, Venezia, 1554–1587* (Bassano del Grappa: Ghedina and Tassotti, 1994), 39.

24. Marino Sanuto, *Vitae ducum venetorum*, ed. Antonio Muratori, Rerum Italicarum Scriptores 22 (Milan: Typographia Societatis Palatinae in Regia Curia, 1733), col. 967.

25. ASV, *Notarile Atti* (hereafter *NA*), busta 515, notary Giacomo de Beni, protocol of 1590, fols. 264v–265r; for another example, see ibid., busta 517, protocol 1592, loose page inserted after fol. 15v.

26. For Giovanna, see Milani, *Streghe e diavoli*, 23; for Corbacino, see Enrico Bertanza and Giuseppe Dalla Santa, *Maestri, scuole, e scolari in Venezia fino al 1500*, ed. Gherardo Ortalli (repr., Vicenza: Neri Pozzi Editore, 1993), 39.

27. Venice, BMC, Donà dalle Rose 174, Procuratia de Citra, Tomo Primo, sec. 4, entitled "Memoria della distributione . . . ," fols. 14 left and 14 right.

28. The original reads, "vecchia, impotente, e poverissima." Ibid., unnumbered page entitled "Informatione de Madre Paula Manfredi. . . ." At one point in his career, Sanuto used the same trilogy of terms in reference to himself. See Franco Gaeta, "Storiografia, coscienza nazionale e politica culturale nella Venezia del Rinascimento," in *Storia della cultura veneta*, vol. 3, pt. 1, *Dal primo Quattrocento al Concilio di Trento*, ed. Girolamo Arnaldi and Manlio Pastore Stocchi (Vicenza: Neri Pozza Editore, 1980), 85.

29. See, for example, the preamble to a rule concerning the officers of the confraternity of the Misericordia in Pullan, *Rich and Poor*, 116. See also, Finlay, "Venetian Republic," 160–61.

30. Quoted in Margaret L. King, *Venetian Humanism in an Age of Patrician Dominance* (Princeton: Princeton University Press, 1986), 143.

31. ASV, *Giudici del Piovego*, busta 3, *Codex Publicorum*, sentenza LXII, 468–77. This case is discussed in Dennis Romano, *Patricians and Popolani: The Social Foundations of the Venetian Renaissance State* (Baltimore: Johns Hopkins University Press, 1987), 23–24.

32. A report of the Provveditori alla Sanità from 1590 defined the Venetian poor as "either sick persons, or boys and girls, or women with numerous children, or aged, crippled or incapable, or finally, persons who have fallen from some kind of high social rank." Quoted in Pullan, *Rich and Poor*, 361.

33. "boni, et antiqui pauperes Veterani navigatores": ASV, *Compilazione Leggi*, busta 309, fascicle "Poveri al Pevere," fols. 390r–391r.

34. Ibid., fol. 414r.

35. Ibid., fols. 401r–403v.

36. The hospital opened in 1503 under the name Ospitale di Messer Gesù Cristo. Semi, *Gli "Ospizi" di Venezia*, 113–14.

37. Ibid., 50–64.

38. Ibid., 128–30, 204, 206–7. For some remarks on the charitable impulses of the trade guilds, see Richard Mackenney, *Tradesmen and Traders: The World of the Guilds in Venice and Europe, c.1250–c.1650* (Totowa, NJ: Barnes and Noble, 1987), 61.

39. For an example of a thirteen-year-old widow, see Sister Bartolomeo Ricco-boni, *Life and Death in a Venetian Convent: The Chronicle and Necrology of Corpus Do-mini, 1395–1436*, trans. and ed. Daniel Bornstein (Chicago: University of Chicago Press, 2000), 95.

40. Semi, *Gli "Ospizi" di Venezia*, 161–62.

41. Ibid., 282; and Margaret F. Rosenthal, *The Honest Courtesan: Veronica Franco, Citizen and Writer in Sixteenth-Century Venice* (Chicago: University of Chicago Press, 1992), 130–32.

42. Monica Chojnacka, "Women, Charity, and Community in Early Modern Venice: The Casa delle Zitelle," *Renaissance Quarterly* 51 (1998): 68–91. For the keeping of pets, see Silvia Lunardon, ed., *Hospitale S. Mariae Cruciferorum: L'ospizio dei Crociferi a Venezia* (Venice: IRE, 1984), 156.

43. Herlihy and Klapisch-Zuber note that in Renaissance Florence an association existed between "poverty and old age (and wealth and youth)." They attribute this to demo-graphics, to the greater number of older persons in poorer households and the larger number of younger people in wealthier households. Herlihy and Klapisch-Zuber, *Tuscans and Their Families*, 196.

44. Frederic C. Lane, "Family Partnerships and Joint Ventures," in *Venice and History: The Collected Papers of Frederic C. Lane* (Baltimore: Johns Hopkins University Press, 1966), 36–55.

45. James C. Davis, *A Venetian Family and its Fortune, 1500–1900* (Philadelphia: Amer-ican Philosophical Society, 1975), 7–8.

46. David Herlihy has argued that aged members of the Florentine elite "passed their last years in permanent tax arrears, and in destitution." He believes this resulted from the need of the merchant elite to distribute their capital to their sons. He goes on to suggest that this pattern was true for other commercial towns of the late Middle Ages as well. This does not, however, appear to have been true of Venice. See David Herlihy, "Age, Property, and Career in Medieval Society," in *Aging and the Aged in Me-dieval Europe*, ed. Michael M. Sheehan (Toronto: Pontifical Institute of Mediaeval Studies, 1990), 151.

47. Dennis Romano, *Housecraft and Statecraft: Domestic Service in Renaissance Venice, 1400–1600* (Baltimore: Johns Hopkins University Press, 1996), 86–89.

48. Davis, *A Venetian Family*, 93–106.

49. Ibid., 101.

50. Stanley Chojnacki, "Subaltern Patriarchs: Patrician Bachelors in Renaissance Venice," in *Medieval Masculinities: Regarding Men in the Middle Ages*, ed. Clare A. Lees (Minneapolis: University of Minnesota Press, 1994), 83–84 and 90 nn. 50 and 51.

51. In 1492 two noblemen came up with a plan to distribute seventy thousand ducats a year to poor noblemen: one hundred ducats a year to nobles over age sixty; fifty ducats a year to nobles under sixty. See Pullan, *Rich and Poor*, 230.

52. In this regard, it is useful to note Chojnacki's assertion ("Subaltern Patriarchs," 81–82) that patrician bachelors tended to hold minor government offices, while their married brothers predominated in the more important posts.

53. They may, as Konrad Eisenbichler pointed out to me, have entered the stage of life defined as "senio."

54. ASV, *Maggior Consiglio, Deliberazioni*, register 22 (Ursa), fol. 151r–v.

55. The original reads, "illustrissimus Princeps noster vacavit longo tempore, ex necessitate personae, a gubernatione Ducatus, et ad senectutem et aetatem decrepitam deductus est, ita ut in totum effectus sit inhabilis." It is printed in Francesco Berlan, *I due Foscari: Memorie storico-critiche* (Venice: Tipografia G. Favale, 1852), 185.

56. For a positive assessment of the situation of elite widows, see Monica Elena Chojnacka, "City of Women: Gender, Family, and Community in Venice, 1540–1630" (Ph.D. dissertation, Stanford University, 1994), 234–36.

57. For an analysis of the difficult situation of younger widows in Tuscany, see Cristiane Klapisch-Zuber, " 'The Cruel Mother': Maternity, Widowhood, and Dowry in Florence in the Fourteenth and Fifteenth Centuries," in *Women, Family, and Ritual in Renaissance Italy*, trans. Lydia G. Cochrane (Chicago: University of Chicago Press, 1985), 117–31. For examples of widows in convents, see Riccoboni, *Life and Death*, 67, 72, 75, passim.

58. The notebook of Procurator Leonardo Donà includes the case of an impoverished noble widow named Trevisana Condulmer who was receiving "some alms" from her brothers. Venice, BMC, Donà dalle Rose 174, sec. 4, fol. 1 right. See more generally Stanley Chojnacki, "The Power of Love: Wives and Husbands in Late Medieval Venice," in *Women and Power in the Middle Ages*, ed. Mary Erler and Maryanne Kowaleski (Athens: University of Georgia Press, 1988), 136–38.

59. For Cristina's activities after her husband's death, see Frederic C. Lane, *Andrea Barbarigo: Merchant of Venice, 1418–1449* (Baltimore: Johns Hopkins University Press, 1944), 34–35. At the time of her will, when she was about fifty years of age, she was still giving instructions to her sons. ASV, *NT*, busta 1238, notary Tomaso Tomei, unbound will number 158. For Foscari, see ASV, *Collegio, Notatorio*, register 10, fol. 34r.

60. Virginia Cox, "The Single Self: Feminist Thought and the Marriage Market in Early Modern Venice," *Renaissance Quarterly* 48 (1995): 543–44; but see also Jutta Gisela Sperling, *Convents and the Body Politic in Late Renaissance Venice* (Chicago: University of Chicago Press, 1999), 6–7, 24, 43, 55, 64.

61. Cox, "The Single Self," 544, 549.

62. Although some elderly women may have enjoyed a certain spiritual authority: ibid., 549. For more on this point, see below.

63. Romano, *Patricians and Popolani*, 133–34.

64. Venice, BMC, Mariegola 173, "Barcaroli del Trageto de San Rafaele et Liçafusina," pp. 182–83.

65. Lorenzo Lotto, *Il "Libro di spese diverse" con aggiunta di lettere e d'altri documenti*, ed. Pietro Zampetti (Venice: Istituto per la collaborazione culturale, 1969), 126–27.

66. ASV, *NT*, busta 372, notary Donato Viti, protocol of wills, fols. 11v–14r (testament 14); for Stella, see Milani, *Streghe e diavoli*, 169. In another example, a *filacanevo* named

Giacomo di Zuanne had gone blind and was dependent on charity. See Archivio Curia Patriarcale di Venezia, busta entitled "Testamenti—Archivio Antico," fols. 172r–173v. And for a notary who went blind on account of age, see Bertanza and Dalla Santa, *Maestri, scuole, e scolari*, 79.

67. Charles Verlinden, *L'Esclavage dans l'Europe médiévale*, 2 vols. (Bruges: De Tempel, 1977), vol. 2, *Italie–Colonies italiennes du Levant – Levant latin – Empire byzantin*, 600. For data about slaves from other areas, see pp. 616, 640–41. It may well be that emancipation of slaves in their thirties and older, who had already been in bondage for as long as twenty years, was motivated as much by a cost/benefit analysis of possible future service as by feelings of Christian charity. For some examples of emancipations of slaves in their thirties, forties, and fifties, see ASV, *Cancelleria Inferiore* (hereafter *CI*), *Notai*, busta 174, notary Giovanni Rizo, unpaginated protocol dated 1422–27, acts dated 24 June 1424, 6 Mar. 1426; and paginated protocol dated 1432–42, fols. 4v, 8r, 12r.

68. The hospital established by the surgeon Gualterio in the fourteenth century was designed to house those who "are no longer able to live by their trade." Giovanni Monticolo, ed., *I capitolari delle arti veneziane*, 3 vols. (Rome: Istituto Storico Italiano, 1896–1914), 1:327. See also Pullan, *Rich and Poor*, 368–69.

69. Creighton Gilbert drew much of the evidence for his essay on old age ("When Did a Man in the Renaissance Grow Old?") from the lives of artists who worked into advanced old age. But, as Erin Campbell notes, several artists, including Titian, came under criticism for precisely this practice. Campbell, "Art of Aging Gracefully," 322–24.

70. Frederic Chapin Lane, *Venetian Ships and Shipbuilders of the Renaissance* (Baltimore: Johns Hopkins University Press, 1992), 76–77.

71. Former nurse Lucia Trevisan, described as "satis antiqua," was raped in a boat while going to the mainland to gather herbs. ASV, *Avogaria di Comun, Raspe*, register 3646, fols. 194v–195r. Although something of an iconographic convention, an old woman selling eggs sits at the bottom of the stairs in Titian's *Presentation of the Virgin* in the Accademia.

72. Venice, Archivio degli Istituzioni di Ricovero e di Educazione (IRE), Der E, busta 62, fascicle 10. For another example of distributing candles to the poor in return for their processing at a funeral, see the will of Marcantonio Morosini, in Jacopo Bernardi, ed., *Antichi testamenti tratti dagli archivii della Congregazione di Carità di Venezia*, 12 fascicles (Venice: Tipografia della Società di M. S. Fra Comp. Tip., 1882–93), 10:26.

73. Romano, *Housecraft and Statecraft*, 173, 203.

74. For Fedele, see Franco Pignatti, "Cassandra Fedele," *Dizionario biografico degli Italiani* 45 (1995): 566–68; and Margaret L. King, *Women of the Renaissance* (Chicago: University of Chicago Press, 1991), 201; for the Zitelle, see Chojnacka, "Women, Charity, and Community," 74–75.

75. Lynn Lawner, *Lives of the Courtesans: Portraits of the Renaissance* (New York: Rizzoli, 1987), 70.

76. Marin Sanuto, *Diarii*, ed. Rinaldo Fulin, Federico Stefani, Nicolò Batozzi, et al., 58 vols. (Venice: Visentini, 1879–1903), 24:151. By contrast, Lorenzo Barbafella, a broker at the Fondaco dei Tedeschi, failed in his effort to install his grandson in his place: ibid., 14:82.

77. See note 64 above.

78. On 3 March 1323, for example, Pietro di Castello emancipated his sons Francesco and Benedetto. That same day, each son agreed to pay him ten lire annually "pro suo victu et vestitu." At the end of the month he emancipated a third son, Marco, under the same terms. Andreina Bondi Sebellico, ed., *Felice de Merlis: Prete e notaio in Venezia ed Ayas (1315–1348)* (Venice: Il Comitato Editore, 1978), docs. 278–81, 309–10. For another example, see docs. 323–24.

79. Semi, *Gli "Ospizi" di Venezia*, 278–80.

80. Ibid., 113.

81. On the fragility of *popolano* families' ties when compared to patricians', see Romano, *Patricians and Popolani*, 56–63; and Ugo Tucci, "Carriere popolane e dinastie di mestiere a Venezia," in *Gerarchie economiche e gerarchie sociali. secc. xii–xviii*, ed. Annalisa Guarducci (Prato: Istituto internazionale di storia economica 'F. Datini', 1990), 848–51.

82. Ibid., 848. It was not uncommon for *popolano* men, like noblemen, to make arrangements for the support of their widows. See Sebellico, *Felice de Merlis*, doc. 911.

83. Henry Simonsfeld, *Der Fondaco dei Tedeschi in Venedig und die deutsch-venetianischen Handelsbeziehungen*, 2 vols. (repr., Aalen: Scientia-Verlag, 1968), vol. 1, docs. 294, 295, 436, 477–78, 479, 501, 507, 526, 816.

84. For example, the widower Andrea Alesio, a former boatman, who had been confined to bed for eighteen years and blind for fourteen, lived in a house owned by the *scuola* of the Misericordia and relied on a certain Caterina (apparently his adopted daughter) to bring him bread on a daily basis. ASV, *NT*, busta 189, notary Girolamo Canal, unbound testament 67.

85. For women living together, see Monica Chojnacka, *Working Women in Early Modern Venice* (Baltimore: Johns Hopkins University Press, 2000), 18–21; for convents as repositories for old women, see K. J. P. Lowe, *Nuns' Chronicles and Convent Culture in Renaissance and Counter-Reformation Italy* (Cambridge: Cambridge University Press, 2003), 174–75; for an example of a *conversa*, see ASV, *CI, Miscellanea Notai Diversi*, busta 1, notary Avidio Branco, testament dated 27 March 1546.

86. See the summary of Lotto's life by Pietro Zampetti in Lotto, *Il "Libro di spese diverse,"* esp. pp. xxxiii–li.

87. ASV, *NT*, busta 1208, notary Antonio Marsilio, unbound testament 365.

88. See note 27 above.

89. ASV, *NT*, busta 372, notary Donati Viti, protocol, fols. 11v–14r, testament 14. In another case, a master agreed to keep his female servant, described as "già vecchia, et impotente" for as long as she lived, but made her agree, in return, that neither she nor her relatives would sue for her salary for the preceding four years or for any future service. ASV, *NA*, busta 426, notary Rocco de Benedetto, protocol, fol. 247r.

90. For Trevisan, see ASV, *NT*, busta 265, notary Ioseph Cigrignis, protocol, testament 6; for Soranzo, ibid., *NT*, busta 191, notary Girolamo Canal, unbound testament 594. Some servants took an active role in seeking to secure their future. One servant, a certain Pasqua, may have tried to oblige her master to her by making a donation to him and naming him her executor and universal heir. See ibid., *NT*, busta 66, notary Priamo Busenello, unbound testament 332. On this practice, see Giovanna Benadusi, "Investing

the Riches of the Poor: Servant Women and Their Last Wills," *American Historical Review* 109 (2004): 805–26.

91. Natalie Zemon Davis, *Fiction in the Archives: Pardon Tales and Their Tellers in Sixteenth-Century France* (Stanford: Stanford University Press, 1987), 88.

92. ASV, *CI, Miscellanea Notai Diversi,* busta 66, testament 38.

93. Romano, *Housecraft and Statecraft,* 202–3.

94. Ruth Martin, *Witchcraft and the Inquisition in Venice, 1550–1650* (Oxford: Basil Blackwell, 1989), 228.

95. Martin (ibid., 239) makes the sensible point that witchcraft provided a means to make a living "for the elderly, the unmarried or newcomers to the city."

96. See Marion Leathers Kuntz, "Ludovico Domenichi, Guillaume Postel and the Biography of Giovanna Veronese," *Studi Veneziani,* n.s., 16 (1988): 33–44.

97. These examples are cited in Finlay, "Venetian Republic," 168–69.

CONTRIBUTORS

Judith Bryce is professor of Italian at the University of Bristol. Her publications range from sixteenth-century Florentine cultural history, including a book on the polymath Cosimo Bartoli, to studies on contemporary Italian authors. Her recent work has focused on later Quattrocento Florence with a series of articles on the dramatist Antonia Tanin Pulci, on women and performance, and the cultural politics of Lorenzo de' Medici. She is senior editor of *Italian Studies*.

Peter Burke is professor of cultural history at the University of Cambridge. He is author of numerous studies, including *Culture and Society in Renaissance Italy, 1420–1540, The Renaissance Sense of the Past*, and *The Fortunes of the Courtier: The European Reception of Castiglione's "Cortegiano."*

Samuel K. Cohn Jr. is professor of medieval history at the University of Glasgow. He is author of several social and economic studies, including *The Labouring Classes in Renaissance Florence, The Cult of Remembrance and the Black Death, Creating the Florentine State: Peasants and Rebellion, 1384–1434*, and more recently *The Black Death Transformed: Disease and Culture in Early Renaissance Europe* and *Popular Protest in Late Medieval Europe*.

Derek Duncan is senior lecturer in Italian at the University of Bristol. His current research focuses on the intersections of colonialism and sexuality. He is coeditor of *Cultural Encounters: European Travel Writing in the 1930s* and of a forthcoming volume on the legacies of Italian colonialism. He has recently completed a monograph on constructions of male homosexuality in twentieth-century Italian literature.

Steven A. Epstein is professor of medieval history at the University of Kansas. He is author of *Genoa and the Genoese, 958–1528, Wage Labour and Guilds in Medieval Europe*, and *Speaking of Slavery: Color, Ethnicity, and Human Bondage in Italy.*

Philip Gavitt is associate professor of history at Saint Louis University. He is the author of *Charity and Children in Renaissance Florence* and a series of articles on such topics as charity and statecraft, infant mortality, and the history of childhood.

Mary Laven is lecturer in history at Cambridge University and a fellow of Jesus College. She is the author of *Virgins of Venice: Enclosed Lives and Broken Vows in the Renaissance Convent.*

Stephen J. Milner is senior lecturer in Italian at the University of Bristol. He is editor of *Niccolò Machiavelli: The Prince and Other Political Writings* and coeditor of *Artistic Exchange and Cultural Translation in the Italian Renaissance City*. He is currently completing *The Cultures of the Italian Renaissance.*

Michael Rocke is the Nicky Mariano Librarian of the Biblioteca Berenson at Villa I Tatti, the Harvard University Center for Italian Renaissance Studies, in Florence. In addition to numerous articles on the subject of sodomy and its control, he is the author of *Forbidden Friendships: Homosexuality and Male Culture in Renaissance Florence*. He is currently compiling an anthology of texts related to homoeroticism in Italy between 1300 and 1700.

Dennis Romano is professor of history and fine arts at Syracuse University. He is the author of *Patricians and Popolani: The Social Foundations of the Venetian Renaissance State* and *Housecraft and Statecraft: Domestic Service in Renaissance Venice, 1400–1600*, and coeditor with John Martin of *Venice Reconsidered: The History and Civilization of an Italian City-State, 1297–1797.*

Kenneth R. Stow is professor of Jewish history at the University of Haifa. He is author of *Alienated Minority: The Jews of Medieval Latin Europe*, the two-volume *The Jews in Rome,* and *Catholic Thought and Papal Jewry Policy, 1555–1593.*

Anabel Thomas is a former lecturer in the history of art at Birkbeck College, University of London. She is author of *The Painter's Practice in Renaissance Tuscany* and *Art and Piety in the Female Religious Communities of Renaissance Italy: Iconography, Space, and the Religious Woman's Perspective.*

Index

MEDIEVAL CULTURES